Against the Law

Against the Law

Labor Protests in China's Rustbelt and Sunbelt

CHING KWAN LEE

University of California Press

BERKELEY   LOS ANGELES   LONDON

University of California Press, one of the most distinguished university presses in the United States, enriches lives around the world by advancing scholarship in the humanities, social sciences, and natural sciences. Its activities are supported by the UC Press Foundation and by philanthropic contributions from individuals and institutions. For more information, visit www.ucpress.edu.

University of California Press
Berkeley and Los Angeles, California

University of California Press, Ltd.
London, England

Library of Congress Cataloging-in-Publication Data

Lee, Ching Kwan.
  Against the law : labor protests in China's rustbelt and sunbelt / Ching Kwan Lee.
    p.   cm.
  Includes bibliographical references and index.
  ISBN-13: 978–0-520–25097–0 (pbk. : alk. paper)
  1. Working class—China—Guangdong Sheng. 2. Working class—China—Liaoning Sheng. 3. Demonstrations—China—Guangdong Sheng. 4. Demonstrations—China—Liaoning Sheng. I. Title.
HD8739.G828L44   2007
331.0951′27—dc22   2006021879

Manufactured in the United States of America

15   14   13   12
10   9   8   7   6   5   4   3

This book is printed on New Leaf EcoBook 50, a 100% recycled fiber of which 50% is de-inked post-consumer waste, processed chlorine-free. EcoBook 50 is acid-free and meets the minimum requirements of ANSI/ASTM D5634–01 (*Permanence of Paper*).

for John

Contents

Preface

At the dawn of the twenty-first century, China is being hailed as the "workshop of the world," poised to assume a pivotal role in the global political economy. Chinese labor conditions have also generated intense interest among American and international policymakers, labor movement activists, and development agencies. The Chinese worker is often imagined as a diabolically exploited, haplessly diligent, mindlessly docile, nondescript, and disposable human being, easily replaced from the seemingly endless supply of identical youthful workers in the world's most populous country. In the United States and also in Mexico, India, and elsewhere in the developing world, the Chinese worker is charged with responsibility for job loss, capital flight, and a plunge in global labor standards. There is a glaring incongruity between, on the one hand, the general recognition of the great significance of Chinese labor conditions and their impact on the world economy and, on the other hand, the public's limited understanding of the complexity of the Chinese experience and, more fundamentally, the humanity of the Chinese worker.

I hope that this book will help to close this cognitive gap through a comparative analysis of the lives and struggles of the two segments of the Chinese workforce that have borne the brunt of market reform and globalization: laid-off and retired workers in China's industrial rustbelt and young migrant workers in global factories in the export-oriented sunbelt. To capture the sharply uneven process of change in this immense and heterogeneous country and to maximize the analytic leverage of the diverse local political economies within its borders, I have selected two provinces that can represent, in oversimplified terms, the death of socialism and the birth of capitalism in one country. It is also in these two provinces—Liaoning in the northeast and Guangdong in the south—that the two respective groups of workers are most geographically concentrated. Once the heartland of the socialist planned economy and home to some of China's most prominent state-owned industrial enterprises, Liaoning has declined into a wasteland of bankruptcy and a hotbed of working-class protest by its many unemployed workers and pensioners. Unpaid pensions and wages, defaults on medical subsidies, and inadequate collective consumption are the main grievances triggering labor unrest in Liaoning. In contrast, the sunbelt province of Guangdong has become a powerhouse of the country's export-oriented industrialization and one of the most popular destinations for the hundred-million-strong migrant labor force. Rampant nonpayment of wages and oppressive working conditions have prompted unrest among these young workers.

The empirical observation that guides this comparative study is that there are both differences and similarities in the patterns of protest and strategies for survival in these two regions. In the rustbelt, I have found "protests of desperation," in which veteran state workers take their grievances to the street rather than to the legal system. Their protests coexist with a survival strategy that relies on the remnants of socialist entitlement, primarily allocated welfare housing, and on informal employment. In contrast, Chinese migrant workers in the sunbelt, indignant over their treatment as second-class citizens by officials and employers, stage "protests against discrimination." These workers resort primarily to legal activism and secondarily to public disruption. Striving to remain employed in the cities, these workers also rely for subsistence on a system of land rights that allocates to rural residents plots of land in their birth villages.

Although unemployment and exploitation, together with working-class resistance and adaptation to these challenges, can be found in many places and at different times, peculiarities of China's postsocialist conditions have engendered features of labor politics that defy conventional categorization. First, the law, fledgling legal institutions, and the rhetoric of legal rights are central to labor protests throughout China, even though very few workers actually believe in the effectiveness of the regime's ideology of law-based government. Second, leading to the formation of neither a national labor movement nor representative organizations, the several thousand worker protests that erupted every year throughout the 1990s took the prevailing form of localized, workplace-based cellular activism. With workers blocking traffic in the streets, lying on railroads, or staging sit-ins in front of government buildings, these demonstrations presented a palpable threat to social stability, at least in the eyes of the national leadership. What must be emphasized, however, is that workers' cellular activism has thus far rarely escalated into large-scale, coordinated, cross-regional unrest. Despite workers' limited organizational capacity, their insurgent identities suggest potential for more broad-based politics. In both the northeast rustbelt and the southern sunbelt, protesting workers have creatively drawn on Maoism, socialism, and liberal ideologies of legal justice and citizenship to stake their claims. This paradoxical mix of localized mobilization and generalized insurgent identities lends an intriguing fluidity to Chinese labor politics of the past two decades.

What, then, is the nature of working-class agitation in this period of marketization and globalization? Why have worker protests been bottled up at the local level, given the familiar accounts of horrific degradation and exploitation suffered by millions of young workers in the export-oriented sunbelt, on the one hand, and massive unemployment and impoverishment suffered by an older generation of workers in the rustbelt, on the other? Alternatively, considering the putatively repressive and authoritarian nature of the Chinese communist regime, what material and moral resources and political opportunities exist for workers to sustain even that level of activism? Finally, what does labor politics tell us about China's transition from socialism? Answering these questions requires a dynamic examination of workers' lived experiences at the point of production and beyond in the context of the contested evolution of the political economic institutions that undergird working-class lives. Above all, I have found that the communist regime's strategy of accumulation, in the form of what I term "decentralized legal authoritarianism," both generates the impetus for and places limits on working-class protests in this period of market reform. This larger political economic context of reform shapes not only collective mobilization by workers but also popular rebellion in general, and therefore is a key to understanding the institutional foundations of China's economic dynamism and sociopolitical tensions.

I should suggest here how my analysis diverges from important works in two major scholarly literatures—transition studies and labor studies—that have influenced our understanding of China and Chinese labor. Transition scholars generally compare China, explicitly or implicitly, with other former Soviet-type societies. To explain the success of the Chinese transition, they usually point to reformed institutions that dispense the right incentives or enable elite interests and alliances to push for marketization in their effort to generate economic growth. Although important, these studies have the collective failing of presenting too laudatory a narrative of China's "successful" turn to capitalism, missing the seamy side of reform that blights many ordinary people's lives. My study, in contrast, begins from "below" and brings a subaltern perspective back to the study of China. My task is not just empirically to document something that transition studies, skewed by its elitist and institutionalist concerns, has omitted. I also seek alternative theoretical frames that allow us to ask hard questions about the nature of Chinese society and the consequences of reform, transition, and globalization. For instance, transition from socialism entails widespread commodification of life processes and resources, including labor, land, nature, and bodies. It also triggers profound shifts in society's normative infrastructure: its standards of justice; the distribution of dignity, entitlements, and rights; and the value of labor. These moral dimensions of commodification, ignored in the literature that privileges the role of material interests and institutions, have causal power in shaping the trajectory of transition as they fuel popular contentions. Moreover, transition studies miss the essence of transition: that because it is a time of unsettled institutional norms and coexistence of old and new ideologies and discourses, it is also a politically poignant moment for a wide range of social activism. The former characteristic allows a greater role for popular struggles to shape the outcomes of conflicts, and the latter furnishes a rich repertoire of moral and congnitive resources for aggrieved workers to frame and make multiple claims.

Labor scholars tell quite a different story about Chinese development. The problem with their studies is not the obliteration of workers' experience in the process of change, but rather a tendency to make a leap of faith from the existence of exploitation to resistance. Some have given us empathetic, if also grueling and graphic, depictions of factory lives inside the Chinese satanic mills, while others predict the emergence of a historic world labor movement, comparable to the Chinese peasant revolution that ushered in the Chinese communist regime. My research in the past seven years has led me to see a more complicated and nuanced reality. Beyond exploitation in the workplace, there are also nonmarket mechanisms for the reproduction of labor power embedded in the rural economy and the urban work unit system that mitigate the worst exploitation workers suffer at the point of production. The much-criticized household registration system that subjects migrant workers to second-class citizenship status, making them a cheap labor pool tapped by global capital, also confers land rights on those with rural household registrations. Likewise, the collapse of the socialist work unit has triggered economic distress and moral outrage, but the work units have also allowed state workers to purchase former welfare housing at subsidized prices. This housing reform has made them private property owners, providing an economic safety net even in the event of enterprise bankruptcy. These institutions also generate a degree of allegiance to the regime. In short, this book depicts a working class that is less wretched and less heroic than many labor studies scholars and progressive observers would be willing to admit.

I have benefited from engaging criticism by colleagues working on transition and labor issues, who take me to task for seeing either too much labor radicalism or too little. I would like to think that, having provoked disagreement from both sides, I may have gotten it right.

During the course of research and writing, I have accumulated numerous debts to people and institutions for their generous support in many ways. First and foremost, I thank friends and colleagues who have made contacts and arrangements that have allowed me to conduct fieldwork on a politically sensitive subject. I deeply regret that I cannot name those who have given me the most crucial contacts, but they certainly know how appreciative I am of their assistance and trust. This study could not have been completed without the courage and cooperation of the workers who accepted me into their world and took the time to share with me their experiences, thoughts, and feelings.

Throughout the course of this project, Michael Burawoy, Elizabeth Perry, Mark Selden, and Shen Yuan have unfailingly provided me with intellectual inspiration, criticism, and encouragement. Since arriving at the University of Michigan, I have been fortunate to find myself in a vibrant and supportive intellectual community consisting of Albert Fuerwecker, Mary Gallagher, Nicolas Howson, Ken Lieberthal, Jeffery Paige, Albert Park, Margaret Somers, George Steinmetz, Ernest Young, and Wang Zheng.

Opportunities to try out my ideas have challenged me to reject or reformulate my arguments. For their valuable and stimulating comments, I thank Michael Denning, Deborah Davis, Gay Seidman, Boy Luthje, Anita Chan, Shahra Razavi, Xin Liu, Ruth Milkman, Kevin O'Brien, Jean Oi, Andrew Walder, and Ian Robinson, as well as participants in seminars at the University of Wisconsin, Yale, the University of California–Berkeley, Stanford, UCLA, Harvard, Wayne State University, the University of Montana, the University of Pittsburgh, Cornell's School of Industrial and Labor Relations, the Woodrow Wilson International Center for Scholars, the Institute for Advanced Study, and the United Nations Research Institute for Social Development.

I am grateful to Naomi Schneider, my editor at the University of California Press, Marilyn Schwartz, and Madeleine Adams for their editorial support and advice. Michael Burawoy, Marc Blecher, and Diane Wolf read the entire manuscript and gave invaluable comments and suggestions. For their research assistance at various stages of this project, I thank Ni Jing,

Qiu Haixiong, Ping Ping, Vivienne Leung, Yim Kit Sum, Li Erjin, Yu Xiaomin, Tan Shen, Greg Distelhorst, Jen Zhu, and especially Liu Kaiming.

Funding for research and writing has been provided by the Woodrow Wilson International Center for Scholars, the National Endowment for the Humanities, the Institute for Advanced Study, the Chiang Ching-kuo Foundation for International Scholarly Exchange, and the South China Program of the Chinese University of Hong Kong. At the University of Michigan, I have received financial support from the Center for Chinese Studies, the Rackham Graduate School, the Institute for Research on Women and Gender, and the Office of the Vice-Provost for Research.

PART I

Decentralized Legal Authoritarianism

1 Chinese Workers' Contentious Transition from State Socialism

DAYS OF RECKONING

For more than a week in mid-March 2002, tens of thousands of workers marched through the streets of Liaoyang, an old industrial town in China's northeastern rustbelt. Some carried a huge portrait of the late Mao Zedong that was mounted on four shoulder poles and accented by a red ribbon knot fastened on the top of the frame. While some people passionately sang the "Internationale," an old woman cried aloud, "Chairman Mao should not have died so soon!"[1] Fueled by simmering anger at the corrupt local government and pressed by economic difficulties after their state-owned enterprises went bankrupt, workers from as many as twenty factories at one point demonstrated in front of the Liaoyang city government building. They demanded payment of back wages, pensions, and unemployment allowances owed them for months, even years. But most shocking to the authorities, they insisted on the removal of the head of the local legislature and former mayor whose seven-year leadership had spawned rampant corruption and wreaked havoc in the lives of the local people. Overseas human rights organizations claimed that it was the largest collective act of defiance since the bloody crackdown of the 1989 Tiananmen Incident. Only this time workers were the major social group present; no intellectuals, students, or private entrepreneurs joined their protests; and the official press censored the incident at both the municipal and national levels.

Liaoyang has the look of many an old industrial town in the northeastern province of Liaoning. A pervasive grayness and an air of morbidity beset what once was a proud and buzzing industrial center boasting a dozen major military equipment factories and a nationally renowned chemical plant built with French technological assistance in the early 1970s. No

3

inkling of such past glory can be found today in the faces of the many unemployed workers gathering in makeshift "labor market spots," holding in their hands or hanging on their necks placards announcing their skills: plumber, electrician, nanny, seamstress, and so on. Abandoned brick workshops punctured by broken windowpanes line the main road leading into this city of 1.8 million, one of which is the Liaoyang Ferro-Alloy Factory, or Liaotie, the epicenter of the protests. For four years, the three thousand employees of this state-owned enterprise had petitioned the local government, charging the enterprise management for financial irregularities and nonpayment of wages, pensions, unemployment allowances, and medical reimbursements. The columns near the main entrance were covered with posters and open letters. One open letter, addressed to "All the People in Liaoyang," read,

> We the working masses decide that we cannot tolerate such corrupt elements who imposed an illegal bankruptcy on our factory. We must take back justice and dignity. We will not give up until we get all welfare payments, unpaid wages, and compensation back. . . . Our respected compatriots, brothers and fathers, we are not anti-Party, antisocialism hooligans who harm people's lives and disrupt social order. Our demands are all legal under the Constitution and the laws. . . . Let's join forces in this action for legal rights and against corruption. Long live the spirit of Liaoyang![2]

Pointed and impassioned, the letters made a resounding accusation against local government corruption and collusion with enterprise management. The panoply of worker compensation specified by central government policy remained an empty but tantalizing promise. Liaotie workers' grievances were shared by many local workers throughout China's cities and especially across the northeast. Yet workers' interests were fractured. A disillusioned former Party secretary of one of the many factories participating in this protest explained to me that different groups of protesting workers participated with their own unresolved "balance books" in their heads. They came together in holding the local government responsible for their plight.

> First, there were laid-off workers who did not get their 180 yuan monthly allowance. Then, there were retired workers complaining about not getting a special allowance promised by the central government two years ago. It was stipulated then that for each year of job tenure, they should be paid an additional 1.8 yuan monthly for their retirement wages. Third, there were retired cadres whose career dated back to the prerevolutionary era complaining about unequal treatment of retirees. There was a policy for military personnel who were with the CCP [the

Chinese Communist Party] before 1949 to get 1,800 yuan a month as pension, but those who surrendered to the CCP at the end of the anti-Japanese War were given only half of that amount. The latter group was of course furious. . . . Then, there were banners saying, "We want to eat," "Return us our wages." . . . People are nostalgic about the time of Chairman Mao, when everyone had jobs and society was stable and equal. . . . After devoting my life to political education work, I now feel my efforts have all been wasted. Since the early 1990s, after they started the director responsibility system, I as the Party secretary was sidelined, and he [the director] could rule and decide on personnel matters however he wanted, no restraint at all.[3]

Thanks to its cross-factory participation and its explicit political demands, the Liaoyang protest received intense international journalistic attention. Despite the rapid collapse of inter-workplace rebellion, its short-lived existence signaled to the regime the possibility of an escalated working-class rebellion beyond the predominant pattern of localized, single-factory mobilizations, spurred by economic and livelihood grievances related to wages, pensions, health benefits, and bankruptcy compensation. In terms of sociological significance, it is this latter type of "cellular activism" that has become paradigmatic in the Chinese reform era. Police statistics on demonstrations, startling as they are, capture only a small part of the phenomenon. In Liaoning province alone, between 2000 and 2002, more than 830,000 people were involved in 9,559 "mass incidents," or an average of ten incidents each involving ninety people every day for nearly three years.[4] Nationwide, the Ministry of Public Security recorded 8,700 such incidents in 1993, rising to 11,000, 15,000, and 32,000 in 1995, 1997, and 1999, respectively.[5] In 2003, some 58,000 incidents were staged by three million people, including farmers, workers, teachers, and students.[6] Among them, the largest group consisted of 1.66 million laid-off, retired, and active workers, accounting for 46.9 percent of the total number of participants that year.[7] The surge in social unrest continued from 2004 to 2005, as the Ministry of Public Security announced a hike from a total of 74,000 to 87,000 cases of riots and demonstrations during these two years.[8]

Rampant nonpayment of wages, pension defaults, and the general collapse of the enterprise welfare system has triggered this trend of increasing labor strife among China's massive laid-off and retired proletariats. The total number of workers in state and collective enterprises who were owed unpaid wages increased from 2.6 million in 1993 to 14 million in 2000, according to official trade unions statistics.[9] In Shenyang, the provincial capital of Liaoning, a survey showed that between 1996 and 2000, more than one-quarter of retired workers were owed pensions, and one-quarter of employed workers were owed wages.[10] Adding insult to injury, the Chinese government has begun experimenting with a one-time severance compensation scheme that translates each year of job tenure into 470 yuan in Shenyang (in 2002). The rates are lower for smaller cities and they vary across industries. Many workers simply reject the idea that "job tenure" can be up for sale; many others find it repugnant that their labor for socialism is now reduced to a pittance, while the state permanently relinquishes responsibility for its workers. With glaring gaps in the new safety net, the estimated twenty-seven to forty million workers shed from their work units in the state and collective sector since 1995 are plagued by a profound sense of insecurity.[11] Across the country, in rage and desperation, workers are wrestling with explosive questions: Who should be held responsible for the collapse of enterprises the regime had for years touted as worker-owned? How much should workers' lifelong contribution to socialism be worth now? Who should be paying? How much for every year of job tenure? Why are pension regulations and bankruptcy laws not implemented? In short, workers are contesting the value of their labor in the broadest sense, not just the amount of severance compensation but also, as this book shows, the meaning of labor, the basis of legitimate government, and the principles of a just society. The 1990s was a time of reckoning between workers who had come of age under Maoist socialism and the post-Mao reform regime.

NEW LABOR BLUES

Veteran state workers are not alone in asserting labor claims. After two decades of market reform, a new generation of industrial laborers has established a solid foothold in all kinds of industries. Hailing from China's vast countryside and toiling mostly in private, joint-venture, and foreign enterprises, the hundred-million-strong migrant population now accounts for 57.5 percent of China's industrial workforce and 37 percent of its service sector employees. In the garment, textile, and construction industries, these migrant workers constitute 70–80 percent of the total workforce.[12] Since the 1990s, these young workers have registered marked increases in protests and strikes, or what the Chinese authorities vaguely refer to as "spontaneous incidents." The overwhelming majority of these conflicts are about wages and working conditions, rather than collective consumption (that is, goods and services that are consumed by the community as a whole). In Shenzhen, China's most developed global export city in the south with some seven million migrant workers, the Labor Bureau officially registered about six hundred such incidents each year during 1998–2001.[13] The annual total of officially mediated and arbitrated labor disputes soared from 54 in 1986 to 13,280 in 1999.[14] Of these disputes, 65 percent were related to wage arrears and illegal wage rates.[15] In Guangzhou, the capital of Guangdong province, the Public Security Bureau reported a total of 863 protests involving some 50,000 people between January and October 2004.[16] For Guangdong province as a whole, the number of arbitrated labor disputes rose from 24,700 in 1998 to 45,790 in 2002.[17] An official survey in 2003 revealed that about 75 percent of migrant workers had experienced wage nonpayment (of varying durations and amounts).[18]

One "spontaneous incident" that has become an everyday phenomenon in Shenzhen involved a court case filed by construction workers. On a balmy morning in the spring of 2002, 188 migrant workers of Jiancheng, a big name in the local construction industry, gathered at the gate of the Shenzhen Municipal Intermediate People's Court. Spirited and hopeful, they were waiting to enter the courtroom for the second hearing of their lawsuit against their employer for illegal deduction of wages and nonpayment of its pension insurance contributions for more than a decade. There were lively exchanges in Sichuanese; 70 percent of the workers came from Sichuan province. At about 8:15 AM, fifteen minutes before the scheduled opening of their case, the judge's clerk came out from the main building to make a surprising and unsavory announcement: the hearing would be postponed until further notice because the court investigators had not yet been able to obtain evidence from the Labor Bureau. The clerk also told one of the five worker representatives that they should be the only ones appearing at the next court date, not all the workers, despite the fact that all of them were plaintiffs. Disbelief quickly gave way to anger, as many workers cried foul, while others cursed the corrupt court system. One man suggested, "Let's go to Beijing, to the National People's Congress!" and others seconded enthusiastically. Their unflappable, shrewd, but gentle leader, Liu Junyuan, tried to assuage the intense indignation of his fellow workers, saying that "the court is working on our case, but it needs more time to gather evidence. Let's go back to the dormitory first." After another twenty minutes of milling and complaining among themselves, and a brief appearance of the Sichuan government representative in Shenzhen to "understand the situation," workers went home, discouraged and disappointed, but, as Liu insisted, also even more determined to fight for their cause, whatever it took.[19] Since the beginning of this labor dispute in March 2001, these workers had tried negotiation and mediation with management, collective petitions to the city People's Congress and Labor Bureau, and writing open letters to the official union, the city government, and the Public Security Bureau. They also ini-

tiated formal dispute arbitration and finally lawsuits, trying every administrative and legal means to assert their demands. Despite their scathing critique of discrimination against migrants, they still believed in the integrity
of nonlocal state authority and the fledgling national legal regime. "It's too
unjust, but we are at the end of our rope," Liu lamented, acknowledging that
the legal system, no matter how flawed, might be the only realistic way to
redress the blatant violations of their collective interest. What he did not
expect was that three months later the court would delay giving a verdict,
prompting his angry coworkers to block traffic outside the court. And when
the judge eventually rejected their claims on dubious legal grounds, Liu
found himself as disillusioned and bitter as his fellow workers, declaring,
"The judge was paid off. . . . If we had to do it again, we would just
protest!"[20]

This is not an isolated case of collective action by migrant workers, nor is
its tortuous course and the legal combativeness of workers involved atypi-
cal. Many cases of labor disputes in the sunbelt are characterized by workers' self-consciously law-abiding principles of action. Going to the streets is
considered a last resort and usually happens only after other bureaucratic
channels have been exhausted. The sentiments expressed during these incidents entail abject vulnerability and intense indignation on the part of
migrants for being treated as second-class citizens by employers and officials unresponsive to their lawful demands.

But why do rustbelt workers take to the street so readily while sunbelt
workers instinctively resort to the labor bureaucracy and the judicial process
before staging protests?

THE PUZZLE

I compare two regional political economies where two distinct groups of
workers bearing the brunt of market reform and globalization are concentrated and display both differences and similarities in their modes of
activism. First, I examine the rustbelt in the northeastern province of
Liaoning. Once the heartland of the socialist planned economy and home to
some of China's most prominent state-owned industrial enterprises,
Liaoning has decayed into a wasteland of bankruptcy and a hotbed of working-class protest by its many unemployed workers and pensioners. Unpaid
pensions and wages, defaults on medical subsidies, and inadequate collective
consumption are the main grievances triggering labor unrest in Liaoning.
Second, I examine the sunbelt province of Guangdong, which has become a

powerhouse of the country's export-oriented industrialization and one of the most popular destinations for the hundred-million-strong migrant labor force. Rampant nonpayment of wages and oppressive working conditions have prompted unrest among these young workers.

In the rustbelt, I have found "protests of desperation," in which veteran state workers, staking their claims on moral and legal grounds, primarily take their grievances to the street, leveraging a strategy of political bargaining by shaming local officials and disrupting traffic and public order, and make only occasional and individual forays into the legal system. Rhetorically, workers' insurgent claims draw on political discourses of class, Maoism, legality, and citizenship. Such protests coexist with a survival strategy that relies on the remnants of socialist entitlements, primarily allocated welfare housing, and on informal employment.

In contrast, Chinese migrant workers in the sunbelt, indignant over their treatment as second-class citizens by officials and employers, stage "protests against discrimination." These workers resort first to legal activism such as filing petitions and lawsuits for collective labor arbitration, mediation, and litigation. Only when this institutionalized channel fails (which it often does) do they resort to public disruption. They stake their claims in the law, clamoring against discrimination by officials and employers and violation of labor rights, identifying themselves as weak and marginalized masses needing the protection of the state. Striving to remain employed in the cities, these workers rely for subsistence on a system of land rights that allocates to rural residents plots of land in their birth villages.

What explains the differences in these protest strategies, one emphasizing street action and the other legal and bureaucratic channels? What accounts for the differences in rhetoric and the claims made to the public and the state?

In addition to these differences, I have also found several significant features of unrest shared by rustbelt and sunbelt workers in this period. One is their passionate appeal to legal justice, assailing official corruption as both immoral and illegal. Also, despite the large number of protests, labor unrest in both regions has been bottled up at either the enterprise or the city level. This kind of decentralized, "cellular" activism seldom evolves into lateral, cross-locality rebellion, and its political target has remained the local government rather than higher-level officials or the central government, with important ramifications for regime stability and legitimacy. What accounts for these similarities in labor activism across two generations of workers and two drastically different regional economies?

We may think of the Liaoyang and Shenzhen incidents described earlier in this chapter as instances of what have been termed, respectively, "Polanyi-type" and "Marx-type" labor unrest. In Beverly Silver's global narrative of labor unrest in the past 130 years, *Polanyi-type unrest* refers to the resistance to the commodification of labor power by workers who have benefited from established social compacts that are being abandoned by the state.[21] *Marx-type unrest*, in contrast, refers to struggles by newly emerging working classes confronting capitalist exploitation in *production*. Marx-type struggles are organized by workers when they have associational workplace or marketplace bargaining *power*.[22] Yet neither Polanyi nor Marx has an adequate theory for explaining the specific modes of mobilization or insurgent identities that constitute labor unrest and workers as political agents. We need, therefore, additional analysis of the state (i.e., its strategies of economic accumulation and regime legitimation), the social organization of collective action, the legal system, the institutions of social reproduction of labor power, and theories of subjectivity and the agency of workers.

This book identifies three levels of analysis forming a configuration of intersecting conditions and giving rise to divergent and convergent patterns of labor activism in reform China. The three levels of analysis are: (1) the political economy of decentralized legal authoritarianism; (2) the two systems of regulation and reproduction of labor, one organized around a "social contract" and work-unit-based collective consumption, the other predicated on the "legal contract" and village-based subsistence guarantees; and (3) a repertoire of insurgent identity claims appropriated from official ideologies. (See figure 1.)

My argument is this: the rising tide of labor unrest in China in the past fifteen years is caused by the commodification of labor, a key component of what has been summarily called "market reform" This commodification process in China is characterized by the Chinese state strategy of decentralized accumulation and legal authoritarianism. This political economic framework and its inherent tensions produce the features of labor protests common across the two regions: cellular activism, local state targets, and mobilizing the ideology of legalism. Specifically, I use the term *decentralized legal authoritarianism* to refer to the twin strategy of decentralized accumulation and legalistic legitimation of authoritarian rule. Whereas fiscal and administrative decentralization has been noted by many scholars as the pivotal strategy of the reform regime, I want to draw attention to a less theorized but parallel state strategy: an attempt to shift the ground of political legitimation from utopian ideology, personal authority, administrative fiat, and violence to a government by law, or rule by law. Together, these

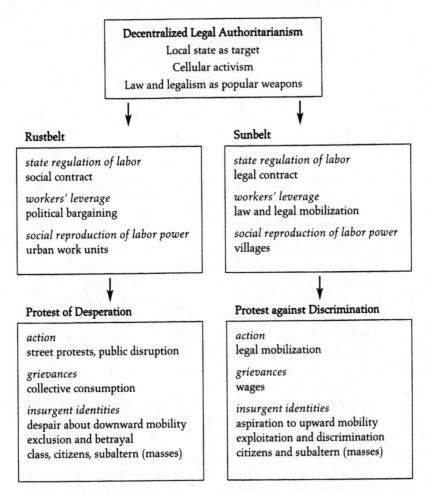

Figure 1. Three Levels of Analysis of Labor Unrest in Contemporary China

strategies of development have profound implications for the patterns and potential of labor activism. In oversimplified terms, decentralization makes local government responsible for developing a probusiness local political economy, while the same local government agents are called on to implement labor laws promulgated by the central government eager to resolve labor conflicts and to maintain social stability. This tension between accumulation and legitimation, between the interests of the local and the central government, gives rise to endemic violation of labor rights and entitlements. The local state becomes the target of worker resistance. Besides, uneven local economic development, a result of both decentralization and the uneven trajectories of global investment, leads to fragmentation of worker interests across localities and work units, producing cellular mobilization. The central government's promulgation of laws and its rhetoric of legality incite popular responses couched in exactly the same legalistic language.

If the common characteristics of labor protests across the two regions have resulted from the national political economic framework of decentralized legal authoritarianism, the differences in worker struggles are shaped by the diverse modes of state regulation of labor and the systems of social provision outside of waged work. Rustbelt workers' employment in state industries usually dated back to the prereform period when a socialist social contract—an implicit state guarantee of employment security and welfare in exchange for workers' political acquiescence—regulated state and labor relations. In the reform era, the transition from social contract to legal contract has been stalled in the rustbelt, and therefore workers still leverage mass action as a means of political bargaining. Betrayed by the state and excluded by the labor market, their protests are fueled by moral outrage and desperation. I call this pattern *protests of desperation*.

In contrast, in the sunbelt, migrant workers have never been part of the socialist social contract. The state regulates employment and workers through legal contract and the Labor Law, which channel collective action primarily toward the institutionalized, bureaucratic system of labor arbitration and litigation. Because the judiciary is not always independent of the local state administration, however, frustrated workers also take their grievances from the courtrooms into the streets. Without urban residency, the reproduction of labor power for migrant workers takes place in their home villages and not in cities. Therefore, their demands center mostly on wage nonpayment and working conditions, not on levels of collective consumption. Instead of committing acts of desperation, these workers aspire to participate in the industrial economy but are incensed by employers' and local officials' collusion and discrimination against them as "outsiders," or second-class citizens. Hence the term *protests against discrimination*.

Finally, the repertoires of insurgent identity claims mobilized by the two groups of workers are necessary causal conditions for the rise of labor unrest and can be understood as derived from workers' collective history and current institutional contexts. In the rustbelt, the lingering validity of the socialist social contract and workers' collective lived experience with Maoist socialism produce a lively discourse of class exploitation and the moral responsibility of the state to the people or the "masses." The current state rhetoric of legality and the central government's attempt to implement a system based on the legal contract adds a layer of legalistic claims on top of rustbelt workers' class and Maoist discourse. In the sunbelt, in contrast, migrant workers have never had any experience with socialist industrialism or Maoist class politics, and therefore there is a conspicuous absence of class identity claims. Even the notion of the "masses" echoes only faintly and is usually subordinate to the claim of laborers' and citizens' legal rights. In the following section I elaborate the theoretical implications of these arguments.

WORKING-CLASS FORMATION: FROM NINETEENTH-CENTURY ENGLAND TO TWENTY-FIRST-CENTURY CHINA

Since Karl Marx, labor scholars have explored the connection between a "class-in-itself" and a "class-for-itself," between the objective existence of workers subjected to exploitation and alienation in production and workers' purposive mobilization to act as a class-conscious collectivity. The rich literature on workers' politics around the world has postulated a close relationship between the development of capitalism, a polarized class structure, and proletarianization, on the one hand, and the rise of modern workers who respond to these economic transformations through collective organization and revolutionary action, on the other. This master narrative (of how capitalist development leads to the formation of the working class) forms the bedrock of the working-class formation literature. Important interventions by cultural Marxists, most notably E. P. Thompson's *The Making of the English Working Class*, by comparative historical sociologists, such as those in Ira Katznelson and Aristide Zolberg's *Working-Class Formation: Nineteenth-Century Patterns in Western Europe and the United States*, and by world-system sociologists, exemplified most recently by Beverly Silver's *Forces of Labor*, have also basically subscribed to this causal argument.

Trenchant criticisms, nevertheless, have come from historical sociologists who maintained that democratic citizenship and legal development, not capitalist economic development, are the driving forces for worker agitations. Reinhard Bendix has argued that industrialization increases workers' demand for democratic and citizenship rights rather than class-based interests.[23] Margaret Somers's research on the effect of local legal culture, rather than the development of capitalism per se, on various English working-class communities' proclivity to mobilization challenges the economic determinism of orthodox Marxian interpretations.[24] Moreover, reversing the causal primacy of objective class structure leading to subjective class agency, recent scholarship has shifted toward a more practice- and identity-oriented approach to class formation. Looking at "cultures of solidarity" forged at moments of class conflict,[25] "narrative identities" based on local cultures of practical rights,[26] or "insurgent identities" developed out of workers' membership in social networks,[27] scholars have accorded a more agentic, transformative role to workers' practices and identities than was found in the previous generation of scholarship.

In short, not only has the teleology of capitalism turning modern workers into a revolutionary class been abandoned, but also economic determinism has been replaced by contingent and concrete analysis of the institutional arrangements of the economy, the political regime, and legal development. Workers' practices and identities, fashioned from a wide spectrum of lived experiences beyond the point of production, are recognized as *constitutive* of collective action, not just as intervening variables. These two metatheoretical reorientations of the traditional class formation theory are particularly relevant to the Chinese case at hand.

First, China's market reform, initially created by the heavy hand of the Chinese communist regime, mixes institutions that can be characterized as both market-oriented and redistribution-based, or capitalist and socialist. Theories that derive from logics of either capitalism or socialism will not suffice to explain the motivations and patterns of labor politics arising out of such hybridity. To understand the dynamics of labor politics in this context of transition, we have to attend to the fortuitous and uneven development of market institutions, state regulation, and legal reform. Second, the fluidity of institutional transformation in transition societies such as China demands attention to popular practices and politics. As a prominent Chinese sociologist observes, in transitional societies such as China, "the totality of praxis transcends structure; it is irreducible to and more than structure."[28] When the political economy and social structure are relatively in flux, workers' willful use of and practical engagement with fledgling economic, political, and legal institutions result in modes of activism that cannot be read off any presumed institutional map. In other words, transitions are times when institutions do not yet produce stable patterns of labor conflict or their resolution. Employers and state agents, dominant as they ordinarily are in employment relationships, are also gauging the parameters of workers' reactions to new policies and practices. Subsequently, multiple modes of activism and insurgent identities are crafted, tested, revised, or abandoned, contingent on their effectiveness in the political process.

Metatheoretical orientation does not specify why and how workers engage in labor strife, however. In the theoretical literature, a long-established proposition holds that workers, especially skilled workers, resist exploitation and degradation in capitalist *production*. Threatened by mechanization and substitution by more vulnerable labor groups, these workers will mobilize to defend their customary control over the labor process, their status system, and their traditional way of life. Unskilled workers, too, demand better working conditions and collective power inside the firm through the establishment of unions.[29] In this perspective, workers' grievances are generated from the antagonism of interests between workers and employers inherent in the organization of the capitalist workplace. Marxist analyses of worker consent to capital's hegemonic domination does not challenge this proposition's basic insight that workers' interests are organized and constituted at the point of production.[30]

Under socialism, it is not so much exploitation in production that prompts resistance but rather conflicts involving the "social contract" between the working populace and the communist state. It has been argued that in return for popular acquiescence to its authoritarian rule, the regime guarantees stable employment and welfare services. Studies have found that erosion of state paternalism is connected with rising trends of open rebellion and covert everyday resistance.[31] Approaching state-labor relations from the perspective of state domination, several seminal works maintain that "organized dependence" on state redistribution of basic livelihood resources and life chances is the crucible of popular acquiescence and consent under state socialism.[32] In brief, if under capitalism worker grievances arise primarily from the realm of production, under state socialism it is the system of redistribution that is pivotal. Either way, these theories explain worker politics by appealing to their material interests conceived as derived from some systemic nature of either capitalism or state socialism, which, in turn, are thought of as political economies with certain coherent logics and tendencies. The empirical case examined in this book defies easy categorization as either socialist or capitalist, and therefore throws into sharp relief alternative mechanisms and logics of labor protests that depart from the prevailing explanatory framework of labor politics. Three points are particularly important. First, the political economy of Chinese reform is characterized by persistent contradictory imperatives and conflicts of interest between the central government and local states. Worker politics derives from these tensions, not from system logics. Second, there is no singular political economy in China. Institutions embedding and enabling the commodification of labor, especially the labor rule of law, are unevenly established in different regional economies, giving rise to diverse local labor regimes and labor politics. Third, worker subjectivity cannot be reduced to material interests. Equally important are workers' sense of dignity, justice, and their need for recognition. Postsocialist transition in China spawns labor unrest because enormous normative violence has been inflicted on workers.

CONTRADICTORY STATE: DECENTRALIZATION, LEGALITY, AND AUTHORITARIANISM

In the transition literature, China's rapid and sustained economic growth has become the gold standard among postcommunist countries. The Chinese state has rightly been at the center of scholarly attention, credited with creating and incubating the market. The emphasis has been on economic decentralization or the state strategy of local accumulation, enhancing incentives among provincial and local communist leaders to liberalize the economy. By allowing revenue retention at the provincial and local levels, fiscal decentralization has generated enormous vested interests among provincial officials to promote and sustain the reform drive, a move to create "a political counterweight to the central bureaucracy and achieve market reform while preserving China's Communist institutions."[33] The positive economic effects of decentralization are captured by several theoretical formulations. "Local state corporatism," for instance, depicts the developmental, market-promoting, and entrepreneurial role of local officials in nurturing the spectacular growth of village and township enterprises.[34] Hard budget constraints and local property rights provide the incentive structure fostering competitive local industries.[35] Elsewhere, the notion of "competitive liberalism" highlights how the center has induced competition among localities to liberalize the local economy and to provide better infrastructure in order to attract capital.[36] Still others have coined the term *Chinese-style federalism* to explain both reform success and the more recent privatization of small and medium-sized state-owned enterprise in the mid-1990s.[37]

A palpable celebratory metaphysics undergirds this literature, whose focal concern is with explaining "successful" market reform via state initiatives and which sees the Chinese state as developmental. Only recently, with rising social unrest, have a few scholars attended to the dark side of economic reform, or the rise of the "predatory state" in China. Minxin Pei, for instance, identified four institutional factors accounting for the decentralization of state predation: the decentralization of property rights, declining monitoring capability, the availability of new exit options, and the erosion of ideological norms.[38] The unavoidable consequence of declining state capacity and appeal of the ruling party is the rising level of rural and urban discontent. Even with this starker perspective, the state is still conceptualized as primarily and solely concerned with accumulation, and as an independent, coherent, and self-contained power structure formed prior to inter-action with social forces. This view also fails to give due attention to the other state imperative, namely legitimation, and to connect particular modes of accumulation and legitimation with modes of social resistance. In con-trast, a dialectical perspective of the state, one that this book adopts, sees contradictions within different state imperatives and insists that state power is not independent of but rather constituted through its engagement with social groups in their acquiescence and activism, triggered by contradictory state goals and policies.

Among existing studies, Zhao Dingxin's study of the Tiananmen protest stands out in that it identifies the gap in state and popular notions of legit-imation as a major cause of the escalation of protests.[39] But his rather crude categorization of the Chinese state as authoritarian, as opposed to demo-cratic, and his failure to point to institutional sites for the state to secure legitimation leave unexamined the nexus between state policies and collec-tive resistance. Elsewhere, Kevin O'Brien and Lianjiang Li contended that the Chinese state suffers from a monitoring problem that induces mis-implementation of central policies at the local level, and thereby creates both the grievances and the opportunities for people to pursue "rightful resistance." They coin the term *rightful resistance* to denote "a form of pop-ular contention that operates near the boundary of authorized channels, employs the rhetoric and commitments of the powerful to curb the exercise of power, hinges on locating and exploiting divisions within the state, and relies on mobilizing support from the wider public."[40] Notwithstanding its heuristic value, the concept of "rightful resistance" does not take us beyond describing a way of "framing" by those involved in resistance, who turn the regime's policy and legitimating myths into weapons of the weak. Giving short shrift to the historical or theoretical conditions for the emergence, mode of mobilization, and dynamics of rightful resistance, O'Brien and Li fail both to illuminate the specific conflict of interest between different lev-els of the state and to connect the modes of accumulation and legitimation to the constitution of interests and action modes among the resisters.

This book moves beyond the simplistic, stark contrast between interpre-tations of the Chinese state as either developmental or predatory and rejects the view that the state is a singular and insulated motor of change. It argues for a dialectical view of the state, pursuing the contradictory interests and tendencies between different levels and units of the state, as well as ordinary people's active engagement with either the developmental or predatory practices of the state. I have found in the arena of legal reform a crucible for the intersection of these two dynamics—a fractured authoritarian state marked by contradictory goals and interests, and a populace interpellated by the law to become citizens rather than subjects.

Unfolding concomitantly with economic reform in the past quarter century, Chinese legal reform entails a remarkable and momentous increase in law-making activities by the central authority, the professionalization of the judiciary and the legal workforce, and the strengthening of the court as an adjudicator of civil, commercial, and administrative disputes. "Ruling the country by law" (yifazhiguo) was formally incorporated into Article 5 of the Constitution in 1999 and has become part of the official lexicon now widely adopted in government, legislature, and Party reports. Between 1979 and 1998, some 327 laws were enacted by the National People's Congress (the corresponding figures were 7 and 122 for 1966–1978 and 1949–1965, respectively) and 750 regulations were issued by the State Council.[41] If authoritarianism was previously predicated on administrative fiat, personality cult, violence, and terror in the Maoist mobilization state, in the reform period it is institutionalized and constructed in the image of a law-based government. Whereas laws and regulations have been used to specify a new framework of property rights to enforce contracts and to organize new market structures, thereby facilitating local accumulation, the central leadership has been equally insistent on the law's political function of maintaining social stability. The president of the People's Republic Jiang Zemin remarked, "Whether it is market regulation or macroeconomic regulation and control by the state, we should constantly sum up our experiences and gradually incorporate them into the law. We cannot possibly foster good order in the socialist market economy in the absence of a sound socialist legal system."[42] Yet legal reform in China has been stalled by two major contradictions besetting the Chinese regime: (1) the contradiction between the local state's imperative for accumulation and the central authorities' concern with using the law to legitimate political authoritarianism; and (2) the contradiction between the need to maintain the political monopoly of the Communist Party and the binding authority of the law over state agents. These two sets of tensions become political only when the populace takes the law seriously, viewing their self-interest and private needs as citizens' rights and public concerns.

Accumulation versus Legitimation

It has been suggested that a twin crisis of profitability and legitimation characterizes the development of historical capitalism.[43] The Chinese reform political economy is also beset by the contradiction between these two imperatives. Economic growth via market liberalization necessarily brings about intensified inequality and dislocation that undermine regime legitimacy. Labor laws and a new safety net are needed to maintain basic livelihood protection for worker-citizens falling through the cracks of the market economy; hence the central government's promulgation of a large number of labor regulations regarding pensions, medical care, insurance, and welfare. But the central authority's strategy of decentralization, entailing the devolution of both fiscal authority and welfare responsibility, creates problems of local implementation. Enjoying unbridled power in economic affairs and standing to benefit personally and collectively from bringing in investment and economic growth, local officials see their abiding interest in accumulation while they scorn welfare reforms as unfunded mandates thrust upon the localities by the center.

In the 1990s, Beijing demanded repeatedly, but in vain, that local governments guarantee payments to retirees and laid-off workers. The lack of local response to this legitimation concern often forced the central government to pitch in emergency funds when worker unrest reached a level to cause central consternation about social instability. In old industrial provinces such as Liaoning, which is saddled with a high concentration of retirees and laid-off workers from bankrupt state factories, the central government had no option but to apportion special relief funds to the provincial governments, out of concern for maintaining social stability. In 2000, the central government pitched in 45.8 billion yuan for local governments to repay owed pensions and laid-off worker livelihood allowances.[44] Leaders and cadres of impoverished inner and northeastern provinces allegedly tried to hold Beijing hostage over the proliferation of labor unrest, in an attempt to demand more central funding for economic development and social insurance payments. In 1998, an extra 300 million yuan was allocated to these provinces as emergency funds.[45] As long as localities give priority to accumulation over legitimization policy, reflecting officials' interest in short-term and concrete financial gains, implementation of labor legislation will be hampered. The pursuit of local accumulation without a corresponding emphasis on welfare and equity has begun to chip away at the regime's legitimacy. Elite obsession with economic growth has generated intense discontent among workers whose livelihood security has been severely undermined by market competition. Perhaps in response to the seething popular discontent expressed through various kinds of social unrest, the new national leadership that came to power in late 2003 has vowed to pursue a broadened agenda of "social development," or "growth with equity." Yet the underlying tension between central and local government power and interests remains.

Economic Liberalization versus Political Monopoly

The difficulty of enforcing central government legislation is related to a second contradiction of the Chinese regime. The persistent monopoly of political power in the hands of the Chinese Communist Party has come into conflict with the legal reform it seeks to establish in tandem with the market economy. The legal scholar William Alford writes of a genuine ambivalence in the Chinese project of legal construction: "On the one hand, they wish to reap the advantages of liberal legality in terms of its perceived capacity to support economic growth, engage the international community, and legitimize the existing regime. On the other, however, they aspire to do so without being unduly subject to its constraints. . . . In effect, this design is the counterpart in law of the larger effort to carry out a substantial transformation of the economy without a commensurate relinquishing of political control."[46]

Without any countervailing political opposition or competition, this contradiction has resulted in an authoritarian regime of "rule by law," not a "rule of law" that can restrain the government itself. Central government law and regulation may provide a wide range of rights and entitlements for workers, but when these are in conflict with local government's procapital interests, the judiciary often succumbs to administrative interference. Poor enforcement of the law is caused by the courts' lack of institutional autonomy vis-à-vis local government. "Local courts are beholden to the interests of local governments. . . . [C]ourt budgets and the salaries and welfare benefits of judges are determined by the local government, not by the Supreme Court of the central government. It is standard procedure to reduce a judge's bonus according to the number of verdicts reversed on appeal, a situation that discourages judges from cooperating with lawyers and from deciding cases according to legal criteria."[47] Labor bureaus, responsible for enforcing the Labor Law, are marginalized and play second fiddle to economic and commerce bureaus in the local bureaucracies. Labor officials have reported extreme difficulties in imposing fines and penalties on employers for violation of the law, owing to the general priority given to creating a favorable investment climate. "Our job is to educate employers on the Labor Law, not punish them," proclaimed one Guangdong labor official.[48]

Like a double-edged sword, decentralized legal authoritarianism both fulfills the regime's instrumental goal of economic growth and political control and generates popular activism by furnishing the aggrieved groups with both a vocabulary and an institutional mechanism to express their demands and seek redress. Combined, the contradictions between accumulation and legitimation and between economic liberalization and political authoritarianism have significant consequences for labor politics. The gap between central regulations and local implementation has undermined working conditions in the sunbelt and collective consumption in the rustbelt. Workers with grievances about nonpayment of wages and pensions and other conflicts demand redress citing central government regulations. Paradoxically, though, the same central-local state tension has led to a bifurcation of regime legitimacy and therefore a localized, rather than national, pattern of labor agitation. The common view found among aggrieved workers is that the central leadership is protective of workers, as evidenced by the numerous laws Beijing has promulgated, whereas local officials are corrupt and unfit to rule because they fail to enforce central regulations. When workers protest, their targets have always been enterprise managerial cadres and their superior officials in local industrial or labor bureaus. Decentralization, coupled with marketization, also contributes to the perception that Beijing can no longer totally determine the economic conditions of individuals and enterprises as economic power has been delegated to local officials. As Vivienne Shue has noted, as legitimate responsibility for the economy has been dispersed and to some extent obfuscated, workers are prone to frame protests in limited and localized ways. "The combined effects of decentralization and marketization have worked to the advantage of the central state, making it somewhat easier for the center to contain and quell those protests that have arisen while simultaneously sustaining its own appearance of legitimacy."[49] It is questionable how long such a bifurcated popular view of a legitimate center presiding over a hierarchy of local venality can be sustained without being replaced by a more integrated view of systemic corruption and illegitimacy. But for the moment at least, what is significant is the prevalence of legal rhetoric as the idiom of activism. "Against the law" becomes the shared accusation used by workers, employers, and officials alike in labor contests.

REGULATION AND SOCIAL REPRODUCTION OF LABOR

If the national political economic structure and its inherent tensions are pivotal in constituting the common features of labor protests (that is, decentralized and localized targets, cellular activism, and legalism), the divergent patterns of protest (that is, protests of desperation and protests against discrimination) have to do with how specific labor systems have been established in various regions. Michael Burawoy's notion of "labor regime" is a powerful analytical tool linking state regulations of labor (through legislation on contracts, minimum wage, social insurance, collective bargaining, and the like) and the social reproduction of labor power (i.e., means of subsistence, daily and generational reproduction of the capacity to labor) to workplace control and workers' capacity for resistance. The idea is that what happens at the point of production between labor and management and among workers is related to how the broader political apparatus intervenes in the regulation and reproduction of labor. In China, as chapter 2 will elaborate, market reform in the past quarter century has entailed a transition between two systems of labor regulation: from one based on social contract to one based on legal contract. It has proved to be a contentious and uneven process, whereby moral, economic, and legal claims and counterclaims are made by state officials, management, and workers engulfed in numerous and intense local conflicts. The social contract "instituted" in the socialist era was a general and implicit exchange between the paternalistic state and a politically acquiescent populace. There was no legal document stipulating the terms of this socialist social contract, only shifting policies that varied greatly according to the political and economic needs of the state in different periods.

In the reform era, the transition from social contract to legal contract was stalled in the rustbelt owing to the challenge of the local economic structure (declining state-owned heavy industries), the financial predicament of enterprises, corruption among local officials, and workers' economic dependence on and moral expectation of state paternalism. Labor laws and regulations were promulgated but not always implemented in practice. The legal and bureaucratic systems were hotbeds of corruption, not responsive or effective in resolving labor conflicts. Rustbelt workers, steeped in the logic of the socialist social contract, saw their leverage in mass action as a means of political bargaining. In contrast, in the sunbelt, the influx of foreign and domestic private investors and the recruitment of young migrant workers, both outside the traditional socialist social contract, compelled the local state to regulate employment and workers through legal contracts and the Labor Law. When conflicts arise, migrant workers' first response was to leverage the only institutional resource available to them—the law and the bureaucratic system of labor arbitration and litigation. Because the judiciary and the labor bureaucracy are not always independent of local state administration, however, frustrated workers who have exhausted their legal options are also prone to take their grievances from the courtrooms into the streets.

The ways in which labor power—the capacity to work—is reproduced on a daily and generational basis shape both the potential and the limits of collective mobilization. In China, as we shall see, dormitories for migrant workers in export factories and residential quarters for state socialist workers are both geographically close to the site of production, forming self-contained, all-encompassing communities where work and nonwork lives take place in the same localities. This residential pattern facilitates communication and the aggregation of interests, especially at the moment of labor conflict. A major difference between the two types of communities, however, is that state workers' residence survives the termination of their employment, in contrast to the itinerant status of migrant workers, whose residence in the cities is contingent on their employment. Thus, labor struggles in the northeast have the potential to last for longer periods, up to several years in some cases, than in the south.

There is another significant way in which workers' capacity is shaped and limited by how labor power is reproduced, that is, by how workers survive beyond their participation in and dependence on waged labor. Here I find that lingering "socialist" entitlements play a key role in limiting both migrant workers' and veteran state workers' capacity to sustain mobilization. Specifically, the birthright of migrant workers with rural household registrations to plots of land in their home villages and the urban housing reform that turned work-unit housing into state workers' private property are buffers against the nonpayment of wages and unemployment. Many state-owned enterprise workers, in some places 42 percent of working-class households, bought the property rights to their previous welfare housing units in the 1990s.[50] Workers can resell these urban properties, turn them into rental units, or pass them on to their offspring, even after retirement or plant closure. Housing is perhaps the most important and enduring of all redistributed goods. In the countryside, land ownership remains collective to this day. Since the dismantling of the communes in the late 1970s, land use rights of the individual peasant have been legally guaranteed by the state, and agricultural land is allocated to the household unit to which that peasant belongs. The most recent 1998 Revised Land Administration Law has reaffirmed the principle of equal distribution of land and peasants' land use rights have been guaranteed for at least another thirty years. This land rights system allows employers and the state to sustain a low-wage labor regime, as the cost of the social reproduction of labor is partly absorbed by the rural communities.[51] It also channels workers' aspirations, sense of belonging, and survival strategies back to the countryside. Many labor disputes end with migrant workers leaving the cities and dissipating into the vast countryside for basic subsistence. As the erosion of peasants' land rights has increased since about 2005, and as the second generation of migrant workers increases in number, we may see changing dynamics of labor politics in the coming years. Yet, up until the turn of the new millennium, the rural land rights system had a dampening effect on urban labor strife.

In short, rural land rights and urban homeownership are forms of state redistribution that cushion workers from destitution and dispossession caused by market competition. These policies produce in each group of workers a degree of dependence and allegiance to the reform regime and the economic order that marginalize them. At the same time, the different entitlements from which the two groups of workers benefit produce and reproduce rural-urban boundaries that fragment the working class from within. They have come to see each other as having fundamentally different life chances and economic interests.

REPERTOIRE OF INSURGENT IDENTITIES: PROLETARIAN, CITIZEN, AND SUBALTERN

Economic and legal reforms entail not just the transformation of institutions but also shifts in standards of justice, values, and subjectivity. The promulgation of laws, and the associated discourse of citizenship and legal rights, for instance, allow workers to view the self as public and to recognize the discrepancies between legal prescriptions and experiences of the absence of legal rights. The making and remaking of the labor subject must be an integral part of any story of labor activism as a force of social change. Examining the micromobilization processes of labor unrest throws into sharp relief how "needs," material and moral, are always defined through the prisms of collectively held sense of dignity, entitlement, and rights. Across the two regions and two generations of workers, the striking similarity is how indignation experienced in the commodification process spurs workers to action. Repeatedly, I have seen that wage defaults and pension arrears were experienced primarily as assaults on workers' prevailing sense of justice, worthiness, and humanity, standards variously defined by socialist ideology and institutions (the social contract) and the Labor Law (the legal contract). The theoretical significance of underscoring this moral and emotive dimension of labor protests, or the labor politics of recognition, is that it reverses the causal logic of a widely accepted proposition that workers resist when they have the capacity or institutional leverage to do so.[52] Given the large labor supply, the prevalence of unskilled and low-wage jobs, and the nonexistence of independent unions, Chinese workers can hardly be described as having much marketplace, workplace, or associational bargaining power. The data presented in this book, however, suggest that the need for recognition and justice can be so powerful that they can prompt mobilization even in the face of formidable political barriers. Mobilization generates political leverage, not vice versa. Beyond China, we find significant instances of "powerless" laborers, such as immigrant workers and low-end service workers, building successful movements based on symbolic power and social justice claims.[53]

This brings us to the third element in my analytical framework: labor subjectivity. Historically, labor studies have documented three potential insurgent identities the modern worker forges in action: proletariat, citizen, or subaltern. The working-class formation theory predicts the rise of modern workers as class actors, who use class as "a way of organizing, thinking about, and acting on society."[54] Class designates a shared position in the division of labor in production, generating shared material interests among class members in opposition to another class. The revisionist argument of Margaret Somers suggests that it was as citizens, not as members of the working class, that workers in nineteenth-century England seized on national labor law to advance their collective interests. The driving force of their collective activities was expectations informed by their understanding of the legitimate rights of membership for all citizens of England's national polity. "The language of rights . . . was the explanatory prism through which class issues and other aspects of social distress were mediated and understood."[55] Elsewhere, the postcolonial labor history of Dipesh Chakrabarty makes a powerful case for a different labor subject in the struggle of the Bengalese working class. He argues that the Indian worker is not the abstract, liberal subject assumed in Marxist theories that take liberal English society for granted. Indian workers are subalterns who, while they labor on the shop floor and participate in strikes and unions, carry with them identities defined by a hierarchical community marked by distinctions based on birth: religion, language, and kinship. "The incipient awareness of belonging to a class remained a prisoner of [their] pre-capitalist culture," he writes.[56]

The analysis of the subject in labor action must be historically and culturally situated, and cannot be determined a priori and in abstraction from theories. Which of these images—the proletarian, the citizen, or the subaltern—reflects the living reality and identity of the Chinese worker in protests? The two snapshots of labor protests depicted in the beginning of this chapter, like many others that are documented in this book, indicate that Chinese workers are experimenting with multiple insurgent identities, drawing on and inventing a repertoire of subjectivity and rhetoric that has roots both in their shared historical experiences under socialism and the new institutional environment in the current reform and globalization era. Instead of fixating and reifying workers' identities, I should recognize their context-dependent contingency and diversity. Contingent on varying local conditions, they invoke and combine class, citizen, and subaltern consciousness and praxis to make claims asserting their dignity, rights, and entitlements. In other words, my account seeks to reveal, rather than reduce to singular theoretical logic, the multiple formations of political agents that mark this period of economic transition and institutional ambiguity. At a time when workers confront the challenge of crumbling old practices and fledgling unpredictable new policies, when it is hard to speak of structured or formal norms, there is more room and necessity for political experimentation from below by those who are ordinarily subordinated. The political poignancy of labor activism in the current period lies in this multiplicity of insurgent identities, their uncertain effectiveness, and their continuous evolution. In brief, what I have found is that workers are testing old and new cognitive, moral, and action frames inadvertently provided by state ideologies, to find out which ones work under what conditions at a time when institutions are in relative flux. If the reform leadership is "groping for the stone as they cross the river" in charting the course of economic reform, a process of experimentation with popular resistance is its mirror image.

Let's consider "class" subjectivity. Workers in the northeastern rustbelt, after decades of official indoctrination with Marxist ideology and firsthand experience with "cradle-to-grave" work-unit welfare, are acutely aware of the rise of new and powerful dominant classes, be they government officials or former state factory managers. Even as the discourse of class has disappeared from the media, academia, and official propaganda, the language of class leads a subterranean existence in veteran state workers' reminiscences of the bygone days of Chairman Mao. A particularly prominent element in working-class subjectivity is workers' claim of collective ownership of their work units. The official ideology of "workers as masters of the enterprise" was a lived experience under Mao, many asserted. From time to time, we see how this "class-based" sense of entitlement, rights, and dignity fuels powerful feelings of injustice and rage and spurs action, as in the Liaoyang incident described at the beginning of this chapter. But the Chinese state allows little political space for workers to form class-based organizations. To date, attempts at lateral coordination among workers have been met with severe sentences imposed by a state determined to nip in the bud any autonomous, organized dissent, whether it takes the form of unions or of political parties. In the sunbelt, the younger generation of migrant workers, who came of age when official ideology had begun deemphasizing class struggle and are therefore less conversant in class rhetoric, nevertheless complain about being dehumanized as "little more than appendages to machines" and deem that not getting paid is the worst form of "exploitation." Workers may relish their fleeting success with strikes that manage to force employers to pay back wages or reduce production quotas. Yet the pressure to make a living and the fluidity of the labor market do not lead easily to collective organizing of any kind. In short, Chinese workers' class consciousness exists as a fading relic from the past, and the persistent weakness of workers' class capacity is not likely to nourish or sustain its development.

The most empowering identity workers have found is grounded in one variation of citizenship—citizens' right to legal justice (*gongmin de hefaquanyi*). Workers enthusiastically embrace the regime's project of legal reform and the construction of a law-based, corruption-free government. Statistics of workers filing for arbitration or lawsuits attest to a rise of rights consciousness. If class struggle was the official ideology in the Maoist era, then legality or *fazhi* (rule by law) is that of the reform era. As workers and the general public learn to articulate their grievances and demands by adopting the language of the state, in this case legalistic language, a process of subject formation takes on a life of its own. As Göran Therborn notes, "people ... are subjugated under a particular force or order at the same time that they are makers and creators of something.... [I]nherent in this double sense of the subject is the always present possibility of transcendence of social and personal givens."[57] When they are subjected to the state-prescribed appellation of *citizens*, workers become qualified or interpellated to act as citizens in the way they define citizenship. But workers' subjectivity is the result not just of ideology but also of praxis. When legal recourse always proves ineffective, owing to the courts' institutional subordination to the government at all levels as well as rampant corruption and collusion between business and government, many workers have become "disillusioned citizens." In trying to exercise their rights, many workers have found that they do not have any. Citizenship is an empty slogan and status, but because it is the language of the state, workers' banners and petition letters are laced with legal terminology and logic. Yet, sometimes the court does follow the law and incites popular usage of the legal system. Under these circumstances, workers-as-citizens are a political agency in the making; they falter in some places but make headway in others. Every favorable arbitral award or court verdict spawns new desire and aspiration among workers to affirm their labor rights and interests through the legal system.

A third kind of insurgent identity and action strategy found among Chinese workers in the reform period is that of the subaltern—in Chinese *qunzhong* (the masses) or, more recently, *ruoshi qunti* (weak and disadvantaged social groups). In protests, petitions, and private conversations, workers refer to themselves as the working masses (*gongren qunzhong*). Tellingly, workers today often use this term interchangeably with *ruoshi qunti*. The "masses," a concept that originated in the Chinese Communist Revolution and the Maoist mass line, consisted of workers, the peasantry, the intelligentsia, and the national bourgeoisie. The masses' interests were harmonious with one another and also with those of the state, and their political energy and spontaneity were to be cultivated and harnessed.[58] Cadres were instructed to guide and encourage the masses to participate in the construction and defense of socialism under the leadership of the Party. Indeed, the masses are conceived as a powerful force in the Chinese polity, and the authoritarian state from imperial times to the Maoist era has accorded them the moral responsibility to rebel against injustice and immoral, venal power.[59] What is notable about the masses as a political agent is that it has survived "class." The appellation *the masses* still occupies a prominent place in official propaganda, most significantly in Jiang Zemin's theory of the "Three Represents," one of which is representing "the fundamental interests of the broad masses." In the 1990s, the new term *ruoshi qunti* became popular, used by the government, the media, and academicians to refer to social groups among the masses that have been relegated to disadvantaged social locations by structural reforms. The central government recognizes the plight of migrant and unemployed workers in the reform era, and it affirms its moral responsibility for protecting them through the legal system or a new safety net. Workers readily invoke this new label of the *disadvantaged masses* to criticize the lack of state protection.

But in embracing such an identity, they also reveal and reinforce a hierarchical political imagination—the central state is the source of omnipotent power and paternal authority from which flows protection for workers. The political logic of the masses also imposes limitations on workers' activism. Ever cautious of the heavy hand of a repressive state authority, workers rarely dare to pursue lateral mobilization across factories, limiting themselves instead to localized disruption that they hope can generate social and political pressure on local officials. That is, workers organize cellular mobilization based on one single work unit, which is usually tolerated by the local government, and petition superior officials who then pressure local officials to respond to workers' demands. At the first signs of official concession or repression, workers retreat for fear of retaliation or lack of organizational resources to press on. But again, the subaltern is a living, reflexive political agent capable of changing practices, not one who is imprisoned in her own traditional culture or predetermined by economic and political institutions. Over time, we may expect Chinese workers to develop greater capacity for solidarity than what they have so far demonstrated.

Processes and identities of grassroots political mobilization everywhere are relational and emergent, sociologists of contentious politics have observed.[60] In China, institutions of state socialism are partially but not totally dismantled, while a contract-based capitalist employment system is being only unevenly instituted. Values, norms, and regulatory frameworks of state-labor-capital relations are in the process of formation and contestation. Within narrow limits, institutional uncertainty generates multiple modes of labor strife and the simultaneous invocation of different worker traditions and idioms of insurgency. In any case, these local sites of struggle are the crucibles of "transition" out of which institutions and subjects are made and remade. The long-term outcomes of labor conflicts are therefore less than predictable. But it would be a misguided oversimplification to suggest that these multiple trajectories of labor politics necessarily portend either successful building of a law-based state or aggravating labor upheavals that would eventually challenge communist rule.

FROM CLASS STRUGGLE TO LIVELIHOOD STRUGGLE

The analytical framework presented here for understanding patterns of labor politics during the Chinese transition has highlighted the conjunctural interaction of (1) the contradictions inherent in the Chinese state's strategy of accumulation and legitimation as providing the structural conditions for popular grievances; (2) the system of labor regulation and social reproduction of labor power as constitutive of labor interests and capacity, and (3) the discourses of class, Maoism, citizenship, and legality as the repertoire of standards of justice and insurgent identity claims. In short, the theoretical framework developed in this book departs from existing theorizations of labor unrest that privilege either capitalism's structural logic, as found in Beverly Silver's elegantly argued *Forces of Labor*, or the Chinese state's incapacity, most conceptually articulated in Minxin Pei's *China's Trapped Transition* and Kevin O'Brien and Lianjiang Li's *Rightful Resistance in Rural China*.

By attending to ordinary workers' lived experiences and collective subjectivities in the making, in the contexts of evolving institutional reforms, this book seeks to document and explain the potential and limitations of Chinese labor as a force of social change. The organizing concept that ties the chapters together is "livelihood struggles." It encompasses both collective resistance in the forms of petitions, protests, and strikes, and individual and familial survival strategies taking advantage of state redistribution and market opportunities. By linking resistance and survival in a single study, I hope to understand both why workers mount a remarkable level of resistance to reform but also why they have not become more radical.

To shift our analytical focus from "class struggle" to "livelihood struggle" is to recognize the multiple dimensions of labor politics and agency. In his *Spaces of Hope*, David Harvey retrieves from Karl Marx's early work the notion of the worker as a living subject. Writing mainly about workers' bodily subjectivity and its multiple positionalities with respect to capital circulation and accumulation, Harvey stresses that the worker is not a singular economic category. "The laborer as a person is a worker, consumer, saver, lover, and bearer of culture, and can even be an occasional employer and landed proprietor."[61] Moments of production, exchange, consumption, and social reproduction may generate different politics. That is why workers in this study protest with the same conviction and resolve with which they exploit opportunities in the market and relish the modicum of redistributive resources at their disposal. The resultant pattern of labor politics, like that of Guha's subalterns, oscillates between "a conservative tendency made of the inherited and uncritically absorbed material of the ruling culture and a radical one oriented toward a practical transformation of a rebel's condition of existence."[62] Or as Harvey notes of contemporary labor struggles under the onslaught of neoliberal globalization, on the one hand, "there is the revolutionary urge to become free of the embeddedness within the circulation of capital that so circumscribes life chances, body politics, and socio-ecological futures. On the other [hand], there is the reformist demand for fair and proper treatment within the circulation process, to be free, for example, of the ugly choice between adequate remuneration in consumption and abject submission in production."[63] Indeed, a deep ambivalence toward China's socialist past and capitalist present lies at the core of the working-class experience in the reform period. "The working class is neither pure combativity, nor pure passive dispersal, not pure institutionalized apparatus. It is a complex, moving relation between different practical forms."[64]

ORGANIZATION OF THE BOOK

My task in this book is to suggest the specific conditions, constraints, and concerns of Chinese workers who participate in these collective mobilizations. The twin questions that thread through the mosaic of stories, events, emotions, and human faces in the following chapters are: How and why have Chinese workers staged as much resistance as they have? And why have protests largely been bottled up in particular workplaces or localities and seldom escalated to larger-scale and more challenging horizontally organized dissent? In short, I ask whether labor unrest in the reform era signals the formation of a Chinese working class in the world's fastest-growing economy with the world's largest workforce.

Chapter 2 is an overview of the uneven transition from social contract to labor contract as a framework for regulating employment relations and reproducing labor power. It is also a brief history of what Polanyi would term "a double movement" of commodification and social protection through state legislation. On the one hand, the restructuring of the Chinese industrial economy has led to the rise and growth of nonstate economic sectors, the shrinkage of state industries, and the recomposition of the workforce. As an older generation of workers were let go from bankrupt or sold state-owned enterprises, a new generation of migrant workers have moved into urban factories producing for a global market. On the other hand, as commodification of labor proceeds apace with market reform, the Chinese state has attempted to put in place an elaborate legal framework, replacing the erstwhile socialist permanent employment system with labor contracts and a new contribution-based safety net. The chapter explains how the various pieces of labor reform have worked or faltered. Owing to the scope of their impact, these institutional reforms have provoked public debate, circulating a range of moral and linguistic resources that would enter into workers' world of resistance and acquiescence. In sum, chapter 2 argues that labor reform is a stalled transition between a system of labor relations based on social contract and one based on legal contract, caused by the local state's priority of accumulation at the expense of legitimation and by the weakness of the legal system under political authoritarianism.

Chapters 3 and 4 examine protests of desperation, or the pattern of labor struggles and survival among veteran state sector workers in the northeastern rustbelt in the past decade. Chapter 3 focuses on the politics of different types of unrest, including protests against pension arrears, bankruptcy, and neighborhood problems. Although cellular activism predominates across these various kinds of protests, on rare occasions, this localized and fragmented mode of popular contention has demonstrated a tendency to become radicalized and politicized. In any case, workers in protests have mobilized three different kinds of insurgent identities, drawing on a rich repertoire of political discourses, including Marxism, Maoism, and legality, that have arisen under Chinese socialism and postsocialism. The chapter argues that the disintegration of the social contract and the informalization of the new contractual system have produced moral and material grievances. From the ruins of the socialist work units, rustbelt workers organized to make claims about the value of their labor, but their oppositional consciousness exceeds their mobilization capacity. Chapter 4 extends the realm of livelihood struggle from protest to consciousness and praxis grounded in workers' everyday life world. Housing entitlements and arrangements, reciprocity within working-class families, and participation at the margin of the market economy allow aggrieved workers and their families to survive, even as the working-class community is in the process of disintegration. Workers' collective memory and assessment of their past and present livelihood reveals a deep ambivalence toward the regime that places limits on their militancy.

Chapters 5 and 6 turn to protests against discrimination by the new generation of young workers in the sunbelt province of Guangdong, where export industries have created a seemingly insatiable demand for this new workforce from China's vast countryside. In chapter 5, I show that despite their difference in age and generational experience from rustbelt workers, despite their coming from a different side of the urban-rural divide, and despite their being employed in a different ownership sector, aggrieved migrant workers, like unemployed and retired rustbelt workers, adopt a predominant mode of mobilization that is cellular and workplace-based. The most common causes of unrest in the sunbelt, however, unlike in the rustbelt, are the nonpayment of wages and exploitation and degradation in the workplace, not collective consumption. Falling outside the moral economy prescribed by a socialist social contract, migrant workers see the law as providing their only institutional leverage in situations of labor conflict. Their mobilization targets local officials and employers and they work through the legal channel, the labor bureau, and the arbitration system. When these institutionalized channels fail to deliver justice, migrant workers turn to the streets and pursue direct action. Instead of desperation growing out of market exclusion and state betrayal, these migrants see their major challenges in exploitation and discrimination, and they demand equal legal rights as citizens. Their insurgent identities are couched more in terms of citizenship and the marginalized and less in the idiom of class than are the insurgent identities of rustbelt workers. Chapter 6 depicts migrant workers' way of life, which entails rural and urban residence, social relations, and economic exchanges. The experience and economics of *dagong*, or laboring for the bosses, cannot be abstracted from the larger fabric of workers' village lives. It is where the social reproduction of labor power is organized: getting married, building a home, raising and educating children, and subsistence farming. Migrant workers' land use rights in their birth villages are a key nexus connecting their work lives with their family lives, and provide an alternative means of survival in times of unemployment or injury. This safety valve, like rustbelt workers' housing benefits, has important stabilizing effects amidst the rising tide of labor unrest. In interesting parallel to the ambivalence of the older generation of workers toward the reform regime, migrant workers also see both progress and injustice in their mixed status as workers and farmers.

Chapter 7 concludes this study with a double comparison: extending from the Chinese rustbelt and sunbelt into similar local political economies elsewhere in the world; and then within China, comparing labor activism with mobilization by farmers and homeowners in the reform period. American workers confronting deindustrialization in the 1980s experienced the same economic and moral dislocation as Chinese workers today, and they also mobilized to demand legislative protection for mortgaged homes, unemployment benefits, and community buyouts of closing plants. Workers in Mexico's export industrial regions and South Korea's light and heavy industries, or an earlier generation of Chinese workers before the Communist Revolution, like Chinese migrant workers today, have fought against exploitation and state repression of independent unionism. Notwithstanding these structural similarities, the chapter also finds that Chinese labor politics in the reform era has come up against particularly daunting hurdles presented by the combined effect of a repressive state-business alliance and a society with little transnational or domestic social movement support. Workers in these other societies have at least benefited from elite cleavage, party or union competition, or social movement associational resources. With so little going their way, Chinese workers' struggle in the past two decades can indeed be considered daring. Finally, returning to China itself, emerging trends of social protests by farmers and the urban middle class point us toward the centrality of the law and legal institutions as a tool of authoritarian domination. Both these latter types of politics share with labor protests the emergent characteristics of legalism, localization, and decentralization. The convergence with workers' struggle on the terrain of the law reinforces a major observation of this study that the law has become a most contested terrain for class and citizenship formation in China.

2 Stalled Reform

Between Social Contract and Legal Contract

The Chinese transition from state socialism has been analyzed in terms of the transformation in property regime, fiscal reform, enterprise governance, economic decentralization, and so on. To this list, this book contributes an additional element—the commodification of labor. Just as it was central to the advent of capitalism in eighteenth- and nineteenth-century Europe, labor commodification is a constituent process of China's turn to capitalism. Karl Marx famously pointed out that a most revolutionary change occasioned by the advent of capitalism is the rise of labor as an object for sale. Like other kinds of commodities, the human capacity to labor can now be alienated from one person and sold to others. Labor has turned into an abstract category of social value and a tangible, material, and physical property of human actors, rather than a life process embedded in concrete and personal social relations. This historic shift entails a radical reformulation of the mode of domination, political subjectivity, social relations, morality, and notions of time and space.[1]

Although labor is turned into a commodity in the process of market reform, it is a "fictitious" one. As Karl Polanyi maintained, a full commodification of labor would destroy human life itself. Societies therefore have invariably moved to provide certain forms of protection for labor. The social history of nineteenth-century Western Europe, Polanyi succinctly concluded, was essentially a story of a "double movement." The spread of the market triggered deep-seated movements in society to resist its pernicious effects, in the form of legislation from above or workers' movements from below.[2] Lacking a theory of class formation or mobilization, Polanyi did not explain the conditions for the rise of either of these trajectories of social protection. But we can still use his insight to trace the Chinese state's initiative from above to provide social protection when the market economy spread and labor was transformed into a commodity.

This chapter begins by outlining the various institutional arrangements that formed the socialist employment system since the 1950s. It then traces how the state has gradually revamped it by replacing the underlying socialist social contract with the market-oriented principle of the voluntaristic labor contract enforced by law. New labor policies regarding pension, wages, and benefits have been promulgated, aimed at transforming workers from a sociopolitical status group to a factor of production for sale in the market. This process amounts to constructing a new regime of labor, or a new political apparatus for regulating labor relations, to meet the requirements of a market economy. It has proven to be a tumultuous process not only because many workers have been stripped of their time-honored entitlements and have become the new urban poor. The new system has also witnessed many gaps and ineffective implementations, depriving many workers of their legal rights conferred by new laws and policies. This stalled transition is a hotbed for the informalization of employment practices heavily biased against workers' interests, especially for the most vulnerable and marginalized groups. Finally, the pivotal role of the employment system in organizing socialism and the scope of its impact on the tens of millions of ordinary people involved has triggered intense debate about labor reform. I shall outline the rationale and rhetoric in the last section of the chapter. The changing public discourse about the value of labor has contained multiple linguistic and moral frameworks that later reemerged in workers' protests.

CHINESE SOCIALISM AND WORKER ENTITLEMENT

Its egalitarian ideology notwithstanding, Chinese socialism had constructed an elaborate social structure of inequalities. In the absence of a market, resources, life opportunities, and welfare benefits were unevenly allocated through bureaucratic redistribution. The most salient and fundamental divide was the one between rural and urban residents, demarcated by their respective household registration status. State power was predicated on people's material dependence on government redistribution. The general population was also subjected to political control imposed through the far-reaching arms of the state apparatus, ranging from the military and the police to the Party cells, which exist on the shop floor, in urban neighborhood committees, or in rural production teams. For the industrial workforce, this web of all-encompassing control and organized dependence operated through the work unit *(danwei)*.[3] From the 1950s until the eve of

economic reform in the late 1970s, intraclass inequality among urban industrial workers, in terms of wages and benefits, was organized and solidified
according to the type of work unit to which workers belonged.

At the apex of this hierarchy were the permanent state workers, or workers in state-owned enterprises with urban household registration. In 1981,
at the beginning of reform, this labor aristocracy accounted for 42 percent of
the entire industrial labor force and produced 75 percent of total industrial
output. Their employment conditions epitomized "socialism's superiority":
cradle-to-grave welfare, permanent job tenure, housing provision, lifelong
medical and pension benefits, and superior wages. Only 32 percent of these
permanent state workers were female. The next group down the industrial
ranking consisted of workers in urban collectives—enterprises that were
initially set up by local government bureaus to absorb unemployed personnel or provide employment for state-dependent workers. Some were subsidiaries of state-owned firms catering to the latter's production needs.
Operating without protection of the state budget, and accounting for 18
percent of urban industrial employment, collectives varied greatly in terms
of their welfare provisions. It was a feminized sector: 57 percent of this
workforce were women in 1981. Beyond these two major groups of workers, temporary workers in state-owned enterprises and workers in rural
industries received even fewer benefits. Their rural residency prevented
them from becoming permanent workers in state and collective factories.[4]
Among permanent workers in state firms, finer differences in the quality
and quantity of welfare entitlement existed among heavy, light, and military equipment industries, and among firms of different bureaucratic ranks.
Within the same enterprise, seniority, Communist Party membership, gender, and personal ties with cadres determined the distribution of bonuses,
training opportunities, housing benefits, and the like. Gender inequalities,
for instance, were manifested in pay disparity, occupational and job segregation, and welfare gaps, despite state efforts to increase women's labor participation rates. On the eve of reform, women's average wage was 83 percent
that of men's; the male-female ratio of Communist Party membership was
2:1; and male-headed households were given priority in terms of welfare
housing allocations.[5]

If not all workers were treated equally, neither were they merely docile
subjects of a totalitarian state. Economic inequalities rooted in the socialist
industrial system, fueled at times by state-inspired factionalism, have periodically propelled different segments of the workforce to engage in collective action and to make economic demands. Thus, even in the prereform
period, Chinese workers claimed a history of proletarian rebellion and

activism, notably in the strike wave of 1956–1957, factional strife and violent protests during the Cultural Revolution (especially in 1966–1967), and workers' participation in the 1976 April Fifth Movement.

Seizing the opportunity of the Hundred Flowers Campaign, when Chairman Mao encouraged dissent from below to preempt larger-scale revolts similar to those in Hungary, workers displaced by the socialization of industries staged more than 1,300 strikes in Shanghai alone between the months of March and June 1957. Launched most fervently by apprentices and temporary workers and those in joint-ownership enterprises, striking workers demanded higher wages, better welfare, permanent worker status, and guaranteed promotion.[6] The Cultural Revolution a decade later offered another political opportunity for labor struggles. Turmoil inside Chinese factories across the nation was partially shaped by factional cleavages created by the Party's network inside the factories, distinguishing the royalists (comprising loyal members of the Party's organization, activists, Party members, shop-floor leaders, model workers, etc.) from the rebels (including a diverse group of ordinary workers who either had been victimized by the royalists or by factory managers prior to the Cultural Revolution or had criticized the Party authority). But labor conflicts during this period were also structured by deep-rooted occupational grievances and inequalities, with apprentices, the unskilled, irregular workers, and younger workers most prominent in making economic demands and joining rebel factions across the country.[7] Then, in the spring of 1976, mass demonstrations and riots with a strong element of worker participation broke out in more than forty places across the country. The backbone of this uprising was young workers, who had been the basis of mobilization during the Cultural Revolution but had been stigmatized for their bourgeois leanings. They used the occasion of the commemoration of the late Premier Zhou Enlai to express their dissatisfaction with the Gang of Four, as well as to protest the political persecution and injustices they suffered.[8]

In the Maoist era of state socialism, the working class as a whole made great strides vis-à-vis other social groups (notably the peasants, the bourgeoisie, and the intellectuals) in terms of political status, wages, welfare, and employment security. Thanks to the egalitarian bent of the Maoist road to modernization, which placed dual emphasis on industrialization and public ownership, Chinese workers (including both blue-collar and white-collar employees in urban areas) benefited from the "urban bias" in resource allocation commonly found in developing countries. Furthermore, Maoist ideology enhanced the position of workers vis-à-vis the intelligentsia and managerial cadres. The latter groups were required to engage in productive labor periodically, sometimes being sent to the countryside for this purpose, and their salaries were capped, following the Cultural Revolution, at only 10–30 percent above that of the highest-paid skilled workers. In material terms, despite a low wage system, workers' real wage levels in 1970 were 35 percent higher than in 1952. Despite periodic setbacks, the revolutionary regime made available unmistakable improvements in workers' living standards—food, housing, medical care, education, and training opportunities.[9] Politically, state paternalism led to both dependence and defiance. Although in normal times, the penetration of the state into workers' everyday life preempted autonomous political activity among workers, there were also volatile periods when marginal workers who felt deprived of their fair share of "socialism's superiority" rose in rebellion against the state.

RESTRUCTURING THE INDUSTRIAL ECONOMY

A quarter century of reform and opening has drastically restructured the economy and the workforce. First, there has been a fundamental shift in the ownership pattern of industrial firms. Table 1 underscores the secular decline in the proportion of state-owned or state-controlled industrial units. The percentage of total industrial output attributable to state-owned enterprises fell dramatically, from 75 percent in 1981 to a mere 26 percent in 1997. At the same time, private, foreign-owned, and joint-venture firms (that is, the category "Others" in table 1) mushroomed, especially in the 1990s when the government made a decisive push to let go of unprofitable small and medium-sized state firms. Bankruptcy and privatization have significantly undercut the numerical and social prominence of the old socialist working class (see table 2).

This industrial restructuring has dealt a severe blow to permanent state workers' entitlements, shattering their prized employment and livelihood security, known colloquially as the "iron rice bowl." Workers in collective enterprises, which had always functioned as subsidiaries of state firms, suffered massive layoffs as well. On the other hand, the rise of the private and foreign sector has opened up unprecedented employment opportunities for the massive pool of peasant migrants. This immense labor reserve was released from agriculture in the wake of decollectivization in the late 1970s, when collective land use rights were redistributed to peasant households. These surplus laborers took advantage of foreign investors' demand for factory hands and the loosening up of the household registra-

TABLE 1 *Percentage of Gross Industrial Output by Ownership, 1993–2003*

Year	State-owned or state-controlled (%)	Collective (%)	Individual (%)	Others (%)
1981	74.76	24.62	0.04	0.47
1985	64.86	32.08	1.85	1.21
1988	56.80	36.15	4.34	2.72
1990	54.60	35.62	5.39	4.38
1991	56.16	33.00	4.83	6.01
1992	51.52	35.07	5.80	7.61
1993	46.95	34.02	7.98	11.05
1994	37.34	37.32	10.09	14.85
1995	33.96	36.59	12.86	16.58
1996[a]	36.32 (28.48)	39.39	15.48	16.65
1997	31.62 (25.52)	38.11	17.92	18.45
1998	28.24	38.41	17.11	22.91
1999	28.21	35.37	18.18	26.14
2000	47.33	13.90	—	64.07
2001	44.41	10.53	—	71.46
2002	40.79	8.68	—	75.73
2003	37.54	6.65	—	80.36

SOURCE: Compiled from National Bureau of Statistics of China, *China Industrial Economic Statistical Yearbook, 2004* (Beijing: China Statistics Press, 2005), table 2-4 [in Chinese].

[a] The numbers in the column "State-owned or state-controlled" before 1996 are data from state-owned enterprises and those from 1996 on are data from both state-owned and state-controlled enterprises. Because some of these firms were double-counted as "others," the sum may total more than 100 percent. The numbers in parentheses represent data from state-owned enterprises.

tion system by the state at that time. Women accounted for about 47.5 percent of all migrant workers in 2000.[10] In some industrial cities such as Shenzhen, women account for 65.6 percent of all migrants.[11] Of all migrant workers, more than 37 percent are employed in industry, with the rest mostly found in construction (14 percent), service (12 percent), and restaurants (12 percent).[12] Reform therefore has spawned two historical processes: first, the unmaking of an entire generation of workers rooted in Maoist socialist tradition and institutions; and, second, the making of a new generation of young migrant workers who are inserted into the orbit

TABLE 2 *State-Owned Enterprise Employment, 1990–2003*

Year	Total number employed (millions)	Industrial workers	
		Number employed in state-owned enterprises (millions)	Percentage employed in state-owned enterprises (%)
1990	63.78	43.64	68.4
1991	65.51	44.72	68.3
1992	66.21	45.21	68.3
1993	66.26	44.98	67.9
1994	65.82	43.71	66.4
1995	66.10	43.97	66.5
1996	64.50	42.78	66.3
1997	62.15	40.40	65
1998	47.53	27.12	57.1
1999	44.28	24.12	54.5
2000	41.02	20.96	51.1
2001	38.38	18.24	47.5
2002	37.29	15.46	41.5
2003	36.72	13.34	36.3

SOURCES: Compiled from National Bureau of Statistics of China, *China Statistical Yearbook, 2004* (New York: Praeger, 2005), table 5-9; and National Bureau of Statistics of China, *China Statistical Yearbook, 1999* (New York: Praeger, 2000), tables 5-6, 5-8.

of capitalism without being fully proletarianized or deprived of their land rights.

UNEVEN INSTITUTIONALIZATION OF
A LAW-BASED LABOR REGIME

Determined to reform the permanent employment system and to regulate the new workplaces and workers, the Chinese state has since the beginning of market reform enacted a series of labor laws. Institutionalizing a labor rule of law has been a protracted process of gradual change over two decades, touching on different aspects of labor relations in different phases of reform. Consistent with the general gradualist approach adopted by the Chinese leadership in other arenas of reform, labor reform usually begins with local experiments or "test points" in certain sectors of the economy.

New practices with proven effectiveness are then adopted by the central government and later promulgated as national laws and regulations. The following sections trace the historical evolution of core changes in labor policy: from the introduction of labor contracts in a small foreign investment enclave, to the promulgation of regulations for handling labor disputes, the passage of a national labor law, and the establishment of a national social security system. Along the way, I will discuss the difficulties of implementing central government regulations at the local levels, leading to a stalled labor transition for many.

Labor Contracts

Labor contracts did not exist under the planned economy. Instead, under an "iron rice bowl" system consolidated since the 1950s, workers were administratively allocated to a de facto job tenure system in urban work units. Labor power, or workers' capacity for productive labor, was not a commodity to be sold and bought by workers and employers in the marketplace. Rather, workers formed a sociopolitical status group whose lifestyle and opportunities were guaranteed and enforced by the state to whom workers would pledge political loyalty and compliance: hence the implicit bargain struck between communist regimes and the populace, or what has come to be known by social scientists as the socialist social contract.[13] By the early 1980s, 97 percent of the state workforce were "fixed workers" with effective lifetime tenure in their jobs.[14]

Labor contracts were introduced in the late 1970s for two reasons. First, the Chinese government was confronted at that time with the political urgency of alleviating the tremendous unemployment pressure caused by the return of some fifteen million "sent-down youths," who had been sent to work in rural areas during the Cultural Revolution.[15] Labor contracts were introduced as a way of expanding employment, by allowing enterprise managers to recruit their own workers and create new employment channels run by collectives and private enterprises.[16] When unemployment pressure abated in the early 1980s, reformers shifted their focus from creating employment to enhancing enterprise productivity. The experiment with labor contracts for new recruits in state and collective enterprises was one such productivity-boosting measure. Other such measures included linking performance with wages and bonuses, using examinations for hiring and promotion, tightening labor discipline, and purchasing more advanced technology.[17] In February 1983, the Ministry of Labor and Personnel issued a formal circular expanding the labor contract experiment from thirteen provinces to all provinces, calling on localities to choose their own pilot enterprises and industries. A second reason for introducing labor contracts was the leadership's decision to allow foreign investment in special economic zones in south China. In enterprises involving foreign capital, provisions for labor contracts were promulgated alongside a joint-venture law in 1979. The government saw the labor contract as an instrument to attract and regulate an experimental economic zone at the margin of the national political economy.[18]

At the beginning, such attempts at overhauling a quintessential socialist institution were greeted with ambivalence and debate. Supporters of labor contracts argued that they were instrumental for realizing the principle of "distribution according to labor," bringing about choices for both labor and management, and clarifying each party's responsibility, power, and benefits.[19] Yet deep disagreement among policy elites and academics, as well as mass anxiety about employment security and worker morale, stalled the universalization of labor contracts for more than a decade. Although the labor contract system was extended to all new recruits in state factories in July 1986, it was not until 1993 that the government set a timetable for implementing the policy nationwide, covering enterprises of all ownership types. The Labor Law, which was passed in 1994 and became effective in 1995, formally requires that all employees sign labor contracts with their employers.[20] Official statistics show that labor contracts had become universal in the state sector by the end of the 1990s, although in many places, signing a contract is just a ritualistic compliance. Neither workers nor managers were serious or concerned about the terms and implications of the contracts. For the nonstate sector, surveys reveal that only about 23–30 percent of migrant workers in private enterprises have contracts.[21] This contract gap, as we shall see in later chapters, would lead to much frustration for workers trying to use the legal system to defend their rights.

Labor Dispute Resolution

Another early attempt by the Chinese government to regulate employment relations through legalization concerns the resolution of labor disputes. A labor dispute arbitration system existed briefly in the early years of the People's Republic but was abolished once private industry was socialized by the late 1950s. Under the permanent employment system and the socialist ideology proclaiming workers "masters" of their enterprise, no formal mechanism was deemed necessary for settling disputes in the workplace. Informal mediation between the workshop director and the aggrieved worker was the preferred method of dispute resolution. But with the introduction of labor contracts in both state and private sectors, the government saw the need to formalize a set of administrative channels for resolving labor conflicts arising from contractual employment relations. In 1987, the State Council promulgated the Provisional Regulations on the Handling of Enterprise Labor Disputes in State Enterprises, which revived the basic three-step procedural structure abolished in the 1950s. It stipulated the mechanisms and the administrative units for mediation, arbitration, and litigation. Then, in 1993, the Regulations for the Handling of Labor Disputes replaced the 1987 Provisional Regulations. The new regulation expanded the scope of conflict resolution to include disputes over matters other than contract termination, such as wages, benefits, and occupational health and safety. Employees of all kinds of enterprises, not just those in the state sector, are now covered. A national hierarchy of labor dispute arbitration committees has been set up. By 2003, there were some 222,888 labor dispute mediation committees in state-owned enterprises, 3,192 labor dispute arbitration committees at the county, city, and provincial levels, and 24,000 labor dispute arbitrators.[22] These committees theoretically follow a tripartite principle and should consist of representatives from the labor bureau, the trade union, and the enterprise. But in practice, most of the cases are heard by one arbitrator wearing a double hat as representative of the union and of the labor bureau. Appeals against arbitral awards can be made to the courts as civil lawsuits.

The construction of this dispute arbitration system turns out to be a double-edged sword. On the one hand, a safety valve is created as the state rationalizes the resolution of conflicts, confining and subjecting them to bureaucratic and judicial processing. On the other hand, the dispute resolution system opens up new opportunities and resources for workers to challenge not only employers who violate the law, but also local state agents who decide what rules must be obeyed and what rights and responsibilities must be recognized. Table 3 shows the staggering increase in the number of arbitrated labor disputes and employees involved since the implementation of the 1993 Regulation. Workers have obviously been keen to use the law as a weapon to protect their interests. Most of those cases were initiated by employees and, according to official statistics, 50 to 80 percent of arbitral awards, depending on localities, were in favor of employees.[23] What these figures conceal, however, is the often elusive boundary separating institutional and noninstitutional activism. When workers are encouraged to seek legal and bureaucratic redress, only to find that the local state often colludes

TABLE 3 *Labor Arbitration, 1994–2004*

Year	Arbitrated labor disputes (cases)	Arbitrated collective disputes (cases)	Number of employees involved
1994	19,098	1,482	77,794
1995	33,030	2,588	122,512
1996	47,951	3,150	189,120
1997	71,524	4,109	221,115
1998	93,649	6,767	358,531
1999	120,191	9,043	473,957
2000	135,206	8,247	422,617
2001	154,621	9,847	467,150
2002	184,116	11,024	608,396
2003	226,391	10,823	801,042
2004	269,471	19,241	764,981

SOURCES: Data compiled from National Bureau of Statistics of China, *China Labor and Social Security Yearbook, 1995* (Beijing: China Statistics Press, 1996) [in Chinese]; National Bureau of Statistics of China, *China Labor and Social Security Yearbook, 1996* (Beijing: China Statistics Press, 1997) [in Chinese]; National Bureau of Statistics of China, *China Labor and Social Security Yearbook, 1997* (Beijing: China Statistics Press, 1998) [in Chinese]; National Bureau of Statistics of China, *China Labor and Social Security Yearbook, 1998* (Beijing: China Statistics Press, 1999) [in Chinese]; National Bureau of Statistics of China, *China Labor and Social Security Yearbook, 1999* (Beijing: China Statistics Press, 2000) [in Chinese]; National Bureau of Statistics of China, *China Labor and Social Security Yearbook, 2000* (Beijing: China Statistics Press, 2001) [in Chinese]; National Bureau of Statistics of China, *China Labor and Social Security Yearbook, 2001* (Beijing: China Statistics Press, 2002) [in Chinese]; National Bureau of Statistics of China, *China Statistical Yearbook, 2002* (New York: Praeger, 2003), p. 794; National Bureau of Statistics of China, *China Statistical Yearbook, 2003* (New York: Praeger, 2004), p. 824; National Bureau of Statistics of China, *China Statistical Yearbook, 2004* (New York: Praeger, 2005), table 23-5; and www.molss.gov.cn/gb/zwxx/2005-12/14/content 99533.htm.

with employers, they are emboldened to resort to mass action to draw the attention of superior levels of government to right local wrongs.

The National Labor Law and Workers' Rights

If reinvigorating the labor arbitration system inadvertently encourages labor activism, the legalization of labor rights is an even more direct catalyst. In 1994, China passed its first ever National Labor Law since the establishment of the People's Republic. As a basic law, it stipulates the legal principles for contractual employment relations, elaborates a range of workers' rights, and redefines the role of the state as regulator of labor relations. In terms of workers' rights, the most important, and interestingly also the most commonly violated, are: the right to get paid for one's labor, the right to rest days and holidays, the right to a safe workplace environment, and the right to receive social insurance and welfare. Another significant feature of the Labor Law is the minimum wage system, the level of which is set by the provincial legislature. The Labor Law also stipulates special provisions to protect women's interests, establishing antidiscrimination principles in recruitment and remuneration, and setting limits on the types of work that may be performed by pregnant, nursing, or menstruating women.[24]

In several fundamental ways, the Labor Law marks a drastic break between "socialist" and "capitalist" employment systems. First, in recognizing the unequal power and disunity of interest between workers and management, the Labor Law jettisons the previous ideological assumption of harmonious relations between employees and employers. The Labor Law was enacted with a view to protecting the legal rights of workers—the weaker party—by placing the state more on their side. Second, the Labor Law abolishes previous distinctions among workers in different types of enterprises—for example, state, collective, private, migrant, temporary, or permanent—and provides a uniform legal framework as well as setting labor standards that are applicable to all workers in all types of enterprises. Third, by stipulating a contribution-based social security system for all workers independent of the ownership nature of their factories, the law shifts the financial burden of worker welfare away from the state and toward the employers and workers themselves. Employment is now a private contractual relationship and the state is a regulator of the labor market rather than an administrator of employment. Whereas the Labor Law lays down the general principles of workers' rights to insurance and the responsibility of workers and employers to contribute to social insurance funds, supplementary regulations and laws have been, and will be, passed to implement those welfare provisions.[25]

From the workers' perspective, the most immediate and sensitive concerns in the Labor Law are those relating to pension, unemployment benefits, medical care, and housing. In the past decade, the transition from a workplace-based and state-funded welfare regime to an employment- and contribution-based system has wreaked havoc on many working-class lives, as unemployment becomes a national social problem.

Pensions

Hailed by the government as a manifestation of the superiority of socialism, a guaranteed pension is widely considered a sacrosanct entitlement by ordinary workers in state industries. The 1951 Labor Insurance Regulation provided pension, medical and disability insurance, and maternity benefits for workers and their family members in enterprises with more than one hundred employees. Such provisions, formulated by Party leaders experienced in skilled workers' unions during the Communist Revolution and modeled after artisans' native-place guilds, were later expanded to include government employees and smaller enterprises.[26] From the 1950s to the mid-1960s, China patterned its social security system after the Soviet model, with insurance plans administered by the official union and the Ministry of Labor. Work units contributed a portion of their total wage bills (about 3 percent) to a pooled fund to cover the expenses for employees' pension and medical expenses. This system was abandoned during the Cultural Revolution (1966–1976), when the official union and the Ministry of Labor were abolished. Since the late 1960s, pensions, along with other forms of welfare, became the responsibility of the individual work units, which paid their retirees directly out of current revenue. The retirement age was sixty for male workers and cadres, fifty-five for female cadres, and fifty for female workers. The replacement rate for cash wages stood at a high of 80 percent (the international average is about 40 to 60 percent), with in-kind benefits continuing at the preretirement level.[27] By the early 1990s, the ratio of pension to preretirement compensation therefore reached 90 percent, depending on the employee's post, grade, and sector.[28]

Based neither on taxation nor contribution and accumulation, this "pay-as-you-go" system at first depended totally on central government appropriation after enterprises remitted all profits. Pensions were drawn from enterprises' employee welfare funds, the size of which varied with the size of the enterprise, and which came from the government. With a massive graying of the working population, the government recognized very early on in the reform process that the old work-unit-based social security was a fiscal time bomb. Reform of the pension system began well ahead of other types of welfare because of the immense demographic pressure. The number of urban retirees increased 7.3 times in fifteen years, from a mere 3.14 million in 1978 on the eve of reform to 25.98 million in 1992. In 2000, China had 36 million retirees. The corresponding ratios of working to retired employees worsened from 30.3:1 in 1978 to 5.7:1 in 1992.[29] By the mid-1990s, retirees were estimated to represent 37 percent of the total workforce of large and medium-sized state-owned enterprises.[30] The World Bank estimated that the proportion of the total wage bill that is used for pensions would rise from 7 percent in 1978 to an alarming 40 percent by 2030.[31] Pensions were also a tremendous financial burden on state sector enterprises, depriving them of a level playing field in market competition.

Following enterprise reform in the mid-1980s, state-owned enterprises were required to generate their welfare funds from their profits. The older the enterprise, the heavier the pension burden on the enterprise's budget and the less profitable the enterprise became. The rise of new foreign firms, joint ventures, and township and village enterprises, which usually employ younger workers, creates formidable competitive pressures for state firms saddled with permanent older workers.

After years of local and sporadic experiments, the government gradually imposed a unified system by issuing several circulars and provisional regulations between 1986 and 1997. From 1997 to 2000, the emphasis was on standardizing local practices into one national system, and centralizing the administration and management of pension insurance plans in the hands of provincial governments, not municipal governments. Employees now are required to contribute up to 8 percent of their monthly wages and employers up to 20 percent of their total wage bills. The funds are deposited into two kinds of accounts: a social pooling account and an individual account, the proportions of which are decided by the provincial government. A retiree's pension will therefore have both pay-as-you-go and contributory components. The Labor Law requires that all enterprises, regardless of ownership category, and all employees, including migrant workers, participate in this contributory system. In light of migrant workers' high job mobility, some localities have issued their own policies allowing migrant workers to withdraw the accumulated contributions in their personal accounts, but not the social pooling account, when they leave their employers. For instance, in Shenzhen, since 2001, migrant workers have been entitled to pension stipends when they reach retirement age if they have made continuous contributions to their pension accounts, and if they have fifteen or more years of employment in Shenzhen.[32] In 2001, the average monthly wage of an employee participating in old-age insurance was 695 yuan and the average pension received by a retiree was 576 yuan, or a pension substitution rate of 82.8 percent.[33]

The implementation of pension reform has met with serious problems. First, in terms of coverage, the state sector has been the most successful in expanding the participation rate, reaching 96 percent in 1998. The coverage rates for collective and all other nonstate enterprises were only 53 percent and 30 percent, respectively.[34] Overall, across all types of enterprises, only 40 percent of firms participate in pension plans. A survey of some 1,500 migrant workers in Guangdong found that 73.8 percent of the respondents did not have any form of social security in 2001.[35] One reason for this limited coverage is the common practice by local governments of allowing employers to enroll only 10 to 20 percent of their employees in social insurance, instead of pressing for the (nearly) impossible goal of full enrollment, as required by law.[36]

A second and more urgent problem is the massive pension defaults and arrears that occurred in the late 1990s, caused by the insolvency of many old state firms with large numbers of retirees on their payrolls. Market reform has brought about financial independence for state companies, as enterprise managers enjoy wide-ranging autonomy in setting wages, determining output prices, hiring and firing, and allocating investment finances. But such independence also means that welfare expenditures have to be drawn from their profits, too. Unprofitable enterprises have nowhere to turn for funding. Many state firms that have nominally joined the pooling system are heavily in debt and have suspended their contributions.

In 2000, for instance, of all the work units nationwide participating in pension insurance funds, about 25 percent of them failed to make their full contributions. Some 43,617 work units were not able to pay full pensions to some four million retirees. And one-third of these retirees were concentrated in Liaoning province—one of the oldest industrial bases in China.[37] In the provincial capital, Shenyang, 26.4 percent of retirees have reported pension arrears.[38] Furthermore, pension burdens sometimes spawn wage arrears. Pension burdens often make enterprises unprofitable, seriously impairing their solvency and ability to pay wages to their working employees. According to official union statistics, the number of enterprises and the number of workers involved in wage arrears have soared (see table 4). A recent five-city survey revealed that 10.6 percent of working-age adults who worked during the 1996–2001 period had experienced wage arrears.[39]

Because retiring workers had often been replaced with their own offspring, a fairly common practice since the 1970s, it is not uncommon to find entire working-class families suddenly being plunged into financial difficulties when the enterprise for which they all work goes out of business. Under pressure from several years of widespread worker protests in the late 1990s, the central government gave additional emergency funding to social insurance funds. Nevertheless, in 2001, despite a 349.4 billion yuan transfer, there was still a shortfall of 2 billion yuan for the repayment of owed pensions.[40] As we shall see later, the rampant nonpayment crisis has led to numerous petitions and protests in rustbelt cities.

Unemployment Benefits

Unemployment has become an explosive social and political problem since the mid-1990s. In public opinion polls, ordinary citizens and officials alike consis-

TABLE 4   *Pension Arrears, 1996–2000*

		Number of units in arrears on pensions to retired and resigned workers	Number of retired and resigned workers with pensions in arrears
1996	National	692,272	1,040,448
	Liaoning	157,365	214,442
1997	National	1,122,486	1,268,098
	Liaoning	194,112	166,955
1998		Data unavailable	
1999	National	29,919	3,647,004
	Liaoning	2,485	443,909
2000	National	43,617	3,881,306
	Liaoning	4,709	1,193,006

SOURCE: Research Department, All China Federation of Trade Unions, *Chinese Trade Union Statistics Yearbook, 2001* (Beijing: China Statistics Press, 2002), pp. 66–67, 79, 88–90.

tently rank unemployment as the primary threat to social stability in urban China.[41] The root of massive unemployment lies in the changing direction of state-owned enterprise reform in the 1990s. Prior to the mid-1990s, enterprise reform focused on enhancing enterprise efficiency by reforming the system of management incentives, autonomy, and governance.[42] The national leadership emphasized enterprise function and the obligation to provide livelihood for employees; acquisition and merger rather than bankruptcy was considered the solution for loss-making firms. Banks were forced to continue their loans to struggling enterprises. But by the early 1990s, the increasingly unbearable burden of subsidizing loss-making state firms finally forced the government to allow leasing, contracting out, and sales of small state-owned enterprises through acquisitions and mergers. Then, after the government formally endorsed the policy of "grasping the big and letting go of the small" (meaning that the government would allow bankruptcy, merger, and acquisition or lease of small firms while reorganizing big firms in strategic sectors) in 1997, bankruptcies (see table 5), production suspension, and privatization became common and unemployment accelerated.

By mid-2001, there were 7.69 million officially registered "laid-off" *(xia-gang)*[43] workers and 6.19 million officially registered "unemployed" workers *(shiye)*.[44] But most academics put the combined estimates at between 19 and 30 million.[45] (See table 6.) These two terms, *laid-off* and *unemployed*,

TABLE 5   *Bankruptcy Cases Accepted by the Courts, 1990–2003*

Year	Number of cases accepted	Year	Number of cases accepted
1990	32	1997	5,697
1991	117	1998	7,746
1992	428	1999	5,622
1993	710	2000	7,219
1994	1,625	2001	9,110
1995	2,348	2002	8,615
1996	6,227	2003	7,673

SOURCES: Data from 1989 through 1996: Cao Siyuan, "Bankruptcy Law in China," *Harvard China Review* 1, no. 1 (1998); data from 1997 through 2001: National Bureau of Statistics of China, *China Statistical Yearbook, 1997* (New York: Praeger, 1998); National Bureau of Statistics of China, *China Statistical Yearbook, 1998* (New York: Praeger, 1999); National Bureau of Statistics of China, *China Statistical Yearbook, 1999* (New York: Praeger, 2000); National Bureau of Statistics of China, *China Statistical Yearbook, 2001* (New York: Praeger, 2002); data from 2002 through 2003: Editorial Board, Law Yearbook of China, *Law Yearbook of China, 2004* (Beijing: Press of Law Yearbook of China, 2005).

denote two groups of workers who are shed from their work units under different conditions and who, in theory, enjoy different entitlements. A "laid-off" worker is one who (1) began working before the contract system was instituted in 1986 and had a formal, permanent job in the state or collective sectors; (2) was let go because of his or her firm's problems in business but has not severed relations with the original firm; and (3) has not found other employment. Many laid-off workers fail to obtain an official laid-off certificate, which they need in order to obtain government assistance but the provision of which implies financial responsibility for their enterprises.[46] "Unemployed" workers are those whose firms have been officially declared bankrupt and whose posts have therefore disappeared. Many former employees who lose their jobs when firms collapse without going through the official bankruptcy procedures cannot be registered as unemployed workers. Therefore, official statistics on both laid-off and unemployed employees are widely considered to be underestimations. Whereas official unemployment rates hovered around 3 to 4 percent in the 1990s, academic researchers reported rates that are three to four times higher.[47]

To maintain social stability in the face of the massive and rapid hike in the number of unemployed workers, the central government has devised

TABLE 6 *Official and Unofficial Unemployment Rates, 1993–2003*

Year	Registered unemployed persons in urban areas (millions)[a]	Official unemployment rate in urban areas (%)[b]	Estimates of total unemployed persons in urban areas (millions)	Unofficial unemployment rate in urban areas (%)
1993	4.20	2.6		3.5[c]
1994	4.76	2.8		3.9[c]
1995	5.20	2.9		18.8[d]
				4.7[e]
1996	5.53	3.0		5.5[e]
1997	5.77	3.1	11.51	15.3[f]
				7.5[g]
1998	5.71	3.1	19.21	10.4[h]
				7.9[i]
1999	5.75	3.1		8.2[i]
2000	5.95	3.1		8.3[i]
2001	6.81	3.6	19.00	7[j]
				8.5[k]
2002	7.70	4.0	30.00	11[m]
			19.20[l]	
2003	8.00	4.3		

[a] SOURCE: National Bureau of Statistics of China, *China Statistical Yearbook, 2004* (New York: Praeger, 2005), tables 2-3, 2-5.

[b] SOURCE: National Bureau of Statistics of China, *China Statistical Yearbook, 2003* (New York: Praeger, 2004), table 2-2.

[c] SOURCE: Hu Angang, "The Current State of China's Economic and Social Development: Analysis and Recommendations," *Reform 5* (2002) [in Chinese]; calculations consistent with International Labor Organization (ILO) guidelines.

[d] SOURCE: "Urban Surplus Labor Survey," compiled by ILO and China Ministry of Labor and Social Security, taken from Yang Yiyong, *Unemployment Shockwave: A Report on the Future of Employment in China* (Beijing: Jinri Publishing House, 1997), p. 48 [in Chinese]. Here, the authors calculated the hidden unemployment rate from all urban enterprises.

[e] SOURCE: Hu, "Current State of China's Economic and Social Development."

[f] SOURCE: Li Qiang, *A Comparative Study of Unemployment and Layoffs* (Beijing: Tsinghua University Press, 2001), p. v. This estimate includes those who are laid off as well as those seeking employment.

[g] SOURCE: Hu, "Current State of China's Economic and Social Development."

[h] SOURCE: Li et al., *Comparative Study of Unemployment and Layoffs*, p. 3.

[i] SOURCE: Hu, "Current State of China's Economic and Social Development."

[j] SOURCE: Mo Rong, "Chinese Urban Unemployment Rate Already at 7 Percent—Appropriate Measures Must Be Taken," *Research Forum 20* (2001) [in Chinese].

[k] SOURCE: Hu, "Current State of China's Economic and Social Development."

[l] SOURCE: Hu Angang, "Chinese Microeconomic Index, 1997–2002: An Analysis of the Previous Administration's Performance and Recommendations for the New Administration," *Hebei Journal 4* (2003) [in Chinese].

[m] SOURCE: Ryoshin Minami and Xue Jinjun, "Estimation of Population and Labor Force in China: 1949–1999," *Chinese Journal of Population Science 3* (2002) [in Chinese]. The unregistered unemployed population and the actual number of unemployed among the laid-off were included in the estimate.

several policies to guarantee a standard of basic livelihood, independent of paid employment. Collectively known as the "three lines of guarantees," these policies include the unemployment insurance system, the "Reemployment Project," and the policy on basic living allowances. Local governments are the key actors in implementing these national policies, resulting in uneven realization of actual protection for workers, depending on the extent of enterprise compliance, the economic structure and history of the province, and the integrity and competence of local officials.

Let us begin with the unemployment insurance system, which first came about in 1986 with the labor contract reform and the bankruptcy law. Before the mid-1990s, unemployment insurance covered only the state sector, where both enterprises and workers contribute to a fund pooled at the "county-ranked" city level. By the mid-1990s, when unemployment increased, all kinds of enterprises were gradually required to participate. Under the 1999 Regulation on Unemployment Insurance, employers contribute 2 percent of total expenditure on salaries and employees contribute 1 percent of their salaries, forming a pooled fund at a prefecture-ranked city administration. Insured employees are paid a monthly allowance set by the local government and for a period of 12–24 months, depending on the length of service of the unemployed.[48] From the beginning, there have been problems with collections as a result of failing enterprises being unable to pay and profitable companies unwilling to join. Although official statistics claim that 78.2 percent of urban employees are covered by unemployment insurance, surveys reveal a grimmer picture: 11 percent of the working population in major cities, 2.8 percent of the unemployed, and 4 percent of those in the private sector at the end of 1999 participated in unemployment insurance plans.[49] An extensive survey revealed that fewer than 30 percent of unemployed men and 25 percent of unemployed women had access to public unemployment or layoff subsidies. One-third to one-half of the unemployed ages forty to fifty—the group most affected by enterprise restructuring—receive no public support at all.[50]

In short, unemployment creates a huge demand for public assistance that has become the administrative and financial responsibility of the local government. Owing to collection problems, misuse of funds, and widespread informal bankruptcy, many workers are deprived of their legal entitlements. Disgruntled and desperate workers have taken to the streets and staged numerous protests, and the central government has responded with circulars, repeatedly urging local governments to take seriously their task of guaranteeing the livelihood of unemployed and laid-off workers. In 2000, the State Council even stipulated that different levels of local governments should increase their budgeted expenditure for social security. At the same time, the central government began a multiyear appropriation to make up the pension and unemployment fund deficits. This special infusion of funds increased from 12 billion yuan in 1998 to 300 billion yuan in 2000. In addition, in 2000, central appropriation for guaranteeing the livelihood allowance of laid-off and unemployed workers reached 458 billion yuan.[51]

The nationwide "Reemployment Project" is the government's response to massive layoffs. The government could not afford to run the political risk of throwing millions of former permanent workers out into the market. Instead, it gives workers continuing access to their work-unit-based benefits, especially pension contributions by their employers through local reemployment centers. Enterprises with laid-off employees are required to partially fund reemployment centers, which are run by individual enterprises, an industry sector, or local labor bureaus. These centers assume trusteeship of laid-off workers for three years, providing them with job training, job placement services, disbursement of basic livelihood allowances, and payment of their social security insurance. Workers have to sign an agreement to terminate their labor relation with their work units upon entering the reemployment centers. At the end of the three-year period, workers are completely on their own or they can register themselves as unemployed. The Reemployment Project has been funded on a "three-three" principle—that is, one-third of the funding comes from each of three sources: local government, enterprises, and unemployment insurance funds.[52] In 2001, the central government announced that reemployment centers would gradually disappear as enterprises were allowed to terminate contracts with employees who become unemployed without going through the transitional laid-off period.

The last measure of livelihood guarantee for the impoverished is a basic living allowance system established in 1997. It targets all urban residents who fall below certain locally determined household income levels. Laid-off and unemployed workers make up a large part of urban poor, estimated to be between fifteen and thirty-one million by the early 2000s,[53] but households with special difficulties, such as those with sick or handicapped household members, are also eligible. The amount of per capita allowance varies according to the living standard of each city, ranging from 100 to 120 yuan in provinces such as Jilin and Heilongjiang and more than 200 yuan in Guangdong and Beijing, with a national average of 150 yuan in 1996.[54] This welfare responsibility falls squarely on city governments, which fund their civil affairs departments to implement this policy. Implementation is far from satisfactory. Many eligible residents are unable to receive benefits because of lack of local funding or local officials' unwillingness to recognize the fact that such residents qualify for benefits. For instance, in Shenyang, only 29 percent of those qualified were paid the basic living allowance in 2000.[55] Again, the central government continued its financial infusion to make up for local deficits. The Ministry of Civil Affairs allocated 8 billion yuan in 2000, 23 billion yuan in 2001, and 46 billion yuan in 2002 to local departments for providing this basic living allowance. Consequently, more people have received the benefits: 3.82 million in 2000, 11.9 million in 2001, and 19.3 million in mid-2002.[56]

Medical Care

From the 1950s to just before the reform era, the vast majority of urban employees (some 94 percent by 1956) were covered under a free medical-care system.[57] The enterprise medical care system provided free services to employees in state-owned and large collective enterprises while the public medical care system provided free services to employees in administrative and nonproductive work units. Dependents of employees were given medical services either free of charge or at half price. The financial burden had always been borne by the enterprise, whether budgeted as part of the enterprise's administrative cost or paid from the enterprise's welfare fund, which was apportioned by the state at a rate of 11 to 14 percent of the total wage bill. Like the pension systems, after the Cultural Revolution in the late 1960s, work units rather than trans-work unit entities (such as the trade union or the local government labor department) became the main provider and administrator of medical welfare. In addition to receiving free medicine and care in outpatient clinics and hospitals, employees on medical leave were paid 60 to 100 percent of their basic wages.[58]

Wasting of resources, hoarding of medicine by patients, and the lack of control over medical expenditures contributed to a fiscal crisis. The average annual growth rate of medical care expenses hovered around 24 percent during the reform years between 1988 and 1994.[59] The rise and rapid development of the nonstate sectors means that a new medical care system is needed to cover employees outside the state sector. Experimental reforms began in 1988, when the State Council led a multiministry committee to study medical reform proposals. Pilot schemes were carried out in Jiangsu, Jiangxi, and Hainan provinces, and they provided the basis for the 1998 State Council decision that required all provinces to implement a basic health insurance program. The new system is basically a contributory, social pooling system whereby employers and employees contribute to a local medical insurance fund, and each employee has an account combining personal and socially pooled contributions. All cities have to set up their programs to be administered by city-level bodies led by the Labor and Social Security Department, and all employers contribute 6 percent of their payroll and employees 2 percent of their wages. All employees' contributions and at least 50 percent of employers' contributions (depending on the length of employment) are deposited into individual accounts, and the remainder to a social pooling account. Below a minimum benefit level, employees have to pay out of pocket for any medical services they need. Above that, payment must first be drawn from employees' personal accounts. Any additional expenses exceeding 5 percent of employees' income are paid from the social pooling component of their accounts and by employees. The percentage of employees' financial responsibility decreases as the cost of service increases. There are other regulations on proportionate reimbursement for different kinds of drugs and hospital care.[60] Yet the overall drift of the reform is to shift the burden of medical care from the state onto employers and employees.

Thus far, as in other arenas of welfare reform, implementation of the new health-insurance system has been uneven, in terms of both coverage and actual access to benefits. Much depends on local economic conditions, local leadership's administrative capacity, and political will. For instance, a recent multicity survey revealed that only 55.7 percent of employed workers had socialized health insurance in 2001, with the highest rate in Shanghai (88.6 percent), compared to a dismal 9.1 percent in Shenyang. Even more important than coverage is whether workers can get the benefits to which they are entitled. Overall, the survey revealed that 22.1 percent of working adults with health insurance experienced expenditure-reimbursement arrears. Shanghai has the lowest rate, at 18.9 percent, while Shenyang registered a high of 27.7 percent.[61] Judging from the coverage rates, local governments are not always successful in enforcing the legal responsibility of employers to contribute to their employees' health benefits. The more impoverished the localities, where workers are more likely to be unemployed, the larger the health insurance gap.

Housing Reform

The trend in housing reform is to turn what was formerly an employee entitlement into a commodity for private ownership. Since 1949, several decades of socialist transformation in cities have basically eradicated private rental housing and substantially reduced owner-occupied housing. Various surveys carried out in the early 1980s concurred that work-unit housing— that is, apartments constructed and allocated by work units to their employees—composed some 60 to 75 percent of the housing stock in urban China,

with municipal housing making up some 20 to 25 percent and private housing about 10 percent.[62] The role of the work unit as a provider of housing
was far more important in China than in other former state socialist societies, where enterprise housing usually accounted for only 10 to 30 percent
of the housing stock.[63] State factories drew on their capital construction
investment funds, allocated by their supervising government agencies, to
construct "welfare housing." Municipalities allocated their housing budgets
to municipal housing bureaus to develop public housing for small and
street-level collective enterprises that were unable to receive capital construction investment. Enterprises could also rent municipal housing for
their employees. The rent charged had remained very low: Between 1949
and 1990, rent in most Chinese cities accounted for only 2 to 3 percent of
total household income, with monthly rent for a typical flat costing less
than a packet of good cigarettes. In the 1980s, the state paid five to six billion yuan each year to subsidize housing maintenance.[64] Large state enterprises and institutions all had residential quarters adjacent or close to their
workshops, and managers and ordinary workers lived in the same compounds, forming very closely knit, cross-class communities. The basic criteria for housing allocation are urban residence and permanent employment
by the work unit. Priorities depended on the status of the employees (for
example, cadres were given higher priority than workers) and length of service. In addition, the size of household and the number of dependent children would sometimes be taken into consideration, especially in the more
informal negotiation with allocation cadres.[65]

The financial burden on the state and the chronic shortage and poor quality of the housing stock are key problems that have prompted reform since
1980. The emphasis has been on commercialization—specifically, the subsidized sale of public housing to current tenants, rent increases, and the introduction of housing allowances for employees to purchase their own homes
on the market. The central government stopped the distribution of housing
to urban employees in 1998 and replaced it with a cash subsidy for private
purchase of housing. At the same time, local governments were asked to
establish a supply system of affordable housing for sale to low-income families. Special central government loans and free land allocation for such
housing projects were introduced in 1994. Local governments were to decide
when to implement housing reform and most found it hard to come up with
the necessary funds to pay subsidies to the many public and enterprise
employees.[66]

Overall, housing reform has turned out to be a slow process owing to
cadres' and workers' vested financial interests in the old system. From the

mid-1980s to the early 1990s, when enterprises were given the autonomy to retain after-tax profits for welfare use, a construction craze occurred and many workers were allocated work-unit flats that were subsequently sold to them at subsidized prices.[67] The caveat was that the buyers bought only part of the full property rights, or the right to use and inherit but not the right to sell in the open market without compensating the work unit for a portion of the profit made on the resale. This complicated property rights issue would become even more confusing when work units collapsed in large numbers in the late 1990s, leaving the partial property right of employees ambiguous and the maintenance of housing stock problematic. Some worker protests have erupted over neighborhood and housing issues. For younger workers in failing state-owned firms or smaller private enterprises, housing allowances simply do not exist owing to enterprise financial difficulties or the unwillingness of employers to contribute. Growing out of a traditional preference for men in enterprise housing allocation,[68] privatization of work-unit housing has tended to confer ownership on men rather than women. But, so far, there are no statistical data to document this gender bias.

For the millions of migrant workers, their rural household registration status excludes them from acquiring either usage rights or ownership rights to municipal and work-unit housing. The housing plans described here are for urban residents only. In some cities, high-income migrants are given special residency permits if they buy housing units locally. But for the vast majority of migrant workers, living in dormitories attached to factories or renting private housing are the only options. Of migrant workers in major cities, 75 to 80 percent live in institutionally provided dormitory rooms measuring about twenty-six square meters, shared by an average of twelve people.[69] This "dormitory labor system" serves employers by keeping labor available on tap, facilitating flexible extension of the workday, inhibiting workers' job-search time, reducing the cost of social reproduction, and strengthening employer control over workers' personal lives.[70]

Trade Unions

There is only one legal union in China—the All China Federation of Trade Unions (ACFTU). Independent unions are illegal and those who attempt to form autonomous unions have been charged by the government with treason or subversion.[71] According to the law, any enterprise with twenty-five or more employees should establish a grassroots union under the auspices of the ACFTU. In 2002, there were 165,800 enterprise-level unions, 30 provincial unions, and 19 industry unions. Historically, the Chinese official union has been institutionally subordinate to the Communist Party and financially dependent on the enterprise budget. For instance, Party organizations at each level are responsible for setting up new unions, the nomination of trade union leaders, and the transmission of Party policies to workers. Financially, enterprises have to contribute 2 percent of the total wage bill to their unions and workers pay 0.5 percent of their wages as membership fees. The Trade Union Law in 1992 transfers the responsibility for paying the salary of full-time union cadres from the unions to the enterprises, making them more dependent than ever on management.[72]

In the reform era, the Trade Union Law of 1950 has been revised twice (in 1992 and in 2002) with the basic goal of strengthening the legal status of the ACFTU. The unions' right to legally represent workers against intimidation by management and to receive enterprise contributions equivalent to 2 percent of total wage bills, as well as the unions' legal role of signing collective contracts and engaging in collective bargaining with employers, are stipulated in the 2001 Trade Union Law.[73] Notwithstanding these legislative reinforcements, the official union continues to be plagued by several fundamental weaknesses, which have only been exacerbated by market reform.

First, industrial restructuring and the rise of the private and foreign-invested sectors have beset the ACFTU with a membership crisis. The shrinkage of the state industrial sector—through bankruptcy, merger, or privatization—has substantially depleted the traditional membership base for the official union. Membership in that sector decreased by about fifteen million between 1990 and 2000. On the other hand, the private and foreign sectors remain quite impervious to union organizations, with the rates of membership remaining near a low of 4 percent and 33 percent, respectively.[74] Many workers simply do not know what unions are about.[75]

Second, the contradiction inherent in communist unions' dual role as representatives of worker interests and promoters of the national, common interest is sharpened under market reform. As market reform has incessantly chipped away at workers' entitlements and tilted the balance of power further toward employers, the weakness of unions as defenders of labor rights is acutely felt. The conflicts in the unions' double institutional identity explain why the ACFTU would spare no effort to preempt the emergence of worker protests and collective actions. At best, official unions have represented individual workers and sometimes groups of workers when they make their claims through state-sanctioned channels such as civil litigation or labor dispute arbitration.[76] This classic dilemma is exacerbated by the particular alignment of interests in the Chinese reform process. Many local governments are establishing partnerships with foreign joint ventures.

Their entrepreneurial interests hold enormous sway over city- and county-level unions, which are themselves part of the local state apparatus.[77] In failing and ailing state-owned enterprises, union cadres are often Party officials or deputy managers.[78] The wearing of multiple hats by union cadres severely hampers the role of unions in defending workers when their interests can no longer be camouflaged as unified with those of the enterprise.

Likewise, in many of the newly established unions in nonstate enterprises, the managerial staff serves concurrently as union cadres. In Special Economic Zones in Guangdong, where unionization rates are reportedly high among foreign-owned companies, a survey found that almost all enterprise union chairs are also enterprise managers.[79] These enterprise unions are concerned with recreation and enforcement of labor discipline rather than with working conditions or labor rights. Management of these firms sees in enterprise unions an additional instrument for controlling workers—a position that ACFTU shares and promotes. For instance, union cadres in Guangdong explained the advantage to foreign managers of setting up unions, saying,

> We propagated the Trade Union Law to foreign investors. We indicated that, if the migrant workers would not be organized under the union, they themselves might organize a "local gang" on the basis of their hometowns, which would destroy the stability of production and create conflicts between different gangs. We also told the employers that, different from western trade unions, the unions in China are a "middle-man" in adjusting labor relations. They will absolutely not organize strikes. Their role is to protect the interest of both parties.[80]

This quotation touches on the sensitive issue of workers' right to strike. Guaranteed by the Chinese Constitution until 1982, the right to strike was revoked by a government haunted by the rise and development of the Polish Solidarity movement.[81] To date, even after the People's Republic of China ratified the International Covenant on Economic, Social, and Cultural Rights, and became a member of the International Labor Organization, the Chinese government still refuses to ratify certain core international labor standards. The most contentious of these are the right to free association, which in its broadest sense includes rights to negotiate and to strike. Some scholars promote the view that the law does not prohibit strikes although it does not legalize them.[82] Nonetheless, Article 27 of the 2001 Trade Union Law explicitly prescribes a proproduction mediating role for unions. In the case of a slowdown or production stoppage, the law requires unions to assist enterprises in recovering the normal state of production as soon as possible, and to reflect workers' "reasonable demands" through negotiation with the enterprise.

Given all the institutional constraints and political subordination of the ACFTU at a time when market reform relentlessly erodes the traditional shield of state paternalism, it is not surprising that ordinary workers are alienated from the unions. Surveys consistently reveal popular disappointment with the emasculated union as a working-class institution. The ACFTU's own survey in 1997 indicated that only 50 percent of the workers polled gave positive evaluations of the union's overall work, and only 34.6 percent of workers found that the union played a significant role in defending their interests.[83] Provincial union and academic surveys have confirmed the declining status of unions. A Zhejiang province union survey found in 1994 that only 13.1 percent of workers sought help from the union about work-related problems, and two-thirds of workers and staff did not believe that trade unions were doing their job.[84] Chinese workers' cynicism toward the official union is hardly unique. A recent study of postcommunist trade unions found that even independent unions have become discredited in the eyes of their own working-class constituencies because of their historical powerlessness and notoriety as a tool of the Party state.[85]

In short, in the reform era, the allocation and remuneration of labor (formerly under the control of government administration and planning) are now to be determined by market demand and supply. Labor power becomes a commodity sold and bought in the marketplace and labor relations are to be founded on contracts, enforced by the law. At the same time, though, there is a counteracting tendency to limit a full commodification of labor. State regulations, through legislations pertaining to working conditions, minimum wage, pensions, unemployment benefits, medical care, and housing entitlements, seek to constrain employers' capacity to extract labor power from workers. As Karl Polanyi maintains, labor, unlike other factors of production, is a "fictitious" commodity whose unlimited exploitation will destroy the use value of the commodity itself. Historically, in nineteenth-century Western Europe, social movements from below or legislation from above materialized in different societies to limit commodification. Likewise, in China, the panoply of laws and regulations passed in the last two decades are poignant examples of initiatives from above. And, despite the absence of an autonomous labor movement, Chinese workers push for changes from below, spurred to collective action by the glaring discrepancies between the existence of labor regulations and the practical application of these regulations on the ground. Overall, the uneven transition of welfare from a work-unit-based entitlement to a universal legal right has led to a general deterioration of workers' livelihoods, especially in the 1990s.

That the law is not always enforced does not mean that legal reform is inconsequential. First, workers still take legal provisions seriously because they are their only ammunition in making claims against employers. The rising volume of labor arbitration cases and litigation are indications of workers' legal activism. Second, flawed local enforcement of the law has, on many occasions, transformed orderly petitions and courtroom procedures into public outrage and protests. Inadvertently and sometimes serendipitously, legal reform has made the state a catalyst of labor activism. The oscillation between the courtroom and the streets—between routine, institutionalized conflict resolution and noninstitutionalized mass action—is a potent source of social instability.

DEBATES ABOUT LABOR REFORM

These institutional changes and tensions have developed in tandem with the rise of new ideological discourses aimed at reorganizing the self-perception of workers and the social construction of the value of labor. Katherine Verdery perceptively underscores the centrality of value transformation in the historic transition to postsocialism, noting that "questions of value, from the most basic (what kind of life do people want to live) to the niggling details of a firm's purchase price, joined with questions of morality to dominate public consciousness. Who ought or ought not to be profiting from the wealth accumulated under socialism—the former managers of state firms? foreigners? the general public?"[86] Chinese workers should not be strangers to such controversies, which have featured prominently in public discourse since the late 1970s. These debates are the linguistic, moral, and cognitive raw materials out of which workers' political claims and identities are forged.

Under socialism, labor was "honorable" *(laodong shi guangrong de),* as many workers still proudly invoke the language of the day, while in the same breath lamenting how embarrassingly passé it sounds today. Not only were one's material well-being, life opportunities, and political status dependent on membership in a production organization, the *danwei,* but also the Chinese state had made labor a primary site for the production of modern identities, even a badge of revolutionary honor. "The state made labor the cultural arena in which women and men crafted the meaning of 'liberation,' proved their socialist moral worth, expressed their nationalist sentiments, and received rewards—or punishments—from the state."[87] The ideological centrality of the permanent employment system made labor reform a politically sensitive issue. Thus, when the post-Mao reform leadership began revamping the socialist labor system, they also unleashed spirited disagreements among political elites and policy makers, reflecting similarly divided popular opinions among different groups of workers. In a nutshell, the contested ideological terrain surrounding labor has been moving from a socialist, class-sensitive discourse in the first decade of reform, through what might be called an individualist, psychological, and meritocratic rhetoric in the first half of the second decade of reform, to a dual emphasis on the legal rights and the structural predicaments of certain social groups from the late 1990s to the present. Later chapters in this book will show how the terms of these debates are selectively and instrumentally invoked by aggrieved workers to bolster their claims in petitions and protests.

During the initial phases of labor reform, reformers criticized the old "iron rice bowl" (permanent employment) and "eating from one big pot" (the egalitarian wage system) as serious obstacles to economic growth. But experiments with recruitment through examination, labor contracts, and differential wage and bonus distribution sparked intense debates. Gordon White's review of that period found a surprisingly wide range of views, reflected in academic journals and mass circulation organs, in response to the basic question, "Is labor power a commodity under socialist conditions?"[88] Answers to this question have ranged from an emphatic no to an equally emphatic yes, with various shades of opinion in between. Traditional views held largely by Party and state officials responsible for organizing the old labor system and by state industrial workers maintained that public ownership was practiced and that laborers jointly possess the means of production and are masters of the means of production. Reformers, in contrast, argued that with the adoption of renewable labor contracts, labor power could become a commodity. Some economists even considered as objective economic law that labor is a commodity. In practice, no consensus was reached on the scope of the application of the labor contract.[89] Amidst confusion and conflict of interests regarding wage and bonus reform, workers also improvised and modified the new skill- and output-based rules by informal work-group norms.[90] "As late as 1988, the economic reformers have yet to arrive at a new definition of the role of labor in a new form of "socialism,'" White concluded.[91]

Implementation of contract management in state-owned enterprises, the expansion of the nonstate manufacturing sector, and entrepreneurial activities stirred public debates on issues of inequality, class exploitation, and the specter of a new "parasitic class" living off speculation in capital markets. While conservative leaders such as Chen Yun called attention to the erosion of socialist ethics of equality and reciprocity, more liberal intellectuals differentiated between "fair inequality" (i.e., inequality resulting from equality of opportunity, market competition, and efficiency) and "unfair inequality" (i.e., inequality associated with criminal and unscrupulous activities). Reformers, such as Xue Muqiao and Yu Guangyuan, defended the socialist nature of Chinese society under reform by emphasizing state ownership of the "commanding heights of the economy" despite the existence of nonstate sectors. They also insisted that formal political and class equality persisted despite uneven economic distribution.[92]

Class-sensitive ideological debates subsided in the early 1990s when Deng Xiaoping pushed for deepening of market reform. By the mid-1990s, legal reform, deemed necessary for the proper functioning of the market economy, accelerated, and with it entered the new official rhetoric of using law to rule the country, or *yifazhiguo*. The building of a "socialist rule of law state" was incorporated into the Constitution in 1999, which might also provide a new legitimacy for the Party. Legal scholars of China have pointed out that the Chinese notion of law-based government is a tool for strengthening, not limiting, communist rule, as the law is intended to curtail corruption and promote economic development.[93] For my purpose here, the most important consequence of this new emphasis on legal reform has been the explosion in the public domain of a legal rights discourse. In the same period, as mentioned earlier, the Labor Law, the basic law for labor-related legislation and regulations, was passed. Academic journals, official publications and the media jointly contributed to the propagation of legal knowledge, offering legal counsel in advice columns or reporting typical court cases to spread the idea of citizens' legal rights. Politically concerned intellectuals, disillusioned and silenced by the state's deadly crackdown on the Tiananmen protests, also see in the law a more promising and realistic way to push for social change.

The flourishing of legal rights rhetoric in the early 1990s coincided with the resurgence of unemployment as a serious social problem. Massive layoffs afflict some twenty-five million workers as state-owned enterprises struggle to become more efficient and profitable in the face of intensely competitive foreign, private, and rural industries. Middle-aged, unskilled women workers in particular were disproportionately susceptible to layoffs. At first, public discourse promoted by the official union, the Women's Federation, and the media explained workers' predicament by referring to workers' individual shortcomings—low educational qualifications and an archaic "employment consciousness" that included a lack of competitive mentality, a dogmatic preference for jobs in state enterprises, and an inertia of reliance on the state.[94] Women workers in particular have been urged to upgrade their individual "quality" *(suzhi)* and to seek new jobs using their natural aptitudes. Successful stories of personal transformation became a staple of official propaganda, featuring entrepreneurial beauticians, seamstresses, domestic helpers, nannies, community volunteers, or simply stay-at-home wives and grandmothers.[95]

From the mid to late 1990s, as opinion polls consistently registered social discontent about unemployment, corruption, inequality, and rural taxation, a new discourse emerged to recognize the existence and predicaments of those who were left behind in the reform process. The term *ruoshi qunti*, meaning groups in weak and disadvantaged positions, of which four have been mentioned explicitly in official documents—migrant workers, the unemployed, retirees or those outside gainful employment, and the handicapped—is now widely used. Adopting various definitions, government officials, nongovernment civil-society groups, the media, and the scholarly community have appropriated the term to urge government protection of those who are disadvantaged by structural changes in the economy.

CONCLUSION

We will see in later chapters that this new collective identification *ruoshi qunti* is being appropriated by protesting workers. From the vantage point of today, what is most revealing about the debate some two decades ago is the extent to which wage labor has been normalized. Totally gone is the political centrality and moral intensity with which labor issues were discussed. Both the unmaking and the making of the Chinese working class are heavily shaped by the state—especially by its construction of a labor rule of law and a new social security system. Broad discrepancies, however, exist between the stipulation and the implementation of these new labor regulations designed to protect labor rights and entitlements. The institutional source of these gaps, this chapter argues, lies in two contradictions inherent in the strategy of Chinese reform. First, the imperative to rely on local accumulation to fuel marketization clashes with the imperative to maintain legitimacy by providing a floor of justice and welfare for the most disadvantaged. Local state agents' overriding concerns and personal interests are decisively skewed toward the former at the expense of the latter. The second contradiction in Chinese reform that is conducive to uneven protection of labor rights has to do with the illiberal nature of the Chinese legal system. The state uses the law as a tool of control over society while allowing itself to remain mostly unrestrained by the law. When it is not in the interests of local officials to enforce labor regulations, there is hardly enough countervailing authority (from the judiciary, for instance) to uphold the law.

The result is that many workers, on seeing their legal rights and entitlements unjustly denied, and pressured by their need to make a living, become rebellious. Sharp increases in labor conflicts are accompanied by proliferation of labor activism, taking both institutional, legal-channel forms (such as petitions, labor arbitration, and litigation) and noninstitutional forms (such as protests, marches, and road blocks). The state has responded with measured mixtures of concession and repression. On the one hand, economic and livelihood demands are recognized and, in many cases, at least partially fulfilled with swift financial compensation doled out by the central or provincial governments. On the other hand, political demands (such as calling for the removal of officials) and cross-factory actions are relentlessly suppressed and harshly punished. Most important, the Chinese government has ardently pressed ahead with social security reform, targeting problem areas such as pension arrears, unpaid wages, unemployment benefits, and medical insurance. Additional earmarked funds are funneled from Beijing to provincial coffers to deal with social grievances that may erupt into social instability. These efforts have focused on reducing the frequency of protests in the rustbelt since 2001. In 2002, the central government forcefully demanded that excessive fees and abusive detention policies targeting migrant workers be abolished by the local governments. There are also plans to systematically institutionalize the provision of legal aid to people who fall below a certain income level. Therefore, the Chinese state has responded to popular demands, if only slowly and selectively. It is to this interaction between labor protests and state power at the local and central government levels that we turn in the next chapter.

PART II

Rustbelt

Protests of Desperation

3   The Unmaking of Mao's Working Class in the Rustbelt

In his dilapidated apartment, with all windows shut and electricity cut off, fifty-year-old Zheng Wu sat on his bed as if the world had frozen in time. Gazing at an old television set and a clock that had long since stopped working, he was bitter and angry about his pitiful conditions after "having worked his entire life for the Revolution" as a factory hand in a rubber plant in Tieling, a medium-sized industrial city in Liaoning. Suffering from a chronic ulcer and arthritis, he had been released from work since 1991, and as his plant went downhill, he saw his livelihood allowance gradually dwindle from several dozen yuan a month to nothing at all. His wife was also an unemployed worker who took odd jobs such as dishwashing and cooking whenever she could find them. His rage was out of proportion to his weak, thin body, which hung like a skeleton. Showing me his wrists inscribed with deep scars from several suicide attempts, he said, "Without wages, I will die either way, whether sitting here or lying on the railroad, so we went lying on the railroad." In 1997, when his coworkers came calling him from the street, he joined them to petition the local government, demanding that their factory pay them the legal livelihood allowance after it suspended production. When the mayor refused to meet with the workers, dozens of them marched to the train station and vowed to board the train to the provincial capital, Shenyang, eighty kilometers away, to appeal to a higher authority. Public security officials came to stop them, and they responded by lying on the rails for several hours, under the watchful eyes of the officers. When darkness fell, seeing no prospect of obtaining any results, they disbanded and went home.

Zheng Wu's situation was hardly unique. Many aggrieved workers find themselves going back and forth between passivity, depression, and even self-destruction, on the one hand, and outbursts of rage, desperation, and heroic acts of collective defiance, on the other. Throughout the late 1990s, as mass layoffs continued unabated, Liaoning became a hotbed of labor unrest. Blocking rail and road traffic became the strategy of choice for workers, so common that the central government even set up penalty rates for every hour of blockage, calculated on the basis of the normal volume of commercial traffic, to be charged against the supervising departments and the factories involved. Communist Party members and cadres in the province received instructions prohibiting them from taking any role in petitions or demonstration activities. Report cards of local government cadres also had an additional criterion, registering the number of "spontaneous incidents" occurring in their areas of jurisdiction. Local cab drivers were even able to infer from experience cyclical patterns of the occurrence of such episodes of public protest: most of these incidents occurred at the end of the month and in the days prior to major festivals and important government and Communist Party meetings.

FAREWELL TO THE WORKING CLASS

This chapter tells the stories of Liaoning workers and their "protests of desperation." The northeastern Chinese province Liaoning was extolled in the Mao era as the "eldest son of the nation" or the "emperor's daughter" for its superior natural resource endowment, strategic location, and early development of basic and heavy industries under Japanese occupation in the early 1900s. As a primary target of state investment and Russian financial aid in the 1950s, the province contributed 71 percent of iron production, 63 percent of steel production, and 58 percent of steel products to the national economy by 1957.[1] The leading province in terms of profit remission to central government coffers, Liaoning was the site of 10 percent of the nation's large and medium-sized state-owned enterprises (SOEs), an industrial structure that has proved crippling to the province's development under the market economy. Since the 1990s, Liaoning has been plagued by the most severe unemployment problem in the nation. By some estimates, as many as 30 to 60 percent of workers in the state sector were without jobs or pay by the late 1990s, a stark contrast with the province's preeminence in the days of the planned economy.[2] The drastic reversal of fortune in the local economy makes labor politics of Liaoning a "critical case" for this study, for it represents the death of socialism in the rustbelt. On the one hand, nowhere are institutional legacies and liabilities of the command economy more pronounced and the Maoist habitus of workers more entrenched than in the many old industrial towns in the province. On the other hand, economic reform has not induced sufficient market opportunity in the form of international capital or private entrepreneurship like that found in Guangdong. Domestic private industries have only a very feeble and shadowy presence relative to the massive workforce shed from the state sector. As in other parts of China where the once dominant SOEs collapsed in large numbers, despair and desperation are on public display everywhere, on the faces of the many peddlers of odds and ends squatting on sidewalks and paddlers on tricycles scouting for passengers.

My main concern in this and the next chapter is to analyze how the characteristics and limits of worker protests are linked to the mode of state regulation of labor and the social reproduction of labor power. I argue that the socialist social contract, in which the communist regime pledged employment security, pensions, and welfare services in exchange for workers' political acquiescence, was still recognized by management and invoked by workers even as market reform proceeded apace and the legal contract was at least ceremoniously instituted during the 1990s. The materials and moral terms of the socialist social contract were reflected in the grievances about collective consumption and the insurgent rhetoric of class, Maoism, and legal rights among rustbelt workers. The strategy of protests, privileging direct street action and disruption of social order, signaled workers' refusal to remain acquiescent when enterprise management and the local government failed to live up to their end of the bargain.

This chapter is organized into three parts, concerning, respectively, workers' grievances, capacity, and subjectivity. Based on worker grievances and demands, I distinguish three types of worker-led protests in the rustbelt: *nonpayment protests* against arrears of wages and pensions; *neighborhood protests* against substandard public service, the lack of heating subsidies, and deteriorating neighborhood infrastructure; and *bankruptcy protests* focusing on job tenure compensation, severance packages, illicit sales or restructuring of SOEs, and cadre corruption. In all three types of protests, workers' demands focused predominantly on collective consumption, which has been organized by the socialist workplace and was instituted through policies and practices, and only secondarily prescribed in laws such as the Bankruptcy Law and the Labor Law. This is because workers' employment usually dated back to the prereform period and most have signed a legal contract only as a formality. Local officials, workers, and management still take the social contract more seriously than the legal contract. Their protests therefore primarily took the form of street action and popular pressure, leveraging the moral political claims of the social contract. Those who have attempted to seek redress through the court and labor bureaucracies have found, to their disillusionment, that these institutions are biased in favor of officials and SOE managers. The common denominator underlying these incidents is a pervasive working-class feeling of betrayal by the state and victimization by the market economy. I therefore call them "protests of desperation." Yet, throughout my research, I have been constantly struck by the heterogeneity of worker interests within the same enterprise or locality, so much so that retired pensioners, laid-off workers, and unemployed workers of the same enterprise see each other as "distinct social groups with different interests." This fragmentation of interest is the result of the array of government policies stipulating different terms of employment and retirement for these different groups of workers. Moreover, economic decentralization also leads to different financial capacities of work units to compensate workers according to policies and laws, creating more fragmentations among SOE workers.

The second set of issues concern workers' mobilization capacity: How are protests possible? What are the units of action and boundaries of solidarity? What limits workers' militancy? My data show that the material and social organization of the socialist work unit has persisted even after production is suspended and the firm is financially liquidated. Living in the same enterprise's residential quarters, workers share grievances related to heat, water services, and fuzzy property rights to their apartments. They can also easily disseminate news about the latest government decrees regarding workers benefits and validate one another's frustration about the enterprise's failure to deliver them. Most important, short notices about when, why, and where to stage protests can be passed by word of mouth or by flyers posted at the main entrances to apartment buildings. These cellular, bounded communities therefore have both mobilizational and containment effects, making it difficult, though not impossible, for cross-unit lateral movements to emerge. When these disparate cellular protests are allowed to linger for a protracted period in the same locality, informal networks of activism may suddenly erupt in action, joining hands in targeting the same group of opponents, for example, corrupt local cadres.

The final issue concerns the nature of political subject, or the emotional, evaluative, cognitive, and instrumental logic structuring workers' collective action. I use the term *subject* to underscore the idea that workers form insurgent identities not just before or even during the course of collective action. More important, as subjects, they reflect and learn from their actions to redefine who they are and what they are capable or incapable of as political agents. Chinese workers' repertoire of insurgent identities draws on both historical experiences and new contemporary discourses, and is always invoked with reference to and in anticipation of state reaction. I shall decipher the context-specific meanings of self-descriptive terms used by workers in protests, including the "masses" (qunzhong), "weak and disadvantaged groups" (ruoshi qunti), "working-class" (gongren jieji), and "citizens" (gongmin). Each of these terms involves a corresponding imagined political community with specific standards of justice, entitlements, and therefore a rationale for a particular course of collective action. The creative combination of these various discourses is a hallmark of the transition period, a time when old and new ideologies coexist in tension.

UNEMPLOYMENT AND ITS DISCONTENTS

Unemployment is not a new problem in China, which has weathered several waves of mass unemployment since the 1949 Revolution.[3] In terms of the rate of unemployment, the current situation pales by comparison with what happened right after the communist regime was established. The official unemployment rate reached a staggering 23.6 percent in 1949 and remained at a high level of 13.2 percent in 1952.[4] Yet, the current spell of unemployment poses unique challenges. Whereas unemployment in the past had mainly afflicted young, new job seekers (as in 1979 to 1981) or temporary rural recruits (as in the post–Great Leap Forward retrenchment), unemployment in the 1990s hit hardest at the bastion of regime support—veteran workers who had held permanent posts in the state sector. It has also been a more prolonged process outlasting the previous shorter cycles. In a matter of seven years, the laid-off population mushroomed to a staggering eighteen to twenty million in 2001, from less than seven million in 1993. Although official rates of "registered" unemployment hovered around 3 percent in the late 1990s, academic estimates of the actual unemployment rate range between 7 and 10.4 percent.[5] And according to some analysts, an additional three to four million urbanites will join the rank of the unemployed every year over the next half decade as China adjusts to a new competitive environment after its accession to the World Trade Organization.[6] In view of the dire political and social consequences inherent in unemployment of such magnitude, the national leadership has accorded top priority to the task of guaranteeing unemployed workers' livelihood. Before his retirement, former president Jiang Zemin warned at the Sixteenth Party Congress in 2002 that poverty and the resulting sense of insecurity among the jobless and poor farmers are the biggest destabilizing factor in Chinese society.[7]

Unemployment in Liaoning epitomizes the immensity and gravity of

TABLE 7 Total Number of Employees in Manufacturing in Liaoning, 1990–2004

Year	Employees (millions)	Year	Employees (millions)
1990	4.618	2001	4.348
1995	4.443	2002	3.943
1998	3.791	2003	1.475
1999	3.532	2004	1.447
2000	3.359		

SOURCES: Liaoning Statistics Bureau, *Liaoning Statistics Yearbooks, 2001–2004* (Beijing: China Statistics Bureau, 2002–2005) [in Chinese].

unemployment among the state industrial workforce. Almost 40 percent of Liaoning's SOEs are large and medium-sized enterprises, and 40.8 percent of state-sector workers were in traditional manufacturing, with only 5.5 percent in the new high-technology sector. With the province's industrial structure skewed toward heavy and resource-dependent industries (76.4 percent of total provincial industrial output), more than 70 percent of its urban workers are in the state and collective sectors. Among these eight million workers in state and collective industrial units in 1997, 21.4 percent were officially registered as unemployed or laid-off workers, 30.77 percent were retired workers, and another 33 percent were redundant workers.[8] By 2002, the total of officially registered unemployed and laid-off workers reached 2.4 million, a figure that was widely considered a gross underestimation by academics and ordinary citizens because it did not capture the numerous workers who were released involuntarily and informally, without any official papers registering their in-limbo status. Although the shedding of manufacturing workers has proceeded apace since the early 1990s, the trend has spiked drastically since 1997, when the government aggressively pursued a restructuring of the state sector, letting go of small and medium-sized firms and holding onto only the big ones in "pillar" industries. Tables 7, 8, and 9 capture only the "registered" furloughed population in the three cities covered by this study, leaving out the majority of the unemployed, whose enterprises evade the official registration process.[9]

Aggregate figures of unemployment outline the general trend of aggravating joblessness but they barely scratch the surface of the gravity of job loss in social and human terms. First, provincial aggregates conceal some particularly concentrated and structurally induced pockets of locality-wide unemployment. Depletion of coal mines and iron ores, and the decline in military equipment industries[10] have meant that jobs for entire communi-

TABLE 8   *On-the-Job Employees in Manufacturing in Three Cities in Liaoning, 1998–2004*

Year	Shenyang	Liaoyang	Tieling
1998	721,180	150,096	87,378
1999	488,034	94,454	44,815
2000	441,942	86,535	41,335
2001	396,395	70,131	35,563
2002	348,724	58,648	31,363
2003	294,017	57,402	28,822
2004	282,683	61,476	27,187

SOURCES: Liaoning Statistics Bureau, *Liaoning Statistics Yearbooks, 1999–2004* (Beijing: China Statistics Bureau, 2000–2005) [in Chinese].

TABLE 9   *Off-Duty Employees in Manufacturing in Three Cities in Liaoning, 1998–2004*

Year	Shenyang	Liaoyang	Tieling
1998	319,244	46,848	68,822
1999	323,116	51,987	80,706
2000	344,215	49,595	77,754
2001	291,191	50,852	74,473
2002	226,615	31,434	53,387
2003	183,710	29,212	37,515
2004	152,884	27,721	33,402

SOURCES: Liaoning Statistics Bureau, *Liaoning Statistics Yearbooks, 1999–2004* (Beijing: China Statistics Bureau, 2000–2005) [in Chinese].

ties have been eliminated, together with family and kin support networks. A 1997 survey revealed that 41 percent of unemployed workers had two or more family members who were also unemployed.[11] Second, unemployment figures conceal the pervasive problem of unpaid wages and pensions among workers who are officially employed and retired. The national total of workers who were owed unpaid wages increased from 2.6 million in 1993 to 14 million in 2000, an increase of 550 percent. The number of enterprises involved increased from 15,655 in 1993 to 79,116 in 2000. One in ten of these workers and enterprises were found in Liaoning. Moreover, of the nearly four million retirees who were owed unpaid pensions, one-third of them were found in Liaoning.[12] The general scenario of widespread urban poverty among the unemployed was underscored by a 1998 survey that found that unemployed residents across the province received a monthly average income of 220 yuan, equivalent to the lowest 20 percent income group, and most families depended on either savings or loans for their livelihood.

Unemployment-related labor strife has increased significantly. Worker activism often begins with collective petitions, which in many cases evolve into collective protests. According to the State Letters and Visits Bureau, in 2000, there was a total of 10.2 million cases of petitions to the Bureau's provincial, county, and municipal offices nationwide, an increase of 115 percent over 1995. Of the petitioners, 76.5 percent were involved in "collective petitions," defined as those involving five people or more. The total numbers of collective cases and collective petitioners in 2000 increased 280 percent and 260 percent, respectively, over those in 1995. Of collective petitions in cities, more than 60 percent were lodged by state enterprise employees.[13]

Liaoning also experienced a remarkable increase in collective petitions. In a survey published by the Communist Party Politics and Law Committee, the Liaoning Party Committee stated that large-scale collective petitions first emerged in 1994, and had increased "several-fold" by 1999. Of particular significance, according to the Party Committee, was the increase in worker-led collective actions, which accounted for 64.5 percent of all collective petitions in the two months following Spring Festival in 2000. Most of these were about unpaid wages and other grievances related to enterprise restructuring. The same report described a trend toward "increased scale of action, rising number of participants, and intensified emotions," with some incidents "developing into blockage of rail and road traffic, siege of government and Party offices, mass assault on individual officials and police, even looting and riots."[14]

Although the provincial reports in the Politics and Law Committee collection stopped short of divulging overall statistics, it is noteworthy that two other provinces in the northeast also registered high proportions of worker-led collective incidents. In Jilin, for instance, collective petitions by state workers accounted for 50 percent of the total number of petitions in 2000, representing a 23 percent increase over the previous year.[15] In Heilongjiang, the Party Committee reported a 2.8-fold increase in incidents of popular unrest involving five hundred or more people between 1998 and 1999; 60 percent of these incidents concerned unpaid wages.[16] When repeated petitions prove fruitless, protests erupt in the form of road and railway blockage, sit-ins in front to government buildings, and sometimes rallies around downtown areas. In what follows, I discuss each of the three major types of worker protests in Liaoning, noting in particular the constitution of worker interests, capacity, and identities. Despite significant similarities in the characteristics and dynamics of these protests, worker perceptions of differences among themselves and their fear of state repression have led to no escalation in the scale of these numerous localized and cellularized protests.

NONPAYMENT PROTESTS

Nationwide, the total number of workers who were owed unpaid wages increased from 2.6 million in 1993 to 14 million in 2000.[17] In Shenyang, between 1996 and 2001, 23.1 percent of employed workers experienced wage arrears, and 26.4 percent of retirees experienced pension arrears.[18] Enterprise insolvency is the major cause of nonpayment: managers of insolvent firms would not fund wage bills or contribute to their employees' insurance accounts. Yet the two groups of workers who are owed remuneration do not usually join forces. To them, pension is a sacrosanct socialist entitlement owed to the elderly, who have lost any competitiveness in the market economy. Although wages should also be paid to the current workforce, it is widely held that younger workers should depend on themselves and find alternatives in the new market society. Therefore, pensions have a stronger moral claim than wages, a consensus I found even among younger workers. Also, different state policies targeting, respectively, pensioners, laid-off workers, and unemployed workers drive deep wedges into the workforce of an enterprise.

Elderly pensioners played a leading role in staging protests in the 1990s as their livelihood was threatened by the chronic nonpayment of pensions. As recounted in chapter 2, pension reform began in the mid-1980s, and by 1991, Beijing replaced the pay-as-you-go enterprise-based system with a contribution-based, social pooling system. The ultimate goal is to transfer the responsibility for financing and distributing retiree benefits from enterprises to "society," meaning contributions from employers, workers, and local governments. From the beginning, pension reform was beset by a confusing patchwork of regulations (e.g., the State Council did not specify which level of local government should regulate pension pools, and there was no attempt to standardize contribution rates) and a fragmented, locally based structure of pension administration. Contributions have been pooled and managed by local governments at various levels and sometimes by agencies of different ministries. Enforcing contributions from enterprises turned out to be a daunting task, as local officials try to be employer-friendly and firms resort to false reporting of payroll records.[19] Many cash-strapped SOEs were too poor to contribute their shares to workers' pension accounts, leading to underpayment or default on pensions. In Shenyang, by 1998, 27 percent of the city's SOEs simply stopped making pension payments. The local finance and labor departments had to step in with a 240 million yuan bailout after waves of protests swept through the city.[20] To make the chaotic situation more complicated, in the transition between the new and the old systems, many retirees' pensions had two components: enterprise-based welfare subsidies and pooled insurance payments. The former has been encouraged by the government as a supplement to the latter. Therefore, even when retirees are paid the mandatory part of their pension, they may still be owed the part instituted by their enterprises.[21]

Pension arrears involve varying lengths of nonpayment periods, ranging from a few months to several years, and depending on the financial conditions of the enterprise and the personal employment history of individual workers, the amount owed to each worker will be different, ranging from less than one hundred to almost one thousand yuan per month. The actual amount owed does not determine action and inaction. Nor does the gravity of workers' financial predicament, an issue that turned out to be more complicated than workers' self-proclaimed impoverishment or the numerous academic income surveys would suggest. One retired worker in Shenyang countered my proposition that hardship households are prone to protest by saying, "What is a 'hardship' household? How do you define 'hardship'? Some worker families have difficulties and others do not. Whether we have difficulties or not, we should still get paid for our labor."[22] The moral imperative is to secure their personal returns on their lifelong contributions to the Revolution and to socialism. The almost universal claim that came up repeatedly in numerous interviews was, "The value of our labor was accumulated in the state and in our enterprise through all those years of low-waged labor." A popular jingle in the northeast captured this moral stance: "We gave our youth to the Party; now in our old age no one cares for us. Can we turn to our children? Our children are also laid off."[23]

Elderly participants in protests boldly claim their revolutionary credentials when confronting young police officers, asking, "Where were you when we joined the Revolution?" Management also feels bound by such moral economic claims of their pensioners. At the enterprise level, many firms in Shenyang, for instance, would rather delay wage payments to their on-the-job workers than stop paying their retirees. In Tieling, a textile mill sold its subsidiary shopping mall to finance its contribution to the retirees' pension fund while it refused to pay wages owed to its laid-off workers. In the government's official language, pensions were elderly workers' "lifeline money" because these elderly workers have lost their labor capacity and cannot be expected to compete in the market economy. Retirees could not agree more, and indeed demand that their contribution to the Revolution and the nation be repaid through their pensions. The moral economic claims of retirees also separate them from their laid-off and unemployed coworkers, constituting the two as different interest groups. The general strategy, as I shall show later, is for pensioners to stage their own protests, so that their moral demand for the government to fulfill its end of the social contract will not be confused or diluted by mixing in the legal but weaker claims of younger workers for owed wages. Although these two groups often pursue separate action, bankruptcy occasions more joint action by the two groups of workers, who normally mobilize separately, because the Bankruptcy Law stipulates that both pensions and back wages take priority over other debts. When they do act together, it is elderly workers who take the lead in rallies, in Liaoyang and elsewhere, lending a shield of legitimacy to their younger fellow workers.[24] I relate here two typical examples of nonpayment protests, one in Shenyang and another in Tieling, to illustrate these dynamics.

Casting Factory

Shenyang is the scene of a large number of pension protests. Let's take an in-depth look at the case of China's largest casting factory, where from 1998 to 2000 several hundred retirees staged some twenty protests by blocking city traffic, demanding full payment of their pensions. The seventy-three-year-old former Party secretary of the production department was a central figure who commanded tremendous respect and trust from his fellow retirees. He was owed a total of 2,400 yuan over a three-year period. During that time, retirees were paid only 60 percent of their total pensions, while the enterprise defaulted on its welfare subsidies (which made up the other 40 percent of the monthly payment). The Party secretary and other workers were angry at such prolonged arrears, although they understood that was just part of the problem of enterprise insolvency. His line of reasoning was typical of retirees in Shenyang.

> Our factory is in serious debt to everyone. In addition to our iron suppliers, it owes the social insurance department hundreds of millions of yuan. More than once, I have seen police being called to investigate debt disputes. . . . Worker action is legal, because pensions are our lifeline money. Even the central government says that. And we don't have any ability to do business or find work in the labor market. It is the respon-

sibility of the enterprise and the supervising department. The "Three Represents" [Jiang Zemin's policy slogan] emphasize the personal interests of the masses, don't they? We block city roads with only one demand: give us our money and we will go home.[25]

Regular participants in these blockage episodes all described them as "spontaneous," without mobilization by any particular individuals. What they actually mean is that there was no formal organization, leadership, or coercion. A former foundry man who retired in 1989 and had participated in six of these protests presented a crisp account of how these incidents unfolded. His vivid narrative underscored several recurrent elements of pension protests I have heard workers reporting in Tiexi district, the oldest and largest working-class neighborhood in Shenyang. These include: (1) the impetus provided by the central government's periodic announcements about the need to guarantee pension payments; (2) the outrage this provokes among retirees who mingle every day in the neighborhood; (3) a strategic selection of traffic nodes to stage a blockage, often corresponding to the degree of the workers' desperation; (4) the restraint of the police; and (5) a minimal stop-gap payment by the enterprise shortly after the protest. Here is his first-person account of how a collective disturbance happened.

> Every time the central government announces publicly that pensions must be paid in full, we are very upset. All of us have television at home and we always watch it. Who would not know about these announcements? Every day, elderly people gather in the elderly activity room in our neighborhood, smoking and playing chess, poker, or mahjong. Someone comments on our unpaid pensions and makes a spur-of-the-moment suggestion to block the road. When we get angry, we just go instantly, or say tomorrow morning at 8 or at 9. Once we arrive at the destination, we don't utter a word. We have no banner or slogan, just stand there. We just want to create public opinion, pressuring leaders of the Machinery and Electrical Works Bureau to talk to the enterprise director. There would usually be several hundred retirees. It's not a large number if you consider that we have 1,500 retirees in the entire work unit. Traffic police would arrive several minutes after we begin blocking. They would not intervene, just ask politely which enterprise we are from. They say they are just doing their job, and urge us to try our best to move toward the sidewalk. Police would come too, and they would even urge the traffic police not to push us too hard. They are afraid that elderly people will get hurt, and then the whole incident will become incendiary. Passersby who are on bikes are very sympathetic and are just curious to know which enterprise we are from. But people in buses or automobiles would swear at us, saying, "Those who should die live

uselessly." . . . Very soon, local government officials would come and we would tell them that we are owed our pensions and have no money to see the doctor. They usually are very patient. Once they promise to investigate or to get us paid the following week, we would just disband and go home. The more workers present, the higher the level of officials who would come down to talk to us.[26]

Asked about the tactic of blocking road traffic, rather than lying on railroads or rallying around town, the old man laughed and offered me a simple explanation.

Look, we are people in our seventies and eighties; our bodies are falling apart. We could barely walk. We could only stand still. Standing there on the road is hurtful enough, let alone marches and rallies. My feet and legs are all sore. When we were young, in the Cultural Revolution, we could roam around town and demonstrate. We are too old for that now.[27]

Although pensioners were cognizant of the disruptive impact of mass action and dared to increase the pressure on the local government by amassing more workers and escalating from minor roads to major roads, they were cautious not to exceed the fine line between what they perceived as legal and illegal behavior, fearful for their own personal safety.

We don't want to block railways. Those are major national arteries. We elderly workers are reasonable and we have a good sense of state policy. In Liaoyang and Anshan, workers blocked railways and bad things happened to them—public security officers were sent in. If any injury or death occurs, the nature of our action will be changed. . . . We are also conscientious about orderly petition. First we approach our own enterprise, and if there is no response, we go to the superior department, and then to the city government. You have to follow the bureaucratic hierarchy of proceeding from lower to higher levels. Then things will be easier.[28]

Retirees felt strongly about the moral righteousness of their resistance. A seventy-five-year-old retiree, a key figure in these protests, forcefully invoked Mao's authority as justification.

We only want to make one statement by blocking the road: superior officials must come to take a look! We only want our pensions paid. Premier Zhu himself promised no arrears when he visited Shenyang. The central government has announced a new forty-nine-yuan extra subsidy for each of us retirees. Work-unit leaders made us sign a paper saying that they would pay us later, but so far nothing has happened. Pension is Chairman Mao's national policy![29]

According to retirees, the dynamic of their interaction with the government is that the bigger the incidents they manage to pull off, the quicker the response by the government and the larger the payment that follows. "Like squeezing toothpaste from a tube," they say, an analogy they use jokingly, which echoes the popular saying, "Big disturbance, big solution; small disturbance, small solution; no disturbance, no solution."[30] Most episodes of road blockages have led to increases in the amount paid, say, from 60 percent to 80 percent of the pension payments owed to workers. Yet, this increase may last only for a few months and then stop again, triggering another round of action, especially if the central government happens to reemphasize the importance of guaranteeing pensions. The target of pensioners' action is quite uniformly local leadership: enterprise cadres and officials of the supervising government departments. This is related to the decentralization and cellularization of pension responsibility mentioned earlier. Under the new pension regime, retirees' benefits are still tied to enterprise contributions to their personal social security accounts. When enterprises fail to contribute, social security offices stop payment of pensions to workers, who therefore hold their enterprises and the supervising government departments or ministries responsible. In Liaoning, where massive bankruptcies create a systemic deficit of funds, the central government has responded with earmarked cash infusions and a quickening of social security reform, using Liaoning as a test site. Between 1998 and 2001, to quell the discontent and disruption caused by pension protests across the country, the central government provided a total of 861 billion yuan to bail out the deficits caused by enterprise and local shortfalls. At the same time, the center also demanded pooling at the provincial level rather than at lower county or city levels to ensure stronger equilibrium between old and new enterprises. Pension payments were required to go through the banking system instead of through the enterprise, avoiding the physical aggregation of disgruntled pensioners. By the end of 2001, nationwide, 98 percent of pensioners receive their pensions through banks rather than through their work units.[31]

A number of factors may explain why pension protests have limited potential to become a militant and broad-based worker movement. First, the government's minimal response, albeit not in all cases, holds out the tantalizing promise that more payment would come and demonstrates the state's recognition of retirees' economic and moral claims. Second, retirees themselves see their interests as firm-specific rather than as a class- or community-based predicament. I was perplexed by the absence of cross-enterprise action, especially in Tiexi, where residents claimed that the majority of enterprises had seen their retirees blocking the streets. Every time I challenged my interviewees to apply their theory of "big disturbance, big resolution" to attempt joint action with other factories, I received this uniform reply: "It is no use coordinating with retirees from other factories, because some firms are more generous or stronger financially, and their workers get more subsidies. Some leaders take our interests to heart while others don't care whether we feel cold or warm." Indeed, even before reform, factories had different subsidy packages for their retired employees, a practice encouraged by the government to increase the benefits of elderly workers whenever their firms could afford it. In the reform period, the problem of pension arrears exists in different degrees across firms depending on their performance and profitability. Bitter accusations of injustice are often expressed by retirees who complain about unequal retirement benefits across firms. For instance, whereas the casting factory paid their retirees an average of 600 yuan a month in 2003, interviewees pointed out that their counterparts in oil, chemical, or electricity companies were paid more than 1,000 yuan.

Third, intrafirm solidarity is also precarious as retirees' interests are fragmented by state policies. Retirees' pension packages often differ according to the starting and termination dates of their employment, differences that are arbitrarily exacerbated by periodic but differential raises given by the central government to, for instance, pre-Liberation workers (i.e., those who started working before December 1948, when the Chinese Communist Party liberated the northeast) as opposed to pre–People's Republic of China workers (i.e., those who started working before the establishment of the PRC in October 1949). Retirees were further divided by policies that gave special preferential treatment to those assigned to "high-temperature" or "low-temperature" job posts, or industries that involved specific occupational hazards and diseases. More highly paid retirees were looked at with suspicion by those paid less because they were able to maintain a more comfortable life even if they were only partially paid. A protest leader recalled being scorned by his fellow pensioners when he tried to stop a protest on a wintry, snowy day with the intention of preventing injury to the elderly workers. He recalled, despondently, "They thought my pension was substantially higher than theirs and therefore I was reluctant to go. They thought I was a traitor."[32]

Protesters also confront the classic free-rider problem. Protests lost momentum as participants were discouraged by poor turnout of their fellow retirees. Frustration was not uncommon, as one participant lamented, "I got discouraged when I asked them to come along and they did not care anymore. Why should I be standing there for you, rain or shine, while you go off to work, earning an extra income? It's not like they would share their income with me, yet they benefit from my effort."[33] Finally, retirees mentioned that their hands were tied in staging protests. They found themselves in a double bind: because their protests would result in fines charged to their enterprises, the more they protested, the heavier the financial burden on their impoverished firms, hurting the chances that they would get paid.

Elsewhere in Liaoning, William Hurst and Kevin O'Brien found pensioners active in worker protests in Benxi, a coal- and steel-industry city. The breaking of the social contract and the subsistence crisis that ensued prompted worker resistance. For Benxi and Shenyang workers, pensions are the single most materially and symbolically important obligation the state should fulfill, they have found. Concurring with this finding, my research also underscores the limitations of pension protests to become a more broad-based and lasting political force, however. A fundamental character of pension protests is their cellular nature. What strikes an outside observer as a homogeneous group confronting common economic predicaments growing out of structural reform is experienced from within the group as fragmented interests, unequal treatment, and mutual suspicion. The sources of such fissures come from both the state and the market. On the one hand, state policies stipulate entitlements for different subgroups of workers. On the other hand, enterprises vary in terms of market performance, leadership competence, and integrity. From the perspective of retirees, the failure of SOEs has to do with both system transformation and specific incompetent and corrupt cadres. This nuanced understanding, in addition to their perception of fissure of interests, often mollifies and mutes their critique against the state as a whole. Finally, retirees enjoy relative privilege among workers in the state sector. At the end of the day, compared with laid-off and unemployed workers, they now at least enjoy the security of socialized pensions. As we shall see later, many retirees have become the main breadwinners in their respective families: their pensions are the major source of stable income supporting their unemployed grown children and the latter's school-age offspring, all crammed into the apartments that SOEs sold to retirees in the course of housing reform in the 1990s.

Valves Factory

Many protests by laid-off workers involved long period of wage arrears before the firm initiated the formal procedure for bankruptcy. The key actors are workers who were still on the payroll, some even showing up on their shop floors regularly, but without actually working. Many did not bother to go and the company was not concerned either way. This situation was called "mutual disregard," or *liangbuguan*. The following protest occurred in China's largest industrial valves plant. In its heyday in 1987, the factory boasted an annual profit of ten million yuan, and a four-thousand-strong workforce. "There were so many workers that it took a quarter of an hour to get everyone through the gate at the end of the workday," one worker recalled proudly. The factory began a downhill slide in the early 1990s. Like other SOEs here, it was plagued by problems of market competition, debt, bad management, and the heavy burden of an aging workforce. At one point in 1992, all workers were required to make a "collective investment" in the firm, each paying 4,000 yuan to save the cash-strapped firm. Then in 1998, it issued "stock," the legal status of which has never been recognized by the local government, and demanded that workers voluntarily convert their investment into stock in the firm, or risk losing any chance of their money being repaid. The general public was also enticed to buy the stock of what to many was the most established SOE in Tieling. Yet, the injection of this twenty-million-yuan investment was not able to avert its decline.

On May Day 2001, some seventy workers blocked the main entrance of the factory with a chain tied around the gate, and formed a picket line to stop other workers from getting in. The factory had stopped wage payments to the entire workforce for six months. A banner declaring "We Want to Eat" and "Return Our Wages" hung at the gate. Even the security guards did not intervene, because they too were owed back pay. Most workers were sympathetic and did not force their way through. During the next three days of production suspension, police cars were seen patrolling the streets surrounding the factory and public security officers looked on, without taking any action to disperse the crowd. One key worker participant emphasized how he prevailed over other more militant tendencies among his coworkers and convinced them to stay within the realm of legal behavior. He recounted how the incident got off the ground due to the ease of communication among coworker-neighbors in the living quarters across the street from the enterprise.

> You don't need much organizing. I was taking a walk in the playground downstairs, and ran into several coworkers who were talking about protesting against wage arrears the next morning. We wanted the director to come out and explain to us. Before that, a dozen of them had visited the petition office of the city government. We got one month's paycheck after that. Then it stopped paying again. . . . There were at first twenty or so of us, gathering at the gate. We were busy debating what to write on the banner. Someone cooked up something really clumsy and long-winded, not crisp enough to be a slogan. I convinced them to go for simple and clear statements, just "We Want to Eat" and "Return Our Wages." On the sidewalk, we used eight plastic bags and wrote with black ink. . . . We waited there for the director to appear. Then, when we

were told that he was heading for a meeting in Beijing and said that he would not cancel his trip because of our protest, workers were infuriated. We immediately put an iron chain around the gate. Some workers yelled, proposing to set fire to company cars, others suggested blocking highways and city streets. I implored them to stay calm, and reasoned with them. I said that asking for unpaid wages is righteous, but if we turn it into a riot, we violate the law. There are regulations against blocking traffic and against public disorder. It will change the nature of our cause. They [the officials] can then put all sorts of bad labels on us.

This worker won the support of most of those gathering on the spot. Thirty people remained stationed at the gate until the evening. When the enterprise management informed the city government of the protest, a delegation of five officials from the Petition Office and city government's Light Industry Bureau came to assuage workers' anger, assuring them that the director had been instructed to take the first flight back the next day. They asked workers to elect their own representatives to negotiate with the director and prepare a statement of demands. Worrying about future retaliation, which had happened at other factories, workers refused to send any representatives, saying that there was nothing to negotiate because they only had one simple demand: that the enterprise pay them their wages. That night, these thirty workers took turns guarding the entrance. The director returned to the factory the next evening, appearing before a crowd of one hundred workers.

He told us our enterprise is experiencing financial difficulty. His trip to Beijing was about something urgent and he had rushed back once that business was over. He was willing to follow the instructions of the government to pay us immediately one month's wages, and will then come up with a more detailed repayment plan. . . . We got wage payments the following two months, but they stopped again after that. No one has ever seen any repayment plan.

The threat of police repression is intense and imminent, leading workers to set self-imposed limits on what actions to take. The sensitive political boundary between enterprise and "society" should be observed if government crackdown is to be averted. Workers feel protected if their activities remain work-unit-bound, where the geography of workplace and residence facilitate communications among coworkers. Within the work unit, workers are also often divided in their interest. When rumors spread that the management of one of the workshops was close to clinching a merger with a private firm from Shenzhen headed by the sister of one of the premiers sitting in the Standing Committee of the Politburo, workers in that workshop were hopeful of resuming work and receiving their unpaid back wages. For workers in workshops that had been "subcontracted" to private, financially independent entrepreneurs, this deal would not benefit them because they had severed their employment relations with the main enterprise and therefore were not entitled to back wages. For the rest of the unpaid workforce, the momentum to engage in further action diminished. When I visited these workers in January 2002, there were flyers posted on the entrance of each residential building, announcing another protest scheduled for November to demand payment of eight months of unpaid wages. That mobilization failed because by then many workers were disillusioned and were busy with whatever alternative jobs they had found. Finally, at the end of 2001, the center's policy of paying a one-time compensation to workers in unofficially bankrupt enterprises resulted in a severance package of 400 yuan per year of tenure. No protest occurred then.

NEIGHBORHOOD PROTESTS

Working-class neighborhoods in Liaoning, as in many major cities, are work-unit-based. Work units built and maintained employees' residences, which were typically apartment units averaging about fifty square meters in an eight-story building. A medium-sized enterprise would have one or two residential quarters (*jiashuqu*) each consisting of six to ten apartment buildings. These neighborhoods have remained intact, even after enterprises have descended into formal or informal bankruptcy. Problems of maintenance, utilities, and public services provision have fallen into an institutional vacuum with the default of enterprise subsidies for a wide range of services to the respective government offices, many of which have turned into independent commercial entities. Based on my fieldwork in Tiexi, the largest and oldest working-class district in Shenyang, winter heating and pipe maintenance have sparked the most collective action, some of which have crossed work-unit boundaries. For instance, in the late 1990s, winter heating became a contentious social issue in Liaoning when only about half of the total heating bills were paid.[34] Some factories had continued paying heating subsidies to the utilities company, while others had stopped. Apartments built in the 1980s or before, when no one anticipated the dismantling of SOEs and the system of work-unit subsidies, were not equipped with individual household meters. The consequence was that the utilities company had no way of recording individual household consumption and could only impose a uniform rate of 1,200 yuan each winter. Many workers said they could not afford it, so no one got heat until everyone paid. Protests by residents erupted in the winter months, when there was no heating in subzero temperatures. The interests of workers as residents were again organized on a work-unit basis. As in the case of pension protests, worker residents simply made use of their everyday social organization, the work-unit residence, for what the government called "extraordinary" activities or disturbances. The architectural infrastructure of the work unit as a social reproduction institution not only survived the bankruptcy of production but also quietly sustained the organizational capacity of workers against their own enterprises and the local government. The target of workers' actions was the enterprise management, which workers held responsible for not paying the subsidies, but they made shrewd use of mass action in public to draw the attention of city government officials, who would presumably leverage their pressure on enterprise management.

There were reports of protests in several northeastern cities that were related directly or indirectly to heat provisions and subsidies.[35] In the winter of 2002 alone, one factory in Tiexi staged three demonstrations outside the heating company. At least one of these was timed to take place before the Sixteenth Party Congress in Beijing, a sensitive time when the central and provincial governments were particularly keen on maintaining an image of social peace and stability. Similar dynamics of organization and action as those found in pension protests underlay residents' protests. This account by the former Party secretary of the factory involved was corroborated by other participants.

> In late October, the heating company began posting flyers in our neighborhood's notice board, announcing that our factory owed them 4.8 million yuan of heating fees and another 4 million yuan of maintenance fees. Each household had to pay 1,200 yuan, otherwise it would stop providing heat this winter. No one wanted to pay and many who were owed wages were unable to pay. When some of us ran into one another in the courtyard and started grumbling about our freezing apartments, we decided to ask people to gather the next day at 8 AM to go to the utility company. So, fifty to one hundred workers would come each time. It's a fifteen-minute walk, and marching on the streets created a scene. Police would come, and once we told them it's about a heating problem, they would leave us alone. The utility company saw us and called our director to come immediately. He promised the company would pay the debt and asked them to resume heating. It's the enterprise's responsibility. By gathering in public, we exerted pressure on city officials. Who among the leadership is not concerned about social stability these days? They cannot afford to ignore problems of heating because those old pipes would crack and burst if they stop heating completely. That's why there is always a trickle of heat in our apartments, not enough to keep people warm, but so the pipes would not explode.[36]

Maintenance of water pipes and supply is another neighborhood issue that has led to public protests in Tiexi. Workers from different factories have joined together as residents of the same neighborhood when they confront the same public services problem. This woman worker from a bridge-work enterprise in Shenyang participated in a road blockade involving hundreds of residents in her neighborhood. They were employees of six enterprises whose apartment buildings were all affected by an extensive leak of sewage pipes. Still relishing the victory of mass action, she recalled with pride and amusement that the Street Committee secretary managed to pull off such a feat of collective dissent. They blocked the major road from Shenyang to Liaozhong, demanding that the local government repair the pipes and stop the flooding of dirty water. Again, the root cause is the collapse of the work unit.

> Pipes inside the apartment building used to be maintained by the work unit. In theory, it should now be the responsibility of the Housing and Property Bureau, as the work unit no longer manages workers' housing. Pipes outside the building should be maintained by the Water Work Company. The problem is that neither of these departments nor the district government want to take responsibility, and the enterprise has collapsed. We have had flooding of white [clean] water and black [dirty] water. . . . We are the masses, the residents; what should we do? We can only complain to the Street Committee *(jiedao)* and the secretary is desperate. One day, he took a loudspeaker and addressed the residents, saying, "For the sake of our neighborhood environment and sanitation, residents please come to block the road." Several hundred people responded, and ten minutes later, we occupied four major intersections of the road from Shenyang to Liaozhong. The secretary said if the police asked, we cannot mention the Street Committee and should all say we came spontaneously without an organizer. . . . Public security arrived first on the scene, and then all the leaders of the enterprises came. Within two months, all the pipes in the neighborhood were replaced.[37]

If incidents like this involve a large number of worker residents from different factories, their demands are very specific and mundane. Once services are restored, the momentum for collective action dissipates. A potentially more serious and knotty problem concerns fuzzy property rights to work-unit apartments that workers and enterprises presumably have shared. Protests involving property rights violations and relocation compensation flared up in major cities across China in the early 2000s. In Liaoning, workers' property rights contentions are inextricably tied to work units. The problem can be traced to the 1980s, when SOEs took advantage of their autonomy granted by enterprise reform and engaged in a frenzy of apartment construction. Around the early 1990s, workers were asked to "buy" their allocated apartments at highly subsidized prices, with the condition that the enterprise retained 30 percent of property rights to the apartments. By the early 2000s, plant closures or production suspensions had workers worried that their property rights were no longer guaranteed, because it was unclear whether and by whom their partial property rights would be recognized. Some enterprises had transferred the management of their housing stocks to the local Housing and Property Bureau, which, according to workers, did not always recognize them as owners. The problem had to do with documentation, with some enterprises issuing property titles to workers while others did not. In other cases, the Bureau claimed that because the enterprises involved had not transferred their share of 30 percent to the Bureau, residents had to foot the bill before their property rights would be officially and fully recognized. A seventy-year-old woman I interviewed was furious that she still did not have her property title. Recently, she and other elderly workers had held several meetings in the neighborhood's elderly activities room and they had decided that they should be given full title of their apartments and the Housing and Property Bureau should issue them title certificates. Her fifty-square-meter apartment in Tiexi, which she "bought" in 1988 for six thousand yuan, was estimated to be worth about fifty thousand yuan today.

> We had several meetings. Each time sixty or so people came, and we wanted to ask the enterprise director to come as well. I called him up during our last meeting, telling him that there were sixty of us witnessing this call. I said we wanted to resolve our property title problems and wanted him to come. I also said that we would play by the rule of first approaching the enterprise. If there is no result, sorry, we'll go to the city government. He was courteous and promised to talk to us directly. We'll see if we need to petition the city.[38]

This incipient protest represents just the beginning of a major movement in Chinese cities. Property rights disputes involving relocation, demolition, compensation, and illicit development of neighborhood land are increasing rapidly, leading to mass petitions and road blockages, and sometimes even self-immolation and clashes with police. When I left Liaoning in the summer of 2003, rumors were circulated in working-class neighborhoods about the local government's plan to develop dilapidated work-unit residential quarters into high-technology parks and commercial districts. Some residents were waiting to see if the compensation plan would give them modest capital to start life elsewhere, while others deplored the imminent disappearance of workers' districts.

In short, both nonpayment and neighborhood protests are driven by livelihood needs and concerns about collective consumption and are mobilized on the basis of highly localized and cellular groupings. Such actions are usually restrained and self-limiting, calculated to avoid state repression but generate sufficient mass pressure so that the local government and enterprise management will yield to demonstrators' demands, at least partially. In the next section, we will see that the propensity for these protests to escalate into more inclusive, broad-based political unrest is heightened when enterprise bankruptcy is involved. In some bankruptcy protests, management's strategy of "divide and conquer" may still prevent retirees from participating in laid-off workers' actions, as the following case studies show. But the two groups are more likely to engage in joint action in circumstances involving bankruptcy declarations because the Bankruptcy Law bundles their rights together, and because bankruptcy always implies cadre corruption and illicit sales of enterprise assets perceived by workers as their collective property. The rage against the violation of workers' "master status," realized through permanent employment and embodied in the physical structure of an SOE, distinguishes this kind of protest from nonpayment protests and neighborhood protests. What to officials and management is outdated machinery or a dilapidated workshop to workers is their collective asset, accumulated through lifelong sacrifice under a low-wage system. When cadres are found to squander these assets, workers' attachment to their factories easily fuels passionate resistance. This extraordinarily deep and unique "class feeling," not to be found among migrant workers in non-state industries, is vividly articulated in many workers' accounts of protests. Bankruptcy becomes all the more incendiary when local government fails to react in a timely fashion, and when particularly daring leadership happens to emerge from among outraged workers. When this occurs, the flames of protests can spread quickly across factories, pitting the local working class against the local state, as events in Liaoyang threw to bold relief.

BANKRUPTCY PROTESTS

Years before the central government formally allowed bankruptcy of SOEs with the policy of "grasping the big and letting go of the small" in 1997, many small and medium-sized SOEs in Liaoning had suspended production in the face of fierce competition from rural industry and private and foreign-owned factories. Since the early 1990s, workers who have not reached retirement age have been released in increasing numbers from these ailing factories, told to "take a long vacation" for an indefinite period of time, or become "informally" retired.[39] Their employment relationship with the firm remains intact, meaning that although they are no longer paid, they are still on the payroll and therefore eligible for health-care benefits and, most important, pensions when they eventually reach the official retirement age for blue-collar workers (fifty-five for men, and fifty for women, with exceptions for workers in heavy industry or in particular posts). The crux of labor contention in bankruptcy protests is the question: Are these middle-aged workers compensated adequately at the time of bankruptcy so that they can enjoy the same floor of security available to current pensioners?

The backbone of bankruptcy protests consists of these middle-aged workers, who are arguably the most disgruntled group in the state industrial workforce in the reform period. Sociologists call them the "lost generation"; these workers describe themselves as victims of state policies.[40] On their collective fate of "running into every major reversal of state policies" (i.e., the Great Leap Forward, the Cultural Revolution, the One-Child Policy, and market reform), a Shenyang woman worker bemoaned,

> Our generation has really suffered a bad fate. As kids, when we were growing up, [there was not enough food as] it happened to be the Three Difficult Years [after the Great Leap]. When we were in primary and secondary school, it was the Cultural Revolution. Then, at seventeen, we were made to leave our parents to go up to the mountains and down to the fields. Just as we got back to the city, there was the "diploma craze." Now at our age, with neither strength nor skills, we become the first target of reform and are let go.[41]

These workers are too young to reap the benefits of socialism but too old to compete in the emerging capitalist social order. Many are sons and daughters of retirees, and returned to the cities and joined their parents' factories after the sent-down movement came to a close between the mid-1970s and early 1980s. A particular state policy of replacement, or *dingti*, allowed these youngsters to inherit their parents' state factory jobs, a highly desirable employment opportunity at that time. SOEs are therefore aptly described by workers and management as "family enterprises" *(jiashuchang)*. By the late 1990s, these relatively younger workers found themselves bearing the brunt of market reform in every conceivable way all at once. Just when their financial and family burdens peaked, with school-age children and elderly parents, they found themselves victims of enterprise restructuring, mass layoffs, wage arrears, and a labor market favoring younger and more educated migrant workers from the countryside. Housing allocation by work units usually benefits their parents, whose longer job tenure translates into higher scores in the allocation exercise. Many laid-off workers who cannot find regular jobs live and eat at their parents' households and rely on the financial support provided by their parents' pensions. Sandwiched between two generations but unable to shoulder the traditional responsibility of taking care of either, this cohort of workers feels particularly hard pressed and vulnerable.

To this generation of workers, not only do they feel betrayed after they sacrificed their youth to erratic state policies and political campaigns in building socialism, but they are also indignant about cadre abuse of power and corruption that deprives them of a fair, level playing field for market competition. A fifty-two-year-old woman worker who took informal retirement when she was forty-eight said,

> We can accept inequality of income, if those who earn more are more capable or work harder. We can only envy their achievement. But the problem today is that the Communist Party people use power, not ability, and that infuriates workers. Even the lowliest cadres have the opportunity to squander the wealth and assets of the ordinary masses.[42]

Corruption is the most popular rallying cry in bankruptcy protests, and as many workers explain, it is immoral because the beneficiaries make no effort and have no merit. These workers approve of higher incomes for entrepreneurs as rewards for their competence and hard work, but they believe that corruption has no legitimacy in either a socialist or capitalist society.

> The problems with our enterprise are about illegal practices. We workers feel totally helpless. People have petitioned the local government many times, and they have sent several teams of investigators. These all ended without result. It's not that the state or enterprise leadership exploits us. We'd rather be exploited. Exploitation is much better than corruption. I find corruption so much more disgusting and despicable. If you [the boss] are capable, and have capital or technology, you are still making a contribution to society. I think this has relative rationality. To a certain extent, I am for exploitation, when it is law-abiding. At the end of the day, what the market economy means is exactly this: private employment relations. Exploitation is more transparent and clean than corruption.[43]

While cadre corruption is common knowledge, bankruptcy procedures involving local government investigation, auditing, and final approval allow workers to learn about the magnitude of the problem and directly implicate workers' personal interests. In the following analysis, I juxtapose several cases of bankruptcy protests in Tieling and Liaoyang to understand how bankruptcy triggers mobilization. Whereas the textile mill protest and the steel window-frame factory demonstration both illustrate the centrality of laid-off workers as the core instigators fighting for severance compensation, the latter case also reveals how and why the local government is under political pressure to concede. The Tieling protest, the third case, shows the powerful force bankruptcy unleashes when both retirees and laid-off workers share economic and political grievances with their counterparts in other factories against an unresponsive local government. Interfactory mobilization emerges, however briefly, only to be met with a heavy-handed crackdown by the government.

Textile Mill

Although protests had become almost a routine affair in this seemingly quiet industrial town of four hundred thousand residents, the textile mill struggle was a local cause célèbre because of the unusual persistence of the workers, who not only petitioned regularly in front of the mayor's office, but also went to the provincial capital and even to Beijing. Workers were bemused that over the many months of interaction, they befriended even the public security officers, who became sympathetic to their cause. Neighborhood shopkeepers would ask for updates of their actions when they went to make photocopies of protest materials or buy other sundry items. Established by the Japanese in the 1920s, the textile mill specialized in producing chemical fiber cloth. Its four-thousand-strong workforce (half of whom were retirees) and fixed assets worth sixty million yuan made it one of the major SOEs in Liaoning's textile industry. The decline of the factory began in the early 1990s, when management made some fateful decisions to take out huge loans to import new technology that later proved to be incompatible with existing machinery in the mill. Competition from township and village enterprises and from SOEs in other provinces also dealt heavy blows to sales. Added to these were problems of rampant cadre corruption and diversion of funds. In 1996, the director announced to the entire workforce that the factory would file for bankruptcy in the local court, so as to get rid of its accumulated debts. He reassured workers that this was a false bankruptcy, only a strategic move similarly taken by many other ailing SOEs to restructure their asset-debt ratios, and that workers would be recalled back to work in a few months. After waiting for three months, to the workers' outrage and dismay, there was no payment of wages or allowances. The government then announced that a subsidiary shopping mall, established in the mid-1980s by the textile mill to generate extra profits, would be transferred to the Labor and Social Security Bureau to cover payment of retirees' pensions. Although retirees were able to collect their pensions every month, younger workers never received the legal minimum allowance of 120 yuan for laid-off workers.

The laid-off workers waited and endured for two years, dipping into their savings or taking up various other forms of employment. Finally, a government announcement sparked worker action. In mid-1997, when the central government pressed ahead with a three-year plan to restructure SOEs, it simultaneously urged local governments to guarantee the basic livelihood of workers made redundant by enterprise restructuring and bankruptcy. "When we heard on television that the government is serious in implementing this livelihood guarantee policy, we began organizing petitions. Every Monday, the 'meet the mayor' day, we showed up in his office," explained Su, who emerged as one of the leaders when the former leader, who was the enterprise union chair, died of a heart attack.[44] At first, workers occupied the union meeting room inside the factory and hung on the door a red banner with the words "Home of the Laid-off Workers." Later, mass meetings were held in the courtyards of the enterprise's residential quarters, which consisted of four eight-story apartment buildings, or in the open in front of the local government office. Smaller meetings for the core leaders were held on a rotating basis in their homes, many of which were within walking distance of one another. Conspicuously absent from these meetings were retired workers, who opposed their planned protests and saw the younger laid-off workers as competitors for the same pot of money. A seventy-year-old female retiree, upset by her son's participation in the protest, was not on speaking terms with him. For her, family relation became tense and fractured from within by the factory's different policies toward retirees and laid-off workers.

For those involved in protests, their strategy was to adhere unflinchingly to the law. Worker representatives diligently amassed evidence, solicited testimony, and drafted sophisticated petition letters, seeking the advice of lawyers and law students. They asked fellow workers to submit testimony of what they knew about management corruption or malfeasance in the bankruptcy procedure. The protest leaders were encouraged when workers in different departments, some very close to top management, would deliver to their doorsteps written testimony with detailed figures of dubious expenditures, embezzlement of sales revenue by cadres, and illegitimate allocation of enterprise housing units to local government officials, and so on. Like many in other protest cases, worker representatives devoured law books and government circulars. A typical petition letter these workers presented to the city and provincial governments reflected thorough knowledge of specific clauses in the Bankruptcy Law or the policy of minimum livelihood guarantee, and evidence of how the enterprise departed from those stipulations.

> With our deepest indignation and a strong sense of responsibility toward the Party, the enterprise, and ourselves, we the entire workforce sustained one hundred days of petition to the city government, demanding thorough investigation into the handling of bankruptcy of our enterprise. There was never any satisfactory reply. Therefore, following the stipulations of the Petition Regulations, we submit this jointly signed petition to you, the provincial government, and we strongly demand that the authorities look into these matters so that we can secure our legal rights and receive justice. . . . Here are the discrepancies between the Bankruptcy Law and the situations of our enterprise. First, the procedure of bankruptcy was illegal. According to Instructions on Bankruptcy of State-Owned Enterprises passed by the Liaoning People's Government Office . . . there must be approval by the Workers' Congress and the superior department of the enterprise. . . . None of this is true in our case. . . . Second, workers received absolutely no livelihood allowance and this is a violation of Clause Four in the Bankruptcy Law.[45]

Reflecting the workers' legal-mindedness and restraint, the banners they raised during petitions read, "We Want to Meet the Mayor" and "Return the Shopping Mall to Us." They wanted the local government to pay them the allowance stipulated in state policy and they wanted to be able to use the shopping mall rental income to make severance payments to all workers, not just to retirees. If they were keenly aware of how their interests diverged from those of retired workers, they also insisted on the difference between themselves and laid-off workers in other local factories. Jealously guarding their unique ownership claim to the shopping mall, one leader said,

> Every factory has its own problems and situations. We have the shopping mall in the best location in Tieling, a spot equivalent to the Tiananmen Square in Beijing. Which other factory has such a prime asset?[46]

Another important factor inhibiting interfactory activism was state repression. Ever cautious to present themselves as "apolitical," these laid-off workers consciously avoided coordinating with other factories involved in petitions. "We do not need networking with others. That would jeopardize our cause. We act within the bounds of the law and we are good citizens," a female leader later explained to me.[47] Instead of lateral organization, to augment pressure on the local government, workers scaled the bureaucratic hierarchy and traveled periodically to the provincial government in Shenyang and submitted petition letters to the government's petition office and textile bureau. They also raised petition funds from workers to finance a Beijing trip for the five representatives in May 1999, and returned with letters from the central departments demanding that lower-level departments expedite their investigations of this case. While in Beijing, they visited a television station known for its exposé programs, but reporters there told them that the textile mill's case was just too common nationwide to be used as material for special reportage. Workers also went to the Textile Bureau and the national Petition Bureau, where they met many other petitioning workers from different parts of the country with similar grievances. They also went to the Justice Department and decided that they would bring their case to the court and press charges against management corruption after getting the issue of pensions and allowances settled. Representatives vowed that they were equally committed to answering the anticorruption call of the central government, although their own livelihood must be the top priority.

A turning point of their agitation came in a meeting with the mayor after worker leaders returned from Beijing. During a heated discussion about the property rights to the shopping mall, workers found out that the ownership certificate of the mall was still in the hands of the director and had not yet been transferred to the Labor and Social Security Bureau. One worker leader who was known for his thunderous temper rushed to the director's office and literally took that piece of paper by force and ran away. The next day, about a hundred workers staged a sit-in blocking the entrances to the shopping mall. In order not to obstruct the businesses of the stall keepers, who were mainly unemployed factory workers, they cordoned off the electricity supply room of the mall. Shoppers went in and out as usual, but business was conducted in the dark. Hanging up banners that read "Return the Shopping Mall to Us," dozens of workers took turns guarding against police action. The next day, local officials backed off and yielded to workers' demands for livelihood allowances. Yet no final agreement was reached regarding the enterprise's contribution to workers' pension insurance accounts, a main concern of laid-off workers who found themselves just a few years away from retirement. Many worried that the lapse in enterprise contributions since the mid-1990s would disqualify them from receiving pensions later. A few leaders adamantly kept up the pressure on the local government, pressing their complaint about illicit bankruptcy procedures. The city government accepted their petition every time they visited the petition bureau, but no concrete progress was made about pensions or bankruptcy compensation. The case dragged on until December 2001, when the central government imposed the policy of the one-time payment to permanently sever the ties between laid-off workers and their enterprises. In Tieling, for each year of job tenure the laid-off worker was paid 400 yuan. Most workers grudgingly accepted, for fear of losing even this pittance of compensation. Others, such as Su Jingwen, chose to wait out this period of chaotic policy to reach the official retirement age. Only five years separated him from the most cherished of all socialist benefits—pension. With tears in his eyes, he expressed indignation typical among workers abandoned by the state's retreat from the socialist social contract.

> I joined the People's Liberation Army at nineteen, and seven years later, came back to join the factory. I am a good citizen, a good worker, a progressive producer in the enterprise. No black spot in my background. I have always believed that as long as the Communist Party exists, they would not ignore our problems. I have been loyal to Chairman Mao from the revolution until today. I gave my youth to the state. Thirty-some years of job tenure, at age fifty-three, with young and elderly dependents at home, you make me a laid-off worker. How can I attain any balance inside? You see how our enterprise has been squandered to this state. I really cannot stand it. I am really unbalanced inside. There are worms in our societies eating us from within. When every one of the state factories is going downhill, the end of the entire society will not be far away. Cadres can go to the office any time they like, and have ladies sitting around the dinner table. Yet we cannot even get our livelihood allowances on time! The Party Central Committee is basically good, but they have problems enforcing the law.[48]

Besides the popular anguish and resentment about the regime's betrayal of the social contract, there are several noticeable features in the mobilization strategy of this protest that are typical of many in the northeast. First, workers use the law imposed by the central government as the parameter and trigger for targeting enterprise and local officials. The gap between central policy and local practice offers the political space for what workers consider legitimate activism. Collective petitions, an institutionalized method for the masses to lodge complaints against local officials, evolves almost seamlessly into collective protests in the interaction with officials who defy the legal procedure of bankruptcy. Second, while the work-unit residential community facilitates collective action, the work unit does not necessarily act collectively, because workers' interests are divided by state policies and management practices (e.g., retirees did not participate in the protest outside the shopping mall). Finally, with the goal of obtaining maximum concrete results, workers consider lateral mobilization across factories less feasible and less effective than leveraging the hierarchal power relations between superior and subordinate levels of government. The next example drives home even more clearly why mass action can generate pressure on local officials.

Steel Window-Frames Factory

Workers' struggle can often lie dormant for months or years and suddenly take on unexpected momentum, fueled by official actions that are equally brisk and sudden. In the case of the window-frame factory, which employed some four hundred workers and suspended production in 1995, workers were sent home without receiving livelihood allowances as required by law. Having argued in vain with enterprise management and the Economic Bureau of the city government, the superior bureau of the factory, workers gave up petitioning and focused instead on making ends meet. Then in April 1999, the government announced that a real estate developer would buy the factory premises for five million yuan, and the enterprise applied for bank-ruptcy and proposed to the Workers' Congress in the enterprise that work-ers would be paid two years of unemployment allowances. Workers went back to the factory to attend the meeting and rejected the offer, demanding that either the enterprise resume production or pay them severance com-pensation pegged to the length of job tenure. In view of the imminent sale, and the rumors that the local government would send in cranes and police to clear the premises, workers living in the nearby enterprise housing area began taking turns guarding the factory's main entrance.[49] Some twenty workers were there holding out day and night, with a red banner hanging up at the gate, reading, "We Vow to Protect Workers' Legal Rights and Interests" and "Stop the Loss of State Assets," both current official slogans. Then, a week later, on June 24, around 2 AM, around five hundred police offi-cers armed with dynamite locked up the dozen workers guarding the premises and, in an hour's time, demolished the several low-rise buildings making up the factory. The noise awakened residents nearby and angry workers living farther away gathered together early the next morning and began a rally in the city, holding up white banners that read, "We Want to Live" and "We Demand Justice." Wang Zhongzhi, an ordinary worker who joined the protest, recalled workers' explosive anger.

> Every inch of grass and every piece of steel in the factory belonged to us workers. They were our sweat and labor. People had tears in their eyes when they saw the fallen pieces of window frames left on the burnt ground. Those were state assets and these officials just squandered them. . . . Two hundred workers gathered and every one was agitated. There were so many different calls to action: block the main highway,

block the railroad, march to the police department. . . . It's really an aim-
less flow of people at that time, marching forward not knowing where to
go, just roaming. I shouted to remind them to stay close together. We
don't want to lose any of them. But frankly, I was very scared on the
inside. Such a huge angry crowd.[50]

A worker representative recalled that it was a rainy day, and the rally
crowd stopped several times under bridges to rest and wait for the rain to
stop. By 6 PM, the two hundred protesting workers arrived at the last train
station on the railway line to Shenyang. Under the cautious eyes and occasional blockage of the police, they decided to walk all the way to the provincial capital, eighty kilometers away. By that time, there were 140 people left
and they stopped to spend the night in a state-owned barn until daybreak.
Around 2 AM, city officials came and wanted to negotiate on the spot. But
workers said they were too tired and would send representatives to meet
with them in the morning. At 5 AM, all the major leaders of the city government came, and to the workers' surprise, they appeared very sincere and
willing to talk about specific compensations and regulations. The government
offered to "buy off their tenure" at a rate of 400 yuan per year. A worker representative explained the calculation by workers and by local officials.

> We accepted, because we heard that the government sets the range at
> 300 to 400 yuan per year. But workers did not trust their verbal promise
> and so we demanded a written agreement. In the end, there were four
> clauses in black and white. Three were about worker compensations and
> the last one was that "workers would never petition to higher-level
> authorities." They [officials] were very afraid that we would bring their
> dirty linen to the attention of their superiors. There were so many ille-
> gitimate accounts inside the factory.[51]

On July 9, all workers went back to what used to be the factory premises
to collect their hard-won paychecks for the last time.

As in the case of the textile mill, we find the same logic of claiming
workers' rights defined by state policy, appropriating official slogans to
legitimize their claims, and the ease of coordination owing to the geographical concentration of some workers living in enterprise housing. Local
officials were pressured to make concessions to workers' demands because
they were concerned that superior and public attention would be drawn to
their management and financial records following an escalation of the confrontation. Many of the workers who joined in the last phase admitted that
the possible settlement of their severance compensation spurred them into
action. Of course, they were outraged that a lifetime's labor was reduced to
a pittance. The land sale seemed like the last chance for them to make a last-

ditch effort to claim whatever the government was willing to give. After several years of receiving nothing from the enterprise, the several thousand yuan everyone got was at least a bittersweet consolation. In short, both the textile mill and the window-frame factory had some concrete assets to be contested: the shopping mall and the factory's land. When workers could see the prospect of a realistic resolution to their problems, mobilization was facilitated.

The conciliatory stance of the Tieling officials in these two cases must be juxtaposed with the other side of a Janus-faced state in response to labor unrest. There are many reports in the international media about worker protests that were put down by armed police and even the military. In a mining town in Liaoning, some twenty thousand miners and their families smashed windows, burned cars, and blocked traffic in March 2000 after the mine declared bankruptcy and offered meager severance packages to the miners. Several hundred soldiers from the People's Liberation Army were brought in from several cities, tear gassing the crowd and firing shots into the air. Leaders of the incident were reportedly arrested.[52] In another incident in July 1997, workers from three state-owned factories in Mianyang City of Sichuan province took to the streets to denounce graft and demand unemployment relief after their factories were declared bankrupt. Armed police were sent in to impose a citywide curfew, after more than one hundred workers were injured in violent clashes with the police and eighty people were reportedly arrested.[53] It seems that state repression is most likely when the number of workers involved is large or when interfactory or community participation appears. Desperate and angry workers, instead of pursuing the tactics of legal petition and cellular activism, sometimes resort to violence against enterprise management. Kidnapping and murder of managers responsible for mass layoffs, and factory explosions purportedly committed by former workers have been reported in different cities.[54] In many other incidents, though, protests erupted under the watchful eyes of local police but died down without violence or concessions by officials.

Liaoyang Ferro-Alloy Factory

The outburst of protests in Liaoyang in the spring of 2002, perhaps the most radical episode in labor activism in more than two decades of reform, raised the specter of a class-based uprising. It involved interfactory coordination and political demands for the removal of city officials. These two features of the Liaoyang incident set it apart from every previous worker protest, and it received enormous attention from the international media and the Chinese regime. While the international media and labor groups hailed it as the largest popular demonstration since the Tiananmen mobilization in 1989, the state came down hard on worker leaders, sentencing two of them to seven and four years of imprisonment, respectively. This is a critical case for understanding the dynamic, potential, and limits of labor unrest. How did it manage to break out of the confines of single-factory mobilization and economic demands? What kind of mobilization strategy was used? And what explained its demise? The following analysis is based on interviews with worker representatives from the Liaoyang Ferro-Alloy Factory and several participants from other factories, as well as journalistic reports in the foreign press and publications of labor organizations outside of China.[55]

All the familiar elements I found in other worker protests were also present in Liaoyang, including the catalytic role of state policy and ideology, work-unit mode of mobilization, diversity of interest among workers, economic demands, popular accusations of local corruption, and appeal to the legality and the authority of the central government. Nevertheless, a *sustained* interaction of these ordinary factors apparently gave rise to something extraordinary. As one worker representative of Liaoyang Ferro-Alloy Factory put it, in a measured and solemnly reflective voice, "The whole struggle went through a conversion, a 'qualitative leap.'"[56] He was referring to the changes from petitions to protests, from single-factory to multifactory joint action, and from economic to political demands. According to workers' accounts, what seems to have happened was that although several years of repeated petitions had failed to bring about a government response, the process of petition itself had taken on a life of its own. Representatives emerged as the government demanded that petitioning workers elect five representatives to present their cases, rather than the government having to deal with massive public gatherings of workers. During numerous visits to the city government, worker representatives from different work units who initiated their action independently came to know one another. The increase of bankrupt firms over time in the same locale led to a transformation in popular consciousness, with a realization that residents' economic woes had common and deeper roots in the corrupt local state. The prolonged process of struggle also witnessed the maturation of core organizers' mobilization skills and established their credibility in the local community. In the end, an incendiary comment on unemployment made by a hated local official was enough to infuriate the public and ignite the dynamite. Had the government in Liaoyang been more responsive, as local officials in Shenyang and Tieling had been, the explosive incident would likely have been preempted. Had individual worker representatives been less daring and committed, workers would not have transcended the cellular confine of their work units.

The Liaoyang rebellion was mainly agitation by workers at the Liaoyang Ferro-Alloy Factory, or Liaotie, where workers had already engaged with the local government for four years by the time of the 2002 protests. Ever since the appointment of Fan Yicheng as director and Party secretary in 1993, the firm's fortunes had slipped, and since 1996 production had been suspended periodically. Beginning in 1998, workers made many attempts to petition local and Beijing officials. They lodged complaints about managerial corruption, illicit transfer and privatization of state assets, and unpaid wages and pensions. All their efforts were in vain; officials did not take any action to alleviate the workers' plight.

In May 2000, more than one thousand Liaotie workers blocked the main highway from Liaoyang to Shenyang and demanded payment of wages and pensions. Armed police arrived and arrested three organizers. The next day, workers regrouped and launched a siege of the city government building, with a banner reading, "Arrears Guilty." They demanded a solution from the mayor, the release of their leaders, and payment of wages. One police source confirmed that at that time, some two thousand workers were still working at the factory but had not been paid for sixteen months since 1998, while two thousand laid-off workers and one thousand retired workers had not received their benefits for three to six months.[57] The leaders were later released but workers still did not get their pay. The only gratification workers obtained was that their action was reported by the Voice of America, which was popular in Liaoyang.

Liaotie workers also tried approaching the Labor Bureau, which, as one worker representative recalled bitterly, refused to process their case because of political pressure.

> We went to the Labor Bureau and tried to register our case with the Labor Disputes Arbitration Committee, only to be told by the officer there that "we cannot handle your case." The city government had instructed them not to touch the case. So, we workers have legal grounds, but to whom can you take your grievance? Our own enterprise trade union chairman reprimanded us for being so foolhardy, saying that "there is the labor law, there is the bankruptcy law, but this enterprise still does what it wants!" Trade unions in China have never defended workers' interests. . . . When elderly workers went to the director for their unpaid pension, Fan [the enterprise director] said to their faces that "the government document is a piece of crap," that it is no use citing government circulars. He could just choose not to

implement the center's policies. It has also become common for petition leaders to be assaulted by criminal gangs. That has happened to the representative of the precision instruments factory.[58]

When I visited this factory at the height of the rebellion in March 2002, open letters and posters depicting the workers' grievances and demands were posted on the walls in the main building. Neatly typed and printed in large, 11.5 × 15 inch sheets of white paper, these posters were intended as calls to action addressing workers outside of Liaotie. In these public statements, charges of official corruption and economic hardship of the masses were contrasted, alongside the gap between central government legislation and illegal behavior at the local levels. In one open letter addressed to the Liaoning provincial head and posted outside the Liaotie premise and throughout working-class residential quarters in the city, workers wrote passionately of the long struggle between two groups, the powerless and the impoverished on the one hand, and the unscrupulous and oppressive officials on the other.

> Since the former director and Party secretary Fan Yicheng assumed duty, our factory began an ill-fated decline. Cajoled by the present president of the local People's Congress, Gong Shangwu, he created a company into which several billion yuan from our factory has been diverted, and lined their personal pockets. . . . Because Fan Yicheng refused to pay our pensions and medical insurance contributions from 1995 to 2001, now that our factory is bankrupt, all employees are left without any source of livelihood. . . . The masses have no other option but to petition and disclose the crimes committed by these corrupt elements. Year after year between 1998 and 2001, our workers went to the city, provincial, and central offices of the Party Disciplinary Committee, the Supreme Court, the Procuracy, the Labor and Social Security Bureau, and the State Council Petition Office. But so far, the masses are still desperately waiting for any official reply. . . . Our city has seen many incidents of mandatory bankruptcy and unjust settlement of job tenure compensation. Helpless workers organized many marches, demonstrations, and even protests by blocking railways. But none of these has been sufficient to draw the attention of the local leaders who just continue with their corrupt and parasitic crimes. We the working masses are all enraged but we find no outlet to vent our burning hatred for these officials. We are about to run out of money to feed ourselves. We can hardly afford the enormous legal fees to take our case to court.

The turning point toward radicalization came in late 2001, when the local government and the court declared Liaotie bankrupt. In another open letter, titled "Government Eats Its Words, Workers Demand Results," workers invoked the Chinese president's speech and the Bankruptcy Law in the indictment of their local leaders.

> President Jiang Zemin said, "All levels of government officials and bureau cadres must care deeply for the masses, be responsible for them and promote their interests." But the behaviors of the Liaoyang's leaders before and after the bankruptcy of the Liaoyang Ferro-Alloy Factory never comply with this instruction. . . . The Enterprise Law and the Bankruptcy Law both formally require an open and thorough accounting investigation before an enterprise can be declared bankrupt. But our city officials join hands with enterprise management to blatantly ignore the People's Republic Constitution, the Union Law, and other laws, ignore the strong opposition of all employees, enlist the threat of force by local public security and armed police and make four attempts to arrest and harass protesting workers, and coerce some worker representatives in the workers' congress to vote for bankruptcy. Why do they do that? Do they dare to explain to the masses? On November 5, 2001, three days before declaring us bankrupt, all the machinery, raw materials, doors, and windows were taken away. Whose fault is this?

The letter went on to list some twenty more economic grievances, such as the lack of certified property rights to housing and unpaid pension contributions for laid-off workers, and demands, such as payment of all owed wages, livelihood allowances (182 yuan per month), retirees' enterprise welfare allowances, and medical and housing subsidies.[59] The appeal to the national leadership, the detailing of the law, and the description of local officials' devious behavior were public expressions couched in the grammar and language of the authorities and intended to bolster the legitimacy of the workers' rebellion. Several times they emphasized that their demands were all based on the Constitution and the law, and that only the removal of corrupt officials would prevent the collapse of the Party and the nation. "When the sky is cleared, there will be righteous officials to protect us and we shall then have a good life." Yet raising the banner of anticorruption as the rallying cry was more than a strategy. It was also a conceptual achievement among workers trying to make sense of widespread bankruptcy.

> We knew that if we did not frame workers' interests as an issue of national and state interests, our problems would never be addressed and resolved. And objectively, we have also seen over the past few years that more and more enterprises went bankrupt and more and more workers lost their jobs, and the amount of unpaid wages kept increasing. It's not an isolated phenomenon and we must talk about anticorruption.[60]

Worker representatives were also quick to point out that the most important trigger for their action was the profound sense of injustice that resulted from seeing the coexistence of corruption and mass poverty in their own neighborhood every day. This vignette during the Spring Festival of 2002 in Liaotie's neighborhood was the harbinger of what would come a month later in the protests.

It all began during the Chinese New Year (in February that year). It was a particularly bad year for many. In my neighborhood, a couple who worked in our factory had only 182 yuan to spend for the Spring Festival. They had a kid and two elderly parents. How could you have a New Year with that little money? They could not even afford cooking oil and were not given any heating allowance. In the same residential area, we saw our cadres living in big apartments and coming home from their shopping sprees with nicely wrapped gifts. They were celebrating bankruptcy! Some elderly workers were particularly upset and they sang the "Internationale" during the New Year. I heard that song several times. The lyrics made such good sense these days—Arise, ye starving slaves! Arise, ye oppressed people of the world![61]

About a month later, at the height of the thirty-thousand-strong demonstration on March 11, protesting workers sang the "Internationale" in front of the city government building. Days before the incident, poster-size open letters were distributed quite widely and were read by city residents who heard the rumor of imminent action. One informant described them as "black newspapers" (heibao) that he saw in public places in Liaoyang prior to the protest. Smaller flyers were posted in Liaotie's residential quarters, announcing the date and time of protests. One Liaotie representative related the ease and success of their mobilizing effort while denying that they were "mobilizing" (dongyuan) others, a term that connotes manipulation with subversive intent.

Workers in this factory have relatives and spouses in other factories, spreading the news and solidarity across firms. . . . We did not mobilize other factories, but we used open letters as a way of encouraging more Liaoyang people to join us. We posted flyers announcing the date and time of gatherings and petitions only in our own residential neighborhoods. But anyone who wants to find out can come and see these flyers. All factories had their worker representatives because of all these years of petitioning the government. The government required that workers choose five representatives to present their case in petition, to avoid gatherings of crowds in public places. These representatives from other factories sought out the specific dates and times of our action and would spread the news to their own factories. People who wanted to come would know when to show up. All workers in Liaoyang had their grievances, but most dare to be angry but not to speak up. They look up to the Ferro-Alloy Factory as a leader, because in 2000, our petition had aroused the attention of the foreign media. Therefore, people knew that our action was effective in creating pressure. They had hopes in joining us, perhaps thinking that it would attract society's attention.[62]

People's long-standing rage flared up when Gong Shangwu, the chair of the Liaoyang People's Congress, who was notorious for his close association with Liaotie's corrupt director, proclaimed on television in early March 2002 in Beijing that there were no unemployed workers in Liaoyang.[63] The actual timing and location of protests were communicated from Liaotie to other factories through workers' petition representatives in each factory, and also by word of mouth, as evidenced by the premade banners brought by different work units. But their coordination was loose at best. Liaotie workers had refused to incorporate representatives from other factories into their core organizer group, fearful of infiltration by the police.[64] The precarious nature of interfactory coordination was evident from the chaotic activities taking place on March 18, 2002. In a group interview, several Liaotie representatives recalled,

> By my estimates, I would say there were one hundred thousand. The police asked me how many, thinking that we the organizers must know. But we did not. All we saw was a long stretch of road from the Liaoyang train station to the city government. It was all filled with people. [Interviewer: Why so many people?] Everyone has some personal interest at stake, interests that have been violated in one way or the other. That's one thing. And then many people were frustrated by many years of fruitless petitions, and they knew about our plan to stage a protest, and responded. Some work units came with their names on their banners, like the precision instruments and chemical factories. Representatives from different factories made their separate speeches to different groups in the crowd. It was so noisy that only people around them could hear exactly what they were saying. But the general thrust was that workers were the victims of reform and our livelihood and future have been taken away. Equally important is that the government simply ignores the law. Workers should have legal rights to get paid for their labor, an hour's wage for an hour's work. But many people have been owed back wages. . . . There were people singing the "Internationale"; an elderly woman worker cried out loud, lamenting that "Chairman Mao should not have died so soon!" . . . There was a huge Mao portrait that an elder worker took from his home, a personal collector's item. We actually had a planning meeting and decided that we should take a Mao portrait with us, because we wanted to show the contrast we felt between the past and the present. In those days, we were paid only thirty yuan, but we felt secure because we were never owed any wages. That's the superiority of socialism. And back then,

Chairman Mao was all against cadre corruption. Bad cadres were
executed and punished. The police asked me why we brought Mao's
portrait. I snapped, saying, "We could not find Jiang's portrait!" And
then I asked him, "Do you oppose this portrait? Is it illegal to bring
Mao's portrait to the street?" And he said, "No, I don't oppose it." But
in the end, the portrait was taken away, and is still in police custody. . . .
Someone has counted that there were a total of ninety-six police vehi-
cles and numerous riot police.[65]

The massive and enthusiastic response of Liaoyang residents was
encouraging to these worker representatives. But as experienced protesters,
they also anticipated a crackdown and arrests. Therefore they had organized
a four-echelon core group to sustain activism in case of arrests. Among the
ten or so people in each echelon, each had clearly defined functional responsibility and all agreed to abide by some basic principles of operation.

We held meetings in the elderly activities center in our neighborhood.
We practiced democratic centralism and elected four echelons of representatives, a total of about forty people. We knew that there might be
arrests, so if the first echelon were taken away, there would be the
second, the third, and the fourth. We elected articulate people with good
reputations and good reasoning ability. In each echelon, we have specific
divisions of labor: people with mobile phones were responsible for communication and coordination, another for maintenance of order and
security, another for emergency medical service. We were concerned
that elderly workers might get sick during the protest. Then there were
people handling external forces [the police]. But after the arrest of four
of our representatives, the second echelon was terrified and disbanded.
Other workers who had a strong sense of righteousness and courage
emerged spontaneously to take their places. Some were elderly workers
who could not tolerate such abuse of Party power by these local
cadres. . . . We were very disciplined and had set down some principles
for our action. No damage of public facilities; no road or rail blockage,
although many workers wanted to; no illegal behavior. We collected
money donated by workers, but we did not allow anyone to use that for
meals or transportation. Mainly the money was spent on photocopying.
We have a financial record book. But it was confiscated by the police.[66]

The core leaders included workers who were motivated by the political
ideal of a law-based and clean government enforcing labor's legal rights, as
well as middle-aged workers who bore the brunt of economic insecurity.
Xiao Yunliang, one of the two jailed workers, for instance, was known for his
independent political views. Back in the early 1970s, when Deng Xiaoping
was the target of a national mass criticism campaign, Xiao publicly refused
to denounce him. For that he was forced into hiding for several months until

the campaign was over. Yao Fuxin, the other sentenced leader, was by all accounts a righteous defender of workers' interests against official harassment. He was a former worker at a rolled-steel factory in Liaoyang, but his wife was a laid-off worker at Liaotie. In his prison letter to his family, he wrote of his "steel-like commitment to democracy" and of his pride and conscience in fighting for "history's trial" of corrupt officials. His acquaintances and relatives provided a portrait of a man of moral and political conviction on behalf of people's rights:

> In 1989, taking a long vacation from his rolled-steel factory, Yao borrowed twenty thousand yuan to invest in a small truck. He became a small transportation entrepreneur and the leader of all the small car drivers in Liaoyang in their negotiation with the government against high taxation on their businesses. For that he was fired from this factory. After his wife was laid off in 1993, they pooled together seven thousand yuan and bought a small grocery store of five square meters. She makes a monthly income of six hundred to seven hundred yuan and now she gets a five-hundred-yuan pension. . . . He always listened to foreign broadcasts, holding a transistor radio in his hand, running around searching for clear transmission. Radios are highly popular items in Liaoyang. He is psychologically prepared for the risk, thinking that three to four years of imprisonment may be likely if the government decides to crack down. But we did not expect the government to be so very unreasonable. Seven years is way too much. Even after the sentencing, he insisted that he did not regret organizing the protest. He looks at it as a seven-year contribution to Chinese democracy. . . . When he appeared in court for his trial, in the only moment when he came close to his fellow workers, his only words were "Did you get your unemployment benefits yet?"[67]

If Yao's personal financial condition was not one of destitution, others in the core leadership group were under greater economic pressure. One of the representatives related his own example as typical. Two years after Liaotie was declared bankrupt, he is still unemployed and only occasionally gets hired as a day laborer, working in individual-owned small firms or on construction sites. His wife works as a waitress in a restaurant for ten yuan per day. They eat and sleep in his parents' apartment, and rely on his father's 540-yuan-per-month pension to pay for his son's education. The whole family has worked in Liaotie. Yet even he admitted that workers rebel not because of destitution.

> No one in Liaoyang that we know of is starving. What upsets people most is the gap between the rich and the poor, and that the money the cadres spend is money from corruption. Even unemployed workers

these days can scrape together a couple of hundred yuan to cover the most basic of basic needs. People can barely hang on. But if anything unexpected happens, like a major illness, or an accident, or if your child gets admitted to college, most people will immediately find themselves in a financial crisis. There is no security, not to mention money to be made.[68]

The prevailing mood among Liaoyang workers from various factories was one of desperation and anger. Liaotie workers received letters of support from other local enterprises, praising the heroic sacrifices of workers in their fight against the "evil forces" of the local government. Expressing ordinary people's angry sadness, one letter said,

Corrupt officials are rising and dancing, while bankrupt workers wipe their tears and hide their faces. People with conscience can only sigh and gaze into heaven. . . . Our heads are lowered and our hearts are broken. Salute to the four comrades [the four arrested labor leaders]!

But staunch state repression quickly stifled the budding impulse of popular rebellion. After reassuring the roaring crowds on March 12 that the authorities were willing to negotiate with worker representatives, and after workers agreed to put off staging more protests to allow time for the government to come up with solutions to their problems, police arrested Yao on March 17. The other three labor leaders, Pang Qingxiang, Xiao Yunliang, and Wang Zhaoming, were arrested on March 20, after paramilitary police forcefully removed hundreds of protesters from the compound of the city government where they had gathered to petition the government. Soon they were charged with "illegal assembly and demonstrations," and "collusion with overseas hostile elements" to damage social security and public order. The government then tried splitting up the core leadership by detaining Yao and Xiao, while bribing one leader with a new job, terrifying another into hiding, and intimidating the rest of the forty to fifty core organizers through surveillance and house searches. Less prominent representatives, some from other factories, were bought off, threatened with arrest, or beaten up by the police. By the time the court indicted Yao and Xiao, many vocal organizers had gone into hiding or abandoned the fight that now seemed hopeless.[69]

The authorities' approach of dividing and conquering worker leaders was supplemented by a parallel strategy of discriminating application of the "carrot and stick" so as to defuse popular support for worker representatives. The Liaoyang government promised to investigate and punish corrupt officials and paid ordinary workers some of their back wages, insurance contributions, and severance pay. For instance, in November 2002, the government arrested and indicted Fan Yicheng, the former director of Liaotie and a prime target of workers' anticorruption demands, together with six other former Liaotie officials. Fan was sentenced to thirteen years of imprisonment on smuggling charges and other former officials were given four- to six-year prison terms for engaging in illegal business practices. The city's police chief was fired and a top Communist Party official was demoted.[70] It was hailed in Party publications as an example of the Party's serious commitment to fighting graft and official corruption.[71] Yao and Xiao were convicted of subversion and sentenced to seven and four years of imprisonment, respectively, in May 2003. Their appeals were rejected in late June 2003 by the Liaoning Provincial High People's Court. The clue to such harsh sentences can be found in the bill of indictment, a seven-page document which emphasizes Yao and Xiao's participation in the outlawed China Democracy Party and their association with "hostile foreign elements" (i.e., Voice of America, the foreign press, and labor rights groups).[72] Their "incitement and organization of the masses" seems almost a minor offence, listed as the last item in the litany of subversion charges. Finally, behind the scenes, the Liaoning government took very seriously the implication of the Liaoyang incident. Bankruptcy procedures have been revised, with strict requirements that before an enterprise can be declared bankrupt, it has to obtain explicit agreement from the local government that the latter will provide financial support for severance payment to the workforce.[73]

CELLULAR ACTIVISM

In all of the three case studies recounted here, bankruptcy is a moment of clarity and moral poignancy, as it not only exposes the collusion of local government and enterprise management more clearly than ever, it also provides a last chance for workers to fight for a final resolution. The Liaoyang protests were unique in that they represented the imminent possibility of citywide upheaval developed out of ordinary work-unit-based rebellion. Such a scenario seems most likely when prolonged government inaction toward work-unit mobilization fans the flames of networking across work units. But this episode also exposed the limits of radicalization. The daring leadership of one single factory, while riding on the wave of mass outrage erupting in the wake of a public lie told to the nation by a hated local official, consciously excluded outside workers from joining the leadership circle. The participation of other factories was as astonishing as it was fortuitous. Also, workers' demands, whether economic or political, were local and enterprise-based. In many of their open letters, workers pledged their support for socialism and the central leadership. Of course, this can be interpreted as a tactic of self-defense, but the fact remains that there was no explicit call to challenge the legitimacy of the communist regime. Once arrests of workers occurred, support from other factories quickly collapsed. And once the government responded to some of Liaotie's demands and cracked down on the leaders, even the momentum for work-unit-based action was impaired.

The basic dynamics of labor protests involving nonpayment of pensions and wages, neighborhood services, and bankruptcies can now be summarized. First, workers' demands are informed by material and moral standards based as much on the socialist social contract as on the current state rhetoric of legality. Direct street action prevails and signals workers' withdrawal of political acquiescence when the social contract is not honored by the state and as legal channels are blocked by venal local officials. Conspicuously absent in the vast majority of labor protests is any hint of demands for independent unionism or for democratic rights of political participation, or challenges to regime legitimacy. The most politicized demand most workers have made to date is the removal of specific officials, without questioning the system of communist rule. I must add that beyond this prevailing pattern of nonpolitical, cellular protests, underground efforts in forming unions for laid-off and retired workers have emerged in several provinces, including Jiangsu, Sichuan, and Shanxi. In Zhengzhou, Henan, a network of clandestine labor activists has assisted workers by offering them advice to resist factory closures. The few available reports describing their activities suggest that they are fervent remnants of the rebel factions during the Cultural Revolution. Others are younger, university-educated New Left–Marxists who are critical of both the excesses of Mao and the reform of Deng.[74] Yet all these precarious attempts have been crushed by police arrests and imprisonment, and they failed to have any significant impact on the massive number of aggrieved workers.

Second, a confluence of institutional factors produces the prevailing pattern of cellular activism. State work units provide the physical sites of communication and coordination, organize workers' interests, and define the boundary of the aggrieved community.[75] It is possible that interfactory activism may evolve from single-factory unrest, but the experience in Liaoyang and even in Shenyang's working-class neighborhood protests shows that lateral mobilization and solidarity are rarely sustainable. Elsewhere, workers in the oil industry have indicated a potential capacity for horizontal coordination after workers in the Daqing oil field sustained a two-month protest against unfair severance packages in 2002. Oil workers in Lanzhou, Gansu in the northwest, and those in Hebei and Shangdong in the east also staged protests against low severance payments. The spread of these actions was facilitated by workers' familial and personal networks across the country, which were in turn spun by government-organized transfers of workers between oil fields. These incidents subsided soon under government pressure.[76]

Third, the central and local governments, in vastly different fashions, play catalytic roles in the growth of unrest. The central government's decrees, circulars, and laws become moral and legal ammunition for ordinary people to challenge local officials. The implementation of central government policies and laws, be they about bankruptcy liquidation or livelihood allowance payments, falls to local officials, who become targets of popular protests. It is also at the local level that workers are asked to choose and send representatives in lodging complaints and in negotiation with local officials, a bureaucratic process that inadvertently creates leaders. Officials' concessions to mass pressure created a popular expectation that within the boundary of work-unit mobilization more activism would bring better results. But more activism at the local level threatens overall social stability, requiring the center to pitch in, by financial bailout and by imposing more regulations and reform, spawning more unrest targeting local leadership. The cycle of state incitement of popular unrest starts anew.[77] The systemic consequence of such state-labor interaction is a bifurcated legitimacy structure that sees local conflicts proliferating while legitimacy at the center is bolstered. The concentration of political pressure on the local governments and enterprise management results from the decentralization of fiscal and economic power to the local levels, as well as the uneven economic conditions produced by market competition. When ordinary workers try to understand the wide-ranging and fine-grained economic conditions across factories, they see both the hands of the local state and the market, while the central government has tirelessly imposed laws and regulations protective of their interests. In short, decentralization spawns cellular activism, and legal authoritarianism spurs an insurgent rhetoric around legality. In the absence of genuine legal reform in the rustbelt, the socialist social contract continues to regulate employment relations. It organizes workers' interests around issues of collective consumption and prescribes direct street action, rather than the court, as their most effective leverage in bargaining with local officials.

THE SUBJECT OF LABOR PROTESTS

The "subject" is the link between social structure and social practice. By "subject" I mean, following Derek Sayer, "the individual as socially represented and empowered."[78] Labor subjectivity refers, then, to workers' situated self-understanding, or "one's sense of who one is, of one's social location, and of how (given the first two) one is prepared to act. As a dispositional term, it belongs to the realm of what Pierre Bourdieu has called *sens pratique*, the practical sense—at once cognitive and emotional—that persons have of themselves and their social world."[79] Collective subjectivities motivate social action enabled by institutional transformation.

What then are the elements defining this Chinese labor subjectivity in protests? Three idioms constantly stand out when workers enunciate their self-identification, rationale, and basis for making claims—workers *(gongren)*, citizens *(gongmin)*, and masses *(qunzhong)* or sometimes more specifically, masses in weak situations *(ruoshi qunti)*. My task in this section is emphatically *not* to decide whether Chinese workers qualify as class actors or citizens defined by theories premised on liberal democratic capitalism. Rather, I seek to understand the indigenous meanings, relations, and institutional context that come packaged with these terms when they are invoked in the rustbelt, often simultaneously.

Class: Masters of the State Factory

"The working class takes leadership in everything" was a popular slogan under Mao and now workers bitterly and self-mockingly describe their situation by turning the claim into "Everything leads the working class." In making public claims to the state, workers seldom invoke the term "class" *(jieji)*, which, with its connotation of antagonism and struggle, has been jettisoned by the regime at the beginning of the reform era. But in their own neighborhoods and in private, workers talk about "workers' personal interests" *(gongren de chexinliyi)* and workers' treatment and rewards *(gongren de daiyu)*. Paramount in these working-class interests are employment security, pensions, and basic welfare. These entitlements are the manifestations of workers' "master status" *(zhurenweng)* in SOEs, the cornerstone of working-class identity that is reactivated in the reform period as that which is ironically lost. This concept of workers as collective owners of their enterprise was not mere ideology of Chinese socialism but a lived reality for Chinese workers who have actually experienced that status in the prereform era. They therefore vehemently resist its disappearance under reform. Bankruptcies crystallize a moment of reckoning of moral and redistributive justice—how to compensate workers' loss of collective ownership over the factory built on the basis of low-wage labor under a social contract of permanent employment and state guarantee of subsistence and basic welfare. Chinese workers' class agency in the reform period is therefore founded on the degradation and exploitation in the redistribution order, not in the production process as a conventional Marxian analysis would argue.

But tying working-class identity to collective ownership over their work units also results in a strongly corporatist, particularistic, and local subjectivity. This corporate anchorage of class has been reinforced by the prolonged lack of labor mobility, the seniority wage and benefits structure, and the recruitment of family and kin members into the same work unit. Workers talked fervently about long years of accumulation of surplus value banked in the enterprise, reasoning that their families' contributions and acceptance of low wages have led to the expansion of the enterprise, but this surplus value is now squandered by corrupt cadres. In this chapter, for instance, worker representatives in the Tieling steel window-frame factory rally alluded to the mass outrage at demolishing the factory, saying that "every inch of soil and grass on the premises" resulted from their sweat and blood labor. When Liaoyang worker representatives explained why they were so persistent, they made references to a "strong working-class tradition," by which they meant, "We saw the enterprise grow from one with only 2,000 yuan in fixed assets to one with 30 million yuan in 1989, the heyday of factory profit." Workers' ownership rights over the fruits of their labor were embodied in the welfare provisions sponsored by the state. That is why in the Tieling textile mill, protesting workers argued with great resolve that "the shopping mall is our child, for supporting our lives when we get old."

Class exploitation is a cognitive tool that frames protests in moral terms, turning the loss of welfare under reform to "exploitation" and dehumanization. A woman worker offered this reflection, without my provocation, on how she came to understand the meaning of "exploitation" *(boxue)*. For her, as for many others I interviewed, it was the denial of her basic needs as a human being that constituted class exploitation.

> In the past, we had many welfare services. For female comrades, the
> most important were the nursery, female sanitary room and sanitary
> napkins, the mess hall, the shuttle, and the barbershop. When this new
> director came, he abolished all these. . . . I now understand what
> "exploitation" really means. We workers are very pitiful now. In the
> past, no matter how bad production became, if you needed housing,
> they gave you a place to live. But for years, not one single apartment
> building has been built.[80]

Therefore, class subjectivity exists in the form of an oppositional consciousness against the violation of workers' ownership over enterprises and entitlement to redistributive resources. Chronic unemployment, however, and the retirement of many from the state sector had, in their expression, "pushed them into society," making them orphans without any work organization to depend on. Working-class rebellion, erupting at this moment of mass exit from the class structure, has to overcome the disappearance of the working class itself. We shall examine in chapter 5 the conditions of the new generation of industrial workers who hail from the countryside and their understanding of "class" relations. At least, we have seen in this chapter the quicksand on which Mao's workers are waging their "class" battle.

Citizenship: Rights Consciousness and Disenchantment

If the state has dropped the language of class and class struggle, it has vigorously promoted the ideology of law-based government and the rhetoric of legality. That is why, in all the accounts of mobilization analyzed earlier, one finds a constant invocation of the law and legal rights in workers' interaction with local officials. But does this imply that Chinese workers think of themselves as citizens with rights and protest against their violation? How do they understand the relationships among themselves, the law, and the various levels of government? Discussions with worker representatives reveal a more cynical and ambivalent orientation toward the law. First, workers are too keenly aware of the lack of strong legal institutions to envision themselves as citizens with guaranteed legal rights. When I suggested to them that they were fighting for citizens' legal rights, they either ridiculed me or made comments such as: "Workers' thinking is not that advanced!"; "Legal rights? What is legal, where is the law?"; "There are laws, but no one implements them"; "The law is just; but its implementation is not." This cynicism and disillusionment is often amplified in the process of petitioning the government, which often turns into a process of discovering deep pockets of local corruption and power collusion. Workers in Tieling and Liaoyang protests, as we have seen, learned firsthand that the court and the labor bureau could not handle their cases because of political intervention by the local government. If they continue to frame their demands in legal terms, it is because the law is the only institutional resource they can use to force official attention. A Tieling worker representative put it most clearly: "Because you are talking to the government, you have to talk about laws and regulations. Otherwise, they can ignore you." Worse, the process of going through legal channels often turns aspiring citizens into disenchanted protesters. During the Liaoyang protests, for instance, one representative brought along a copy of the Constitution and cited her rights of assembly when police interfered.[81] She also filed an application for the rally, hoping that the police would leave the protesters alone.

> We filed an application for a rally after March 11, giving the Public Security Bureau everything that is listed in the law: the route, the time, the organizers' names, and then they said they did not approve it because it was handwritten and not typed! So, the next time around we submitted a typed application for the April 16 march. They still rejected it. The PSB chief said to me that he would impose on me any number of charges to stop me from leaving Liaoyang. If I tried to get to Hong Kong, he would detain me by charging me with something like an outstanding fine of 250 yuan. There is no one you can reason with in such a big country. Anything ordinary people do is allegedly illegal.

In short, the more experienced these worker representatives are in dealing with the government and using the law, the more they find the rule of law elusive. They keep adopting the language of legality and citizenship as a tactic, not out of a sense of empowerment or entitlement. Yet the labor subjects in these protests do aspire to have their rights protected by law and enforced by the government, although the civic citizenship they have in mind is one that dovetails with the regime's project of "rule by law" rather than a "rule of law" system. There is no criticism of the lack of popular participation in legislation, no demand for independent worker organizations, no questioning of the adequacy and rationale of law and policy set by the central authority. Cynicism and disenchantment notwithstanding, workers' demands for legal rights generate popular pressure on both the local and the central government, which, after all, embraces legal reform as a necessary complement to market reform.

The Masses: Supplicants or Rebels

The third term of self-identification that workers use is "the masses," *qunzhong,* and sometimes "the working masses," *gongren qunzhong,* or, more recently, "weak and disadvantaged group," *ruoshi qunti.* What all these terms have in common is the reference to a hierarchical political community in which the Party state commands moral and political authority over the populace at large. The led masses are placed in the position of supplicants to the state, which in turn has a responsibility to protect and lead. What gives this subordinate identity its political potency is the idea that the masses have the spontaneity, the capability, and indeed the moral responsibility to rebel against immoral leaders. This aspect of Chinese protest politics, argues Elizabeth Perry, is unique among authoritarian regimes, in that the Chinese communist regime has periodically encouraged or even compelled its citizens to express criticism publicly in state-sponsored mass campaigns. In this sense, Mao's mass line shares with the early Chinese philosopher Mencius's Mandate of Heaven the belief that "to rebel is justified."[82]

Originating in Maoism dating back to the communist movement in the 1930s, the appellation *the masses* still occupies a prominent place in official propaganda, most significantly in Jiang Zemin's theory of the "Three Represents," one of which is representing "the fundamental interests of the broad masses." Not surprisingly, this collective identification of workers as the masses appealing to the Party state as the representative of the general interest to fight against internal sabotage by local cadres can be found in workers' banners and action strategies. In the Liaoyang protest, there were banners demanding "Serious Implementation of the Three Represents," "Liaotie Workers Want to Meet with Honest Official Bo Xilai" (Bo was the governor of Liaoning at that time), and "Punish the Thirteen Corrupt Official Worms." In several of their open letters, workers deplored their demotion "from worker aristocracy to weak and disadvantaged group *(ruoshi qunti)*." In their letter to the Party's Central Disciplinary Committee, which by and large echoed other open letters, Liaotie workers emphasized their shared interests with the Party and the state, and maintained that their target was those who sabotaged the common project of the state and society. The following excerpt shows how workers reasoned as supplicants and appealed to the center as the masses.

> From the time when Chairman Mao promoted "serve the People" to General Secretary Jiang Zemin's "Three Represents," the core principle of the Party has been to serve the interest of the broad masses. . . . The working masses *(gongren qunzhong)* love our motherland, love the Communist Party, and support the construction of socialism with Chinese characteristics. . . . But they hate all those corrupt elements, those big and small vampires and parasites, who go against the law for their own selfish interests, to try and topple the socialist flag, destroy the basis of socialist economy. Yet, their goal will never be realized. The Party and the government and the broad masses are determined not to let them harm state policy or the people, and will bring them to the trial of history.[83]

In Shenyang, retirees deployed a strategy of mass pressure to draw the attention of higher officials to the suffering of the masses. Some elderly workers recalled how in Mao's time (during the 1957–1958 rectification movement and the Cultural Revolution), ordinary people *(laobaixin)* once had a powerful recourse—political campaigns—to rectify cadre work style and corruption. A retired mechanic looked around the neighborhood in Shenyang and regretted the disappearance of mass struggle meetings.

> Everyone here says this: our lives would be so much better if there were still struggle meetings and political campaigns. . . . Back then [in Mao's time], we the masses had a weapon against corrupt cadres. Many people miss mass campaigns. People always say these cadres would have been criticized and executed many times over now for the amount of their graft.[84]

Also significant was the continual use of petitions or letters and visits by workers in the northeast. Letters and visits are long-standing methods by which the masses participate in communist politics. The first formal bureau to facilitate these methods of mass participation was instituted in 1931 in the base area of the Chinese Soviet government. After the establishment of the People's Republic, in 1951 the central government adopted regulations calling on all local and higher-level governments to establish departments for handling letters from the people or reception rooms for receiving visitors.[85] To date, workers still respect this bureaucratic procedure and emphasize following rank by rank the bureaucratic hierarchy in petitioning, and not skipping steps (yueji). A significant number of petitions have evolved into protests, either because petitions fail to bring about results or because the gathering of petitioning masses easily generates unanticipated action dynamics. But workers' activism has almost always started with a petition to the enterprise or the local government. Then as now, petitions do not force the hands of officials, who can choose either to respond or to ignore petitioners.

In Liaoning, most workers repeatedly express their approval and trust in the central leadership. Even though workers are vehement in accusing enterprise managers and their conspirators in the local state bureaucracy as "enemies of the people" or "worms" in society, their faith in the moral and political integrity of the central state has remained largely unwavering. Time and again, workers declare their conviction that the "nation" (guojia) or the "center" (zhongyang) has designed good policies to protect workers, and the problem is local failure to implement them. When I asked what made them trust the center, one said, "You can see that on television: central leaders always emphasize the need to guarantee laid-off workers' livelihood. But when it comes to the local level, things are distorted and good policies are not always implemented." So the mere promulgation of protective laws and regulations seems to have buttressed the legitimacy of the regime in the eyes of the populace, who limit their critique to the local agents responsible for the law's implementation.

The finding that to date the political subject of protesting rustbelt workers is "the masses" appealing to a protector central authority in no way precludes the potential for change. For one thing, workers' continual appeal to the central government as protector results from the lack of alternative political authority. One protesting worker bemoaned tellingly, with palpable frustration, "Where else can we turn but to the government?" In many of my interviews, workers expressed in unmistakable terms that every leader has to be careful of the potential power of the masses, who may cause instability. The image of people's power surfaces with poignancy among the most articulate worker representatives, who have contemplated privately a more radical break with their docile politics of supplication. One of the most eloquent worker representatives in this study offered this thoughtful reflection on the possibility of a large-scale uprising against the regime itself, not just its local agents. The "masses" he had in mind were those in the 1989 prodemocracy movement and the more significant ones in the Communist Revolution that brought about the current regime.

> It's a pity that the student protests were abruptly suppressed. Students had foresight that we did not: the problem of corruption is still with us today. . . . We the masses understand that reform will bring with it waves of instability, that we understand. But you [cadres] cannot ask us to sit and watch while you pocket tens of thousands of dollars. It is not easy for us the masses to summon the courage to confront the cadres. Only when we have no alternative are we forced to challenge the government [i.e., enterprise]. We only want to get a verdict of justice from the officials. . . . During the revolution, why could a small communist army defeat Chiang's nationalists? It's because it had the support of the people. Without the people, would there be any cadres or nation?[86]

CONCLUSION

This chapter has focused on the demise of the socialist employment system and rustbelt workers' forced exit from the class structure. Beneath the surface variation in worker grievances is the common pattern of worker unrest organized around localized, bounded work units or their subgroups, whose boundaries are defined and fractured by state policies. Cellular activism deviates from the mode of organized labor movement à la Polish Solidarity. It is also different from the quiet, hidden, and atomistic forms of everyday resistance characteristic of socialist industrial workplaces or authoritarian political systems. What then are the institutional and cultural logics that generate cellular activism? I broached these questions by examining workers' strategic interaction with the local and central governments, and their moral and cognitive resources and political subjectivities. Cellular activism is not the result of myopic worker consciousness, nor is it simply a concession to state repression against cross-factory networking. Its prevalence has to do with how workers' interests are constituted in the reform period. My research indicates that decentralization of economic decision making, from the central to the local government and down to enterprise management (in the name of enterprise autonomy), has constituted localized communities of interests and responsibilities. Workers lay the blame for pension and wage arrears on their enterprises and local governments because these agents have been given the power and responsibility to manage SOEs. Decentralization is coupled with market competition, giving rise to uneven and unequal economic conditions of enterprises even among those located in the same region or city. On top of these differentiations, state policies continue to accord different, albeit minuscule, entitlements and compensations to workers in different industries, cohorts, or forms of unemployment, resulting in bewildering variations of worker interests. This fragmentation of the working class into cellular interest groups does not paralyze collective action, but it does drive wedges among workers and channels them into dispersed units of activism.

Some students of Chinese labor have suggested that labor unrest is a form of moral economy protest. Nostalgic of lost subsistence rights, they argue, Chinese workers draw on prereform ideological legacies of state paternalism and the old rhetoric of class to demand a restoration of traditional entitlements.[87] The argument of this book is that this moral economy interpretation is valid but not adequate. Although workers' resistance has been driven by a restorative and subsistence ethic, I have also found other coexisting political and cultural logics that impel worker activism. Rather than seeing workers as locked in some traditional political mentality harking back to the past, it is more accurate to see a repertoire of multiple worker subjectivities formed through workers' participation in ongoing institutional transformation. Legal reform, no matter how partial and uneven, imparts new conceptions of worker rights, interests, and agencies, as does the regime's continual adherence to Mao's notion of the masses. Citizen's rights to legal justice and the legitimacy of the masses to rebel against corrupt officials are equally powerful frames of labor mobilization. This book therefore emphasizes the coexistence of the working class, the citizen, and the subaltern as equally important, if also shifting, political subjectivities through which workers are interpellated to act. Again, following Göran Therborn, my argument is that Chinese workers, as social actors or subjects, can turn ideology into power, becoming qualified to act and resist by the same ideological appellations that are intended to subjugate them.[88] Like the making of class, we cannot predict the outcome but can explain the trajectory of when and which ideological interpellation underlies what collective action. In the process of waging these struggles, workers also contribute to bringing about legal and welfare reform in new directions.

In this drama of evolving labor insurgency, Chinese government's reactions to popular unrest command particular attention. Devising a "carrot and stick" approach to divide and conquer leaders and ordinary workers, and differentiate laterally organized dissent from local cellular mobilizations, the government at both the local and the central levels present themselves as a Janus-faced authority, setting clear boundaries between zones of indifference, even tolerance, and forbidden terrains. Within the limits of the former, the government can selectively concede to workers' most urgent livelihood grievances or make concrete improvements in the collection of social insurance or the implementation of bankruptcy procedures. Once workers veer toward organized political dissent, however, the state cracks down ruthlessly, arresting and imprisoning leading agitators. Thus, the state is responsive to popular discontent, though in a slow and erratic, and at times repressive, manner. Labor unrest is not a catalyst to challenging the political system in China, but it generates pressure for social policy changes. Most important, analysis of workers' bifurcated perception of the legitimacy of the central and local state throws into sharp relief the tensions between the central and local governments, or between the imperatives of legitimation and accumulation.

Even though cellular activism has been the dominant tendency in the past decade, my analysis here does not preclude the possibility or proclivity of workers to transcend cellularity and build networks of resistance. In Liaoning and elsewhere, I have found instances of workers' bold attempts to go beyond the confines of the work unit to create cross-factory actions, industrywide protests, or underground union movements. To date, these have been rare undertakings that either have been swiftly crushed by the state or have run out of steam for lack of popular persistence. In the next chapter, I explore another important institutional factor that has limited worker militancy—the way labor power is socially reproduced or the means of survival outside industrial employment. If this chapter captures Mao's working class at heroic moments of street protest, the next will delve into workers' quiet ambivalence about the communist regime and the market economy.

4 Life after *Danwei*

Surviving Enterprise Collapse

We saw in the last chapter the various kinds of protests workers staged to demand government action to solve their livelihood problems. But the puzzle remains: how did workers survive long periods of unemployment, wage arrears, and pension nonpayment? Alternatively put, why is there not more militant resistance, given the pervasiveness and severity of economic difficulties in the rustbelt as a whole?

To answer these questions, this chapter depicts core features of working-class life after the collapse of the socialist work unit. First, it explains the social reproduction of labor power, or the ways in which livelihood resources are found outside of waged work. Specifically, I will analyze workers' material survival and the strategies of eking out a livelihood at both the individual and familial levels. Second, I will attend to what Raymond Williams perceptively terms the "structure of feelings" in the reform era. The concept refers to workers' emerging collective impulses, which are not yet articulated as a well-formed counter-hegemony but are "affective elements of consciousness and relationships: not feelings against thought but thoughts as felt and feeling as thought: practical consciousness of a present kind."[1] This dual focus on both the material and cultural aspects of working-class transition flows from an analytical perspective informed by David Harvey's discussion of workers as "living laborers."[2] Seen in this light, Chinese workers are not just an economic category in the process of production but are also property owners, private entrepreneurs, participants in the informal labor market, members of household economies, and bearers of collective memories of Chinese socialism. This broadened conception of the worker will generate a more complex and ambivalent view of "labor politics" that goes beyond the moment of collective resistance to incorporate the latter's shadowy border with collective acquiescence.

Before the reform, urban China was aptly termed a "*danwei* society," one in which the workplace formed a "minisociety" or "minor public." Encompassing economic, social, and political functions within their walls, work units controlled and funneled essential livelihood resources and opportunities from the state to their employees and dependents. Andrew Walder's influential *Communist Neo-traditionalism* (1986) offers the most systematic analysis of this institution of "organized dependence." Market reform has ushered in a gradual and quiet death of this *danwei* way of life, rending the social fabric of many working-class communities and individual family economies. Rustbelt workers, as much as they rebel, have devised ways to survive the collapse of the *danwei* by triangulating resources from state redistribution, familial reciprocity, and participation in the informal economy. Living through the reform over the years is simultaneously a cultural process of rethinking what socialism was about and what postsocialism has become. Constitutive of and inseparable from improvising a new way of life is a new mentality, a conceptual achievement of some sort by ordinary people to make sense of the past, the present, and the future. In this cultural experience of transition, collective memory turns out to be a terrain as wrought with contentions and emotions as collective protests.

Throughout my fieldwork, three salient elements in post-*danwei* working-class lives have surfaced. This chapter is accordingly organized into three parts. First, housing resources and arrangements provide a glimpse into several processes, including the functioning of the working-class family as an economic unit, the informal privatization of socialist welfare into private property, and the minimum floor of subsistence that the transition generation of urban workers may enjoy perhaps for the last time. In theoretical terms, these are the mechanisms for the social reproduction of labor power. In chapter 3, I showed how the collapse of welfare organized by work units led to localized protests on issues of collective consumption. In this chapter, the discussion focuses on the effect of work-unit-based housing reform in limiting worker resistance. Second, the informal economy nurtured by overall economic growth for the past quarter century has kept many poor blue-collar families afloat. Workers participate in the market economy in various ways with different resources and outcomes, generating a wide differentiation of economic conditions within the same community. As in housing matters, the working-class family is a source of both resources and strains. Finally, everyday conversations are punctuated with recollections of and comparisons with the past. Workers' historical consciousness and collective memory mediate their handling of present predicaments and opportunities. I have found a rich mosaic of personal and collective assessments of the regime's record from the past to the present, consisting of both nostalgic and traumatic recollections. It is this heterogeneity and ambivalence that puts limits on worker solidarity and resistance.

HOUSING: FROM WELFARE TO PRIVATE PROPERTY

Whereas joblessness is ubiquitous, there is no sign of homelessness even in the worst-hit areas in the rustbelt. Near universal provision of housing is perhaps one of the most significant keys to the regime's capacity to maintain overall social stability even in the midst of rising and massive unemployment. Fieldwork for this research has taken me into many a worker's home. I was struck by the wide variations in the quality, the size, and the interior decor of these apartment units. In Shenyang, the most spacious apartment I visited was about 120 square meters. There, an unemployed woman worker at a textile mill lived with her husband, who was a manager at another state-owned enterprise (SOE). The sun-filled and airy living room had big windows on two sides, and the hardwood floor was shiny from a recent waxing. A gigantic thirty-two-inch television set sat quietly next to a home entertainment system with hi-fi and DVD player. The woman's teenage daughter was playing the piano in her own room. The golden or brass-colored light fixtures in the apartment were eye-catching. The kitchen had what are considered the basic appliances in the vast majority of working-class households—refrigerator, microwave, stove, rice cooker, and dish sanitizer (a small refrigerator-like cabinet that purportedly keeps out germs for glasses, china, and dinnerware). At the other end of the spectrum, in Shenyang I interviewed an unemployed male worker in his thirty-square-meter, unheated one-bedroom apartment. Shivering in this cold, decrepit, dark, and dingy home on a frigid winter day of −12 degrees centigrade, he talked about the inconvenience of everyday life when his wife and his two grown sons all had to cram into this space already stacked with clothes, bedding, and a tiny wooden table that serves all purposes. The little kitchen was carved out of a balconylike three-foot-wide corridor leading to the toilet. Every corner of this apartment was filled with old furniture, small appliances, and everyday items of all kinds. Even in the daytime, he had to turn on a small lightbulb hanging naked from the living room ceiling so that he could see his way in his packed homestead.

There are many reasons for the wide discrepancy in workers' housing conditions. None of these observations implies that workers are satisfied with their living conditions. Variation in firm profitability, workers' seniority, rank, and family size, and managers' commitment to improving employee housing all affect what kind of apartments workers obtain. Also, workers with second incomes or spouses in lucrative sectors such as oil or telecommunications tend to enjoy better than average housing obtained from these other work units. Higher family incomes allow them to invest in modern interior decor. Workers harbor substantial grievances about the inequities in housing allocation, the dilapidated conditions of some of the housing stock, and the ambiguous property rights they hold. But no matter how incongruous, these complaints coexist with the reality that workers are provided with basic housing. No matter how destitute, they have a home to go back to at the end of the day.

Allocation of apartments to SOE employees was a long-standing practice during the prereform period. It became more important to workers' lives in the 1980s when reform gave more autonomy to enterprises to improve employee welfare as a means of boosting incentives and productivity. As I outlined in chapter 2, in the 1990s commodification of the housing stock became a reform policy and enterprises began selling work-unit-built apartment units to their employees at subsidized prices. The privatization of work-unit housing has turned many state-sector workers, who had been tenants, into private property owners.[3] According to national statistics, 42 percent of households in which the household head is a worker have purchased their homes from their work organizations. Nearly 50 percent of urban households that purchased their housing units by the year 2000 paid less than 20,000 yuan.[4] In Shenyang, for example, workers in my study reported paying between 10,000 yuan and 30,000 yuan for their apartment units, or about 40 percent of the market price. Depending on local regulations, these working-class owners have acquired varying types of rights: right of occupancy, use rights, partial rights to generate profits by renting or reselling after a certain number of years of occupancy. Even after their enterprise has been declared bankrupt, their ownership rights remain intact. As property owners, they can also bequeath ownership rights to their children. In times of financial difficulties, a popular income-generating practice among residents in enterprise housing complexes is to take in boarders or rent the entire apartment unit to outsiders.[5] A top-floor unit of fifty-one square meters in the working-class neighborhood of Tiexi, sold to workers at the subsidized price of 14,000 yuan in 1991, could fetch 50,000 to 60,000 yuan when sold in the open market in 2002. Deborah Davis has noted the windfall reaped by sitting tenants at the time of housing reform in late 1990s, remarking in particular how management and cadres benefited disproportionately owing to their power to allocate more and better housing to themselves.[6]

But not all workers benefit from the government's commodification policy. Workers who cannot afford to purchase their apartments remain tenants and pay monthly rent to the local Housing Bureau. Rents used to be nominal, accounting for 2–3 percent of workers' income. Housing reform throughout the 1980s has aimed at restructuring rents to enable basic housing construction and maintenance, and by 2000, rents in the public sector had increased to levels that cover basic construction and maintenance costs, plus investment interest and property tax.[7] Some families can no longer afford rent. In an old neighborhood in northern Shenyang, as reported by one woman, tenants spontaneously refused to pay rent.

> My factory pays me only 110 yuan, and rent costs 60 yuan per month. How can I afford it? If I pay rent, how am I supposed to buy enough food to stay alive? I would say 80 percent of all tenants in this building refuse to pay rent and the Housing Bureau officer has stopped asking for payment. I have stopped paying rent for several years.[8]

Among those who have purchased their apartments, private ownership of one's apartment is widely viewed as the most important financial asset ordinary workers in Liaoning can realistically accumulate at the end of what they consider "a life-long contribution to socialism." Most workers see owning their work-unit apartments more as an entitlement they deserve than as a benevolent policy of the state. Some even complained about being forced to dig into their savings to buy something that previously was theirs to use almost for free. A retired lathe turner complained,

> We used to pay only 28 yuan per month as rent. Then they made us pay 8,000 yuan for the same apartment. What's the advantage to us? And only now does the City Housing Bureau tell us that we own only 70 percent of the property rights. They said we need to pay an additional 3,000 yuan to obtain full rights to the apartment.[9]

Stories abound about workers who persistently and strenuously maneuvered to obtain more than their usual share of apartments, and these are often told with extraordinarily intense emotions. Family feuds and suicides have occurred growing out of conflicts in housing allocation, and the quality of worker-management relations in an enterprise could hinge overwhelmingly on whether or not workers' housing needs have been satisfied.

> There are workers who file for fake divorce so that they obtain two housing units instead of one. We workers labor our whole lives and the biggest reward we get is an apartment. It is very important. In my factory, an elderly male worker committed suicide because of housing distribution. He had four sons and all lived in one apartment unit. One of

his sons was so upset about his father's inability to obtain individual units for each of the four brothers that he had an argument with his father after getting drunk. The honest old man went to talk to the factory director, who refused him. The next thing we knew, he hanged himself on the front gate of the factory. His son was outraged and assaulted the director. In the end, they got one more apartment unit.[10]

In another case, a middle-aged worker in the cable factory in Shenyang jumped off the factory building after a failed request for a work-unit apartment. The man was paralyzed, but he got his apartment. Ever since this tragedy, workers with housing grievances had flocked to the director's office to lodge complaints.

These examples illustrate not just the economic significance of having an allocated apartment. More important, perhaps, they reveal how Chinese working-class familial reciprocity crucially mediates workers' plights. Especially middle-aged workers in SOEs, who are the hardest hit in the reform process, find shelter in inherited housing property. Mr. Jin is one such example. A foundryman in one of Shenyang's oldest factories, Mr. Jin inherited his factory job from his father, who retired in 1985, at a time when the national *dingti* (replacement) policy allowed for early retirement as a way to create employment opportunities for younger workers returning from the sent-down movement. In 1992, his father bought the fifty-square-meter apartment the family was living in for ten thousand yuan. It was passed on to Mr. Jin when the old man died several years ago. Mr. Jin is a divorcé and a laid-off worker, taking up temporary transportation jobs riding his motorcycle. To supplement his irregular income, he has rented one of the bedrooms to a friend for a modest amount of money. Like many laid-off workers, he is struggling to make ends meet but his inherited apartment unit has at least given him a stable dwelling even while he is unemployed.[11]

Filial obligations and intergenerational transfer in Chinese society have usually taken the form of the younger generation supporting the older generations. This "tradition" has inadvertently been preserved in urban China by socialist institutions after the 1949 Revolution. Bureaucratic allocation of employment tends to keep parents and children in the same city if not also in the same enterprise. Service shortages also compelled exchange of multiple kinds of assistance to cope with the demands of daily life. Pensions, medical insurance, and other benefits that have been guaranteed to elderly urbanites make them fairly nononerous to their grown children.[12] What seems to have occurred in the 1990s is a reversed pattern of dependence whereby grown children of elderly workers rely on the latter's housing benefits and pensions to survive periods of unemployment and wage arrears. I have discovered that housing allocation in Liaoning is skewed toward older male workers, who usually score higher in housing allocation exercises due to their seniority in the enterprise and the gender bias of allocating housing to male household heads. When bankruptcy began to appear, many middle-aged workers found to their dismay and desperation that they would not be allocated any subsidized housing in the future. Married couples have to stay put in crammed conditions in their parents' apartments. Some of these young couples with school-age children are in such dire financial straits that they have to move in with their parents and become dependent on them for meals, education fees, and living expenses. A worker representative in the Liaoyang protest was painfully ashamed of his dependence on his parents.

> My wife is also a laid-off worker and she now washes dishes for ten yuan per day. I don't have a job now and I have moved in with my parents. The whole family is dependent on my father's monthly pension of 540 yuan. I have no option. For the sake of my kid, that's the only way to survive. Of course, I feel the psychological pain all the time to be still dependent on my folks when I am forty-five.[13]

He is of course not unique in sustaining a reversed pattern of intergenerational transfer. In a multicity survey of urban workers' livelihood, it was found that among workers who left their jobs involuntarily, 34 percent of men and 54 percent of women reported relying on the income of other household members. Personal savings is the primary source of support for 23 percent of men and 12 percent of women among the same group of workers. The same survey also shows that unemployed workers tend not to live in nuclear family arrangements. Only 38 percent of the unemployed lived in households with two or fewer adults.[14]

Intergenerational family reciprocity keeps many workers afloat in hard times. This example of income and care pooling is typical. In Shenyang, a fifty-three-year-old woman who coordinated with other residents in refusing to pay rent took early retirement at the age of forty-five. Her valve factory had owed her several months of pension payments and the government-stipulated 170 yuan minimum living allowance, giving her a monthly subsidy of only 110 yuan. Her husband received only 300 yuan, 200 yuan less than the full amount of his 500 yuan pension. They live with her daughter, who is a clerical worker at the *Shenyang Daily*. Her 500 yuan monthly income is an essential part of the meager household economy. In return, she relies on her parents to take care of her out-of-wedlock baby.[15]

Welfare housing and its transformation into private property are the only remaining benefits that ordinary workers see as their last defense against market competition and insecurity. Even destitute workers have a dwelling to go back to after protests or blocking traffic. As the government decided to redevelop Tiexi, and the northeastern rustbelt in general, into a modern, high-tech commercial district, however, a crisis is developing. A retired engineer who has worked for many years as a heat casting worker in the Shenyang tractors factory grudgingly condemned the government's policy of tearing down working-class neighborhoods for redevelopment. He said, "There are graffiti on the walls of buildings destined to be demolished. People wrote, 'How can the government be so cruel to its own people?'" Forced relocation has not yet occurred, but workers are already discussing the pros and cons of the compensation plan, wondering where to find jobs if they can afford housing only in more remote areas. In other major cities across the country, housing demolition and urban renewal projects have already prompted millions of residents to protest against inadequate compensation and forced relocation.[16]

THE INFORMAL ECONOMY:
PETTY ENTREPRENEURS AND "FLEXIBLE" WORKERS

Many times during my fieldwork, I was baffled by workers' response to a seemingly straightforward question, "Do you work now?" (Ni xianzai you gongzou ma?) They would say no. But as the conversation grew and expanded, they would mention working for a relative, a former coworker, or a collective enterprise in a nearby rural area. As it turned out, many take what Chinese labor officials have euphemistically termed "flexible employment" (ninghuo jiuye) or "hidden employment" (yingxin jiuye). Workers, too, differentiate formal work from informal work with their linguistic invention of the term bucha, literally meaning "making up the difference" between regular earnings and arrears. Bucha is not considered "real work," which in Liaoning workers' lexicon is restricted to permanent employment in the state sector.[17] These linguistic nuances undergird some puzzling discrepancies in (un)employment statistics. According to a survey that includes Shenyang and other major cities, only 29.1 percent of former SOE workers who had left their work units between 1996 and 2001 were able to find reemployment within one year. By the end of 2001, 64.5 percent of these workers were still unemployed.[18] Yet official statistics on hidden employment suggests a different picture. In the Blue Book of Chinese Employment compiled by the Institute of Labor Studies of the Ministry of Labor and Social Security, which is intended as the research basis for government policy formulation, officials estimated that by the year 2002, out of an accumulated population of 25 million laid-off workers in the state sector, 15 million had engaged in some form of flexible employment.[19] If the figures of laid-off workers from both the state and collective sectors are considered together, the proportion of laid-off and unemployed workers involved in flexible employment reaches 80 percent.[20] Flexible employment, as a form of employment, includes workers who are employed as seasonal, temporary, subcontracted, or day laborers in state-owned, collective, private, and microenterprise firms, the self-employed, and independent service workers such as peddlers and domestic helpers. Flexible employment can be found in different occupations, principally in community services (e.g., care for the elderly, maid service), urban sanitation (e.g., garbage collection, street cleaning), secondary production services (e.g., packaging, parts, and components), and personal service (e.g., hair salons, bicycle repair, concession stands, moving, and transportation). The same report also notes that these jobs are usually low-paying, low-skill, short-term, and unstable, and they lack legal contracts and welfare and social security contributions by employers.

In Liaoning, I found that workers bemoaned the loss of permanent and formal employment in state factories, and they suffered financially as a result of payment arrears and unemployment. They see themselves as "without jobs," owing to the inferior working conditions, the high intensity of labor, the instability of wage payments, and the lack of benefits. Yet the reality is that intermittent and unstable employment in the many categories of jobs enumerated in the aforementioned employment report has provided some means of livelihood to many of these workers. The most daring and prosperous are those who have ventured into some form of entrepreneurship, setting up their own small businesses. The majority, however, have oscillated between self-employment and casual jobs. "Hardship households" *(kun nan hu)* can be found among those who have been plagued by both chronic illness and prolonged unemployment of family members. The following discussion covers some of the most typical patterns of employment strategies among Liaoning workers I have encountered in the past six years. Together, these personal stories convey the salient reality of intraclass economic differentiation and inequality. At the bottom of the working-class structure are hardship households, which are plagued by prolonged unemployment of more than one family member, usually aggravated by chronic illness within the family, and lack the means or capacity to become petty entrepreneurs or casual workers. I introduce some typical cases from my fieldwork to explicate each of these conditions—petty entrepreneurs, casual workers, and hardship households.

Some workers early on had entrepreneurial ambitions. Even before massive plant closures in the rustbelt, at the time when most SOEs experienced a production boom and rising wages in the 1980s, these workers sought and found opportunities to try their luck in petty trades. One of the most entrepreneurial working-class families I encountered in the Tiexi neighborhood began their business ventures back in 1982, at the very beginning of market reform. Over the next fifteen years, Ms. Wang and her husband, a worker in a bridge works enterprise in Shenyang, tried selling women's clothes, household appliances, and opening first a salon and then a restaurant. Most of these attempts did not last long, and she claimed that they did not make much money. But still their home was among the better maintained, with hardwood floors and new stainless steel window frames. Their twenty-four-year-old daughter, a clerk in a joint-venture swimming pool facility, was playing the piano in her room while I talked to Ms. Wang in the living room in front of a large-screen television set. Never satisfied with the rigid and disciplined working life of a factory worker, Ms. Wang applied for "internal retirement" when she reached the eligible age of forty-five, receiving a fraction of her basic wages and then her full pension when she finally reached the official retirement age of fifty. She boasted a long career as a petty entrepreneur.

> When the "market" first appeared in Guangzhou in the early 1980s, I was very curious to know how people do business. I found some excuses to get a long sick leave to visit my relatives in Guangzhou. I was very adventurous, finding my own way and asking people who spoke only Cantonese. I even brought back some clothes to sell to people in Shenyang. My husband is also interested in trading and doing business. In 1982, he already began his own seafood trade, buying from Guangzhou and selling in Shenyang. He later shifted to soy beans, buying from Heilongjiang. Even when I was still working in the tractor factory, I already had a second job selling home appliances in a neighborhood mall. After I retired in 1996, I first tried operating a small salon in the neighborhood. Rent was only two hundred yuan per month. Hiring migrant women to do shampooing and hair cutting cost another several hundred yuan per month. . . . Later on, there was too much competition and I closed the salon and tried selling clothes in the downtown underground mall. It's difficult to make a lot of money . . . but I feel much freer when I work for my own business. I don't like being controlled by the factory. I have relatives in rural Liaozhong. My uncle opened a large restaurant there with a loan from the Agricultural Bank. I was inspired. It's cheaper to operate a restaurant in a rural area. I found a three-story building, recruited some waitresses and hostesses—you need to have hostesses; otherwise no one will patronize the restaurant. I invested

seventy thousand yuan and in the end I did not make any loss. Unfortunately, my uncle became jealous and sent a group of gangsters to harass my employees and me, to make me quit. I was too disillusioned. . . . I sold the restaurant.[21]

Elsewhere, two laid-off workers in a Tieling rubber factory had tried their hands in the farm business in the countryside, starting farms and raising rabbits, sheep, and fish. In Liaoyang, one of the jailed worker representatives, Yao Fuxin, opened a small concession store after he was dismissed from his work unit in the mid-1990s. His store became a major gathering and meeting place for organizers of the protests. Other businesses accessible to former workers include food stalls, neighborhood restaurants, and vegetable counters in the street markets. Some workers have made good use of their apartments to launch businesses. The retiree who led several pension protests in Tiexi turned his married son's bedroom into an ant farm, raising medicinal ants in wooden drawers lining the walls. A forty-three-year-old laid-off woman worker in a Shenyang rubber plant invested 3,300 yuan to launch a pure-bred dog business at home. She reports that in Shenyang's pet market, it is not unusual to find people bringing foxes, cats, pet hogs, and other small animals they breed at home for sale.

> I started breeding this kind of dog [she calls them small deer dogs] several years ago. I was wandering aimlessly and went into the pet market just for fun. I was inspired when I saw that a little dog could be sold for seven thousand yuan. I asked people there and one said he could sell me a three-thousand-yuan dog for breeding. I bought it, together with another three-hundred-yuan dog to make a pair. I never talked about my business to neighbors and coworkers. The dogs always stay home, so the neighborhood committee people know nothing about it. I have printed some business cards and distribute them in the pet market. When someone is interested, I show them my wares at home. I now have eight dogs, and each can be sold for three to four thousand yuan. I have to raise them for only forty days after they are born. Buyers are usually businesspeople who nowadays give pets as gifts. Sometimes I get phone calls from people who happen to have a copy of my business card. I can make about ten to twenty thousand yuan a year. It's pretty good. It's still labor, and labor is honorable. I am not like people who speculate in the stock market: they play mahjong all day long and just wait for prices to rise and fall.[22]

In some neighborhoods, the local government has implemented a preferential policy to help laid-off workers start their own vending businesses. In smaller cities such as Tieling and Liaoyang, it is quite common for men to become tricycle drivers, taking residents around town and making several hundred yuan per month. In Shenyang, a number of workers I interviewed reported a 50 percent reduction in rent in certain local markets if they can present their "laid-off certificate." Some sell homemade steamed buns during the morning breakfast hours; others hawk vegetables, fruit, and snacks.

Taking advantage of the neighborhood committee's registration fee waiver for laid-off workers, one forty-eight-year-old woman worker from the Shenyang petrochemical company joined together with two other laid-off women workers from another factory to run a "family service center," a form of community reemployment touted most enthusiastically by the official media as the ideal career for middle-aged laid-off women workers. Ms. Ma spoke proudly of her entrepreneurial success.

> Other people refer to us as "iron women"! We have developed special skills and techniques to clean stoves and range hoods. Many households need this service every few months. We also clean apartments, take care of sick elderly, chaperone schoolchildren, prepare meals. . . . One of us has a ground-floor apartment and we turned that into a storefront. [Interviewer: How much capital did you need?] We bought a big umbrella, fifty yuan, to set up a stand with a company sign. We also bought plastic cleaning gloves and cleaning agents, but we took buckets from home . . . so a total of one hundred yuan was enough. We did not pay any management fee or tax for three months. After three months, the neighborhood committee charged us a monthly fee of only thirty-five yuan to defray all state taxes or miscellaneous fees.[23]

For the majority of unemployed workers and retirees who do not have the money or the capacity to become self-employed, casual employment is the most common way out. Given the relatively young official retirement age for workers (fifty for female workers and sixty for male workers), it is not unusual for retirees to continue some form of gainful employment.[24] Ms. Zhang is a seventy-year-old retiree from a Shenyang casting factory, and has been active in the factory's elderly activity room, especially in organizing residents to pressure their director to pay additional money to the Housing Bureau, which will then recognize workers' full property rights over their apartments. After her retirement in 1989 with a monthly pension of 200 yuan (increased to 470 yuan in 2003), she had always been able to continue her profession as an auditor, working for private companies and earning a monthly income of 500–800 yuan. She had stopped working only two years before I interviewed her, at the age of sixty-eight. Despite her discontent with her work unit's delay in granting workers full property rights, she spoke of the unmistakable material improvement in ordinary workers' lives. Her remaining worry was medical fees.

> People are lying if they say there is no improvement in our living standard. I now have an apartment in a high-rise building. We once lived in barracks used by the Japanese army! We [workers] are now the bottom stratum in society, and our living standard is of the lowest level. You need about 500 yuan per person to cover all the basics. But things have become cheaper over the years. I can wear a blouse for ten years, and it costs only about ten yuan. Food prices are also stable. One kilo of rice is only 0.8 yuan. Fish, meat, and vegetables are always available in the market. Rural production has increased and we city folks can eat cheaply. The government has kept a close watch on prices. My husband can even afford a few drinks occasionally. . . . My greatest burden is medical expenses. My husband has diabetes and need to get four shots per month. The consultation fees, needle fees, and asepsis together cost 500–600 yuan per month, more than his living expenses. Between the two of us, we have to spend all we earn. In the past, the work unit provided free medical care and free hospitalization. But then, we were so young and strong that we did not even have the flu. Now, when there is no state guarantee, we become old and sick.[25]

Some workers got burned by their small business ventures. Ms. Zhang's fellow retiree, Mr. Zhou, a former skilled worker in the casting factory, had also worked for two years after his retirement in 1989. He continued his mechanic work in a suburb of Shenyang, working for the collective enterprise that had been set up to absorb surplus family labor of the casting factory. Like many locals in Shenyang, Mr. Zhou explicitly denied that he had a "job" (*gongzuo*), insisting that was only "making up the difference" (*bucha*). Mr. Zhou's retirement stipend was about 300 yuan at that time (increased to about 500 yuan in 2003), and his income from this moonlighting job was 200 yuan. With declining health, he stopped working in 1992. His wife received a monthly retirement stipend of 300 yuan from her collective enterprise making tractors. When their two sons, who were workers in other state factories, were laid off several years ago, they dipped into their personal savings and gave them fifteen thousand yuan as start-up capital for business ventures.

> One of our sons began his business as a merchandiser of casual clothing. He bought merchandise from Zhejiang and transported and distributed it to small vendors in Shenyang. But he was cheated, and never got his money back from the vendors. My second son also tried selling video compact disks, renting a retail counter in a shopping arcade. He did not have any luck either. The price of VCDs dropped precipitously after he

opened his stall. He could not recover his investment, but still had to pay upfront a monthly rent of one thousand yuan for his counter. That fifteen thousand yuan was my personal savings over the years. It's all gone now.[26]

Finding temporary jobs is not nearly as hard as holding on to a job and getting paid. The litany of jobs many have held after being laid off reflects the pervasive instability and insecurity of employment even when jobs are available. Ms. Han of Tieling's rubber plant has experienced job change every year since her factory stopped production and sent all workers home. When I talked to her, she was working as a clerk in a video rental store, earning ten yuan per day.

> It's been like this since 1994. By now, I really feel discouraged. There's never any stability, and I don't know how long I can continue *dagong* [working for the bosses]. I have sold tickets on a minibus, traveling all day with the driver. The following year I was a cashier in a restaurant, and then I became a helper in a friend's restaurant. Last year I came to this video store. Sometimes I really have the idea of committing suicide. It's easier to be dead than to be exhausted like this. It's so meaningless.[27]

Moreover, the main peril of holding such odd jobs is wage default. As a rule, no labor contract is signed, depriving employees of legal recourse to redress any violation of their rights. Ms. Jiang, a forty-three-year-old laid-off worker from Shenyang's casting factory, is willing to settle for a low-paying job as a kitchen assistant in a local school, which she thinks is less likely to default on wages. Her erratic work history is typical of middle-aged laid-off workers in Liaoning.

> My factory began imposing long vacations in 1992. I did not go to work but nominally was still on the payroll. For seven or eight years, I worked full time as a sales clerk in the shopping mall, earning a basic salary of two hundred yuan plus a 1 percent sales commission. The year 2000 was particularly bad for retail, so I took another job, wrapping dumplings in a restaurant for 350 yuan per month. I worked every day continuously for three months, no rest days. Then I found a kitchen assistant job in the canteen of No. 36 High School, washing dishes, cleaning, and picking vegetables. They only hire people younger than forty. I am too old for them. But I convinced them that I'd be a responsible worker. I now work twelve hours per day, five days a week, for only three hundred yuan. It's a private contractor, but I thought it's still part of a government school. It's not likely to default on wages.[28]

Hardship households are those whose income falls below a local government—set threshold. Established in the mid-1990s, the minimum living standard program for urban dwellers entitles these households to an income supplement equal to an amount by which their per capita family income falls below the minimum living standard.[29] During my fieldwork, workers reported that the family monthly income threshold set for a minimum living standard was 220 yuan in Shenyang in 2002 and 180 yuan in Tieling. (See also chapter 2.) Yet only 29 percent of qualified residents in Shenyang, for instance, were paid, owing to the city's financial difficulties, bureaucratic red tape, and malfeasance.[30] Also, unemployment subsidies for registered unemployed and laid-off workers were not available to the majority of affected workers. In a survey that includes Shenyang, it was found that fewer than 30 percent of unemployed men and 25 percent of unemployed women had access to public unemployment or layoff subsidies.[31] Urban poverty has become a visible social problem in China, with the Ministry of Civil Affairs estimating an urban poverty rate of 4–8 percent, or 15–31 million urban citizens.[32]

Among workers in this study, the Tieling worker Zheng Wu, who lay on the railroad in the incident I described at the opening of chapter 3, was representative of the situations of the multitude of urban poor. Like many of his fellow impoverished citizens, Zheng Wu had to confront the combined predicaments of chronic illness, unemployment, divorce, and family dissolution. I was told later that several years after our interview, he had become mentally ill, but still refused to step out of his shuttered apartment. The deep scars on his wrists resulting from several suicide attempts were indicative of a huge problem among the urban poor. Tragic stories of suicides were staples in my interviews, as were accounts of elderly workers dying of chronic illness without medical care. A woman worker told me with moving rage and contagious sorrow an unforgettable, haunting case. As we strolled down a street in her Tiexi neighborhood lined with women and men squatting in front of the heaps of odds and ends they were trying to sell, she said,

> When my sister's factory closed last year, she became a fruit hawker and she told me about this horrible incident she witnessed in the market. A middle-aged woman was caught stealing a piece of pork in broad daylight. When the hawker and the surrounding crowd accused her of stealing, she broke down in tears. It turned out that her son had begged her to cook him some meat, after he was offered some in his classmate's home. She was unemployed and too poor to afford pork at the dinner table and so she stole. People were sympathetic and let her take the pork home without charging her anything. The next day, in the daily paper, people were shocked to read that a family of three was found dead after eating some poisoned pork for dinner. It was that woman who stole the pork, who apparently took her own life and those of her family members.[33]

Some of the unemployed workers in Shenyang introduced to me by their coworkers had taken to drinking and gambling. On several occasions, when my worker informants finally convinced these workers to leave their poker games to talk to me, they were obviously drunk and were not able to hold coherent conversations in the middle of the day. I also heard that in some cases, their wives had left them or had turned to the sex trade to support the family. Such experiences of social dislocation have spawned satirical jingles *(shunkouliu)*, which are counter-hegemonic colloquial expressions, collective political statements in the guise of rhyming folk wisdom. In Liaoning, for all the reasons this book analyzes, the plight of unemployed workers and corrupt management were prominent themes. This one was made up by a group of workers in China's leading heavy machinery plant, where workers had staged spontaneous work stoppages after the plant delayed wage payments for four months.

> We don't know the date of wage payment
> We don't have gloves as labor protection
> We don't have soap for washing our hands
> We don't know how much we earn
>
> *kaizhimeiyouhao*
> *laobaomeishoutao*
> *shishoumeifeizao*
> *zhengduoshaobuzhidao*

Others had less specific origins but were circulated and appreciated widely among locals in their daily conversations. When workers I encountered offered these to me, it was always to make an implicit statement about the resilience of the human spirit and the wit of the masses, no matter how desperate the circumstances.

> Don't you worry, unemployed big brothers
> Go pick up guns or choppers
> Our leaders' homes have everything you need
> You must fight with your fists when you need to
>
> *xiagang dage xin mo huang*
> *shuangshouzhuaqi dao he qiang*
> *lingdaojiazhong shadouyou*
> *gaichushoushi jiu chushou*
>
> Don't you shed tears, unemployed woman worker
> Put on makeup and go to the nightclubs
> Fifty yuan for drinking with you
> One hundred yuan for sleeping with you

xiagang nugong mo liaolei
dabandaban qu yezonghui
wushiguaiyuanqian peinihe
yibaiyuanqian peinishui

Directors and managers travel across the oceans
Midlevel cadres travel to Shenzhen and Zhuhai
Workers and the masses descend into the bitter seas

changzhangjingli piaoyangguohai
zhongcengganbu shenzhenzhuhai
gongrenqunzhong diaojinkuhai

The factory looks small
The director drives a Bluebird
The factory looks a mess
The director drives a Crown

biekanchangzixiao
changzhangzuonanniao
biekanchangziluan
changzhangzuohuanggguan

In short, long gone are the days when every family knew what their neighbors' incomes were and when people felt that they were more or less economic equals. In the age of reform, families face different opportunities and predicaments, depending on idiosyncratic circumstances such as the economic fortune of a spouse or offspring, the availability of start-up capital loans from relatives or friends, the timing of one's retirement or layoff, knowledge or social connections to get one started in a business venture, and luck. Inequality is painfully visible. My ethnographic field data indicate the pivotal significance of individual sources of income and housing assets and subsidies as the two greatest sources of inequality in urban Liaoning. This finding agrees with the national pattern that Khan and Riskin have found for urban China as a whole in the period 1988 to 1995.[34]

For the purpose of understanding working-class experiences of market reform, this chapter so far has mapped the range of survival strategies and the resultant disparity in material well-being among unemployed workers. This intraclass heterogeneity and the multiple sources of inequality must be emphasized when broaching the subject of the limits of labor activism, solidarity, and radicalism. The next question is: How are objective inequality and material hardship perceived and filtered through workers' cognitive, moral, and historical lenses? In what follows, I turn to what seems to me the third and final parameter of labor's lived experience of accommodating to and surviving market reform—workers' collective memories and assessment of the present.

NOSTALGIA AND CRITIQUE: WHAT WAS CHINESE SOCIALISM AND WHAT HAS IT BECOME?

The pivotal significance of collective memories for understanding labor politics in the reform era dawned on me soon after I started my fieldwork in Liaoning. Day after day, as I went from one home to another, conversations with workers about protests and survival today inevitably returned to "the past," that is, "in the time of Chairman Mao" or "under the planned economy." Rarely could my interviewees articulate and describe the present without invoking the past. The intense moral indignation and righteous anger triggered in recalling the past and contrasting it with the present furnish the emotional energy that "puts fire in the belly and steel in the will."[35] These emotions were compelling forces fueling many of the protests described in chapter 3. Yet, when I probed deeper into workers' collective memories, I found complexity and contradictions in their historical experiences, not just nostalgia for the good old days.

In this final section of this chapter, I present some of the salient but diverse themes emerging in workers' narratives, which together point to working-class ambivalence about the socialist revolution and postsocialist reform. The socialist period, remembered fondly by most as a time of employment security and relative equality in material rewards, was not a time of unmitigated bliss, as it was also a period of material shortages, and political campaigns meant that the masses had a relative degree of power, but also that violence and interpersonal distrust were pervasive. For most people, it was a mixed bag of social and personal experiences too complex to be reduced to a simple narrative of progress or decay. Some aspects of the past were good and some others bad, and they are often expressed in the same breath. The present predicaments hurt, but many see progress in the reform era. Caught between two concrete historical realities, two ways of life, each with its own pitfalls and merits, workers feel ambivalent and torn. Constrained by the varying availability of political and organizational resources, they oscillate between acquiescence and critique, inaction and action.

Nostalgic Memories

Several themes stand out in workers' positive remembrances of the socialist period and these encompass both personal livelihood conditions and more macro political and social concerns. The most oft-mentioned characteristic of their lived experience under Mao is livelihood and job security. Many workers made the distinction between material standard of living (which was lower at that time than in the current period) and psychological well-being (which was better in the past). The second element in workers' nostalgic memory centers on their labor experience within SOEs, especially occupational pride based on skills acquired in the factory, the relative equality of wages, and, most important, the political power of ordinary workers over cadres. The third component in workers' positive memories emphasizes workers' contribution and dedication to national development, and the collective purpose realized in production work. In many narratives, these themes are interwoven pieces mentioned in one single breath, as workers depicted in broad strokes the gestalt of an era. Another noticeable feature of these narratives is that they are seldom strictly about the past. The striking regularity in the juxtaposition and contrasts between the Maoist and post-Mao periods suggests that the present is an enabling device for workers to make sense of their past.

Livelihood and Employment Security   The following account was given by a fifty-two-year-old woman worker in a Shenyang textile mill. When I met her in 2000, she had taken "early retirement" and was getting an allowance of about two hundred yuan per month from her enterprise. Recalling the past, she sighed and shook her head constantly throughout the interview, although she lived in a very respectable, roomy, and well-heated seventy-square-meter apartment allocated by her husband's work unit under the Railroad Bureau. They bought it at a subsidized price of twenty thousand yuan. The past stood out as a time of material and psychological security.

> At that time, I always felt that life had a natural rhythm: I worked, collected wages, retired, and then my children would inherit my post. But now, there is no guarantee for pensions, children's education, or employment. I don't know on whom to depend in the future. Many young people cannot find jobs and they have to depend on elderly parents. I cannot feel the bottom of my heart. In the past, I never felt this empty inside. When I was sick, I had labor insurance, free medical care, and the union to depend on. Now, when I am sick, I cannot ask for reimbursement. I cannot even afford to cure minor illnesses, let alone major ones. At that time, I could approach the work unit and the Party. Now, where can you go for help? . . . Openness and reform work only for those with ability, culture, and knowledge and for those who are sneaky. For honest, ordinary, and mediocre people like us, Mao's egalitarianism was much better. My family ate steamed buns; your family also ate steamed buns. The next day there were the same steamed buns. My heart felt balanced and relaxed. And there was no corruption. During the Cultural Revolution, my neighbor's family member was jailed for ten years for stealing one thousand yuan. On the contrary, today, even if you lined up all officials in the work unit and shot all of them one by

one, you would still miss others who were corrupt. . . . I feel unbalanced not because others make more money. If people get rich by working hard and doing legitimate business, I can only be envious. But now, workers are outraged because it is all about power. Tens of thousands of yuan of bribes are all ordinary people's money. "Eating from one big pot" may not be good for our country's development, and it impoverished and exhausted workers, but psychologically we felt better.[36]

Another woman worker in Tieling, a forty-nine-year-old worker in a textile mill, echoed an attachment to the needs-oriented redistributive system of Mao's day. She emphasized the regime's commitment to fulfilling workers' welfare and livelihood needs. Workers were treated as "human beings," and she saw that as a consequence of the more powerful role of the masses under Mao. In her case, she explicitly explained that her recognition of a distinct past era resulted from the contrast the present thrust upon her, when she was deprived of enterprise welfare.

Our old factory director was very concerned about workers' welfare. For women workers in particular, we had a clinic—they distributed sanitary napkins to women—a nursery, a mess hall, a factory bus, a barber shop, a workers' culture palace [a Mao-era institution for movie screenings and other cultural events]. . . . When the new director came, there was nothing left. Now I understand what *exploitation* means. We are really pitiful. In the old days, if you needed housing, the factory would give you housing. Now, no single apartment has been built. Mine is a three-person household and still we cannot buy our own apartment unit. Instead we rent an eighteen-square-meter unit from the city Housing Bureau, paying thirty yuan per month. Gradually, all kinds of power the masses had under Mao have been taken away bit by bit.[37]

The importance of "welfare" and "needs" in the Maoist period was also central to male workers, although some of them associated "needs" with skill training and work conditions rather than reproductive services. For instance, a fifty-year-old driver at a machinery factory said,

In the past, when my kid was sick or my family had any financial difficulty, I went to the union chair. He would study the problem and come back to me with allowances. This is gone now. Our Workers' Congress has not had a meeting in years. The union chair works only for the director who appoints him. Workers have no protective gear on the shop floors, no working shoes, antitoxic masks, soap or towels, nothing. They cannot even reimburse you 50 percent of your medical expenses. In the days of Mao, no matter how poor, the factory could not ignore you when you got sick. Now, without money, you just wait for death when you get sick.[38]

A Shenyang welder, boasting a twenty-nine-year job tenure in the same factory, spoke at length about the superiority of Maoism, focusing mostly on skill acquisition and workers' commitment to quality production. His lively demeanor and colorful voice expressed vividly his excitement about the past and anger about the present.

> The current system in our country slights skills. But when we first joined the factory, we spent many hours taking skill classes. Every Monday, Wednesday, and Friday, every week, in the evening we stayed in the factory after work to learn systematically different types of welding, different raw materials and their mixture, and how to read blueprints. These days, when young workers come in, they know nothing and learn nothing in the factory. Our country is regressing. . . . When the Chairman was alive, poor students who really wanted to go to school and did well would get scholarships. It was a way to preserve the strength and the quality of our nation. Now, without money, you cannot send your child to school. I really miss the Chairman. You see, I have his portrait in my living room. At that time, we did not consider rewards. We just had faith. The more difficult the production task, the more willingly we worked. I was a Youth League member, very eager to join the Party. Once a fire broke out in the factory. I took the lead in fighting it. I was not afraid. . . . Now, no more. I don't care if I make substandard products, because the factory defaults on my wage payments. It's natural that we are producing many rejected goods because no one feels responsible for their work. What a contrast with the past, when we volunteered to study how to improve production. Now everyone says, "This is so meaningless."[39]

Economic and Political Equality   The sense of security and stability described by these workers is closely associated with the relative economic and political equality workers remembered about the socialist period. An articulate fifty-five-year-old male technician, who was once honored as a model worker in one of China's largest valves factories, gave a compelling depiction of working-class mentality at that time.

> At that time, people's class feeling and standpoint *(lichang)* were very simple and pure. Eight hours of work was our responsibility to society. I did not have big dreams or lofty ideals. Even though propaganda sang the praises of good people and their good deeds, most of us did not aspire to those high goals. There was no time to think about those things. I only worked and worked, because I felt that society treated me well. As long as I worked hard and well, I did not have to worry. The work unit took care of my housing, children's employment, and pension. I was very content. . . . They used to say the working class was

the leadership class. At that time, I believed it because of our status in
society and in the enterprise, and our wages were not low. . . . Our living
standard was not high, it's true, compared to the present. But we were
worry-free. For my own interest, I would prefer going back to the time
of the planned economy. Society was stable and the masses had a sense
of purpose. At the time of old Mao, the planned economy served our
country. In 1949, there were only foreign goods. No domestic industry.
At that time, even if we had wanted to open up our economy, no one
wanted to be open with us. We could depend only on ourselves to build
up our foundation. The most important things are stable development,
social stability, and that people can be carefree.[40]

Workers' positive memory of the relative political equality in the past
was commonly invoked by their palpable discontent about cadres' abuse of
power and corruption, and workers' powerlessness to restrain officials.
Strained Party-mass relations *(dangqun guanxi)* were vehemently criticized
by reference to past practices such as big-character posters and political campaigns. A fifty-year-old truck driver in Shenyang made some of the most
passionate indictments of management in the reform period, centering on
workers' desperation in the face of rampant cadre corruption. Big-character
posters and union power have given way to fatalistic passivity and anger, he
said.

Northeastern workers today harbor rebellious mentalities *(yifanxintai)*.
The twenty-somethings look toward the West and those in their forties
and fifties long for Mao's time. I think the 1990s is like the 1960s, only
now we do not have to eat bark. But we Chinese still have to eat a lot of
bitterness and bear much hardship. . . . If only the top leaders can take
the lead and set the example of sharing the pain with us. Today, you see
all those factory leaders, it's too common for them to go out with ladies,
spending several thousand yuan, while workers have no money for
medical treatment. This is antagonism and opposition. Cadre-masses
relations have become extremely tense. . . . The most important thing is
that today's workers have no power, the power that Mao gave workers,
the power to criticize the director and to write big-character posters.
Now it's illegal to write big-character posters. They will arrest you. . . .
Our union is a yellow union, just as Marx and Lenin said, and the union
chair is the running dog of the capitalists. He is just a dog. Maoism
urged cadres to "serve the People." I really believed that was true. When
we went to school, we were poor but we were given the chance to attend
school. But the current government does not care at all about people's
interests. . . . I don't have a religion, but let me tell you this story about
our director. Our director had a beloved BMW. His son had returned
from college in Japan, and had learned how to drive the car. The son's
wife was an ordinary woman worker in our factory. The whole family

went visiting his hometown in the countryside to show off his wealth and status. But his car crashed, because he was driving too fast. The director's son and daughter-in-law were both killed! When workers heard the news, they all said, "Heaven cracks down on corruption when workers cannot." The car was not his; it was a state asset, the sweat and blood of workers![41]

Many workers recalled, either fondly or cynically but always with nostalgia, their occasional exercise of mass power over cadres during political campaigns. A sixty-eight-year-old retired manual worker in a military equipment factory offered a typical comment.

> People today always say, if the Cultural Revolution came again, these corrupt cadres would all be executed many times. In the past, cadres were criticized and persecuted just for harboring bad attitudes toward workers, meaning that they were too wooden or their voices were too harsh when they urged workers to work harder. There was absolutely nothing like the kind of corruption we see these days. Now, there is hardly any cadre who is not corrupt. The problem today is twofold: first, there are no more campaigns; and second, even if there was a campaign, it would be impossible to nail officials down because they collude and protect one another. The auditor is always an acquaintance of the director. You can never get the proof to charge them.[42]

Working-Class Contribution to National Development Workers recalled a striking sense of collective purpose in their mundane factory labor. Many conveyed having the experience of involvement and commitment in a national project of economic construction. Wage levels were low and stagnant, and working hours long, sometimes lengthened by political meetings and voluntary work. Yet what is remembered is not complaint or resentment, but willing submission, even fervent belief in the national and factory leadership. That sense of community is now lost but missed, as remarks by two woman textile-mill workers reveal.

> Even in the early 1960s, when we had to endure hunger, we did not complain. People without ability are all nostalgic about Mao's time. We had to do voluntary labor. Perhaps because we were young and strong, we never complained. It was something we "should" do. I saw my father working in the factory continuously during the Great Leap Forward and coming home to rest only once every two weeks. He did not get extra pay. Back then, earning thirty yuan was sufficient for supporting the entire family. . . . Workers became lazy and calculating only after the Cultural Revolution. When bonuses were introduced, workers became reluctant to work if the bonus was small. People also had more conflicts with one another on how to distribute bonuses.[43]

I was a 1968 sent-down youth. When I returned to the city, I was particularly enthusiastic and progressive, probably because we were educated
in Maoist thought. Whether I was in the village or in the work unit, I
worked particularly hard, without any impure thought. You can almost
say I lived up to the standard of a Communist Party member. . . . At that
time, production was for our country, for building socialism. I had a
very advanced mentality. [Interviewer: Was it only a slogan?] It's what
the slogan said, but it's also my genuine feeling. We were very different
then from young people today. . . . It's true that I had my own struggle
when I was sent down to the countryside, with no hope of returning. . . .
At the beginning of my return to the city, I felt particularly excited and
content because I could learn new technologies. I was very hardworking.[44]

Another worker in the same textile mill explained how an esprit de corps
was forged by a delicate mix of political and social pressure, and a workplace
culture of competition.

When I started working in the textile mill in 1975, there were still
many political activities, meetings, emulation, competition, posters,
small-group evaluations, group discussions of workers' thinking, and so
on. We were already exhausted after work, but we still had to attend
meetings. If you did not go, you would be criticized and you lost face.
Every week they posted a huge table of outputs for each worker. It made
you look really bad if you fell behind others. For the sake of saving face,
you would work hard just to be in the middle. Otherwise, you felt very
uncomfortable. That was the time when politics was in command. It was
really something; those meetings were nerve-racking. Who was good
and who was bad were all discussed. But I must say, those criticisms
were usually reasonable. Moreover, if you really fell behind, several
Party members next to you would follow you all day long, to encourage
you or help you, all day long. If you did not meet your quota, they
would drop their work and came over to work with you. I did not know
whether they were really nice or were just fulfilling their political task.
But they did help you.[45]

In short, collective memories of the Maoist era were essentially the
workers' revisiting a standard of justice now lost in reform. In rallies and
demonstrations in Liaoning, banners proclaiming "We Want Justice," "We
Want to Live," "We Want to Eat," and "Down with Corrupt Officials"
reflected what they considered the basic conditions of a "just" social order.
In the absence of a public forum for workers' articulation of their interests
and of organizations of worker resistance, shared emotive and moral frameworks have come to play a heightened role in fostering solidarity.

Critical Memories

Several themes are prominent in workers' negative remembrances of the prereform past: the violence and fear induced by campaigns, the despotic power of work-unit leadership, and inequality produced by socialism. The most bitter criticisms I heard came from middle-aged workers who joined the workforce in the early 1970s and were too young to benefit from pensions when enterprise bankruptcies deprived them of all the traditional socialist workers' rights. Yet by that time, they already had put in almost two decades of labor and had sacrificed the best years of their youth.

Violence and Fear   Although most people glossed over their years during the Cultural Revolution, giving general statements rather than specific details, their avoidance and occasional forays into that period reveal glimpses of their memories of fear and violence. A seventy-five-year-old Grade Eight worker, boastful of a work history that began "before the establishment of the Republic," remarked sarcastically but with trepidation,

> In the past, production was interrupted by politics. Today, production is arrested because of economics. . . . Reform brought a better life, that's for sure. We don't have to endure hunger, as in the days of Mao. I now eat rice every day. I don't like noodles. In the past, we chanted the "working-class leadership" slogan because that's what leaders wanted. No one could avoid it. We chanted whatever slogans were given us. I could not care less whether those slogans were true or not. I only knew that if I did not chant, I would be branded a "backward" element. . . . Three workers on my shop floor died: one committed suicide, the other two were beaten to death. One was named Liu. He was accused of sabotaging a big project. But he was a Grade Seven or Grade Eight worker. In hindsight, I don't think it was a case of sabotage, just a technical error with the casting mold. But at that time, once someone charged you with sabotage, you were certain to be found guilty, whether you admitted it or denied it. The real problem was his political viewpoint and some leaders wanted to get rid of him. He soon committed suicide. . . . If leaders admired you, you were good; if they criticized you, you were bad. It was not up to us. I just wanted to avoid mistakes. Everyone was afraid of struggles every day at work. But then production was hectic because people were afraid of being labeled as saboteurs. We cast eighty tons of iron every day at that time. Now, we don't make that much in a month. . . . It's hard to say which period is better, Mao's or now.[46]

A similarly ambivalent experience of fear and acquiescence was reported by a seventy-year-old male worker in a Shenyang military equipment factory. He joined the electronic equipment factory in 1954 and had retired by the time I talked to him in 2000. Yet what also stood out in his memory of the socialist period was workers' contribution to national development.

> During the Great Leap Forward, production went on nonstop. It was a contribution to the country and to socialism. It was what we should do, without bonuses, but from our hearts. I was genuinely willing. But it's also true that people dared not resist, because no one wanted to fall behind. The common thinking at that time was to be progressive, ambitious, and positive about work. People at that time dared not cultivate *guanxi* to get away from work. We had to report our thinking to the Party, or report coworkers with ideological problems, or who sabotaged production. When I missed my family in Sichuan, I reported this to my superior and he advised me to take a different perspective about my feelings. They made me realize that it was more important to do well in production. At that time, those leaders had people's trust, and they were not corrupt at all. One of them had an affair with a woman and he was kicked out of the Party, branded as a case of corrupting bourgeois mentality. . . . During the Cultural Revolution, there were always meetings, like two hours every day, until eight or nine in the evening. All kinds of criticisms and confessions. The Red Guard organized us to write big-character posters, and we spent day and night writing. We also went to other factories to participate in struggle meetings. Everyone had to go, otherwise you got criticized. I was very afraid at that time, and could only go with them. . . . When I was thinking of finding a marriage partner, the Party helped me to check potential spouses' political backgrounds. I did not find this repellent because everyone was like that. Indeed, for certain personal information in people's dossiers, you had to rely on the Party to find out.[47]

Cadre Tyranny   Although many workers recalled with amazement that workers actually once occasionally wielded the power to criticize management, they also remembered the institutional power and privilege enjoyed by cadres. Female workers were particularly vulnerable to sexual harassment. A forty-three-year-old woman recalled the sexual abuse she and her coworkers had to endure when shop-floor cadres held despotic and total power over pay and bonuses. She joined the casting factory in Shenyang when her father retired in 1978. Many workers on her shop floor operated cable cars controlling the mixing of molten iron and alloy materials. The absolute power of the foreman was the most vivid, if also most hated, aspect of her years as an SOE worker. She was so disillusioned that she became very distrustful of the "quality of the working class."

You could never antagonize the foreman or the section head. They had myriad means to make life miserable for you. They could allocate you "good" work, so you could sleep through your shift, or they could give you impossibly hard work. Among the fifty of us in the section, only ten were men, elderly men. So all the women workers tried every means to placate the section head, giving him cigarettes, home-cooked food at lunch, or sweet words. They surrounded him all the time, organized their daily lives around him. Why? All for a few yuan of bonus every month. . . . When I first joined the shop floor, I was only nineteen, and one day the foreman said he wanted to teach me how to operate the cable car. I followed him up the cable car and when the door was closed, he put his hand on mine and his body pressed hard against mine from behind. I was horrified and when I went home, I complained to my father. He was furious and said that the foreman had a problematic work style. My father knew him and talked to him. He dared not touch me again. But very soon, he spotted another new woman worker who was even younger than I was. He first bought her goodies and then took her out during lunch break. Later someone found out that they made out in a secret place near the railroad. . . . They were discovered by the police and both were criticized. But they still remained in the work unit, just on different shop floors. Another foreman came, but still the same problem. The Women's Federation even came to investigate. But I was on good terms with this foreman. There were times when I needed to attend to my moonlight job during the day and wanted to work the night shift, so I gave him cigarettes. I gave him one carton at first. He refused. I gave him a second carton, and he agreed. I got night shifts for two weeks. After that, I had to give him more for more weeks. I really hated this. Now I work outside the *danwei*, and I don't have to cultivate this kind of relation. I rely on my own ability. As long as I am good at my work, I don't have to cajole anyone. I don't miss the *danwei* at all. For the first few years in the *danwei*, I was a model worker, because of the quality of my work. But these leaders and their work style really disgusted me. I don't believe in the quality of the working class anymore.[48]

Sacrifice and Betrayal Quite common among middle-aged workers are cynicism and criticism both of socialism's demand for personal sacrifice and of the lack of payback by the state now that reform has rescinded many of the benefits older workers enjoyed. Their rejection of the past is prompted by their misery in the present. A demobilized soldier and a Party member, a fifty-one-year-old technician in Tieling spoke angrily about the betrayal of his generation. He has to support two school-age children after being laid off. He has become so disenchanted by his current predicament that he disparaged his own past as only an illusion.

I am just a victim of deceit and lies. But sacrifice for what? In the past,
I was very active in debating what were socialism, communism, and
capitalism. But they were all instruments of political struggles. They
deceived ordinary people to serve the interest of politicians. . . . Since I
was a child, I had always believed in the Party. At that time, I felt I had a
religion, and psychologically was very peaceful and balanced. I willingly
gave my best effort at work, so as not to fall behind. We were the masters of the enterprise, I thought, just as the propaganda said. But now,
I know that I was fooled. Only 312 yuan [severance pay] per year of
job tenure. Is this fair treatment for "masters"? How can a technical
employee of the best-equipped factory in China become so pitiful? Is
this not cheating?[49]

Workers in their thirties and forties expressed the most negative experience of socialism. Many recognized their plight as a generational phenomenon. A typical memory of the socialist past depicted a collective experience
of suffering owing to radical shifts in state policies. Not surprisingly, during
a large-scale protest in Liaoyang, a labor leader passionately invoked a popular satirical jingle that expressed the desperation of victimization. Mass
emotion was spurred to a high point when he lamented on behalf of the
crowd,[50]

We gave our youth to the Party
Now in our old age no one cares for us.
Can we turn to our children?
Our children are also laid off.

In the northeast, workers have an aggravated sense of victimization
because of a strong regional identity. *Northeastern workers* is a common
collective reference they use to describe themselves. A seventy-year-old
engineer-turned-worker in Tiexi, the largest and most established working-
class district in Shenyang, elaborated at length on the sacrifice made by
Shenyang Tiexi workers.

Tiexi was the famous Ruhr of the East. Industries here began in the
Japanese colonial period. Then with Soviet aid, many of the 156 projects
were located here too. It's the eldest son of the Republic's industrialization, and many national number ones [flagship factories] were born here.
Now, workers' villages have become laid-offs' villages. At the beginning
of the Republic, many technical workers submitted to government allocation and were moved from other cities to work here. Our government
owes them too much. In the past, there was provision for basic needs.
Now, everything is gone. Some time ago, a former model worker sold
his National May First medal because he needed money to see the doctor. The local community was really shocked.[51]

Another Shenyang worker echoed the same regional identity of sacrifice.

Northeastern workers have a very glorious history. The liberation of
China depended on the northeast. Without the industrial resources of
the northeast, how could the Communist Party have made its way to
the south? Even after the Liberation, it was the northeast that led the
country to industrialize. Workers here, unlike those in Guangdong,
gave their lives and fates to the factory once they got in. They loved
and respected their work. There was not much opportunity to moonlight, unlike in the south. We worked for very low wages, and all the
surplus went to build up the nation's military. But all this nation-
building sacrifice is wasted. Now that we are approaching old age,
we cannot even get our pensions on time.[52]

In a nutshell, working-class memories are fragmented and ambivalent.
Diversity of worker memories most prominently follows a generational
pattern, perhaps a consequence of changing realities in state factories and
different amounts of time spent as a worker. Workers in their sixties or
older recalled a more "revolutionary" experience in which sacrifices were
made in the name of socialism and national development, and relative
equality and employment security were lived experiences in the past. In
contrast, those who started their factory careers in the 1970s had more cynical and less passionate recollections of their working lives. Their memory
narratives were more negative, emphasizing cadre tyranny, unrewarded sacrifice, and state betrayal. This is probably the result of their position in the
social structure. Caught between the old and the new economies, these disgruntled workers neither benefited from pensions nor have the youth and
educational advantages to succeed in the marketplace. One interesting
caveat is that although their personal experiences informed their critical
memories of socialism, they also drew on their parents' experience to articulate an imagined memory of Maoism. This imagined Maoism, consisting
of themes of equality, security, and mass power, is invoked in petitions to
local government.[53] Among people of the same generation, there is no linear relationship between current conditions and the emphasis of memory.
That is, workers who feel secure in their lives under reform are as likely to
be nostalgic for the socialist era as those who experience deterioration in
their current lives.

SURVIVAL, MEMORIES, AND FEELINGS

This chapter has attempted to illuminate the fabric of everyday survival and
structures of feelings that are continuous with but distinct from moments

of collective action. Holding these two elements together, we see that after each episode of protest or petition that we examined in chapter 3, workers go back to their private abodes. And between acts of collective defiance, they are preoccupied with making ends meet in the marketplace. Although righteous rage, outcries against injustice, and nostalgia for the Revolution and the socialist past are the emotional energies that constitute labor resistance, acceptance of some of the practices and values of market reform prevails as a quiet undercurrent of working-class feelings. Both sets of emotions are informed by workers' collective memories of socialism, a terrain marked by profound ambivalence.[54]

This argument is slightly different from what has been suggested in the literature on worker politics in the reform era. On the one hand, Marc Blecher has found that workers in Tianjin accept a "market hegemony," subscribing to the core values of the market peddled by the dominant class and the state.[55] For instance, he found that workers believed that market allocation of income and competition were both right and were more effective than the planned economy was. They also believed that the economic health of their enterprises was a matter of luck, the result of an agentless, natural, and inevitable market process. Such hegemonic acceptance, for Blecher, explains the absence of a coordinated worker challenge to the state. On the other hand, William Hurst and Kevin O'Brien found a more black-and-white situation in two ailing mining towns, where "all the working-class interviewees expressed open hostility towards market reforms, claimed that they and the country had been better off before reform began, and expressed varying degrees of desire to restore large parts of the Maoist social order."[56] Rather than positing these two scenarios as contradictory and mutually exclusive, the present study finds that both hegemony and counter-hegemony coexist in workers' attitudes. Instead of underscoring either rebellion or hegemony, I have tried to clarify the terms of each and the circumstances under which they are activated and translated into a mix of collective action and inaction.

In chapter 3 and this chapter, I have depicted how and why rustbelt workers staged protests of desperation while they managed to scrape together a mode of survival in the shadow of widespread bankruptcy and unemployment. I have argued that this pattern of protest and survival was shaped by the political economy of decentralized legal authoritarianism and a labor system in the rustbelt that still organizes the social reproduction of labor power around the work unit and that attempted a transition from the social to the legal contract, which stalled. Next, we move on to another regional political economy and a different pattern of labor struggles and survival. In the sunbelt province of Guangdong, I found protests against discrimination by a new generation of young, migrant workers in nonstate manufacturing, construction, and service firms. Although their backgrounds, interests, strategies, and identities diverge from those of rustbelt workers and despite working under a labor system predicated more on legal contracts than on the social contract and to a reproduction of labor power based in villages rather than in the urban work unit, the features of cellular activism and legalism are rooted in the same political economy of decentralized legal authoritarianism. It is to these protests against discrimination in the sunbelt province of Guangdong that the next chapter turns.

PART III

Sunbelt

Protests against Discrimination

5 The Making of New Labor in the Sunbelt

On the afternoon of May 9, 2002, the courtyard outside the Petition Department of the Shenzhen City Labor Bureau was crowded with young workers still in their blue uniforms, with factory identity cards pinned to their shirt pockets. They were ordinary workers and line leaders of a Hong Kong–owned electronics plant making hair dryers and toaster ovens for export to the United States. After the company announced a "wage reform" that substituted piece rates for hourly wages, workers walked out of the factory on May 7 and marched to the Labor Bureau in Nanshan district in Shenzhen to launch a collective petition. After unsuccessful negotiations with management, they decided to strike again and this time they decided to appeal to the Shenzhen City Labor Bureau instead. The Nanshan district police, anxious to prevent angry workers from causing a disturbance within their jurisdiction, blocked traffic and demanded that the buses carrying these workers suspend service. Undeterred, workers decided to walk for three hours to downtown Shenzhen. Police officers "escorted" them until they left the Nanshan district boundary. Hours later, these workers showed up in the Shenzhen City Labor Bureau downtown. One worker representative explained the cause of the strike.

> We always knew we were not getting the legal wage rates. But nobody stuck his neck out to do something about it. And as long as we could get by, we didn't want to create trouble. But this time, management pushed us to rebel. The wage reform is a wage cut in disguise. They say it can raise productivity, but the assembly line is already moving so fast that we'll become robots to make a living wage under the new piece rate system. Four years ago when I first came, we were making 360 hair dryers per hour in each production line. Now, we are turning out 440 pieces an hour. It's impossible to work faster.[1]

As worker representatives presented their case to the Shenzhen City Labor Bureau officers inside the petition room, their fellow workers waited eagerly outside and filled the courtyard with lively conversation, occasional laughter, and angry cursing of the police who had stopped their buses. A dozen Shenzhen police arrived, standing by without intervening, while "black market" lawyers handed out business cards, offering legal advice about the 1995 Labor Law and encouraging workers to file a lawsuit against the factory. When the Nanshan District Labor Bureau chief emerged from the building and tried to address these several hundred workers, asking them to return to the factory located in his district, he drew howls of protest from workers who wanted to drown out his voice. Eventually, the Shenzhen City Labor Bureau chief came out of his office and announced his solemn pledge to resolve the dispute to the workers' satisfaction. Everything would be resolved according to the law, he vowed, and workers would get a labor contract, legal wage rates and overtime compensation, and pension benefits, all of which had been denied them by their employer. Around 5:00 PM, the Shenzhen City Labor Bureau chief deployed his fleet of employee buses to take workers back to their dormitories, to "ensure workers' safety."

Workers in another subcontracting factory manufacturing for Wal-Mart also approached the government. Like their counterparts in the construction company, their struggle for legal wage rates, overtime pay, pensions, and decent dormitories was a protracted one, lasting more than eighteen months.[2] The incident had evolved from writing complaint letters to management to collective visits to the city government, strikes and work stoppages, mediation and arbitration by the local Labor Bureau, public demonstrations outside the city government offices, and finally the court. In this case, six worker representatives had received a call from the court saying that the authorization letter signed by workers at the arbitration stage was no longer valid. They had to come up with an updated authorization, something that was almost impossible because workers had already left the factory and had given only their rural home addresses to the representatives. The court suggested mediation, asking if workers would accept a settlement of five hundred yuan for each plaintiff. When they accepted, the clerk in the court went to the Labor Arbitration Commission and somehow managed to obtain a revised updated authorization all by himself. One worker leader, reflecting on the "mediated" result of the lawsuit, was ambivalent about the workers' success: "Financially, we lost. We were owed more than five hundred yuan each. But morally, we won. The court affirmed our righteousness."[3]

THE FORCE OF LAW AND PROTESTS AGAINST DISCRIMINATION

These two episodes of labor conflict illustrate a typical dynamic of labor contentions involving migrant workers in southern China. Labor unrest is closely intertwined with the law, the courts, and the government's labor bureaucracy. The trajectory of working-class formation involving young migrant workers hailing from the vast countryside in the reform period evolves differently but parallel to that of veteran workers in the rustbelt. Whereas the exit of the older generation of urban workers from state industries occasions collective mobilization, it is the mass entry of about one hundred million migrant workers into cities producing for the global economy that gives rise to labor contentions. One group protests against its exclusion from the market and betrayal by the state, the other against capitalist exploitation and state discrimination. Also, whereas the contestation involved in the unmaking of the socialist working class is driven by the socialist social contract, labor conflicts between migrant workers and their employers are regulated and engendered by the fledgling legal system and the legal contract. That is why the law, the courts, and the labor bureaucracy become the crucible of labor mobilization in the sunbelt. The discrepancy between the legal prescription of rights and the lived reality of the absence of those rights has prompted workers to raise their voices against discrimination.

The project of building a law-governed state is not a unique Chinese concern; many postsocialist states strive for new legitimation through reconstituting state power based on legality, distinguishing themselves from the previous socialist state based on terror, fiat, arbitrariness, and deceit.[4] It is a Herculean task of such historic proportions that the legal scholar William Alford vividly compares it to the construction of "a second Great Wall."[5] The outcome depends significantly on how social groups respond to and use the law, and what powers and cultural processes shape the law's actual operation in social life. As detailed in chapter 2, a series of labor regulations and the National Labor Law were promulgated in the reform era to allow the government to regulate labor relations after it removes itself from direct management and allocation of labor (its role under the planned economy). Of particular relevance to migrant workers are the Labor Law (1995) and the Regulations for the Handling of Labor Disputes (1993).

In this chapter, I examine how workers actually use the law and how they interact with officials charged with instituting this fledgling system. As "a social field of force," as Bourdieu suggested, the Chinese juridical and bureaucratic fields are sites of competition for control in which everyone is constrained, however unevenly, by the constitutive structure and principles of the legal field.[6] That is, corruption, prejudices, or other caveats notwithstanding, law and regulation's universalizing logic imposes terms and limits of contestation and may be seized and transformed by workers. I have found that, on the one hand, many migrant workers have successfully used the law to obtain back pay and pension contributions owed to them by employers. My fieldwork finds that their positive experience with this tantalizing legal system encourages other migrant workers to follow suit, constituting a social force that bolsters the central government's project of constructing rule by law. Yet, on the other hand, for every worker who finds vindication in the system, there are many more who, in the process of their long and arduous legal battles, lose faith in the neutrality of the court and develop negative dispositions toward the integrity of the state itself. These workers become inclined toward noninstitutionalized, bordering on illegal, modes of actions, or what they themselves describe as "radical action."[7] Therefore, the transformative effect of the law is open in the sense that it can become a new wellspring of criticism and discontent, and yet at the same time it may lead to enhanced state legitimacy or the spread of popular demands for the right to legal justice. Either way, the uncertainty of the outcome in this field of force has propelled rather than inhibited labor activism.

In a nutshell, this chapter uses ethnographic and interview data to unpack the processes of contentions in the corridors of the Labor Bureau, the dormitories of factories, lawyers' offices, and the courthouses. I find that migrant workers, feeling deprived of the socialist social contract available to state-owned enterprise workers, see the Labor Law as the only institutional resource protecting their interests vis-à-vis powerful employers and local officials. From the perspective of migrant workers, their inferior legal status in the cities, enforced by the household registration system, leaves them no choice but to turn to the state bureaucracy and the law as the only protections available. Hailing from the countryside and shackled for generations to the farm, many migrants regard urban jobs as a major means of upward mobility. The Labor Law defines them as workers with legal rights and therefore furnishes institutional leverage amidst all kinds of disadvantages. Workers are inclined to resort to the government labor bureaucracy and the court whenever conflicts erupt in the workplace. The unpredictable and often corrupt bureaucracy and the legal system may, however, add insult to injury and end up producing more frustration and desperation than the initial workplace disputes did. Collective mobilization at that point will overflow from the Labor Bureau and the court into the streets, and legal activism will be transformed into direct street action. This oscillation between rationalization and radicalization of labor conflict is what underlies the volatility of the labor regime in South China, where the law and the legal contract are purportedly the major means of state regulation. Mirroring the analysis in chapter 3, I analyze workers' grievances, action strategies, and subjectivities in the following sections.

The first part of this chapter discusses the industrial economy and growth of Shenzhen in relation to the proliferation of labor conflicts. Through workers' narratives of their own workplace experience, I depict features of workplace degradation, exploitation, and discrimination from which labor grievances and conflicts flow. The core part of the chapter traces how migrant workers come into contact with the Labor Law, how they navigate the treacherous mediation and litigation processes, and how they confront labor officials, employers, lawyers, and judges. Such interactions between workers and the legal system often work to contain conflicts within the officially prescribed channels of resolution but occasionally and subsequently they also lead to street protests. Either within or outside the institutionalized channels of labor contention, the prevailing mode of mobilization is that of cellular activism, as is the case in the rustbelt, engendered by the state strategy of decentralized legal authoritarianism. Finally, I return to the discussion about labor insurgent identities at the end of the chapter, noting both commonalities and differences between migrant workers in the south and unemployed state workers in the northeast. The sharp consciousness of legal rights is shared by workers in these two vastly divergent political economies.

REVISITING THE SOUTH CHINA MIRACLE

The site of my fieldwork is Shenzhen, in the southern Chinese province of Guangdong. A stark contrast to the old industrial cities of the northeast, Shenzhen, with a population of about 7.8 million, is China's major link to the global marketplace. In 2000, Guangdong province accounted for 42 percent of all China's exports, 90 percent of which came from eight cities in the Pearl River Delta area, led by Shenzhen.[8] Driven by international industrial investment and domestic private firms, Shenzhen boasts a staggering average annual gross domestic product growth rate of 31.2 percent over two decades of reform, and remains to this day the most popular destination for China's eighty to one hundred million migrant workers.[9] One in three migrant industrial workers in China lives in Guangdong and some six million of them worked in Shenzhen as of 2000. Despite the ubiquity of savage industrial capitalism in its factories, Shenzhen is also the frontier of labor law and labor arbitration reform, making it a most contentious city in labor relations. Almost one-fifth of China's arbitrated labor disputes occur in Shenzhen.[10]

In 1992 and 1993, I worked as a factory hand in a Hong Kong–owned export-processing electronics plant, as part of the fieldwork research for my dissertation. Back then, I was exploring the mechanisms of labor control and the reproduction of power behind an economic success story founded on the use of female laborers. I characterized the factory regime there as "localistic despotism."[11] It was a system in which local state intervention in and regulation of labor relations was minimal, thanks to the clientelist relationship between foreign investors and local officials. Such a political economy allowed despotic management to rely on the use of coercive and punitive discipline. The social and gendered organization of the labor market was such that localistic networks among workers were incorporated into the shop floor, subjugating a predominantly female workforce by constituting them as docile maiden workers. My theoretical project there was to engender Marxist understandings of the labor process so that gender hierarchies and identities become integral elements in theorizing production-based class relations. I was more interested in the organization and reproduction of power than collective resistance to control.[12]

Despotism, Growth, and Conflict

Now, a decade later, I revisit this pioneering border city to find the export-driven economy continuing to thrive apace and, along with it, a relentless intensification of the labor process. The city boundaries have sprawled in all directions to accommodate an ever-increasing workforce that hails from villages all over the country. Shenzhen's migrant labor population has grown from 1.3 million in 1990 to 6 million in 2005, about 75 percent of whom find jobs in industry. Although many international and domestic firms have relocated to more remote, inland locations in search of cheaper land and labor, Shenzhen has witnessed the persistent growth of foreign and private investment. The largest number of firms are export-processing projects and foreign-invested projects, with a total of twenty-one thousand establishments at the end of 1999, accounting for 80.9 percent of the city's industrial output.

Fueling such impressive expansion of the industrial economy are numerous "satanic mills" running at such a nerve-racking pace that workers' physical limits and bodily strength are put to the test on a daily basis. In the early 1990s, a factory operator regularly worked a ten- to twelve-hour day, six days per week. During my visit in 2002–2003, I had extreme difficulty scheduling meetings with workers whose regular work cycle consisted of a grueling fourteen- or even sixteen-hour workday, and, with very few exceptions, no rest day at all throughout the month except on payday. It has become "normal" to work four hundred hours or more every month, especially for those in the garment industry. One study conducted by the Communist Party Youth League in six cities in Guangdong polled 1,800 migrant workers in December 2001. It found that 80 percent worked more than ten hours per day. Most worked twelve to fourteen hours per day, and 47.2 percent said they rarely had any holidays or rest on weekends.[13] In contrast, the Labor Law stipulates, among other things, a forty-hour workweek, a maximum of thirty-six hours of overtime per month and at least one day off per week. Although aggregate statistics on industrial injuries, strikes, and labor disputes reported in the following pages may convey a general picture of hardship, they nevertheless flatten the gravity of the situation, which can occasionally be glimpsed in "extreme" cases. The phenomenon of "overwork death" *(guolaosi)* is one such example. During my fieldwork in the spring of 2002, a headline in the *Southern Metropolitan News* announced the death from exhaustion of a young woman worker who vomited blood and then dropped dead outside the gate of her garment factory, after two weeks of continuous overtime. Every year, a dozen or so workers die from overwork in Shenzhen.[14]

Horror stories of managerial mistreatment, extremely long hours of work, occupational diseases, and injuries are regular features of popular newspapers such as *Southern Metropolitan News, Shenzhen Legal Daily,* and the most critical of all, *Southern Weekend.* Official figures show steadily rising trends in all indicators of labor conflict. The number of arbitrated labor disputes rose from a modest 359 cases in 1990 to 13,280 cases in 1999.[15] According to the Shenzhen City Labor Bureau, "large and important labor disputes," those involving more than thirty people, rose from 11 in 1989 to 556 in 1998, and the yearly total of petitions increased in the same period from 317 to 23,218.[16] In 1993, there were sixty cases of strikes, large and small. By 1999, there were 110 incidents of large-scale strikes alone.[17] Shenzhen City Labor Bureau statistics reported that officially handled "spontaneous incidents," meaning large-scale collective protests and petitions, totaled 556, 540, and 682 for 1998, 1999, and 2000, respectively.[18] All these, conservative estimates at best, have earned Shenzhen the notorious title of "the worst mainland city for labor disputes."[19] It seems that as the Chinese economy becomes more integrated with global capitalism, manufacturers are confronted with ever more intense competition and shrinking margins of profit, so much so that plant closures, relocation, and restructuring are happening more frequently. Inside factories, these competitive pressures turn into longer production shifts, declining real wages, neglect of production safety, consolidation of production sites, and subsequent mass layoffs. The turn of the twenty-first century is also marked by a rising number of disputes related to social insurance contributions by employers, as a new law prescribing this payment to migrant workers was implemented in 1999. A new national law on the prevention of occupational diseases and injuries, promulgated on May 1, 2002, is also expected to usher in a large number of lawsuits against employers who fail to provide workplace safety facilities or pay for injury insurance.[20]

Worker Grievances: Exploitation and Degradation

Migrant workers confront three major types of workplace grievances that often lead to labor arbitration, litigation, and protests. They are (1) unpaid wages, illegal wage deductions, or substandard wage rates; (2) disciplinary violence and dignity violations; and (3) industrial injuries and lack of injury compensation. Underlying these predicaments is what may be called a "precapitalist" institution of labor relations, underscored by the lack of contractual and legal guarantees for the market exchange of free labor power. The treatment of Chinese workers in many of these conflicts goes beyond the Marxist notions of exploitation and alienation. I offer examples for each type to illustrate the precapitalist nature of Chinese labor relations, despite attempts by the state to impose a labor rule of law and to bring about a regulatory framework amenable to the emergent capitalist economy.

If getting paid for one's labor is a fundamental feature of capitalist employment relations, strictly speaking many Chinese workers are not yet laborers. In 1998, 65 percent of arbitrated labor disputes, that is, disputes registered with and handled by the Labor Bureau, were about nonpayment of wages and illegal deduction of wages. The proportion of these two kinds of disputes rose to 70 percent in 2002.[21] A survey published in 2003 by the official New China News Agency found that nearly three in four migrant workers have trouble collecting their pay. Each year, scores of workers threaten to commit suicide by jumping off high-rises or setting themselves on fire over unpaid wages. These desperate acts become more common in the weeks before the Chinese New Year, when many return to the countryside for family reunions.[22] Although contracts are required by the Labor Law, a national survey shows that only about one-third of the workforce employed in private enterprises have signed labor contracts with their employers. Another one-third of the workers have verbal agreements, and the rest have neither written nor verbal contracts.[23] Even among those who have signed contracts, many workers report that their employers did not allow them to see the terms stipulated in the document, and sometimes simply forged workers' signatures. Another common practice is for employers to submit to the Labor Bureau a certain number of signed contracts so as to keep up the appearance that they abide by the law. The lack of contractual regulation of employment puts workers in a vulnerable position when employers delay payment. Moreover, the exigency of survival dictates that as long as employers provide food and lodging, no matter how primitive, minimum day-to-day subsistence can be maintained, prompting workers to continue working instead of quitting. Workers have no choice but to withstand prolonged periods of wage arrears, sometimes lasting for months, because the more money they are owed, the more vested interest they have in staying with the same employer and the fewer resources they have to find another job. The following is a typical example of how workers are trapped working for an employer who does not pay them wages for months. In their dimly lit and crowded dormitory room, the representative of some sixty angry workers in a private electronics factory related their ordeal. They had not been paid for four months.

> We walked three hours from our dormitory to the Labor Bureau to lodge a complaint because we had no money. Many of us have not eaten anything in the past two days, because the boss does not allow us to use the canteen when we refuse to work. We have not been paid since the beginning of the year. He only gave an "advance loan" of one hundred yuan each to older workers. Our boss is from Jiangxi and when we demanded that he pay us, he insulted us by saying, "It's difficult to find four-legged chickens, but human beings with two legs are everywhere in Shenzhen. You can leave if you are not happy here. I can replace you in an instant." . . . We have never signed any contract. But recently, he suddenly wanted older workers to sign a contract with a monthly wage of three hundred yuan. That's an illegal wage rate. Some of us refused to sign, and we went to the Labor Bureau to complain about that as well. . . . But we have continued working here because as long as we show up at work, we can eat in the canteen and sleep in the dormitory.[24]

Sometimes, workers are recruited through acquaintances' recommendations and the employment relationship is established on the basis of a very general verbal agreement on wage rate. The common practice of deferring the payment of wages for a month means that workers as a rule have to count on employers' good faith to get paid for the first month of labor at the end of their second month of employment. A Sichuan garment worker with more than ten years of work experience in this highly competitive and time-sensitive industry recounts a grueling work life with little guarantee of collecting wages.

> There are fifteen workers in my group. They are from all over the place: Henan, Jiangxi, Hubei. I brought some of them with me when I quit the previous factory. One of my Sichuan fellow villagers *(laoxiang)* knew this boss and he introduced me to her. It's an undergarment factory. She promised each worker at least 1,600 yuan per month. But since we started working four months ago, workers have gotten only two hundred yuan per month, and I as the group leader have gotten only five hundred yuan. I asked her why the rate was so low, and she said, "I am the boss. This is my factory. I can pay what I like to pay." It's an unregistered factory, no time card, no record of the number of hours we work on the pay slips. We worked every day until 11 PM, same for Saturdays and Sundays. That's a total of 190 hours of overtime on top of eight hours every day, seven days a week. With rush orders, we worked until 2 AM continuously for weeks. In those days, every time I got up from my sewing machine, I would immediately fall over. We did not take any lunch break away from the machine. That's the same for all garment factories. The normal run of a typical order is ten days. Then, if there are no more orders, we have no work and no pay. Garment shops are particularly awful because of the dust. It stays in your throat and it's so thick that you cannot even spit it out at the end of the day. And our hands are always colored. No mask, no gloves. It's a much harsher industry than electronics.[25]

The second type of workplace conflict that has sparked labor protests is disciplinary excesses and assaults on workers' dignity. Although hardly quantifiable under the rubrics of official statistics on worker grievances, the Chinese press has carried in-depth reports of foreign firms' mistreatment of workers whose indignation has propelled lawsuits and protests. These incidents reveal almost unchecked disciplinary and physical violence used by employers to enforce everyday control over the workforce. In a Taiwan-invested hat factory in the Pearl River Delta, several workers suspected of theft were ordered to kneel for hours in front of other workers, with placards hanging from their necks announcing, "I am a thief." The entire workforce of six hundred, initially shocked and frightened, eventually organized a strike and marched to file a collective petition with the local government.[26]

Elsewhere in Guangdong, a strip search at the end of the workday of all the workers leaving the factory is a common practice that has caused much indignation among workers. In a private gem factory near Guangzhou, when a bag of four gemstones was discovered to be missing, eighty young female workers were forced to sign an agreement for the factory to conduct body searches. "We are all teenage, single women, and have never encountered such humiliation and assault," said one worker. In a huge glass-partitioned shop floor, supervisors ordered all eighty women to take off all their clothes, including underwear and shorts, and even sanitary napkins for those who were menstruating. All the clothes were then shaken out and screened for traces of gemstones. Many inexperienced workers cried as they took off their clothes, while the more mature ones protested that this was illegal. After two hours of searching, nothing turned up and workers were allowed to go back to the dormitory. Thirteen daring workers protested against the mistreatment and forced management to negotiate. When they were offered one thousand yuan each as compensation and asked to waive their right to any legal action, many reluctantly agreed to the settlement, out of fear that the company might retaliate if they pushed any further.[27]

In a Korean-owned wig factory in Shenzhen, fifty-six women workers were ordered to fold their arms behind their heads while female supervisors searched their bodies, putting their hands into their undergarments, for alleged missing wigs, while male supervisors looked on. At first workers were terrified and shaken by the violation, and many sobbed during the ordeal. Sleepless in their dormitory, many cried together. "This is a serious violation of dignity. We are traditional women from the countryside and we feel the utmost indignation at having others touch and fumble all over us while men look on," said the work group leader. The next day, a few women took the lead to complain to the local government and approached a labor lawyer to press charges. Factory management in the end agreed to a mediated settlement, and most workers quit the factory after receiving their wages and the small sum of four thousand yuan each as compensation.[28]

Finally, the use of violence as a means of disciplinary punishment is also common. Extreme cases involve security guards incarcerating and beating up workers on charges of theft or disobedience, sometimes causing deaths or injuries.[29] In a Hong Kong–owned textile mill in Guangdong, a wage arrears dispute evolved into open conflict, when workers with rocks fought with factory security wielding iron sticks during several days of riots within the factory compound.[30]

Besides nonpayment of wages and physical abuse, industrial injuries are also a common cause of labor disputes. There are no systematic official statistics on the magnitude of workplace injuries, although a few government-controlled newspapers report an average of more than ten thousand cases of workplace injuries per year in Shenzhen alone since 1997.[31] An investigative report in 1999 by a local journalist found that an average of thirty-one industrial injuries happened every day, with one work-related death every four days in Shenzhen in 1998.[32] An Amnesty International report concurs about the gravity of the situation, stating that in Shenzhen in 1998, an average of thirteen factory workers per day lost fingers or arms, and during the year, 12,189 workers were seriously injured and eighty died. This occurred against a national backdrop of 110,000 deaths from industrial accidents in 2000, rising to 140,000 in 2002.[33] A 19 percent increase in industrial deaths at factories and construction sites was registered between 2002 and 2003.[34]

Many accounts I collected reflected the same set of accident-prone conditions: gruelingly long work schedules, inadequate rest for workers, outdated machines in disrepair, little technical supervision or maintenance, and intense pressure to skip safety procedures to reach higher production quotas. The following account given by a twenty-four-year-old male worker illustrated a pervasive danger in some of the most labor-intensive factories in Shenzhen. Cao Shue had quit a plastics factory after a seventeen-year-old fellow worker had her arm cut off by a stamping machine. But he found it hard to avoid dangerous workplaces when they seem almost ubiquitous. He was injured in a Taiwanese-owned factory making medical masks from synthetic cotton.

> Our shop floor was very demanding. Thirteen to fourteen hours per day, and the machines never stop. We did not stop for lunch. We ate while tending the machines. Five of us had to tend to many machines and it was always dusty, noisy. When the accident happened, it was shortly before the Chinese New Year, and one of the more experienced workers quit and went home for the holiday, leaving me to operate a machine I had not worked on before. Only me, no technicians or masters around. It's a huge machine with a large conveyor belt and a wheel with sharp cutters. At first my hand was pulled into the machine by the belt, and then half of my body was drawn into it. Seven of my ribs were broken, and my hand was crushed. Four of my teeth were knocked out, blood gushed out of my lips, which were torn open. I basically fainted right away and lost consciousness for two weeks. When I woke up, I could not move my body at all. I could only see that my shoulder was gone.[35]

Another injured worker reported extreme exhaustion on the day both of his hands were cut off by another stamping machine in a plastic mold factory.

> I was injured at two o'clock in the morning. I had been doing the night shift for a month, because of the many rush orders we received. My body could not stand night work, and many times I felt like I could not walk or move after work. The manager wanted us to use one hand instead of two. The Labor Bureau stipulated operating with both hands, putting in the materials and closing the cap of the stamping machine

and taking the product out with two hands. But the boss wanted us to work faster. Six workers had lost their hands or fingers before me. Sometimes it was because the machines were not working properly. Other times, they were just too tired to pay attention.[36]

A twenty-three-year-old male worker from Sichuan was operating a presser in a Hong Kong–owned plastics factory when his hand and forearm were crushed. He also had seen workers poisoned by glue used in a toy factory where he had worked for several months before quitting.

> I inhaled that glue ten hours per day for almost a year. The glue tasted sweet on the tongue but it made you dizzy. I could not eat after work. When I saw food, I just wanted to vomit. I worried at that time that my body could not stand it. Every time I told my boss I wanted to quit, he would increase my pay. In the end I could tolerate no more and quit. One month later, some thirty workers got seriously sick and they were admitted to a local hospital. I considered myself very lucky at that time. Then I got into this plastics factory, because I had some Sichuanese friends there. That day, I started my shift at 7 AM and the person from the night shift was so exhausted that he left me with a broken machine. I thought I had turned it off, but actually it was still on. As I put my hand into the wheels, it moved and cut off two of my fingers. When my coworkers rushed to switch off the machine, I saw my two crushed and bloody fingers trapped in the machine.[37]

There are occupational injuries that are less visible but no less pernicious and damaging to workers' health. The pressure of working in some of the higher paying, foreign-invested firms can generate severe depression, stress, and mental illness. In one of the world's largest hard-disk manufacturers, a former line leader from Hunan reported that in her seven years there she saw seven workers going crazy at work. All were then committed to mental hospitals or sent home. Such injury is as insidious as it is invisible, especially as it hides behind the modern facade of a "high-tech" global firm.

> The girls thought it was a curse in the factory. But I think it's because of the indescribable stress at work. Management was ruthless and reprimanded workers for the most minor mistakes. You got scolded, humiliated, and fined for a loosened screw, or dropping something on the floor. On the shop floor, foremen always threatened to "deduct your 107." That's the amount of monthly bonus. Any minor mistake, like being late for a few minutes or taking a day of sick leave, can cost us 107 yuan. Some young girls did not know how to deal with this kind of abuse and they just took it all inside themselves. You can see the pain and distress in their deadly silence. At some point, they could take it no more and lost their minds.[38]

Injured workers who sued employers for compensation reported hor-ridly primitive and dangerous working conditions. As in the case of wage arrears and nonpayment, many industrial injuries occur in the context of informal employment relationships, without contractual regulation. And when injured workers seek assistance, their first reaction is to appeal to employers' benevolence and compassion, not their legal responsibilities. Rarely do workers ask for or sign formal contracts, which are largely con-sidered nonbinding by employers and workers alike. Employers willing to pay some compensation can usually placate aggrieved workers, some of whom even stay on as handicapped workers in a reduced capacity or in lower-paying posts. But when employers go to the extreme of denying workers any compensation at all, workers seek official or legal resolution. Among these several types of labor conflicts common in Shenzhen, unpaid wages and disciplinary excesses are more conducive to collective action and collective lawsuits than industrial injuries, which are often individual-based.

INSIDE THE LEGAL LABYRINTH

Observers of the Chinese labor scene have rightly chastised the Chinese state for failing to guarantee the legal rights of migrant workers. A ringing critique can be found, for instance, in the carefully documented works by Anita Chan, especially *China's Workers under Assault*, in which she rea-sonably charges the central and local governments with not consistently upholding the Labor Law.[39] But I have found that, even with flawed imple-mentation, the mere formal existence of such laws and regulatory institu-tions has significant political and cognitive consequences. In what follows, I focus on the actual practices and effects of these bureaucratic and legal pro-visions. The Labor Law, the Labor Bureau, and the Labor Dispute Arbitra-tion Committee figure prominently in the trajectory of migrant workers' struggles.

Beginning with the moment of workers' first encounter with the Labor Law, the labor bureaucracy and the court, no matter how biased, help frame workers' grievances as public and legal matters demanding state interven-tion. A remark by a woman worker encapsulates the impact of the discov-ery of the law on collective conceptual transformation: "once we saw the terms of the Labor Law, we realized that what we thought of as bitterness and bad luck were actually violations of our legal rights and interests."[40] Moreover, at every step along the legal labyrinth, going through the motion of formal procedures takes on a life of its own. Gross injustice in the labor arbitration process or indignation experienced in the courtroom will at times solidify workers' determination to seek justice, and if injustice persists, workers will be radicalized to take their grievances to the public. I will report cases from my fieldwork to show that at each of the three stages of the official labor dispute resolution process, practices of labor officials and judges have directly caused labor protests. As this is labor politics embedded in the legal system, legality is the vocabulary of worker resistance as well as state control.

Learning about the Law

Let us begin at the beginning. How do workers get to know the law? Serendipity plays a role, but most consequential is the presence of the Labor Bureau. A strike in a handbag factory is perhaps the most illuminating case of the political effect of the Labor Law, and also the fortuitous way in which it comes to workers' attention. Surprisingly, it was the employer who brought knowledge about the Labor Law into the factory. In January 2002, two thousand workers participated in a plantwide strike that shut down production for two days. For years, workers had endured a punishing pace of work and overtime shifts for wage rates below the legal standard. They decided they could take no more only when management imposed a "training session" every morning, drilling workers in the "correct" answers in anticipation of an upcoming labor standards inspection by the factory's American customers. This episode was a moment of awakening, as a security guard who participated in the strike recalled with his fellow technicians.

> The girls in the sewing department started it. They work the hardest but their pay has always been very low—too low—and their hours extremely long. The factory makes workers sign pay slips to show that they get about eight hundred yuan, but they actually get six hundred yuan, including overtime pay. Management lowers the piece rates once workers begin to earn more. Overtime is a must, almost always until 11 PM or midnight every night. Never a Sunday off. It's a bad factory. During the training, workers were given model answers about the Labor Law, and they had to memorize them so that when customers' inspectors come and ask, they will deliver the line, "Five-day workweek, eight-hour day, Sunday off, two hours maximum overtime each day and not more than five nights per week. We are all very satisfied with our work schedule." It's the first time we learned the details of the Labor Law, and what we were not getting.[41]

Likewise, in the case of a labor dispute involving construction workers, the employer had been violating the law for many years, forging workers' signatures on labor contracts and denying workers access to the terms of the contract. After one worker managed to seize a copy of the labor contract from the company administration and saw the terms of the Labor Law mentioned in the labor contract, several worker representatives decided to check out the law on their own. They stationed themselves in the Shenzhen Book Center, a multistory comprehensive bookstore downtown, and started reading.

> For two weeks, we had only one meal each day and we read everything on the Labor Law and labor dispute arbitration in the bookstore. Before this, we had no idea what the law said about us migrant workers. For many years, we had only heard about the labor contract, but we did not press the company hard enough when they refused to give us a copy. We always felt it was unjust that we were treated unequally, always inferior to workers with Shenzhen residence registration. Since we started this struggle with the company, many workers have begun to read newspapers. Some even cut out labor dispute stories for circulation in the dormitory. The more we read these legal reports, the more we understand the legal issues involved in our own case.[42]

Most often, workers come into contact with the law by visiting the Labor Bureau located in downtown Shenzhen. Usually a useful educational experience, this first step also generates ambivalent reactions among workers toward the state and the law. During my numerous visits to the Labor Bureau accompanying workers filing arbitration requests or seeking legal information, I observed that state agents treated migrant workers with condescension, looking down on them as ignorant supplicants rather than fellow citizens with rights. The reception rooms of the Petition Department on the ground floor and the Labor Dispute Arbitration Committee on the fifth floor are as a rule crowded. On the fifth floor, the two overworked female clerks routinely yelled at workers who flocked around their desks, anxiously pressing their faces against the partition windows. They dished out insulting remarks, ordering workers to read the terms of the Labor Law themselves rather than explaining to them what those terms are. In many cases, upon receiving a dispute arbitration application from workers, these clerks would initiate mediation with employers over the phone while the workers involved sat and listened to the dialogue. If workers refused to accept what the clerks considered an acceptable settlement, the clerks would authoritatively discourage workers from taking further action, reminding them that a formal procedure would take a long time, or that resourceful employers always prevail in lawsuits. Their message was that workers should be content with a mediated deal, even one that falls short of the law, because most employers will not fully adhere to the law anyway.

Official contempt for migrant workers is also evident in the corridors of the Labor Bureau. One day, I was with a group of workers who had gathered outside the reception room to discuss their strategy for the mediation meeting with their employers that was to begin in an hour. Exhausted, they squatted on the ground in small groups, while labor officials passing by glared suspiciously, and one yelled, "Go! Go! Go! Who says you can hang around here? Go back to the factory!" Workers, visibly upset and filled with indignation, dared not utter of word in reply, but made the concessionary gesture of moving toward the stairways. As soon as the officer entered the elevator, everyone returned to the original position in the corridor and continued the discussion. This kind of ritualistic confirmation of official superiority and mass deference happens in many guises inside the Labor Bureau. Local state power is personified by these arrogant officers, and workers approach the bureau more as subjects than citizens.

Nevertheless, no matter how much the exchanges between street-level bureaucrats and workers border on verbal abuse and humiliation, officials distribute information about the law and procedural rules for launching an arbitration application on a daily basis. Representatives of a cement factory, for instance, tried to file an application for dispute arbitration, and despite rude treatment by the clerk there, they were directed to the publication office on the twelfth floor, where they purchased books laying out the details of specific regulations on which to base their complaint. The courtyard outside the Petition Office, which is attached to the main building, is also a vibrant marketplace for legal know-how. "Black lawyers," individuals without professional registration but who charge a service fee for providing legal representation in court, congregate to offer advice and moral encouragement to potential clients. Petitioning workers from different factories also exchange experiences and grievances with one another.

Another public source of information for workers is found in the hospital wards that treat workers suffering from industrial injuries. The site of tragic and heart-rending scenes, it is also the place where fellow patients provide solace and, more important, legal knowledge and referrals to otherwise lonely and helpless victims. A woman worker who recalled thinking about committing suicide after seeing her hand crushed by a machine in a plastics factory recalled,

> There were many injured workers in the hospital. It was a horror scene. New patients came in everyday, with their fingers or hands cut off by machines. They [fellow patients] told me not to be afraid, and they talked to me about workers' legal rights to get insurance compensation. . . .
> Then, when I put on my artificial hand, another patient handed me the

business card of a lawyer. A home-village friend of hers was also injured
and she knew this lawyer. I also bought books about the Labor Law and
began reading.[43]

The concentration of factories in Shenzhen also facilitates the circulation
of knowledge of the law and regulations. Rows of multistoried factory buildings line an entire district, with factories occupying one or two floors each.
Here, workers from various factories can easily socialize, their ties sometimes further cemented by common provincial or hometown origins.
Although most factories build and manage their own dormitories, the
Shenzhen government also rents dormitories to smaller establishments.
These dormitory buildings provide social space shared by workers from different plants in the district. A woman worker representative in a labor dispute at an electronics factory explained how word about successful labor
action in another factory spread and workers in the same district learned
about their legal rights regarding dismissal compensation.

The forty-nine workers who dared to lead the strike on April 29 and
went to the Labor Bureau insisted that the company should compensate
us when it terminated our contract. . . . Some time ago, another factory
in the next building folded, and workers got compensation according
to the Labor Law. Some of us had friends in that factory, and they came
to visit us in our dorm. That's how we learned about the legal compensation. That's why we were not afraid.[44]

Due to the geographical concentration of factories, it is not surprising that
"contagious" strikes sometimes occur among companies in the same locality.
A report on "spontaneous labor incidents" stated that, in Guangdong
between 1994 and 1995, there were 182 cases of strikes involving more than
four hundred people, accounting for 28 percent of all strikes in the province
in that period. Usually lasting for two to five days, these strikes tend to
expand in scale through emulation by workers in neighboring factories.[45]

In sum, these stories suggest the powerful transformative effect of legal
knowledge. The law facilitates a reframing of workplace grievances from
normal hardships and unavoidable "bad luck" to wrongdoing proscribed by
the state. The law is at once a crucial power lever for workers confronting
employers and an authoritative reference on the "value" of labor. With few
alternative references to determine "fair" wages, most workers accept the
government's standard of minimum wage as a reasonable wage "floor." In
mid-2002, it amounted to 574 yuan per month or 3.3 yuan per hour in
Shenzhen City and 440 yuan or 2.7 yuan, respectively, in other districts
under Shenzhen's jurisdiction. A worker explains the typical mentality:

We are not greedy or jealous of others making more money than we do. We just want the legal minimum. If the boss did not push us to this desperate situation [not paying them for three months], we would be happy with what we used to get: 2.05 yuan per hour. As long as we can get by and save one or two hundred yuan per month, we don't want to create trouble.[46]

Similar logic applies to workers seeking compensation for workplace injuries. The government compensation standards are usually accepted by workers as reasonable rates of compensation for injury or loss of arms, hands, or fingers. Many maintain that whatever the legal standard, they will accept it as just and fair compensation "because it is the law."

Plant Closure and Exit Solidarity

The effect of the law in instigating labor activism is heightened when workers are collectively dismissed. Worker solidarity peaks at the point of collective exit from the factory, occasioned by plant closure or relocation. A mass layoff unites workers who are otherwise divided by shop floor, local origin, rank, and skill level. Fear of dismissal also recedes as workers feel they no longer have anything to lose in asserting their demands. The sense of urgency and desperation that prevails at the moment of plant closure also leads workers to pursue multiple modes of struggle. Take the case of a May Day labor dispute in an electronics factory making adaptors. On the eve of the week-long holiday celebrating Labor Day in 2002, sixty workers walked out of their afternoon shift and together went to the Labor Bureau to lodge a complaint against their employers' refusal to pay dismissal compensation and pension insurance. The firm had announced its relocation from Shenzhen to a nearby town in early April but had not yet made clear its policy of compensating those who did not want to move to the new factory. Afraid that the boss would "escape" during the week-long holiday, and having failed to obtain a registration number at the overcrowded Labor Bureau reception office, the workers marched to the city government and sought emergency help. The Labor Bureau Inspection Team, bowing to the pressure of the mass presence of workers still clad in their blue uniforms, called a mediation meeting between management and worker representatives an hour before the factory closed for the holiday. In the end, the employer conceded and promised to compensate workers according to the law. He calculated that his new plant was located in a township falling within the Shenzhen government jurisdiction, and keeping a good record with the government would be important in the future.

Another example of "exit solidarity" among migrant workers can be found in the electronics subcontractor for Wal-Mart mentioned at the beginning of this chapter. This Hong Kong–invested export-processing factory, established in 1988, committed all the most common violations of the Labor Law. The firm did not sign labor contracts with workers, did not pay the legal minimum wage, did not follow the overtime wage scale established in the Labor Law, and never contributed to workers' pension insurance. These practices had gone on for years, and workers complained in vain by writing opinion letters to management and even to the local Labor Bureau. Then, after a drastic reduction in production orders from the United States in the aftermath of the terrorist attacks in September 2001, the factory frequently suspended production and imposed no-pay vacations on the entire workforce. Then, in late December, the factory announced that it would cut production capacity and relocate to Dongguan. According to one worker leader,

> Line leaders became concerned and they jointly organized the girls in their lines to petition to different government departments, demanding allowances during this no-work period. Line leaders saw that their interests were compromised like those of the workers. And eight hundred workers signed the petition letter to the Labor Bureau.[47]

Workers divided themselves into three groups and marched to the Labor Bureau, the district government, and the district court, respectively, deliberately putting public pressure on the authorities to pay attention to their plight. Thus began a tortuous process of negotiation with management, mediation by the Labor Bureau, an appeal lawsuit initiated by the factory, and finally a court settlement. It is obvious that workers were prompted to act collectively because of the imminent plant closure, a time when stakes were the highest, solidarity the strongest, and opportunity cost the lowest. It is a time of reckoning when all accumulated grievances over the years can come together in a single explosive action.

The Contested Terrain of Illiberal Legality

Whether driven by newfound awareness of the law and workers' legal rights or spurred to action by plant closure and relocation, aggrieved workers confront an arduous legal terrain founded on an illiberal regime of "rule of law." The central government sees the law as an instrument indispensable for creating an attractive environment for investment, managing social conflict, and maintaining social and political stability.[48] But at the local government levels, local officials' overriding concern to develop the local economy easily fosters a procapital regulatory environment detrimental to labor interests and rights. Some government bureaus, however, have their own departmental interests in helping workers to use the law or at least in promoting the ideology of legality. The raison d'être of the legal aid centers, labor dispute arbitrators, and Letters and Visits Bureaus is tied to workers' interests and the implementation of labor regulations, no matter how compromised. These forces and interests work at cross purposes in some cases but in unison in others, leaving room for routine arbitration and litigation to evolve into less predictable episodes of mass action. Following the three-step procedure of labor dispute resolution, I illustrate how workers surmount with varying success the barriers posed by local government, legal professionals, and employers. At every turn, the pressure and exigency of eking out a living at the margin of a freewheeling capitalistic city often compels opportunistic compromises with employers' financial concessions.

Step 1: Mediation   Because the promotion of "harmonious" labor relations and a stable society stands at the heart of China's labor law regime, informal steps such as conciliation and mediation play a key role in the process. Although mediation is optional, meaning that either party in the dispute can reject mediation, it is strongly encouraged. Mediation is to be followed by arbitration, a necessary precondition for litigation.[49] Most workers who come with grievances to the Labor Bureau will first be directed to the Petition Department, where the on-duty officers does an initial screening of the facts of the case. Even here, the clerks will attempt mediation, as will those at the arbitration application department, the first step in entering the arbitration process.[50] Workers wanting official intervention, whether in the form of arbitration or mediation, have to file an application with the Labor Dispute Arbitration Committee housed in the Labor Bureau within six months of the alleged violation of their rights. It is incumbent on the employees to establish the existence of an employment relationship with the employer in question. For that, they have to show a labor contract or evidence of employment (such as wage slips or factory identification cards with their names). They also need to submit a copy of the commercial registration record of their employer, for which they have to pay sixty yuan to obtain a photocopy from the Bureau of Industry and Commerce. Table 10 shows that from 1986 to 1999, about 90 percent of all labor dispute cases handled by the Shenzhen City Labor Bureau involved mediation. In 1999, for instance, of the 13,280 disputes handled, 11,062 went through mediation, including those that reached the arbitration stage.

The express principles of mediation, according to the State Council Rules for Handling Labor Disputes in Enterprises (1993), should be their founda-

TABLE 10 *Handling Methods and Results of Arbitrated Labor Disputes, Shenzhen City, 1986–1999*

	Total	1986	1987	1988	1989	1990	1991	1992	1993	1994	1995	1996	1997	1998	1999
Total cases arbitrated	70,351	54	193	402	500	359	322	316	2,900	6,792	8,941	10,983	13,179	12,130	13,280
Handling Method															
Mediation	63,807	38	111	260	338	236	177	164	2,660	6,506	8,611	10,442	12,267	10,935	11,062
Arbitration	3,779	0	11	37	41	36	38	42	69	81	93	246	542	894	1,649
(Appeal)	(2,211)	(0)	(4)	(7)	(10)	(16)	(5)	(29)	(36)	(12)	(56)	(109)	(341)	(781)	(805)
Other	2,765	16	71	105	121	87	107	110	171	205	237	295	370	301	569
Result															
Favorable to entrepreneurs	9,840	8	31	71	87	62	55	45	463	1,039	1,254	2,001	3,194	638	892
Favorable to employees	48,544	34	105	203	247	196	186	207	1,896	4,861	7,003	7,724	5,812	10,569	9,501
Favorable to both	11,967	12	57	128	166	101	81	64	541	892	684	1,258	4,173	923	2,887

SOURCE: Shenzhen City Labor Bureau, ed., *Constructing Harmonious Labor Relations* (Beijing: China Labor and Social Security Publishing House, 2000), p. 170 [in Chinese].

tion in law and their voluntary nature. Yet, in actual practice, and depending on the individual labor supervisor or the willingness of the employers, workers report varying degrees of noncompliance and even blatant violations of these principles. Mediation quite often inadvertently spawns more unconventional actions than it manages to contain, especially because labor officials tend to take workers more seriously when they appear in large numbers. In the following incident, a worker representative learned the hard way that small-group petitions never bear fruit. Only when all 154 workers participated in a strike in their factory did the Labor Bureau arrange for mediation.

> Six or seven of us had lodged complaints against low wages several times before, but the Labor Bureau couldn't care less about us migrant workers. All they said was that they would come to investigate, but nothing happened. This time, after three consecutive months of receiving only seventy or one hundred yuan, we really had no choice. Soon we would starve to death. We lodged another complaint with the City Labor Supervision Team but the company did not budge. When the factory demanded that public security arrest our coworker [for sabotage and deliberately cutting off the electricity supply], all of us were furious. We stopped working and protested outside the factory. . . . We were about to march to the city government when the Legal Aid Center intervened and the Labor Bureau immediately arranged for mediation.[51]

In another collective dispute, five hundred workers gathered outside the Petition Department of the Shenzhen City Labor Bureau one afternoon, after they found that the district Labor Bureau was toothless and not interested in workers' plights. The district officers there left the factory even when mediation conducted two days earlier did not satisfy workers' demands for a labor contract, legal wage rates, and social insurance payments. But when hundreds of workers showed up at the Shenzhen City Labor Bureau, the bureau chief reacted promptly. The bureau chief personally came to talk to them, and the chief of the Labor Supervision Department showed up together with the district Labor Bureau chief. One worker representative was bemused by this cordial official attitude, especially the Bureau's offer to provide free transportation with their official fleet of coaches.

> Once the chief at the petition department saw so many of us, he took up the case immediately. No need to wait in line. . . . Workers were infuriated to see the district Labor Bureau chief, and when he tried to explain, workers shouted, "We don't believe you anymore," and they drowned out his speech. When the Shenzhen chief talked, they all quieted down and listened. . . . He also said that, to ensure our safety, the Labor

Bureau would dispatch commuter buses for their employees to take us back to our factory. Many of the workers had walked three hours from Nanshan district to Shenzhen City, because police came and stopped their buses on the way here.[52]

Frustration with the futility of mediation and the compromising attitudes of labor officials easily discredit the bureaucratic process and lead workers to resort to protests and demonstrations at the city government building. Offering a rare glimpse of the prevalence of such radicalization of labor arbitration, national official statistics on arbitrated labor disputes in 1997 reported that, out of a total of 70,792 arbitrated cases handled, 854 protests (or 1.2 percent) were triggered by the arbitration process itself. If we use this rate as an estimate for other years, incidents of arbitration-related labor unrest amounted to 1,568 in 2000, 1,455 in 1999, and 1,107 in 1998.[53] These figures capture but the tip of the iceberg of the total volume of labor mobilization.

Worker representatives often notice with disdain the government's overwhelming priority of reaching a mediated agreement even at the expense of the law. Instead of adjudicating legal rights and wrongs, labor officials placate employers to get them to agree to a settlement. A woman representing fifteen workers owed wages by their employer recalled how they were flabbergasted at the mediation meeting at the Labor Bureau.

> The labor officer was almost cooing to our boss. He said in a very sweet and gentle tone, "I beg you, Madame, to have pity on these workers who work for you. Do a good, charitable thing. Workers' lives are very hard. Please don't force them out of the factory." We scolded him at once for talking like this. We did not want any pity! She owed us our rightful wages!. . . . It was only when our boss ignored him that he changed his attitude and became more helpful to us.[54]

For labor officials, mediation is a strategy to defuse tension and minimize administrative costs expended on any one case. Workers have urgent and real existential need for a quick resolution at an early stage of the dispute. Given their excessively long workdays and high mobility across factories, migrant workers normally cannot afford the time, energy, and opportunity cost of resorting to litigation. But workers also expect a law-based resolution. A labor representative in the Wal-Mart subcontracting factory explained workers' disappointment and tactics when she found that the Labor Bureau officer handling the mediation cared only about reaching an agreement, without any interest in enforcing the spirit and letter of the Labor Law. Eventually, disgruntled workers took to the streets.

The officer from the Labor Bureau did not care about who was right and who was wrong. He just wanted to stand in the middle, asking both sides to concede. It's so apparent that workers were the victims in this case, but he did not place legal responsibility on the company. . . . We think that they are anxious not to antagonize investors, and that's why they care only about getting an agreement. It's the company that illegally deducted our wages, but the Labor Bureau did not impose any compensation or fine. The whole thing upset us so much that we lost interest in negotiating. All we thought of was to organize a demonstration at the city government.[55]

When workers distributed handbills drafted by their line leaders about the routes to the city government, management reacted by calling public security and the Labor Bureau. Officers came to lecture workers and threatened arrests if they demonstrated. One worker recalled, "The vice-chief of the Labor Bureau said, 'It [workers' action] damages the city's image.' But I just thought that it could only be legal for us to petition the city government. Some workers were scared by his threat of arrest. So, in the end we started negotiating with the management one more time."[56]

In other cases, mediation before arbitration does bring immediate if less than law-based relief for workers. The Labor Bureau still carries considerable weight among investors who plan to stay or even expand their businesses in Shenzhen. The intervention of a labor supervisor will in many cases extract sufficient concessions from employers to appease workers. An employer agreed to negotiate and implement the agreement with workers after workers showed up at the gate of the city government and petitioned the Labor Bureau, demanding economic compensation and repayment of their insurance contributions when the factory relocated to a smaller township in Shenzhen. He showed his disdain for workers appealing to the government, lecturing them in the negotiation like a domineering patriarch reprimanding his own children.

You should not stage that kind of sit-down strike. It's very uncivilized, and it indicates your low quality. . . . I know people in the court, and I know how I can use the court to drag workers into the legal process, three months or a year. You cannot afford to play this game with me. I have built a new factory worth tens of millions of yuan. What's workers' compensation compared to this investment? I'll give you that money, if only out of charity. But you have to promise me not to complain to the Labor Bureau again.[57]

In the end, the employer paid workers the legal compensation, but the workers were hardly empowered by the episode. As in the corridor of the Labor Bureau, normally articulate and feisty worker leaders turned compliant and reserved around the negotiation table, taking the boss's verbal beating with lowered heads and occasional tears rolling down a few faces.

Step 2: Arbitration   The second step in the three-step formal process of labor dispute resolution is arbitration. Any party may initiate arbitration proceedings by submitting a request for arbitration to the local Labor Dispute Arbitration Commission within sixty days from the date of the dispute. At this stage, mediation may still happen and result in a written agreement. Following the national pattern,[58] most cases brought for arbitration in Shenzhen are resolved through mediation facilitated by labor arbitrators.

In Shenzhen, at the city and district levels, there are twenty-one full-time arbitrators, and sixty-eight part-time arbitrators. Some 80 percent of all disputes are handled by a single arbitrator, although complicated and collective cases are usually arbitrated by a committee, with representatives from the city union, Labor Bureau, and business association. Some 70 percent of arbitrated cases in Shenzhen from 1995 to 1999 were handled by these grassroots units, although serious and collective cases were usually handled by the Shenzhen City Labor Bureau. The quality and legal knowledge of labor arbitrators are often uneven. One former Labor Bureau official also points to poor legal training and inadequate supervision of arbitrators' performance.

> The many part-time labor arbitrators receive only a one- to two-week crash course on the Labor Law and relevant regulations. Of the full-time staff, only two out of more than twenty have formal training in law. In general, civil servants in the Labor Bureau have low status compared to other branches of the government, and you cannot expect to find the best and brightest here. . . . There is absolutely no systematic assessment or supervision of their work. If either party is not happy with the arbitral award, they can only appeal to the courts.[59]

A group of 150 workers involved in two cases of arbitration, one on wage rates and another on an illegal contract, found to their dismay that the two arbitrators handling their cases were not equally competent. One handled the case legally and professionally, and the other was so incompetent that he gave them wrong instructions.

> The first arbitrator did not say much during the hearing. He basically looked at the evidence. We accused the company of charging us illegal deposits [to guarantee that workers will not quit arbitrarily], and we had the receipts for that. But the company's lawyer still argued that the company had not taken any deposits. The arbitrator smiled, finding that absurd. When the arbitrator asked the company's lawyer how the company calculated wages, the lawyer said he did not know. The arbitrator

then reprimanded him and asked him not to come if he continued to know nothing about the company. We thought that this arbitrator was fair. He followed the legal procedure. But the one in charge of our contract dispute was totally different. He told us to go to the Public Security Bureau to verify our contract, but the Public Security Bureau said they did not handle civil cases! He also asked us to obtain photocopies of our contract. When we turned them in, he said we should not have done so because we said the signatures were counterfeits. He's a piece of shit, and knows nothing. We have decided to appeal to the courts.[60]

Another problem is local protectionism in grassroots labor dispute arbitration committees. At the township level, where many foreign-invested and private export-processing factories operate, a layer of Labor Relation Conciliation and Dispute Arbitration Subcommittees, attached to the local Labor Bureau office, has been set up. By the end of 1999, there were forty-nine Conciliation Committees with 264 coordinators and twenty-one Labor Arbitration Subcommittees at the township level.[61] Staffed by personnel drawn from local village committees and township heads, these committees are fertile soil for employer-government collusion. The village and township governments depend on employers for revenue and often are themselves coowners of these firms. The employer-bias of many of these grassroots arbitrators gives rise to widespread disillusionment about bureaucratic neutrality and legality at the local level.

Besides the varying quality of labor arbitrators and intervention by local officials, many of whom have a conflict of interest, workers have to overcome another hurdle in the bureaucratic process. They are responsible for gathering the necessary documentation about the company and evidence of its wrongdoings. For workers who are owed months of back wages, dismissed by employers, and kicked out of the dormitories, some cannot afford even regular meals. The logistical costs (e.g., for obtaining the business registration certificate of their factory, photocopying, cell phone or pager, and transportation) involved in arbitration and litigation are prohibitively expensive. On top of that, some government departments join in the fray to extract exorbitant fees for paperwork needed for arbitration. Several lawyers criticized the government's predatory fee scales in our interviews. One lawyer's remarks are typical.

Workers initiate arbitration because they don't have money. But they have to pay up front an arbitration fee (4 percent of the targeted compensation), in addition to a fifty-yuan case-handling fee. Then, the Industry and Commerce Bureau *(gongshangju)* charges a sixty-yuan fee for a copy of the factory's commercial registration. The Labor Arbitration Commission requires this payment before it opens a case.

It's absurd that the *gongshangju* fixes its own fee schedule for looking up company records in their computers, fifty yuan for ten minutes, one yuan for a page of photocopy. And there are lawyers' fees.[62]

Yet local state interests are fragmented. Not all units of government are one-sidedly procapital or have an interest in denying workers' rights. On the contrary, there are government units that have departmental interests in championing workers' legal rights. Legal aid centers run by the judiciary may not have all the manpower needed to fully meet workers' needs, but on-duty lawyers do offer legal advice every day, and some workers in this study find them very accessible and resourceful, giving indispensable help in their legal battles. They run the nationwide "148" hotline offering legal counseling services to all who call, and legal representation is given to applicants fulfilling certain economic criteria. In the Baoan district of Shenzhen, twelve full-time staff members (six of whom are registered lawyers) have been serving a migrant population of 2.5 million since 1997. Every year, an average of two hundred workers receive assistance, mostly regarding industrial injury compensation and wage arrears conflicts.[63] During one visit to this center, the lawyer on duty was visited by a young peasant whose sister had suddenly died in the apartment provided by her employer. In a harsh and condescending tone typical of Chinese officials, he did not mince words when the helpless and nervous peasant showed signs of ignorance about the legal procedure. Bureaucratic mannerism aside, however, the lawyer dutifully took up the investigation, answered all queries, and provided professional advice on how to seek employer compensation. Moreover, workers have reported encountering fair and helpful labor arbitrators and judges. Although the labor rule of law is often subject to the personal caprice of officials and may be twisted by economic and political forces, the laws and regulations are universal principles that are available for use by well-intentioned labor officials and legal professionals.

Overall, of workers who manage to sustain their effort within the official resolution system, some have seen their rights upheld. According to official statistics, the rate of favorable arbitral awards or mediated settlements for employees far outweighs that for employers. Table 10 shows that employees' winning rate stood at a high of 70 percent over a fourteen-year period between 1986 and 1999. This pattern dovetails with the national one in which most disputes are also resolved in favor of employees. For instance, in 2000, employees won 58 percent of the cases handled through labor arbitration, and in an additional 31 percent of the cases, the resolution partially favored both parties.[64] Of course, we cannot tell from such statistics what the state means by "in favor" of either party. Neither do these statistics suggest anything about how effective the court is in enforcing its award decisions.

Step 3: Litigation This brings us to the stage of litigation. In Shenzhen, between 1995 and 1999, some 50 to 70 percent of arbitral awards were appealed in the courts, although the absolute number remained relatively small compared to the total number of cases handled by the Labor Arbitration Commission.[65] Within fifteen days of an arbitral award being issued, either party can appeal the award in the courts. From then on, the case is adjudicated under the Civil Procedure Law, and heard by a three-judge panel *(heyiting)*. A civil case has to be concluded with judgment within six months of the filing date. If an adverse judgment is appealed, judgment on the appeal must be completed within three months. In normal circumstances, a case that undergoes all three formal steps will take at least a year or more to obtain a final verdict.

Many employers prefer arbitration and litigation to mediation. Whereas implementing a mediated agreement incurs immediate financial losses by way of repaying docked wages, dismissal compensation, or pension insurance contributions, employers can always count on their financial advantage over workers to wait them out in the litigation process. Lawyers term this abuse "litigation exhaustion" *(cansu)*, a common strategy by employers to exploit employees' "litigation fatigue" *(sulei)*.[66] Even among the most determined worker representatives, the seemingly interminable waiting time for a court hearing and decision strains the limits of their financial resources, mental resolve, and solidarity, especially under the constant pressure to eke out a livelihood without much protection or support from society or the government in Shenzhen. A woman worker related her experience with her employer's manipulation of the legal system.

> When we first went to the Labor Bureau, the petition officer suggested mediation, and we agreed because we needed the money right away. The boss refused and claimed that she had already paid us. We went right away to register this case for arbitration. Fifteen days later, the arbitration hearing began. The arbitrator was sympathetic to us, encouraging us to speak clearly and not to make factual mistakes in what we said. He reassured us that we were asking for our rightful dues from the boss. He helped us compile a form on the amount of back wages and deductions. . . . We waited for another fifteen days for the second hearing, the boss was a no-show again, and then we won an arbitral award. We took the award immediately to the Nanshan court to ask for immediate payment. On the last day of the fifteen-day period, the boss responded to the arbitral award and took it to the Lowu [Luowu or

Luohu?] court for appeal. So, we were again made to wait for the court to inform us. It was the Spring Festival, a long holiday. We waited for another month, and then the court decided that neither party had an address in Lowu [Luowu or Luohu?], and the case could not be tried there. It was a deliberate tactic of the boss, just to prolong the process so that we would quit. So we waited for the courts to transfer the case. . . . We kept calling the court to urge them to act. I was angry at their inaction and yelled at them that they should think about workers' hardship. . . . In the end we finally received notification that the case would be heard on May 16. Fifteen of us had already dispersed to different jobs. Had we not called the court all the time, we would have missed this hearing because they failed to contact the worker representative, who happened to be temporarily out of town.[67]

Another factor contributing to the unpredictability of court decisions has to do with the judiciary and legal professionals. Official attempts to modernize and upgrade the qualifications of judicial personnel only confirm how rudimentary that establishment remains today.[68] Judges' salaries come from the local government budget, which in turn is dependent on taxation and business investments. A labor lawyer specializing in industrial injury compensation cases uses this telling example in a township court in Shenzhen to illustrate the general situation of court-business collusion.

At the end of a court hearing, the judge said to me in public, "Lawyer Zhou, if the court adheres to all the laws and regulations of the provincial government, all these factories would move elsewhere and the local economy would collapse. Who would be responsible then? You?" He later on even stated explicitly to my client that the two basic levels of the local courts in neighboring Dongguan City have reached a consensus that they could not follow the letter of the law. Judges in the mainland are part of the local government, just like officials of the Labor Bureau. Their rice bowls depend on the income of the local government and they in turn depend on private and foreign enterprises.[69]

The fledgling legal profession, like the judiciary, constitutes an additional obstacle to justice for aggrieved workers.[70] Plagued by the profession's low status and financial insecurity, many Chinese lawyers avoid taking on labor cases because the returns are too low. Ethan Michelson's study on this subject has found that Chinese lawyers are prone to screening out labor cases, adopting tactics of discouragement as an indirect refusal mechanism, and misinforming and miseducating clients about the legal merits of their cases.[71] In my fieldwork, lawyers I interviewed explained that they would take on labor cases only when the cases are big and have a social impact, which would mean that the law firm would receive publicity. In the few cases where workers manage to pool their funds to hire a certified lawyer, there is no guarantee that they will obtain high-quality legal services. In one meeting with their lawyers, worker representatives whom I accompanied spent the entire hour wrangling with their lawyers about legal fees demanded by the latter for writing a short paragraph in the arbitration application. "I am taking losses with your case," a lawyer uttered with contempt to two female workers representing some two hundred workers who had already paid him thirty thousand yuan for simply showing up during two fruitless negotiation meetings with the employer.

The result is the emergence of a market for unregistered legal representatives. In 2002, there were an estimated 1,700 registered lawyers in Shenzhen, and a few hundred "black-market" or "barefoot" legal workers. Since Chinese courts allow unpaid legal representatives to represent an individual in court, these "black lawyers" can take advantage of this provision and charge fees under the table. There is a thriving market for black lawyers in Shenzhen, despite government campaigns to eradicate them.[72] No matter how inadequate and uneven their qualifications and competence, in many cases their experience with the court system gives confidence to workers who are otherwise easily intimidated by administrative procedures, court personnel, and legal language.

Watching workers in courtrooms speaks volumes about the enormity of the disadvantages they confront. Even the most articulate workers feel inhibited when challenged by the demand of linguistic precision, the authority of the bench, the technicality of evidence, and the letter of the law. Moral righteousness is insufficient to win a legal point in the courtroom. Many times, I saw workers failing to answer the simplest of questions, such as when they quit the factory, whether they still lived in the dormitory, or whether they had signed labor contracts. Whether out of distrust of the court or fear of being trapped by trick questions, workers give very clumsy and long-winded details in places where the judge wants precise and direct responses. Palpable frustration and anger simmers on both sides.

In the case of the 188 construction workers with which I opened this chapter, several times during the final hearing, workers expressed their impatience with the court's seemingly interminable process of gathering and examining evidence, howling aloud in court, "Give the verdict now!" And when the judge asked one of the workers to get proof from the Ministry of Civil Affairs to show that he was directly recruited by the employer through a poverty alleviation quota, an uproar broke out among workers, protesting what they considered an unrealistic request. "He will never get it!" they shouted. It had been eight months since they first petitioned the Labor Bureau. Since then, they had seen the hearing postponed three times before it first took place in May. Many workers felt so alienated by the entire process that some preferred bringing the case to Beijing's National People's Congress instead of waiting any longer. With immense pent-up disillusion, aggravated by the economic pressure of survival after being dismissed by their employers, workers took radical action on June 5, 2002, the date of the three-month deadline for announcing a judicial decision. Unable to obtain any verdict from the court, angry workers decided immediately to block the roads outside the courthouse, holding up traffic for more than twenty minutes. When armed police arrived and threatened arrests, workers retreated back to the courthouse to meet with the vice-director of the court. A worker representative spoke of his fellow workers' utter distrust of the law and the government.

> The practice of the court violates the law! In previous times, whenever the court was scheduled to hear our case, it was either canceled or postponed. Same thing this time. When we tracked down the judge and asked her on May 30, she guaranteed that there would be no more delay. Then only five days later, it was delayed again. Workers can take it no more, and how can anyone not take up radical actions? It seems that if we did not resort to radical actions, they would not resolve our case. I really want to ask, whether the "big" in the title "Big Judge" (da faguan) means big justice without self-interest (dagongwusi) or just big and powerful people?[73]

One week later, the final verdict was handed down with the heavy presence of one hundred police officers. Even before the formal court session, workers realized that the company they worked for had prepared small payments to be given to workers on the spot, indicating that the company had received advance word from the court about the verdict. In the end, workers were totally dismayed by what they considered a rigged decision: the company was found not guilty of its decade-long deduction of 8 percent of workers' wages and default on pension contributions, and the court recommended that it pay each worker a small compensation (about 4,800 yuan) on a voluntary basis. With this result, even the usually calm and determined worker representative muttered, "The judge was paid off. . . . The laws are good, but the legal system doesn't work. . . . If we had to do it again, we would just protest."[74]

Radicalization of conflict may occur in any stage of the arbitration-litigation process. When workers with standing grievances find legal grounds for their case, they expect official attention. But bureaucratic red tape and political pressure from big companies or state firms may affect whether workers can even lodge a complaint. Feeling unjustly abandoned by the government, workers react with mass sit-ins, collective petitions, and strikes. The following episode of traffic blockage throws into sharp relief the process of radicalization. On the morning of May 22, 2002, more than sixty construction workers went to the petition office of the Shenzhen city government. The office directed them to the Labor Bureau, which then said that because the workers had no written contract with the contractor and could not prove the registration of the construction company they worked for, the Labor Bureau was unable to investigate the case. By that time, workers were already very frustrated and emotional. They went back to the city government to seek help. When the officer there insisted that he could not do anything, workers yelled at him, "Why is no one taking care of workers' affairs now that we are under Communist Party rule, and not Republican rule?!" Angrily, they marched down the main road aimlessly, and when they arrived at the intersection in front of the huge Deng Xiaoping portrait in downtown Shenzhen, several of the workers decided to sit down in the road. Others quickly followed, forming a human chain that held up traffic for about fifteen minutes. Soon, some twenty policemen arrived, grabbing and pulling workers to the sidewalk without arresting them. One of the three worker representatives talked to me about the workers' anger and predicament.

> All of us are from Sichuan. We have worked for three months for this contractor, and have completed five to six floors every month, working twelve hours each day. But we have never been paid a penny. The boss [the contractor] only loaned us money, several hundred yuan per person from time to time. He said the big boss [the construction company] has a cash problem and there is lots of work coming in. We struck twice and each time they promised to pay in a week. The last time we struck, on May 17th, the boss even threatened us, announcing in public, "I'll kill anyone who dares to lead a strike again." Once he said that, we realized that we could not trust him anymore, and we began to worry about our personal safety. . . . We workers work legally and tried legitimate means and got no response. They [the government] are forcing us to shed blood, to take the criminal route. As we left the city government and walked on the street, some of us suggested bombing the company, others cursed that it's better to be run over by cars than to work without getting paid. . . . We did not plan this action, it's so natural for everyone to follow once several workers decided to sit down in the road. When police came to remove us, some workers told them that being arrested was good. At least we wouldn't have to worry about food and lodging.[75]

In another incident, about one hundred restaurant workers took to the street to protest against unpaid wages by their employer, who fled during the SARS outbreak in April 2003. At first, they approached the city government Petition Office and the Labor Bureau for help. But because they had neither labor contracts nor proof of past wage payments to prove a labor relationship, the Labor Bureau delayed tapping into the fund earmarked for wage arrears complaints to bail them out. In the meantime, the Labor Bureau distributed an emergency allowance to each worker, the equivalent of 20 percent of the city's average wage. When the cash-strapped workers realized that it might take one hundred days before the investigation would result in government payment of back wages, they became restive. They organized a march through downtown Shenzhen, hoisting banners reading, "Return Our Sweat and Blood Money," "Please Help Us Working People," and "Down with Wang Simin" (the owner). One worker leader explained,

> The march is inspired by what we saw on television and in the newspaper. There was a case of wage arrears that took only one week to resolve. That's because the workers managed to get their story into the newspapers. We organized the march and contacted several newspapers, *Guangzhou Daily, Shenzhen Special Zone Daily, Southern Metropolitan News,* and *Crystal News,* in the hope that the media would report our case. In the end, reporters came but no report made it to print. . . . We are not afraid, because we know we have done nothing illegal. The law should not coerce the public. We agreed before the march that if anyone was arrested, all should come forward to confront the police. For an hour, we walked through major roads in Shenzhen. The dozen or so traffic police came and followed us all the way, asking us to keep to the sidewalk. We were a big group, so the government had to intervene. If we were just a few people, they would've ignored us. Of course, we are legal illiterates. Otherwise, we would have insisted on signing a contract with the boss, or we would have kept some evidence of wage payments.[76]

In the end, the Shenzhen government paid every worker at least the average monthly wage. Those who showed proof of wage payments in the past could collect the full amount of owed wages. In this case, bureaucratic flexibility was prompted by the central government's demand to keep migrant workers in the city at the height of the SARS epidemic. Impoverished unemployed migrant workers were the most volatile, and became beneficiaries of this special policy.

It is important to point out that not all labor dispute arbitration and litigation end in seething anger and frustration. In the case of fifteen garment workers who were owed two months' pay, the court verdict vindicated their charges. The workers have not yet been able to collect payment, however, as the court was not able to locate their employer, who has apparently closed the shop and relocated elsewhere. Some of the workers involved in the lawsuit found comfort in their moral and legal victory, while others have long since returned to the countryside to recuperate from the unrelenting work pressure of the garment industry. A year after their employer kicked them out of the dormitory and refused to pay them wages for the previous two months, amounting to two thousand yuan each, the final verdict brought little financial relief, only nagging ambivalence: they were not sure whether all the trouble of litigation and appeal had been worthwhile.

There are other workers in this study who have more positive experiences with the labor arbitration and the legal systems. Yang Qin, a migrant worker in her midthirties, has worked in the handbag industry for more than ten years, moving up the ranks from assembly worker to shop-floor production manager. When her husband, who worked in another factory, was dismissed without reason or compensation, she represented him in his arbitration hearing and won the case. Since then, she has become a quasi expert in labor arbitration, advising and accompanying aggrieved friends and acquaintances in their disputes with employers. One day, during one of my visits to Yang's apartment, her hometown friend from Guangxi came over to discuss his plan to sue the village leaders back home for illicit requisitioning. His farmland in the village had been confiscated and sold to developers, and he suspected that cadre corruption was the reason for the low compensation that villagers received. Emboldening him was not only Yang's positive experience with the law but also his own successful arbitration award after his arbitrary dismissal.

CELLULAR ACTIVISM, LOCALIZATION, AND LEGAL RIGHTS

The sunbelt pattern of labor unrest can now be summarized. The Labor Law and the legal contract have given migrant industrial workers crucial institutional leverage in their contests with employers about violations of labor rights. The strategy of choice for migrant workers is to approach the labor bureaucracy, the arbitration apparatus, and the court, owing to workers' precarious social and economic status in the cities. Thanks to local officials' procapital interests, however, and their influence over labor officials and the courts—a result of the central government's strategy of decentralization and local accumulation—legal injustice experienced during the processes of mediation, arbitration, and litigation often fuels as much unrest as the original workplace disputes. Therefore, I have emphasized the dual tendencies of China's illiberal "labor rule of law" toward pacification and radicalization of labor strife. Like actions taken by their rustbelt counterparts, direct and disruptive actions by migrant workers usually falter when police appear on the scene, when workers find jobs in other factories, or when they temporarily return to the countryside. As I will elaborate in the next chapter, this exit back to the land and subsistence farming has dampened migrant workers' political will to sustain their collective action in the cities.

In a pattern of labor unrest similar to that prevailing in the northeastern rustbelt (see chapter 3), migrant workers pursue cellular activism organized on the basis of the factory. In major cities, 70 to 80 percent of migrant workers live in institutionally provided dormitory rooms. The vast majority of private and foreign-invested factories prefer this dormitory labor system because it allows employers the convenience of having labor available on tap, facilitating flexible extension of the working day, minimizing workers' job search time, reducing the cost of social reproduction, and strengthening employers' control over workers' personal lives.[77] Dormitories have facilitated communication, coordination, and the aggregation of interests and demands.

The lack of independent unions or workers associations to connect, aggregate, and build on disparate activism is another reason for cellular activism. The few attempts by underground unionists to form independent unions among migrant workers ended in arrests and imprisonment. For instance, in the aftermath of the Tiananmen uprising, student-intellectual activists formed the backbone of several independent unions. The Free Trade Union of China *(Zhongguo ziyou gonghui)* was formed in late 1991 by two workers, a teacher, and a small trader, who were also members of either the Liberal Democratic Party of China, or the Chinese Progressive League, two underground political groups. Its members were soon imprisoned for two to twenty years. In March 1994, Yuan Hongbing, a university lecturer, Zhou Guoqiang, a lawyer, and others formed the League for the Protection of Laborers' Rights *(Laodongzhe quanyi baozhang tongmeng)*, but were soon either arrested or put under labor reform. Also in 1993 and 1994, several fresh college graduates formed the Wage Workers' Federation *(Dagongzhe lianhehui)* in Shenzhen, focusing on migrant labor rights and publishing two short-lived newsletters, *Wage Worker Exchange (Dagongtongxun)* and *Wage Worker Square (Dagongguangchang)*. Three members were soon arrested and given two to three years of labor reeducation.[78]

Given the clandestine nature of these organizations, it is not surprising that not much has been documented about their organizers and their modus operandi. The following first-person report by an activist involved in the Wage Workers' Federation may not be typical of other underground labor organizations, but it provides a rare glimpse into the precarious nature of such an undertaking. Li Minqi was a student activist in the 1989 movement, a member in the circle of student leaders. He reflected on the political lessons these student activists learned from their involvement in Tiananmen:

> The failure of the 1989 democratic movement exposed, on the one hand, the serious contradictions between the different social classes and groups in the movement, especially that between the middle-class intellectuals and the urban working class, and on the other, the fundamental limits of a democratic movement led by liberal intellectuals under the guidance of Western bourgeois ideology. . . . I began to look to Marxism and later became a Marxist.[79]

Arrested in 1990 for making an antigovernment speech and imprisoned for two years, he went to Shenzhen in 1993 to meet two of his college-educated friends from Hunan.

> They somehow realized that the 1989 democratic movement failed because it failed to mobilize workers effectively. Therefore, to achieve democracy . . . the democratic movement must "make use of" workers (that's how they literally talked about it) just as the Polish bourgeois intellectuals made use of the Solidarity Union to accomplish capitalist restoration. This is how they began to be interested in the workers' movement.[80]

Li's friends started a night school, consciously imitating the experience of the Chinese Communist Party, but so few workers came that the school nearly failed to get started. Using his own money, Li himself typed up and printed the ten-page *Wage Worker Exchange*, and circulated it to some twenty to thirty workers. Shortage of money forced him to stop publication, and he left Shenzhen. Another Beijing University student came to Shenzhen and circulated three issues of *Wage Worker Square*. Li himself left for the United States in 1994 and became a graduate student in economics at the University of Massachusetts, Amherst. His associates were arrested and imprisoned.

Since the mid-1990s, and in response to the hostile political environment and taking advantage of new resources and political space, workers, concerned intellectuals, and professionals have attempted another kind of labor activism. The rise of labor-oriented nongovernmental organizations (NGOs) that have strategically shunned the rhetoric and organizational mode of trade unions is a significant development in the new millennium. Echoing the official emphasis on migrant worker "education" and "services," these new organizations exploit the institutional spaces allowed for by the Ministry of Civil Affairs and business organization licenses, and rely on funding from international foundations, overseas churches, academic institutions, international human rights organizations, and even foreign governments. Some of these social entrepreneurs are first-generation migrant workers who have either been seriously victimized by industrial accidents or have developed a strong sense of justice for fellow migrants. Other activists are lawyers, journalists, academics, and students. In Beijing and the Pearl River Delta region, several of these organizations have quietly expanded their activities over the past five years. As in the many disparate incidents of labor strife documented here, these labor NGOs put a premium on protecting workers' legal rights and all have active programs to provide legal advice and education.[81] In the long run, these grassroots organizations may empower workers individually and foster their collective capacity. As of today, however, they have reached only a tiny minority among the teeming millions of migrant workers.

The Chinese state has handled migrant workers' activism using multiple strategies. While cracking down on underground union organizing, the Chinese government has been tolerant of everyday isolated unrest and has initiated reforms to remove some of the most oppressive policies against migrant workers. Most significantly, in October 2001, the Ministry of Finance and the State Council Planning Committee jointly issued a circular that in one stroke removed the panoply of administrative fees charged to migrant workers, including the temporary resident management fee, the family planning management fee, the city expansion fee, and the labor power adjustment fee. A temporary residence permit, which used to cost three hundred yuan per year, now costs only twenty-five yuan in Shenzhen (elsewhere in the country it is five yuan). Government departments issuing other kinds of certificates can charge migrant applicants only a few yuan of the production cost of certificates.[82] Also, in the same spirit of simplifying the regulatory regime for migrant laborers, the State Council prominently promulgated a circular in January 2003 demanding the abolition of local restrictions on the kinds of jobs migrants can take. In particular, it highlighted and condemned the pervasive problem of wage arrears and illegal deductions. The same circular also required local governments to facilitate access to education for migrants' children in the city by removing differential school fee schedules. Legal aid services have also received more official recognition and are earmarked for more institution building. Some academics have played leading and vocal roles in galvanizing public pressure on the government to respect the constitutional rights of migrant workers, especially with regard to police power of detention.

Legal scholars wrote petition letters to the legislature, criticizing police abuse of power and protesting against the deaths of migrant workers. In 2003, the state revised its long-standing vagrancy laws, explicitly prohibiting illegal detention.[83]

INSURGENT IDENTITIES

Irrespective of court verdicts or strike outcomes, the trajectory of labor strife involves willful human agency. In this section, I ask the same questions about migrant workers' insurgent identities as I did in chapter 3 about unemployed and retired workers involved in labor unrest in the rustbelt. What collective identification—or participation identity, as Roger Gould calls it—is invoked or contested when migrant workers participate in labor resistance?[84] I have found that class identity is more muted and ambivalent among migrant workers than among rustbelt workers, whereas claims made on the basis of equality before the law and of citizens' right to legal justice are impassioned and firm, as in the rustbelt. Workers also identify themselves as the marginalized and the subordinate in society, and therefore deserving of state paternalism and protection against employers and their official accomplices. In short, there are commonalities among these multiple insurgent identities, but as I shall emphasize, the cultural logic and practical circumstances undergirding their formation are different for migrant workers than for their counterparts in the rustbelt.

Muted Class Consciousness

Rarely do migrant workers speak of themselves as the "working class" *(gongrenjieji)* and "workers" *(gongren)*. Even workers who have worked in urban factories for more than a decade and have known no other form of waged employment except as factory hands still consider themselves peasants *(nongmin)*, a place-based, ascribed status unambiguously marked by their rural household registration. Many also identify themselves as "non-state workers" *(mingong)*, "peasant workers" *(nongmingong)*, or "outside workers" *(wailaigong)*. In prereform China, the systems of household registration *(hukou)* and the work unit together defined the structural location of the working class. That is, a worker is an urbanite employed in a state or collective industry. Lacking an urban *hukou* and working outside the state sector, migrant workers in Shenzhen logically do not see themselves as real "workers," much less as the politically and ideologically privileged "working class." The discourse of class and working-class power is so tied up with state socialism's ideology and institutions that it has inadvertently functioned as an exclusionary identity for the new generation of workers who now unambiguously confront domination by the capitalist class.

Besides the historical construction of the bona fide working class as those employed in state work units in the cities, according to some of the more discerning migrant workers, the unorganized existence of migrants is the key element that disqualifies them from becoming part of the working class. One worker representative said, "We are a pool of loose sand. Without a union, we are not a collective, not a group. A working class should at least have some organization."[85] Indeed, the failure of the official union to penetrate the numerous private and foreign-invested firms, the eradication of guild and native-place organizations by Mao's regime, the lack of a developed civil society, and government repression of independent unionism all leave workers without much organizational space to develop their own institutions. Native-place ties exist in the form of informal cliques on the shop floor, or loosely organized and flexibly defined friendship circles among those who happen to work in the same locality. Migrants rely on these social connections for financial assistance, emotional support, company, labor market information, and communication with families and relatives back home. But these ties are just as easily dissolved as forged, following the ebbs and flows of a highly mobile labor market.[86]

Although migrant workers do not explicitly invoke a rhetoric of class, there are palpable indications of an incipient class consciousness in formation. In chapter 3, I argued that state-sector workers' class consciousness is achieved through their collective experience of Maoist political campaigns and the institution of permanent employment in state enterprises over which they claimed ownership. Reform dismantles both pillars of class experience and sharpens the reality of class subordination. In contrast, migrant workers' critique of class exploitation and alienation is grounded more in their encounter with market and capitalist forces, and in terms of denial of human dignity, loss of personal autonomy, and employer dishonesty. Cheating of wages by management, in the forms of concealing the rates of payment, discounting the volume of worker output, and delaying and docking wages, constitutes the most common experience that reveals the corrupt and adversarial nature of the capitalist employment relationship.

Bodily degradation and physical exhaustion often take place in unregulated private and foreign-invested factories and spark rebellion. Corporal punishment is so frequently meted out to workers that a common yardstick for workers to assess an enterprise as good or bad is whether "the boss hits workers." Everyday physical deprivation engenders critical consciousness indicting capitalist managerial practices. Many migrant workers sustain withering critiques of "inhumane" managers who transform workers into "appendages of machines" or outright "slaves of the boss."

> There is no fixed work schedule. A twelve-hour workday is minimum. With rush orders, we have to work continuously for thirty hours or more. Day and night . . . the longest shift we had worked nonstop lasted for forty hours. . . . It's very exhausting, because we have to stand all the time, to straighten the denim cloth by pulling. Our legs are always hurting. There is no place to sit on the shop floor. . . . The machines do not stop during our lunch breaks. Three workers in a group will just take turns eating, one at a time. . . . The shop floor is filled with thick dust. Our bodies become black inside working day and night. When I get off from work and spit, it's all black. . . . In the factory, your entire body is under his [the employer's] control. You lose control over yourself. You have to do whatever he wants you to. It's like you're sold to him.[87]

> He [the boss] treats workers like machines. As long as we can earn him money, he does not care about workers' health and bodies. . . . It's like in the old society, I give you money and you become my slave, a lesser human being. In the countryside, even if you are poor, people look down on you but still as a human being.[88]

The strongest sign of class solidarity appears at work during struggles against employers. As the many instances of strikes and protests reported in this chapter show, workers experience their strength in numbers, and the government responds to their large presence on the street or in the Labor Bureau. Yet this solidarity occurs mostly at the moment of imminent exit from the factory. After a dispute or a strike, workers will disperse again, going along with the ebb and flow of the labor market. No organization exists to sustain connections among workers, who often leave one another without a telephone number, only a home village address, or among workers across factories.

Second-Class Citizens

Can the regime's legal reform and promotion of "socialist legality" at least nurture workers' rights consciousness, inspiring and inciting them to act as citizens defending their legal labor rights? For migrant workers involved in collective disputes with employers, the Labor Law has proven pivotal in labor contentions as it accords, on paper at least, all laborers the same contractual status and rights regardless of social origin and ownership sector. In the several examples I cited in this chapter, workers experienced a cognitive transformation about their predicament through the lens of the law. A worker representative offered his own reflection on the consciousness-raising role of the law and labor officials.

> Had we only read a case like our own in the newspaper, we might not have become so insistent. But after both the labor inspector and the legal aid lawyer said that these [back wages] are the law, there was no turning back. To us migrant workers, they represent the will of the government.[89]

But if the law gives lofty promises of labor rights, its uneven enforcement gives rise to a groundswell of disenchantment. Once migrant workers engage the Labor Bureau and the court in their battles with employers, they quickly realize that rights on the books are sabotaged by an authoritarian mode of governance in which the law cannot effectively constrain local official caprice. Everyday treatment by street-level representatives of the government, especially public security officers, reminds them constantly that, as migrants with agricultural household registrations, they are second-class citizens and permanent outsiders in the eyes of local officials and residents alike. House raids are a typical harassment detested by migrants.

> We are second-class citizens, and not even that sometimes, just beasts in the eyes of the police. When they came to raid our houses in the middle of the night, they rode roughshod over us, forcing us to squat on the ground, with our hands raised and folded behind our heads. They treated us like criminals. Even if we could show them our temporary residence permits, they would tear them up, and ask, "Where are your papers?" Migrant workers have no rights at all, because we are not locals.[90]

Urban prejudice and everyday harassment are commonplace experiences of migrants, be they laborers or entrepreneurs.[91] Police are not the only predatory street-level state agents who prey on migrant workers. I have discussed the abrasive language used in the hallways and reception room of the Labor Bureau. And despite workers' faith in what they perceive as the greater integrity and justice of Shenzhen's legal system as compared with that in their hometowns in the interior provinces, the legal system often looks like a daunting bureaucratic monster filled with hurdles and straining their resources as a subordinate group. Therefore, even that sense of empowerment by the law is ambivalent and mixed with an ingrained distrust of the powerful.

> The law does not seem to protect us migrant workers. It only refers you to different departments. Today it's the Labor Bureau, tomorrow it's the Industry and Commerce Bureau, or this or that court. Always delay and

rescheduling. . . . The boss can afford it. We don't have an inkling of citizen rights *(gongminquan)*. There is no government department responsible for punishing bosses who don't pay workers. They can still open another shop somewhere else. I find this mind-boggling.[92]

Finally, migrant workers' status as second-class citizens is perpetuated by regulations other than the Labor Law. Unequal treatments are also stipulated in local regulations for pension insurance and medical insurance. Even when local regulations have, since February 2001, entitled all workers in Shenzhen, irrespective of *hukou* status and enterprise type, to monthly pension payments at retirement, migrant workers are still treated differently. Whereas workers with Shenzhen *hukou* need only ten years of contributions before they are entitled to such payments, nonlocal workers have to accumulate at least fifteen years. Medical insurance for local employees covers outpatient care and hospitalization, but for migrant workers, only the latter is provided. Finally, until 2003, all migrants were required to pay a range of fees to obtain and renew documents such as the temporary residency permit and the temporary resident's marriage and reproduction certificates.

The lack of medical welfare is perhaps most sorely felt. A worker representative who fell ill during the heady days of negotiations with management went to a local hospital to receive a shot for his cold. He later used this example to explain why migrant workers are second-class citizens in the eyes of the government.

> It costs me three hundred yuan for an injection and some medicine! Just a cold. If we were Shenzhen locals, or state-owned enterprise workers, we would not have to pay that outrageous amount. We are a pitiful lot in the city. We get no welfare from the government even though we contribute our labor.[93]

In short, the law both empowers and disenchants migrant laborers. It interpellates aggrieved workers to act as citizens with legal rights, but the illiberal legal system also disenchants many who find the court beholden to local government and business interests. This aspect of workers' demand for citizenship in accessing legal justice and rights is the common ground for workers in both the rustbelt and the sunbelt, and is in significant ways induced by the regime's strategy of legal authoritarianism.

Subaltern: Double Subordination

The third articulated identity found among migrant workers is that of *ruoshi qunti*, meaning social groups in weak, subordinate, and disadvantaged positions. Almost all worker representatives in this study mention that they are a "subaltern group" and that the law and government officials have the responsibility to protect their rights and interests from infringement by capitalists. In the open letter written by the 188 construction workers of Jiancheng, they plead for support from the Guangdong provincial government, the Shenzhen city government, the Shenzhen People's Congress, the Trade Union, and the Public Security Bureau:

> We implore you not to push migrant workers to the end of the road, not to force our wives and children into the street. The law should "protect the weak," the government should "protect the weak." Who cares about a weak group like us?

As I discussed in chapter 3, rustbelt workers also invoked the term *ruoshi qunti* in their petitions and protests. Emerging in the mid-1990s in the official media, policy circles, and academic writings, this new social category entered popular parlance in the late 1990s.[94] After Premier Zhu Rongji mentioned it in passing in his government report delivered to the National People's Congress in early March 2002, urging government departments to better protect the *ruoshi qunti* from the negative effects of reform, a more precise definition of the term was then given by a director of the Labor and Social Security Ministry, who referred to four subgroups: unemployed workers, the elderly and handicapped, migrant workers, and retirees with small pensions. Since then, a deluge of commentaries in the national and local press, supported by social scientific analyses of leading academics, shed light on the existence of subalterns. The general opinion reflected in speeches of provincial and local government and union officials is that the government *should* protect the livelihood of groups in disadvantaged positions through the law and the construction of a national social safety net.

The designation *subaltern groups* underlines migrant workers' objective, collective subordination in a new social structure, and it resonates with their feelings of being doubly subordinated by the market and the state. But inherent in *ruoshi qunti* is also a hierarchical political community presided over by a protective, righteous, and benevolent state, with workers as supplicants. In another study of Shenzhen migrant workers' petitions, it was found that aggrieved workers referred to themselves as "the people," "the workers," and "the masses," appealing to officials as their "protectors," identifying them as "father and mother of the people," "protective god," "fair judge," "uncles," "directing comrades," or "servants of the people."[95] This logic of the masses led by a hierarchically arranged political leadership also explains why some workers threatened to appeal to the National People's

Congress in Beijing when the local court failed to give them legal justice. Again, as among veteran state-sector workers, we see here a bifurcated view of the state: a righteous and legalistic center far removed from corrupt and predatory local agents. The people, like Mao's masses, are responsible for exposing these local malfeasances and bring them to the attention of the central leaders.

The coexistence of different normative principles embedded in the collective identities of "workers," "second-class citizens," and *ruoshi qunti* parallels the multiple insurgent identities I have found among unemployed and retired workers in rustbelt protests. In the sunbelt province of Guangdong, however, class is largely a muted collective identity among migrant workers, whereas "citizen" and "the masses" are more empowering identity claims to which migrant workers aspire. Depending on the different channels of appeals, workers in both the northeast and the south deploy different frames and mobilize different elements of their normative and political repertoire to maximize the chances for optimal official responses. When filing for labor arbitration, they use legalistic language. On the other hand, in lodging complaints to petitions officials, workers emphasize social and normative injustice and inhumane treatments they suffer. Finally, protests on the street involve using direct mass pressure, enlisting media support, and leveraging popular disobedience to embarrass local officials by attracting the attention of their superiors.

NORTH-SOUTH COMPARISON

Labor unrest involving unemployed workers in Liaoning and migrant workers in Guangdong shares the significant pattern of dispersed, localized, cellular mobilization. The industrial workplace and the dormitory or the residential quarter organized around it can be inadvertently turned into sites of rebellion. But labor struggles in the northeast have the potential to be sustained for longer periods of time, up to several years in some cases, largely because urban state-sector workers are permanent residents in their allocated housing units, which survive the termination of their employment and enterprise bankruptcies, in contrast to migrant workers' itinerant status and lack of permanent dwelling in the cities. The few instances of networking of aggrieved workers across factories and cities and clandestine union organizing in both provinces do not have any lasting or wide impact on the much more numerous and "ordinary" labor protests.

The cellularity of labor resistance, its economic demands and local official targets reflect the institutional dynamic of market reform, which empha-

sizes fiscal and economic decentralization, enterprise autonomy and competition, and subsequent differentiation in economic conditions across firms,
industries, and localities. The fragmentation of worker interests, at least the
fragmentation as perceived by workers themselves, is also caused by refined
differences in state labor policies and regulations according varying entitlements to diverse categories of workers within the state sector. Besides the
internal fissures among the different groups of state-sector workers and
migrant workers, a clear boundary is maintained between these two segments of the working class, which have never shown any inclination to join
forces or form an alliance. They perceive their interests, life conditions, and
social status as worlds apart from each other. The rural-urban dualism in the
larger social structure, unmistakably marked by the draconian household
registration system, finds its mirror image in the structuring of labor
resistance.

Nevertheless, are these two major groups of workers as different as they
would tend to imagine? Juxtaposing the materials in this chapter and chapter 3, we can identify certain similarities in their insurgent identities, besides
their common adoption of cellular activism. Both groups have variously
invoked Marxist, Maoist, and liberal normative principles and identities. I
have tried to show how class identities have grown out of the socialist social
contract among the older generation of workers, and have been muted
among the younger migrant workforce. Rustbelt workers, having lived
through the Mao years when workers were permanent employees and
therefore collective owners of their enterprises, show a stronger class identity than younger migrant workers, whose incipient class consciousness
arises from experience with degradation and exploitation in the production
process. But lacking the discursive resources available to the older generation of workers, barred by their rural household registration status from
permanent residency in the cities, migrant workers do not identify themselves as the working class as readily as the veteran urban workers do.

More unifying than the respective cultural and historical constitutions of
their class consciousness, both groups make strong claims based on the law
and workers' legal rights stated in the Labor Law and related pension and
bankruptcy regulations. When they are frustrated by the ineffectiveness of
this fledgling institution, both groups of workers are prone to use direct
action instead of pursuing the more institutionalized bureaucratic channels
of conflict resolution. Their common predicament is the illiberal nature of
China's legal system. The regime's project of constructing legality is inher-
ently shaped by a dogged commitment to its monopoly of political power
and the refusal to subject itself to the constraints of the law. Local govern-

ment's imperative to enhance economic growth and investments leads to widespread violation of the Labor Law. The local courts are politically too weak and financially too dependent on local governments to counter this resistance to genuine rule of law. We have seen how labor activism oscillates between the court and the streets, or between the tendencies of rationalization and radicalization. An ineffective and illiberal legal system may derail the tendency toward more peaceful labor relations and may erode state legitimacy. Already, many desperate workers are seeking redress from the central government, after failing to obtain justice at local levels marred by corruption and incompetence. In these popular petitions, workers adopt the identification of the Maoist "masses," as supplicants pleading for protection by a paternalist political authority.

If the Chinese regime's highly repressive stance toward horizontally organized dissent generates self-limiting action among workers in protests, cellular and localized actions still call for concrete responses if these stirrings are to be contained. Thus far, in both the northeast and the south, with respect to grievances of the two groups of workers, the local governments have responded to their most urgent livelihood needs, while ignoring political critiques of cadre corruption and business-government collusion. But rampant corruption that sabotages legal reform and intensifies inequalities may become the lightning rod sparking social protest by groups as disparate as peasants, workers, private property owners, religious sects, relocation refugees, and many others. This does not mean the brewing of a social revolution from below. It only suggests that the state has to deal with challenges from an increasingly assertive society with pluralistic interests, resources, and claims to express discontent.

6 *Dagong* as a Way of Life

Given the pernicious working conditions and the common problem of wage default affecting tens of millions of migrant workers in southern China, why has labor rebellion largely remained tame and nonmilitant? Are there other factors besides state repression that have contained the rebellion of the new generation of workers? On a more mundane level, how do workers survive during periods of unemployment and nonpayment of wages?

This chapter answers these questions by examining migrant workers at the moment of the reproduction of labor power and consumption, to supplement the previous analysis of labor politics at the points of production and exchange. It also analyzes workers' experience of state power in the countryside and the city, together with their collective memories of rural socialism. This chapter runs parallel to chapter 4, which tackles the same set of issues for rustbelt workers. Only by moving beyond the narrow and single-moment confines of "production," and reinstating a holistic livelihood context of the living laborer can we understand worker politics as a human and historical phenomenon, with all its attendant contradictions and nuances. More specifically, I argue that in order to understand why China can boast a seemingly bottomless supply of cheap and docile labor, we have to link the world of labor with that of the farm, and the most important nexus in the city-country linkage is the system of rural land rights. Access to land and its associated functions for the social reproduction of migrants' labor power helps reduce employers' burden to pay adequately for workers' survival and limits workers' propensity to sustain labor strife in the cities.[1] In other words, for the tens of millions of migrant workers, *dagong*, or selling labor to the bosses, despite its connotation of being an urban experience, is actually a way of life that straddles two worlds, one in the countryside and the other in the city. This double existence is at once economic, political, and cultural. Grasping these dimensions and the centrality of the rural economy and society for migrant laborers is essential to understanding their interests and grievances, and the limits to their resistance in the cities.

The first section discusses the *economics* of *dagong*. It begins with migrant workers' returning to their home villages in times of temporary unemployment or between jobs. It discusses how migrants' right to agricultural land, the rural household economy, and the division of labor make possible and compel migrants' double existence as both farmers and workers. Tilling the land and toiling in factories complement and require each other. For many migrant workers, agriculture provides a floor of subsistence and city jobs allow for material improvement for their families and better life opportunities for the next generation. For others in impoverished households and villages, *dagong* is not an option but a necessity. For these farmers, farm income shortfalls necessitate additional cash income in order to survive. Overall, it must be emphasized that villages are sites of social reproduction of labor, that is, resources and social relations in the villages allow migrant workers to reproduce themselves on a generational basis and to subsist when waged work is not available. Many married migrant workers use their urban income primarily to prepare for their final, permanent return to the countryside. For single younger migrants, returning to the village looms large in their plans for the future. What this means for labor politics is that wages and working conditions, not collective consumption, are workers' primary concerns in the cities and therefore the most important trigger for protests. Yet migrants' land rights allow for subsistence in times of unemployment and nonpayment of wages, forming a buffer that has thus far prevented workers' radicalization.

The second section turns to *dagong* as a political experience. Workers' narratives of their urban-rural experience underscore a double powerlessness brought by an ascription-based or place-based subordination to the state in both the city and the countryside. As a result, they are very skeptical of the state rhetoric of contractual and legal rights even as they become urban workers. The argument here is that these migrant workers harbor no illusions about their position and potential in a market society, even as they see the law as the only institutional resource they can leverage. Domination in the city and the countryside is transparent rather than opaque: in the city, the frequency of wage nonpayment reveals the nakedly exploitative relations between workers and employers favored by the local government; in the village, domination is equally concrete, arbitrarily exercised by local state agents who exact fees and enforce fines. Having a cash income allows some escape from bureaucratic domination that targets peasants as castelike, locality-based subjects. The continuity in the lived experience of power in both city and countryside does not preclude resistance in both locales, but it does surface from time to time to cast doubt among migrant workers on their capacity to effect changes in the larger social and political system.

The third section addresses *dagong* as a collective cultural experience. I explore the existential meanings of *dagong* as they are currently constructed by migrant workers while also embedded in a larger mnemonic narrative of socialism in the countryside and workers' aspirations for the future. In the conjoined urban-rural worldview of migrant workers is their vivid memories of and aversion to poverty associated with collectivized agriculture. This has produced an overall narrative of relative "progress" in the countryside through the past several decades, overshadowing or diluting the brunt of present-day urban and rural misery. Bereft of an alternative vision of the social order, except perhaps a desire for more political accountability of local cadres, migrant workers focus on individual fortune and aspire to rural entrepreneurialism as a personal means of transcending past poverty and current hardship. As this book goes to press, however, Chinese researchers and labor activists have noted the rise of a new generation of migrant workers—second-generation migrants—who are more determined to put down roots in the cities. Widespread rural decay in interior provinces has thwarted any desire to return to the land. The character of China's working class is likely to change in the years to come.

THE ECONOMICS OF DOUBLE EXISTENCE: LAND AS ASSET AND LIABILITY

In chapter 5, I showed that labor disputes in Shenzhen were often spurred by an "exit solidarity" among migrant workers. That is, at the time of plant closure or relocation, migrant workers are acutely aware of their common interest and the urgency of confronting their employers about labor violations. Equally striking, though, is the rapid dispersal of migrant workers once the factory is closed or moved. While many are under financial pressure to seek new jobs, others simply take the opportunity to go home for short-term visits. Peng, a twenty-nine-year-old woman from Hunan, is one of the four worker representatives for the eight hundred workers involved in a labor dispute with Seagate, a hard-disk manufacturer. The dispute was caused by Seagate's failure to contribute to its workers' pension fund in Shenzhen. Scheduled for relocation to Jiangsu in April 2002, the factory dismissed most of the workforce. Meanwhile, some of the more educated workers discovered that migrant workers were legally entitled to pension contributions by their employers. Worker representatives began collecting signatures from fellow workers and hired a lawyer to represent them in negotiations with the company and in approaching the Social Security Bureau. Peng has worked at Seagate for seven years and is married to a fellow Hunan worker. While the couple stayed in Shenzhen to continue the process of petitioning and filing for labor dispute arbitration, many of Peng's coworkers left the Shenzhen dormitory after the plant closure and many had temporarily returned home. Seeing the disappearance of their fellow workers back to the countryside was one of the most dispiriting aspects of the struggle. After being kicked around like a football by different government departments and being charged extortionary fees by an irresponsible lawyer, Peng and other representatives simply gave up.

Such an exodus of migrant workers back to the countryside often saps the will of worker representatives and dampens the mobilization momentum in labor disputes. Tough economic times in the city also prompt workers to return to their villages, where subsistence is still possible. Xia, a thirty-year-old worker from Chongqing, Sichuan, was committed to fight for his and other workers' rights at the beginning of a wage dispute with the owner of an electronics factory. Tirelessly visiting the Labor Bureau, seeking advice from fellow complainants he met at the Labor Bureau, and eagerly absorbing all kinds of legal information he managed to collect from newspapers and booklets in local bookstores, he himself talked about returning to the countryside.

> All of us who come to the city to *dagong* have a psychological goal. For myself, I need to make at least two thousand yuan net per year, or about six hundred yuan per month. Otherwise it is not worth leaving home. Shenzhen's 574 yuan minimum wage is barely enough. The situation turned from bad to worse when our factory stopped paying us for three months when there was no order. Not even livelihood allowances. How can we survive? In my home village, growing rice and corn alone does not make any money. But peasants can earn about two thousand yuan by selling vegetables, grains, or fruit. I am thinking of going home for good. Some of my coworkers from Sichuan have gone home. It's not worth it, working in the city.[2]

What makes this return to the countryside a viable alternative is the system of land use rights and land contracts. Land rights are almost universal for migrant workers holding rural household registrations, or *hukou*. Since 1956, China has ended all private ownership of land: urban land and natural resources are state-owned, accounting for some 53 percent of China's territory in 1996, and suburban and rural land, taking up 46 percent

of the national land mass, are collectively owned. Under the planned economy, farmers were grouped into production teams, which in turn formed
larger units such as brigades and communes. Agricultural land was worked
collectively, with only a small portion of land being allocated to farmers as
private plots. Since the rural reform of the late 1970s, with the adoption of
the household responsibility system, brigades and communes were dismantled. The village collective or the village committee contracts agricultural
land to rural households, based on household size and composition.[3] The
length of the land contract was originally set at three years, but was
extended to fifteen years or more in 1984. Under the 1998 Revised Land
Administration Law, to improve tenure security, land is contracted for
another thirty years. Land leases are adjusted periodically to take into
account changing population due to births, deaths, and women marrying
into and out of the localities. By the late 1990s, at least 80 percent of the villages in China had adjusted land allocation at least once.[4] The size and quality of their farmland vary across localities, but the national average in per
capita allocation of arable land is 1.2 mu in 1997.[5] Typical of many migrant
workers originally from Sichuan in this study, for instance, is a contract of
one or two mu of paddy field and an equal amount of dry land. One Sichuan
woman's situation is representative. Her land contract has been renewed in
1998 for thirty years. Since both she and her husband are in Shenzhen, her
mother-in-law and relatives farm the land for them.

> I have one mu of farmland and one mu of wetland that remain in my
> native village. We grow fruit trees or corn on farmland near the hills
> and rice on the wetland. I got married in 1993, and my husband has
> two to three mu of paddy and dry land, and his mother has a similar
> amount. My child is only nine years old and he is waiting in line to be
> allocated his own land. Even if he is allocated his own plot, there is no
> manpower to farm it.[6]

Another woman worker has worked in Shenzhen for eleven years. While
her sixteen-year-old son is still at home to finish high school, her husband
and their daughter all work in Shenzhen. When her mother-in-law died, she
inherited her land, and the whole family of four together farm six mu of
land. By law, and in actual practice, women are entitled to the same land
allocation as men, resulting in a general expectation among migrant workers that agricultural land allocation is a birthright of a rural resident.

> My maiden share of land is still in my native village. After I got mar-
> ried, my sister-in-law got my plot because she has transferred her
> hukou to our village. Now we have our neighbors till our land. We
> only pay the taxes, and the rest is their responsibility. Land is of

course important. We will eventually return to the village. My son is
an out-of-quota child and he has no land right. He can only inherit
ours.[7]

A male worker has 1.5 mu of wetland and 1.5 mu of farmland back home.

My parents keep my land certificate, and I do not know much about
what's written there. The village committee divides up the land and the
production team does the practical work of assigning specific plots of
land. I am not worried that I will lose my land right because I work in
Shenzhen and have other people farm my land. As long as I live, the
land is always mine, whether I make money or not, rich or poor. I am
not a city resident. As long as I am a peasant, I should have my plot of
land. My son can inherit and use the land, especially if he turns out to
be mediocre in other lines of work. At least he has this last resort of
returning to the land.[8]

Younger workers are more likely to have no experience in farming and
are vague about their land rights. An eighteen-year-old woman knows that
she was allocated a small plot of land in the early 1980s, and that her brother
was born too late to be included in the first allocation exercise. Still, land is
in the back of her mind when she thinks about the future.

I got a little bit of land, but I don't know how much. . . . I have never
done farm work. The land is not important to me now. Many farmlands
in the village lay fallow. But it's better to have some land rather than
having nothing. But if I go back, I'll want to run a small restaurant or a
small business. We are too young to think about these things. Perhaps
when I get older, I'll think about it. We are from the countryside, so we
must one day return to the countryside.[9]

Is rural land an asset or a liability? Most workers see it as both. Workers
in their thirties have a better sense than their younger counterparts of the
cost, income, and tax burdens involved in farming. Still, the consensus is
that land functions as informal social insurance. Migrant workers see the
land as a birthright to which they are entitled, a functional equivalent of the
state provision of grain and pensions given to urban residents. When I visited the home villages of some of the migrant workers from central Sichuan,
they and their families reported that owing to the consistent decline in grain
prices but ongoing high fertilizer and pesticide costs, farming alone was not
adequate. Sideline production, such as growing vegetables and raising poul-
try, supplemented by incomes from the city, is needed to make ends meet.
Among the thirty-five families interviewed, the average cost of agriculture
production and basic living expenses combined was between three thousand
and five thousand yuan per year per household, with an additional three

thousand yuan spent on education, medical care, and communications. The average deficit per household was about two thousand to three thousand yuan per year.[10] Incidentally, in another study of Sichuan migrants, it was found that the average amount of remittance sent by migrants to their home villages in 1999 fell within this range, at about 2,853 yuan.[11] Nationwide, in 1999, nonagricultural income accounted for 40.7 percent of rural households' income.[12]

These figures have to be interpreted against the background of wide regional disparities in China. Scholars have conventionally divided rural China into the eastern, central, and western regions and underscored the enormous intrarural disparities in income. In 2000, the average per capita rural income in eastern provinces was 2,994 yuan, 2,030 yuan in central, and 1,557 yuan in western provinces. In 2001, when the per capita income of peasants nationwide was 2,366 yuan, in rural Shanghai it was 6,860 yuan, and in some western provinces, it was about 1,000 yuan.[13] Migrant workers in this study have come predominantly from the middle-income region in central and interior provinces, where rural industry is less developed and agriculture is still the mainstay of the local economy. Average income for rural Sichuan in 1999, for instance, was 1,843 yuan, below the national average of 2,210 yuan.[14] There is an apparent symbiotic relationship between waged work in the city and income from farming, with some migrant worker households more dependent on wages to sustain agriculture than those who can use waged income for building better houses or sending their children to better schools in nearby towns. But many migrant workers in this study report that two-thirds of their household income now comes from earnings in the city. Therefore, whether as a necessity for or a supplement to farming, wage income from *dagong* has become a pivotal component of the rural economy, for local governments as well as for individual households. Sichuan's fifteen million migrant workers, out of a total rural population of sixty-eight million, for instance, sent home forty-five billion yuan in 2002, or 1.5 times the amount of the province's fiscal revenues of twenty-nine billion yuan.[15]

SOCIAL REPRODUCTION OF LABOR POWER: MARRIAGE, HOUSE BUILDING, AND EDUCATION

For the individual family, the village land entitlement is not just a resource for subsistence in the present, but a site of long-term social investment and generational reproduction. Migrant workers return home periodically not just to have a respite from the unrelenting pressure of work in the city.

Some of them are forced to go home during spells of unemployment. At certain life-cycle stages, young adults see the countryside as the ideal place to get married and start a family before venturing into the city again. Still others return home to take care of elderly family members or young children. A 1999 survey carried out in Sichuan and Anhui, two of the largest sending provinces for migrant workers, found that among returnees, 56.6 percent go home because of employment difficulties, and the rest mainly for family reasons.[16] Among women workers, a common practice is to quit their city jobs for several years when they reach an age to marry and bear children. A young mother worked in factories and restaurants in Shenzhen for four years and went home to marry her husband, who came from a nearby village. Holding her seven-month-old daughter and sitting next to her mother in their home in Sichuan, she explained why it was better to come home to find a mate.

> Although I do not believe in arranged marriage, it's still more assuring to find someone at home. Acquaintances here are more trustworthy. In Shenzhen, you meet people from different provinces and it's hard to tell the good ones from the bad. . . . My husband went back to Shenzhen after we were married. If he decides later that he wants to be back, he can find a job in a nearby town or raise more pigs. But we need the wage income to stay even. 80–90 percent of our income comes from our wage employment. Maybe my child will quit the countryside and farming, but most important of all, now, is to have enough money for her education.[17]

For workers with longer histories in Shenzhen and more family responsibilities, going home between jobs allows them to visit their spouses, parents, and children. In some cases, women workers end up having truncated careers as a migrant workers because of these familial obligations. A thirty-three-year-old woman with two children spent five years working in an electronics factory in Shenzhen and returned to her Sichuan family because of her father-in-law's cancer and her children's education.

> Rural women who stay [in the villages] are usually those with elderly parents to look after. If they [the elderly] are sick, there is no one to take care of the children. Now that I cannot work in the city, I have to raise more pigs, ducks, or silk worms, or other sidelines such as weaving bamboo baskets for harvest. My eldest daughter has just begun her primary school education. It's not just about paying a one-thousand-yuan per semester school fee. It's also about having someone to supervise her schoolwork.[18]

Indeed, education is one of the biggest items of expenditure among

212 / *Part III*

migrant worker families, who see in education the best strategy to achieve social mobility for the next generation. Many migrants are convinced that a good education is more important than an urban *hukuo* for the next generation, and therefore the academic performance of their children is a top priority. A child's high school education in the countryside costs between six hundred and eight hundred yuan per semester, and an extra two hundred to three hundred yuan for room and board. Some workers have brought their children to the cities and placed them in urban schools, which ask for "sponsorship fees" for these migrant children. Others pay extra money to get their children into township high schools near their home villages. All harbor an intense desire for social mobility for their offspring. Without their hard-earned city income, there is no chance of holding out this hope. A woman worker recalled the money needed to get her son into a preferred junior high school.

> Because we do not have any *guanxi* (social connections), and because my son's score is ten marks less than the minimum requirement, the school asks for an extra-quota fee. At first, they wanted six hundred yuan per semester, and I said that I am a poor migrant worker and cannot afford that much. They lowered it to three hundred yuan per semester, plus five hundred yuan room and board and other sundry fees. I have to spend a lot on his education.[19]

Another male worker pays an extra eight-hundred-yuan sponsorship fee, in addition to a five-hundred-yuan school fee and another two-hundred-yuan room and board fee each semester so that his daughter can attend a new experimental high school in his township. But he faces a dilemma that many migrant parents have to confront. Parents' absence exacts a heavy toll on children's learning.

> Children need parents' supervision, or else their studies will suffer. Working away from home, we can give them only little love and guidance. She always says on the phone that she wants her mother home, that she misses us. . . . Grandma spoils her excessively. But in this society, this is the contradiction: you want to give them an education and a better life, so you have to *dagong*. But *dagong* means that you have to leave home and cannot take care of them. I hope she can become a teacher or a doctor. That will depend on whether or not she can get into college. I can only provide her with the best opportunity. I have only very limited knowledge and I don't have any alternative. But I do not want her to stay in the countryside all her life. It's too miserable and poor there.[20]

Echoing the same concern, a woman migrant worker who has worked for twelve years in cites in Guangdong lamented her nephew's experience.

If women peasants come home from working in the city, it's usually for the children. Take me as an example. If I didn't return, my kid will likely fail his high school entrance examination. It's a serious dilemma for us. If I did not work in the city, even if he had high scores, we could not afford to pay. But if we were both away in the city, no one would supervise his school work and he would not get high marks. . . . My sister has a nine-year-old. She has left home for work all these years and her mother-in-law takes care of her child. He can barely talk, and he does not like talking either.[21]

A twenty-year-old woman relates how growing up without her migrant parents had an adverse effect on her school performance.

I used to be a very good student but once I started senior high, my scores plummeted. I was so ashamed that I felt I did not have the face to continue. It's partly because my parents were not there for me. I felt I had no support, no shield, no confidence. It's also partly because our village is too remote. No decent road, no telephone, no television. Every day, we had to walk an hour each way to go to school. When it rains, the road becomes impassable, and we had to carry a lunch box, a school bag, and an umbrella. It's too tough.[22]

Having quit school after graduating from junior high, her goal now is to earn enough money by working in Shenzhen so that she can save up ten thousand yuan to attend adult high school in the township near her village. In the meantime, she spends all her spare time in a computer school in Shenzhen.

I paid nine hundred yuan for a whole program that teaches us the Internet, Photoshop, and other software. There is no fixed duration. We take as many classes as we want, until we get everything. I go there every day at lunch and I spend all my days off there, from morning till night.[23]

The foremost material goal of most migrant workers is building a new, well-constructed village house made of cement and bricks, to replace the old, derelict huts made of mud or straw. Even among those who return only several times over a period of ten or fifteen years, sending money and building a house back home are of paramount economic and social significance. First, mud houses are not just dilapidated, uncomfortable, and drab; they are also a hazard to live in. Moreover, building a new house is the ultimate symbol of a family's social status, material success, individual competence, and effort. It is such an important status symbol that it is considered a necessity for parents looking for desirable marriage partners for unmarried offspring. Third, it is also an investment for the future, when migrants eventually return to a rural way of life. Even if they do not farm, they need permanent dwellings. Therefore, building houses cannot be dismissed as irrational and unproductive consumption. As one relative in the home village of a Sichuan worker puts it,

> The status of a migrant worker family in the village is totally changed. Eighty percent of these families have built new houses. No more straw sheds. It's a matter of image, but also real needs. Sheds are dangerous dwellings and can collapse anytime. Even without any interior decoration, new concrete houses are much safer.[24]

Field studies of migrant returnees in other parts of China confirm that house construction is a primary concern regardless of the level of local economic development. Rachel Murphy, for instance, finds that in Jiangxi, among rural households with migrant laborers, house building was by far the most important area of remittance usage, followed by education, daily livelihood, and farm inputs.[25] Sally Sargeson summarizes the motivations prompting the so-called rural house-building craze in the more prosperous Zhejiang countryside.

> Housing . . . is an investment in the family's future. A new house accommodates increasingly diverse, individualized lifestyles and thereby allows for family extension. It conveys to the world information about the wealth and status of its inhabitants, giving sons a wider choice of potential partners. Unencumbered by debt, young couples can channel money into business and education. Finally, a new house offers security and sanctuary to out-migrants and serves as a conduit through which the wages they earn can be drawn back into the family.[26]

One couple has been in Shenzhen for thirteen years. The husband is a construction worker and the wife has worked in various factories before becoming a sanitation worker sweeping city streets. The eldest son is in high school at home, and the younger son is in junior high in Shenzhen. So many of their closest relatives have come to Shenzhen that they feel little need to go home for the Spring Festival. They return home only every three or four years. Nevertheless, after careful and elaborate consideration, they borrowed money to build a new house in a nearby town and they rent it out to generate extra income. The house and the piece of land it is on are insurance for the future.

> We spent sixty thousand yuan building a new house. Half of that amount was borrowed from my wife's brother and ten thousand yuan from my own brother. It's by the road in our township, about a mile from our village. It's built on the newly requisitioned land that has become part of the township. Now we rent it to a fellow villager for

1,200 yuan per year. Now that we have a house, if we return in the future, we can still take a boat to our farmland. Even if we don't do any farming, we at least have a place to live. If we waited until that time, there might not be land or houses for sale any more in the township.[27]

When I was in Sichuan visiting the home villages of some of the workers involved in labor disputes in Shenzhen, kin and families of migrant workers almost always drew my attention to the contrast between the new and old houses, often standing side by side. To these peasants, these structures are solid proof of hard earned status and self-respect. Wang Chang Wu, one of the Shenzhen workers, was taking a break from *dagong* while waiting for a final court decision on the labor dispute with his employer. Having been dismissed from his previous job, he was able to find work as an electrician on a short-term basis. After a year or so, he decided to go home to check on his newly built, two-story house, and his parents, wife, and children. He has rented the ground level of the house to a local family business making bamboo sheets for construction sites. Going past a half dozen workers operating several simple machines that cut up bamboo trunks into threads and weaving them by hand into large flat sheets and containers, he elaborated his design ideas for the second floor of his house. The roomy 1,200-square-foot space was practically empty except for a weathered wooden bench and a television set. Pointing to a raised platform that marked a split-level, he relished his own design idea. "This split-level can be used as a small dinner area, leading to two bedrooms and a bathroom. I still need to do some interior decoration work, and add the drapes, and so on. We have spent more than one hundred thousand yuan on building this house. Now there is nothing left for furniture. We borrowed thirty thousand yuan from relatives and another thirty thousand from the agricultural credits cooperative."[28] His wife had worked in Shenzhen for six years, but came back to Sichuan when his father was diagnosed with cancer. Treatment for the illness had cost them several years of savings from their earnings in the city. His wife raises hogs, sold for five hundred yuan apiece, to supplement the family income.

The irony, in many cases, is that accumulating resources for building a house necessitates leaving home for an extended period of time. The material and emotional well-being of the family are always in tension. The most vivid example of deferred gratification is the story of Lei Juan, whose childhood was one without parents and whose new family house has been left vacant ever since it was built. Lei is now twenty years old and has worked in Shenzhen since 2001. Her mother is a sanitation worker and her father works in construction. They live together with two other families in a room with three sets of double-deck bunk beds, each family paying 280 yuan monthly rent. Her parents left for Shenzhen when she was two, and she and her brother were raised by one relative after another.

> Before 1995, we had a mud house. Now it's a brick house. But it's almost empty, no other furniture except a bed and a table. None of us has lived in that house. My father began working in Shenzhen since 1988 as a construction worker and my mother followed him when I was two. My brother and I were first raised by my mother's sixth sister, then my father's third sister, and then my father's elder brother, moving from relative to relative. Sometimes, my brother and I lived in different households so that it would not be a big burden on our relatives.[29]

LIVED EXPERIENCE OF POWER AND SUBORDINATION IN VILLAGES

If the availability of subsistence farming and the vision of an eventual return to the countryside undermines migrant workers' willingness to sustain collective resistance in Shenzhen, their lived experience of power in the countryside may also have imparted a sense of futility and cynicism about migrants' political effectiveness. Since the 1949 Communist Revolution, Chinese with rural household registrations have for decades been victimized by the urban bias inherent in the Chinese government's macroeconomic strategy. The state, through central planning, has siphoned resources from collective agriculture into urban heavy industries through low-priced compulsory grain procurement. Not only was mobility strictly regimented, but also rural residents confronted disadvantages in a panoply of redistributed resources and services such as health care, social security, and education. This urban-rural hierarchy constitutes one of the sharpest sectoral divisions underlying the social structure of Chinese socialism.[30] Some observers even compare this ascription and place-based system of inequality with a caste society.[31] As a political cultural category, Chinese farmers are collectively referred to as *nongmin,* or "peasantry." It is a term coined by the Chinese state with the connotation that the rural population is " 'backward' and a major obstacle to national development and salvation. For them [the political elite], rural China was still a feudal society of peasants who were intellectually and culturally crippled by 'superstition.' "[32] Even twenty-five years into the reform period, when a relaxed rural-urban migration policy allows farmers to travel and work in the cities, an ingrained and internalized sense of inferiority is still palpable among most of the migrant workers in this study. A telling example is Yang Qin, who is the informal big sister of many of her coworkers and native Guangxi friends in Shenzhen. Fiercely articulate and talking jauntily about her victories in several labor arbitration cases, Yang becomes derisive and scornful when the subject turns to her status as a peasant. She declares very forcefully her contempt for the uncultured peasants, including herself. "As peasant, I just feel naturally inferior. I cannot explain why."

Psychological inferiority is exacerbated by glaring income gaps between rural and urban residents. Between 1998 and 2003, the official urban-rural income ratio has increased from 2.51:1 to 3.23:1.[33] A schoolteacher in a Sichuan village emphasizes the importance of money in the current social order, in which peasants always find themselves among the lowest-income groups.

> People with money look down on poor people. I am a peasant, but I myself despise peasants because we are so poor. According to Chairman Mao's teaching, there exists no hierarchy among occupations, only division of labor. But how can you maintain this view when you observe that peasants always have inferior clothes, food, dwellings, and means of travel? Peasants are the most numerous in this country, but they are also the poorest.[34]

The income gap is only one reason for the pervasive sense of powerlessness and inferiority among rural residents. An equally important factor is their political subordination to a predatory regime of local government. Throughout the reform period, peasant burdens and the abuse of cadre power in extracting fines and grain from the peasantry have triggered widespread discontent in the countryside, threatening rural social stability. Naked power is wielded and exercised in the countryside by local officials. Grassroots elections, which are still largely controlled and managed by the Communist Party, have not been effective in fostering official accountability. The consequence is that for migrant peasant workers, whether in the city or in the village, there is no escape from cadre caprice, abuse, and corruption. Their accounts of interactions with officials in rural areas echo the similarly arbitrary and transparent domination by employers in Shenzhen. In both, the threat and the use of physical violence, not the silent compulsion of the market or the law, plays a manifest role in the exercise of power. Like employers who have private security forces on site or who threaten to deploy criminal elements to quell worker resistance, local officials in the countryside commonly use violence, according to one peasant worker.

> Rural cadres hire thugs to beat people up and to collect fines for out-of-quota births, for example. If peasants cannot afford the fines, these thugs climb onto the roof of the house and damage it. Or they take away furniture or pigs. Since the 1990s, there are pure peasants who

cannot afford paying all kinds of fees. Households with migrant workers fare better and usually have cash to pay fees.[35]

Moreover, peasants often fall prey to official corruption in myriad ways. Bribes have to be paid to resolve land disputes or to lay the foundation for building houses. Peasants are also forced to participate in dubious investment schemes with their meager incomes. The following stories are just a few examples.

> Whenever there are disputes among peasant households about the boundaries of their contracted land, village cadres care only to protect their own acquaintances, or those who have good relations with them. Or when the production teams agreed to pool money to install additional electricity lines, the head of the village committee would simply announce a lump sum to be collected from each household. No one dares to ask how he arrives at that amount. There's a lot of corruption going on, and we tolerate it quietly. And then there is the fishpond that was built by the production team, and later contracted out to team members, but we have never received any dividends from the profits. The Water Authority has allocated more than one hundred thousand yuan for an antidrought grant to the village for repairing the water dam. Where has that money gone? There is more corruption in the village than in Shenzhen. In Shenzhen you see more justice. The Letters and Visits Bureau there will at least receive you, no matter who you are. Here in the countryside, when peasants approached the township government to complain about levies, cadres argued with them and later on public security officers even arrested some of them. My parents told me this when I returned home for a visit.[36]

> My son had to bribe the cadres when he built his house. If you are not related to these cadres, you pay ten yuan a square meter for the foundation. If you are an acquaintance, you pay five yuan. In the days of Chairman Mao, there was no karaoke and no dance hall. How could you become corrupt in such poverty? We have a saying here, "In the past, you could not buy life even if you had the money; now money can buy the lives of those who should die."[37]

> Several years ago, our Fujia township Party secretary asked the provincial government for special funding to "restructure" agricultural production. Peasants were told that Pipa is a good export product and so every family got a non-interest-bearing loan of 1,900 yuan to plant four hundred Pipa trees. Somehow, later on, the terms of the loan changed from 0 percent to 7 percent interest rate and now it is the credit cooperative that lends the money. The Party secretary has been reassigned elsewhere and no one knows what happened to the original funds.[38]

A Hunan woman worker relates another typical form of local official extortion that derives from cadres' regulatory power over private matters such as marriage and fertility.

> You need both good *guanxi* and bribes to get things done at home. My husband is a demobilized soldier and I am a peasant. When we got married, we did not know where to go to get a migrant population birth permit because we are not from the same place. After I got pregnant [in Shenzhen] and came home to rest, I frantically applied for the birth permit. I needed the permit before I could give birth, otherwise no hospital would take me in. Local officials kicked us around like a football. I was six months pregnant, and it was hard for me to go from one department to another. Finally, my father asked our village head to seek personal help from the township head. This township leader just meted out a fine on the spot, saying that one month of pregnancy is fined 1,500 yuan, and six months is 9,000 yuan. The village head said good words for us and convinced him to reduce the fine. The next day, we went again, bringing one hundred yuan worth of cigarettes, a watermelon, and eight hundred yuan cash. He agreed to issue us a birth permit.[39]

Popular consciousness and discontent with bureaucratic domination are particularly acute in Renshou county, the native place of some of the migrant workers in this study. I went home with them, visited their villages, and talked to their relatives and fellow villagers to understand the link between waged employment and peasant household economy. A decade ago, in 1992–1993, peasants in this part of central Sichuan launched an impressive spate of "riots" and demonstrations against brutal and abusive cadre behavior. Ostensibly triggered by an extremely unpopular and coercive road construction levy and by popular outrage about local (provincial and county levels) defiance of central government's 5 percent cap on rural taxation, these collective mobilizations also resulted from discontent with official use of violence in extracting fines for out-of-quota births and tax evasion by peasant households. Peasant leaders were ardent promoters of central government laws and regulations, and their public speeches made in local markets faulted local officials for failing to implement central decrees to reduce peasant burdens. Escalation of confrontation led to the beating and arrest of leaders, peasants holding officials hostage, burning and smashing of cars, and finally deployment of armed police to quell the unrest. The county Party secretary was replaced, other high officials were dismissed, and four peasant leaders were arrested. The province allocated a special emergency fund to complete the highway project.[40]

Different residents draw different lessons from the lore of collective resistance. Some of the villagers proudly suggested that peasants have learned to be more conscious of their legal rights and would not comply with local policies that contravene central directives. But most were jaded and intimidated by the severity of the sentencing of the leader of a popular and innocent attempt to popularize government regulations. "The leader of the riot spent almost ten years in prison. Who dares to come out and lead again? People are afraid of approaching the government," said the brother of one of the migrant workers in this study. The Renshou incident therefore mostly comes down to a sense of the futility of collective and radical confrontation with the state. Discontent and critique of power holders are explicitly articulated in everyday conversations, but they are not easily conducive to collective unrest, especially after the state flexes its repressive muscles. It only breeds cynicism and unobtrusive, individual resistance. For instance, even after the implementation of the "tax-for-fee" reform in 2001,[41] which drastically reduces peasant burdens by half in this area, many peasants still find the cash-for-corvee payment as unreasonable. They see this charge as contributing nothing to rural welfare but only camouflaging farmers' financing of local cadre salaries. But instead of filing collective petitions with the county and township governments, individual households merely refuse payment. A schoolteacher in Fujia district, one of the thirteen districts in Renshou, reflects on the chilling effect of state suppression.

> Three peasant leaders were jailed. Xiang Wenqing got the longest sentence, twelve years. That incident was a sober lesson for both the officials and ordinary people. Law enforcers now dare not use excessive means to collect taxes. The masses, on the other hand, dare not voice their grievances. They give up on going to the officials because they think it is useless. They find the tax slips confusing, with all the unexplained items. Many people complain about the *yiwugong* payment [i.e., paying the fees to substitute for the four days of corvee labor per capita each year]. Some households simply refuse to pay instead of making any noise.[42]

What I have found among migrant workers' experience with local state agents suggests some divergence from the more optimistic scenario described as "rightful resistance" by Kevin O'Brien and Lianjiang Li.[43] They found that peasants often appeal to central policies to protest against local distortions of these policies by local officials. Rightful resistance in rural China, they argue, has been the product of the spread by participatory ideologies and patterns of rule rooted in notions of equality, rights, and rule of law and is a sign of growing rights consciousness and a more contractual approach to political life. It appears as individuals with new aspirations come to appreciate common interests, develop an oppositional consciousness, and become collective actors in the course of struggle. This formulation of rural contentious politics may apply only to the initial phase of some of the popular resistance that has emerged around issues of election and taxation. But it misses the rapid downward spiral that the process of popular resistance and official suppression often unleash. If we follow through farmers' experience of fighting against corruption and abuse of cadre power, the darker side of collective resistance often surfaces—futility of collective action due to official inaction or repression, popular disenchantment in their purported rights enshrined in the law, and erosion of any incipient sense of citizenship together with regime legitimacy in the eyes of ordinary people. Although more research needs to be done to differentiate when and how popular rebellion leads to either empowerment or disempowerment, my limited fieldwork among farmers and migrant workers cautions against a one-dimensional, linear development toward greater democracy and accountability.

NARRATIVES OF POVERTY AND PROGRESS

Despite their youthfulness relative to veteran state workers in the rustbelt, and their much shorter collective biography, the life stories that migrant workers tell of themselves, like the collective memories of older workers in the state sector, contribute to the construction of agencies. Three salient themes emerge in these narratives: abject poverty in the past, hardship but material improvement in the present, and an aspiration for rural entrepreneurialism as a personal strategy for transcending peasantry and industrial work.

Poverty

I asked migrant workers in this study to tell me their feelings and observations about village life and their family life during the collective period and the reform period. Almost unanimously they began with food supply. This construction worker from Sichuan recalls,

> When reform began in 1978, I was only seven years old. I remember eating yam, millet, and corn, not rice. So I understand hunger and poverty. My father died early, so our family did not earn enough work points for food from the production team. We had to borrow food and grain from other households in those days. Even after we contracted our own lands, we still owed the team a certain amount of grain. I do not know if we eventually paid back the grain, but we had a grain debt. After the village divided up the land, the grain problem was solved. People now produce enough rice and we are no longer hungry. In the past, we would have meat only if my mother worked for other households from time to time.[44]

The childhood of a migrant worker born in 1967 spanned both the collective and household responsibility eras. His overall assessment of the collective era was that it was a period of poverty and ignorance.

> I have never experienced starvation, but my brother had days when only corn and millet were available, no rice. I remember times when we could eat meat only a few times per year, because no one raised pigs in the collectives. As school kids, we usually brought leftovers to school for lunch. We had no money to buy lunch at school. . . . Collectives were badly managed, ignorant, and unscientific. We were told to sow seeds 10 cm apart; now people do it 15–20 cm apart. We were planting the seedlings too close together. The crops did not get enough sun and air. On top of that, the quality of fertilizer, feed, and seeds was all inferior.[45]

Although scarcity of food and poor nutrition are most frequently used to illustrate poverty, workers also pointed to illness and the lack of financial resources as prevalent conditions of migrant workers' childhood experience. In an otherwise very animated and spirited conversation, a Hunan woman broke down in tears when she recalled how poverty nearly took her father's life.

> My parents have three daughters and one son. Altogether we were allocated seven mu of land. But during the collective period, our family had little manpower but many mouths to feed. My grandparents died early and so only my father earned work points. We were very poor. . . . I was in junior high when my father came down with a serious lymphoid condition. We did not have money and he went to two quacks who gave him two totally different prescriptions, one after another. He took both prescriptions three times and vomited blood. [Sobbing heavily] We were very scared and took him to the township hospital. We had to borrow money from relatives. My eldest sister had to go to Changsha to work and earn an income to support the family. She was paid ninety yuan per month, and every month she sent home ninety yuan. She did not leave even one yuan for herself. [Sobbing heavily][46]

Workers' memories of poverty often develop into stories of progress for the family and themselves largely through personal perseverance, hard work, and steel will. Yang Qin, the Guangxi woman who is proud of her big-sister status among her friends, seamlessly weaves together a personal story of climbing the social ladder, from a high school dropout in her native village, to an ordinary assembly worker in Shenzhen who, twelve years later, becomes a shop-floor manager of the production department in a large handbag factory, earning a monthly salary of 2,500 yuan. She emphasizes that she got all these promotions by passing examinations, sometimes beating applicants with college degrees but no experience in shop-floor production. And her income is responsible for all the modern trappings of her family's home back in Guangxi. She declares proudly,

> When I was young, we were so poor that there were times when we could not afford salt. . . . After my father injured himself and became paralyzed, my mother was the only able-bodied laborer doing farmwork. We had five girls and one son in our family. I am number four. When I came home from school and saw my mother tending sugar canes and sweet potatoes by herself, I often could not help crying. . . . When I got my first paycheck, I sent it all back home, leaving only five yuan for my own expenses. . . . Overtime shifts often ended at around 11:30 PM but I felt energetic, as though it was still daytime. I did not feel tired or sleepy. I liked doing overtime because I could earn more money. If you don't have work to do and go out, you'll have to pay for everything. Skating, karaoke, things like that all cost money. . . . Sometimes I saw recruitment flyers in the neighborhood, offering higher salaries. I sat for the tests and moved. . . . Today, everything in my mother's house is bought with my money, the large television and hi-fi.[47]

Hardship

"Hardship" *(xinku)* and "ambivalence" *(wunai)* sum up many migrant workers' experience of selling labor to the bosses. Both agricultural and industrial production involve physically demanding labor. The following comparisons given by three experienced women workers in Shenzhen are typical, although they disagree about which kind of labor is more grueling.

> The blazing sun is on your back. Your feet were sunk deep in muddy and slippery ground. Your back aches from bending down all day. And you have no control over the harvest, if the weather decides not to cooperate and turn bad that year. Inside the factory, at least there is a roof above you![48]

> Farming is of course more tough than factory work! During harvest time, no matter how intense the sun is, we just have to endure it. When we are done with the field, there are poultry and hogs to take care of. But in factories, you get days off, or Sunday off. At home, there is no rest day. Women always have housework around the house. Men have to take up other odd jobs to supplement incomes. Farmers' work is more demanding.[49]

> Overtime work at night gives me black spots on my face. The doctor says it's due to inadequate sleep. Overtime shifts go into early morning, and at the end of the shift, I sometimes don't even feel my own head, like last year in the factory in Nantou. I cannot stand up straight in the morning, and I cannot walk to the morning meeting. Farming the land is also hard work. But it's hard work only during the day. You can rest

at night and take a nap in the afternoon. Except in sowing and harvest times, there is not much to do, just periodically check on the crops. That's why many people in our village play mahjong. In the past, in the collectives, there was more work. Even when it rained, you still had to report to the production team. Now, individual families decide when to work and rest. When the sun is too intense, you can choose to stay indoors. The worst thing is that farming does not make money.[50]

But she also immediately adds the disclaimer that neither kind of work offers any guarantee of economic return or freedom to the producers.

Back in the village, you are physically free but you are financially hard pressed. Working in factories in Shenzhen does not give you any freedom. You are confined within the factory most of the time. But you get paid, usually. Yet that again is no guarantee. Last year, when we were owed wages and wanted to sue the employer, I had to make numerous and long bus trips to the courts. That's really tough, given our brutal work schedule. At home, you can walk to almost all places.[51]

The hardship of working for the bosses, as these quotations suggest, is embodied. Factory discipline and the brutal production schedule often leave indelible marks on workers' bodies, in the form of permanent damage to workers' health. With nine years of working experience in Shenzhen's factories, a twenty-nine-year-old woman worker lamented,

People at home can only see the visible and positive results of *dagong*. You make money and they will be enthusiastic about you. But my body and my health pay the highest price for *dagong*. I almost never got colds before. Now, I am very vulnerable to colds. Between the factory and the dormitory, we have to walk for about thirty minutes. If it rains, we may get wet on the way but we have to work in an air-conditioned room no matter how wet we are. And my back always aches, whenever I stand, walk, or lie down a little longer. Like many of the workers in the factory, I have a throat condition. There is always something blocking my throat, something I cannot spit out. I lose my appetite easily too. It's an occupational disease due to the chemicals in the air in the factory.[52]

There are other kinds of hidden injuries. After years of a double existence as both peasant and worker, migrants report a sense of lost identity, that they are neither peasant nor worker. One Hunan woman expresses a typical realization that migrant workers cannot take up either agricultural or industrial work as a permanent or long-term career.

We [migrants] are neither peasants nor workers. I don't know how to farm the land anymore after so many years away from home. When I was young, people planted seedlings by hand; now they use a new throwing method. . . . We are not real workers either. With so little education and skills, and the job market so fluid, we can be dismissed anytime. How can you build a long-term career, when there is no security and we have no skills?[53]

An eloquent worker representative from Sichuan relates at length his "contradictory" feelings, both wanting and not wanting to return home.

Ever since I started working in 1987, I have always worked in Shenzhen. If I judge my own ability, I feel I am better than I was in the past. But then, I also feel that after fifteen years, I still have not earned much money, that I am not as good and competent as other people who can start their own businesses here. . . . I returned to my village in 1994, 1997, and this year [2003]. Every time, I was reluctant to go home. But once I got home, I was reluctant to come back to Shenzhen. When I am home, I say to myself: in the past, this place was so backward and poor; but even after so many years of *dagong*, I still have very little surplus. So, I don't want to leave. But once I am in the city, I am anxious to earn more money to improve the life of my family, and therefore I don't want to return home so soon. Most of the time, I don't even know what I think or want, village or city?[54]

For younger women, working in the city is also a contradictory experience. Zhang Xiao has worked as a factory hand and a restaurant server in Shenzhen for two years. Her parents and brother are also migrant workers here. She is torn between the security and the stagnation of village life.[55]

At home, I have a shelter protecting me from storms. But we have to enter society eventually. Growing up in the countryside is like a tree growing without sunshine. . . . Here in Shenzhen, we also have happy times. I am the happiest on payday. We go to parks or shopping malls, to window shop.

But like most of her peers, she cannot imagine settling down in the city.

I am sure I won't stay here and work for the bosses forever. I am sure I'll go home one day. I don't know why I think so, but that's what I believe. I know I'll go home and farm when I get older. But I have never done any farmwork.[56]

In terms of return to expenditure of labor, the net income of many factory workers is about the same as that from sideline production in the village. Waged employment in construction or shops in townships near to home villages also bring comparable net incomes, although the job markets are more limited than those in major cities such as Shenzhen and Shanghai. For some workers, waged work brings a more assured and immediate income. One worker relates what many see as the advantage of waged employment over agriculture.

You get an immediate return for your labor when you work in the city.
You work one month and the boss pays you the next month. With
farming, you work and can get something back only the next year.
Moreover, farming can provide subsistence only, not surplus. And even
when you stay in the village, you need to spend money on different
things; it's like in Shenzhen, you need money. On balance, I spend as
much at home as I spend in the city.[57]

Yet as he elaborates the comparison between these two ways of earning a
living, he realizes how elusive the difference is. Employers can easily get
away with unpaid wages or illegal deduction of wages, the two grievances he
and his coworkers have in the labor dispute they are involved in. "The
biggest contradiction is that we don't get what we should get. There is a
minimum wage law and all that, but many workers cannot get the legal
minimum, especially women working in assembly lines. How can we say it's
fair?"[58]

The same ambivalence applies to workers' sense of personal freedom.
Many experience the contradiction of economic bondage and geographical
mobility. Low wage rates and long hours of work deny them the opportunity to explore the sights and sounds of Shenzhen. Their lives are very con-
stricted in the factory premises and the immediate environment. Extremely
long and punishing work hours do not leave much time for urban explo-
ration. A vivid account of a woman worker captures the lack of freedom of
industrial work in a Japanese-Chinese joint venture making sneakers for
export. It was her first job in Shenzhen.

It's a piece-rate factory and we basically worked as much as we could.
From 8 AM to 2 AM, if there were outstanding orders. No rest day at all.
The only rest time was during power outages, and we just threw our
things on the floor and would fall asleep right away, right there. I almost
never saw daylight. I still remember one day when summer came, I
went out at lunch to buy a mosquito net for my bunk bed. When I first
stepped outside and saw the sun, I could not open my eyes. I was very
weak. . . . For six months, I did not think of going anywhere except from
the dormitory to the factory. Only after about a half year did I sneak
into the famous theme park near Xiangmihu. Work was totally
exhausting.[59]

Progress

Consumption is a very powerful experience of personal and societal
progress. Married male workers often mentioned buying or planning to buy
big-ticket items such as household appliances. The list of basic electrical
goods includes color televisions, washing machines, and refrigerators. The

more advanced and luxurious items are air conditioners and audiovisual entertainment systems. Many married women workers purchase gold or silver jewelry for their symbolic and investment value. Younger workers use their money to pay for short-term courses, especially to learn computer and Internet skills, or vocational classes such as cooking, sewing, and bookkeeping. They report wide-ranging spending behavior, with some very frugal and others inclined toward free spending. Clothes, meals, cigarettes, and beer are the most common expenditures. The excitement associated with personal consumption and material possession quickly gives way to the realization that their wages can hardly afford much beyond daily necessities. Theft in the city has a chilling effect on their desire to purchase more valuable items. Like many young women workers in Shenzhen, a twenty-one-year-old Sichuan woman speaks of both joy and despondence about spending her own money.

> The happiest moment of *dagong* is collecting our wage payments. Women workers would take a walk in public parks or to the shopping mall to look at clothes, just window shop. Actually, I can only afford a summer blouse not more than twenty yuan apiece, and about forty yuan for a winter suit. Usually I buy three each summer and another three each winter. We have work uniforms, so we don't spend much on clothes. I have also bought a cell phone, but it was stolen very soon. Now, I want to buy a computer for my brother at home.[60]

Others who have bought jewelry painfully saw their necklaces or earrings stolen. A married male worker was not enthusiastic about consumption, having spent most of his savings on building a new house. He sighed,

> I have never bought anything for myself, except a two-thousand-yuan television set and a necklace for my wife. But last year during the Spring Festival, when we visited home in Chengdu, someone snapped her necklace. . . . I bought a cell phone several years ago but I lost it very soon. I don't have one any more.[61]

Consider the case of another veteran migrant worker who has more than a decade of work experience in the garment industry. Zhao Rong, a Sichuan native, became a migrant worker in 1991 when she was thirty, and in 2003, her eldest daughter joined her in Shenzhen and began her own migrant worker career in another garment factory. Her husband is a demobilized soldier and has worked as a factory hand, security guard, and kitchen assistant. The narrative she gives of her life story is one of surmounting the crippling backwardness of the countryside through enduring the unendurable, and making way for the next generation by giving them the best education she can afford.

I came to the city to work in 1991. I was already married with two children. I have always been very interested in sewing and making clothes. So I told my mother that I wanted to take classes to be a seamstress. Then I saw a recruitment notice in the township, and I went to Shanghai and from there to Shenzhen after a few years. Garment is the toughest of all industries. The dust is unbearable. It is so thick that it always clots my throat. There is no way of spitting it out. Our hands are always dirty with color dyes. No masks, no gloves. It's much harder than electronics factories. I usually do not take any lunch break, and even when all the workers have left the shift, I would still be there working. That's why my production volume is always the highest, anywhere I go. I was already earning 1,400 yuan ten years ago! At times, I even made 2,500 yuan. No ordinary seamstress makes that much money. The whole industry uses the same remuneration system: piece rates and overtime shifts whenever there are orders. No order, no shift. For longer orders, the work pace can be more lax, and we get some rest. But for short orders, there is no flexibility and the daily quotas are very tight. Normally, each order lasts ten days. . . . I sent one thousand yuan home to my mother, to take care of my two sons, one in high school, the other in primary school. So most of the money goes to their education. After that, I hope to buy a house in our township. It will cost seventy thousand yuan for the land and the construction. In the village, people respect those with money. Because my husband was in the army and has a township *hukou*, they respect us. They may think that one day, they'll have to ask us for loans. So they are very willing to help my mother with her farmwork.[62]

Entrepreneurship

When migrant workers look into the future, entrepreneurial aspirations abound. Almost without exception, they articulate a desire to become their own boss back in the countryside in the future. "Open a small business" and "open a small shop" *(kaixiaodian)* are the two most general terms for operating a small business concern, such as a restaurant, a grocery store, a bicycle repair shop, a beauty salon, a clothing shop, or even a small factory. When pressed for more concrete details, migrant workers usually have relatively little to offer, except to say that they will think about it when they have amassed sufficient savings, in the neighborhood of tens of thousands of yuan. Being a little boss *(xiao laoban)* is an attractive personal goal, as it implies someone with status, independence, and modest wealth.[63]

Since their marriage in 1993, a thirty-four-year-old woman worker and her husband have never farmed the five mu of land they have contracted. Their plan for the future, typical of many migrant workers, underscores a refusal to see either agriculture or industry as a viable long-term way of making a living. Their hope lies in petty rural entrepreneurship.

> Farming is really meaningless, but factory work is hard. With so many unemployed people in the city, we are sure that one day we will have to return to the village. Back in the countryside, we don't earn much, but we can survive without wages or going to the market. But in the city, you cannot live without money. It's true that as a family you can earn a couple thousand more each year working in the city, but living in the city, you have to spend that money. . . . When we first came to work in Shenzhen, our only goal was to build a house. Now that we have built it, we are still here. My husband does not want to return to the land. In the future, when we eventually return for good, we want to run a small village store or a small business. Farming is the last resort; it's only good for subsistence.[64]

The reality is that very few returnees are able to realize their dreams of entrepreneurship. In Sichuan and Anhui provinces, for instance, a survey in 1999 found that returnees accounted for about 29 percent of current and past migrants, and only 2.7 percent of them engage in nonagricultural businesses (among them, 2 percent own small service businesses, 0.3 percent own productive facilities, and another 0.3 percent engage in transportation).[65] Murphy's field study of Jiangxi, another major migrant sending province, seems to suggest a more promising opportunity structure for returnee entrepreneurs, with these former migrants making "significant" contributions to local private enterprises. For instance, in one county in 1997, returnees accounted for one-third of all individual entrepreneurs in services and manufacturing, and they contributed 14 percent of tax revenue returned by this sector.[66] Successful entrepreneurship is more likely for men than for women, for those with higher levels of education, longer durations of urban sojourn, greater advancement (usually in white-collar positions) in the urban labor market, and better contacts at home. The sectors they work for in the city usually serve as "incubators" for these aspiring entrepreneurs, who tend to set up shops in the same sectors in which they have worked.

CONCLUSION

A major institution that plays a key role in the reproduction of migrant workers' labor power is the land rights system in rural China. Since the late 1970s, decollectivization has unleashed millions of peasants to enter the city in pursuit of waged employment. But the dismantling of the Chinese communes does not lead to "accumulation through dispossession" that Marx analyzed with respect to the enclosure movement of the English country-side. Nor is it an instance of the kind of predatory process in third-world countries whereby various collective forms of ownership are converted into private property rights.[67] Rather, the distinctiveness of the Chinese agricultural reform is that it returns farmland to the village collective, which then allocates land use rights to individual peasant households. Most of the migrant workers holding rural household registrations are entitled to a renewable land lease in their native village. As agricultural prices drop and the cost of agricultural production rises, farmers increasingly need cash incomes to sustain farming and to pay rural taxes. Therefore, land is both an asset and a liability; it reproduces the labor power of migrant workers but it also compels their participation in waged employment. A piece of rural land is also the most significant material anchor for migrant workers' identities as peasants. The availability of rural land and the subsistence economy it supports act as a safety valve for their city survival, and dampens migrant workers' resilience in sustained labor struggles. Yet by 2005, land seizure and illegal requisitioning of villagers' land by local officials led to intensified rural unrest and undermined the economic and political buffer offered by the peasants' land entitlement. The erosion of this institution may enhance the radicalization potential of labor protests involving migrant workers in the years ahead.

Migrant workers' experience with the local state in both the city and the countryside has convinced many that the political system is beyond their influence. In chapter 5, I showed that the flawed and subordinate legal system and the violation of labor contracts expose migrant workers to naked and personal domination by employers, sometimes compounded by discriminatory treatment by state officials. As a result, many migrant workers do not harbor any "liberal illusion" that they enjoy equal rights and legal justice as urban residents. In this chapter, I traced their experience back home, and found that domination in the countryside is equally marked by concrete and transparent domination by local cadres through taxation and levies, birth control, coercive investment, and other kinds of financial extortion. Popular anger against cadre abuse and corruption has at times led to collective rebellions, found in the home towns of some of the workers in this study. Many have apparently been discouraged by state suppression and terrified by the heavy penalties inflicted on farmer leaders, however. As long as economic opportunities exist, migrant workers see more promising prospects in using personal and economic strategies to escape bureaucratic abuse and control.

Finally, the collective biography migrant workers construct reveals how the meaning of *dagong* is assessed in the context of rural poverty and immobility. Working in the city is a strategy for limited upward mobility, especially for the next generation. Juxtaposing the memory narratives in chapter 4 with the personal stories reported here, one sees many contrasts. Whereas there is ambivalence about state socialism among the older generation of workers, there is a much more acute and clear-cut sense of making progress from abject poverty to relative stability and sufficiency. This dominant narrative of progress coupled with an aspiration for entrepreneurship fosters not a sentiment of collective desperation, like that found among unemployed and retired workers in the northeast rustbelt, but rather anger and criticism of discrimination when these rural villagers become diligent workers in cities but are denied legal wages and rights.

PART IV

Conclusion

7 Chinese Labor Politics in Comparative Perspective

> In the cotton and flax spinning mills there are many rooms in
> which the air is filled with fluff and dust. . . . The operative of
> course had no choice in the matter. . . . The usual consequences
> of inhaling factory dust are the spitting of blood, heavy, noisy
> breathing, pains in the chest, coughing and sleeplessness. . . .
> Accidents occur to operatives who work in rooms crammed full
> of machinery. . . . The most common injury is the loss of a joint
> of the finger. . . . In Manchester one sees not only numerous
> cripples, but also plenty of workers who have lost the whole
> or part of an arm, leg or foot.
>
> FRIEDRICH ENGELS, *The Condition of the Working Class in England*, 1845[1]

> There is no fixed work schedule. A twelve-hour workday is
> minimum. With rush orders, we have to work continuously for
> thirty hours or more. Day and night . . . the longest shift we had
> worked nonstop lasted for forty hours. . . . It's very exhausting,
> because we have to stand all the time, to straighten the denim
> cloth by pulling. Our legs are always hurting. There is no place
> to sit on the shop floor. The machines do not stop during our lunch
> breaks. Three workers in a group will just take turns eating, one
> at a time. . . . The shop floor is filled with thick dust. Our bodies
> become black working day and night indoors. When I get off from
> work and spit, it's all black.
>
> A CHINESE MIGRANT WORKER IN SHENZHEN, 2000[2]

The haunting parallels between these two depictions of working-class life,
one in mid-nineteenth-century Manchester and the other in twenty-first-
century China, underscore both capitalism's historic global sprawl and
workers' common predicaments. In the world's many rustbelts, too, workers' experiences with unemployment and plant closure bear striking similarities. Whether it is the closing of a steel mill in the American Midwest in
the 1980s or the bankruptcy of a state-owned textile factory in northeastern
China in the 1990s, deindustrialization has inflicted similar collective
injuries on blue-collar communities. Consider these two workers, worlds
apart yet almost identical in their consternation and indignation.

235

Joe Smetlack has been "pushing" a cab for the last two years. He's very angry. Joe's thoughts are never far from the money he believes he was cheated out of. When Wisconsin Steel closed, Joe was entitled to severance payment, supplementary unemployment benefits, and vacation pay totaling $23,000 by his count. But he's gotten nothing. . . . The experience has made him bitter. "I resent very much what they do to us. Right now, I'm looking for revenge. . . . I stood behind the government in the 1960s. I would have went to 'Nam. The form of government we have here, you can't beat it. But it's being corrupted. . . . The American Dream? That's dog eat dog. Rip off as good as you can. Integrity don't mean a damn thing anymore."[3]

I joined the People's Liberation Army at nineteen, and seven years later, came back to join the factory. I gave my youth to the state. Thirty-some years of job tenure, at fifty-three, with young and elderly dependents at home, they make me a laid-off worker! How can I attain any balance inside? Cadres can go to the office any time they like, and have ladies sitting around the dinner table. Yet we cannot even get our livelihood allowance on time![4]

These personal snapshots tellingly suggest that workers in the global sunbelt and rustbelt face similar challenges of exploitation and exclusion. What then is unique about the Chinese labor protests documented in previous chapters? In this concluding chapter, I approach this question from two directions. First, I make schematic comparisons between labor protests in China and those in other places and times, and speculate on parallels and contrasts. This is necessarily a heuristic excursion that can only claim to be suggestive of plausible comparative analysis in future studies. Second, I pursue a cross-class comparison within China and analyze the strikingly similar features of protests by workers, villagers, and urban homeowners during the reform period.

In a nutshell, comparing China with other parts of the world, I discover that the propensity and capacity of rustbelt and sunbelt workers worldwide to stage collective protests tend to be enhanced by (1) competition among political elites, parties, or trade unions; (2) skills leverage over integrated production; or (3) community-based associations or social movement allies. Chinese workers confront the unique challenge of not having any of these opportunities or resources. If this "China and the rest" comparison shows what China is not, the second, cross-class comparison within China shows perhaps more directly what China is. The features of labor protests I have identified—decentralization, cellular activism, and legalism—also characterize collective mobilization by other aggrieved social groups. All these struggles tend toward a convergence on the law as the terrain of refashioning state-society relations, class and citizenship formation, and collective mobilization. Juxtaposing labor unrest with instances of peasant and property owners' mobilization will spotlight a uniquely Chinese path of contentious politics that pivots on a politics of the law: popular insistence on using the law, working through legal and bureaucratic channels, while equally readily breaking the law, taking to the street, and assailing official corruption for violating the law and justice.

In what follows, I will first sum up the arguments this book makes about labor politics in China. Drawing on other scholars' reports on other segments of the economy and the workforce, I offer some speculative propositions on the tendencies of labor politics in China. The second section moves on to look at the politics of deindustrialization, plant closure, and unemployment in the United States and Russia. The third section returns to the sunbelts of the developing world and compares labor conditions in the Chinese export base with *maquiladoras* in Mexico and export industries in Korea and prerevolutionary China. The fourth and final section discusses popular resistance in reform period China by peasants over land seizures and by middle-class homeowners over property rights.

PROTESTS OF DESPERATION, PROTESTS AGAINST DISCRIMINATION

Since the 1980s, the Chinese communist regime has pursued a dual developmental strategy of fiscal decentralization and "rule by law" authoritarianism. This book seeks to understand how this developmental strategy of decentralized legal authoritarianism affects ordinary workers' collective capacity to foster or resist social change. Broadly speaking, it examines the linked transformation of state power and worker power in a vast country whose diverse regional economies offer ample opportunities for comparison. Jettisoning the monolithic notion of China as a single unit of analysis and the homogenizing view of the labor force as an immense pool of nondescript factory hands, I have chosen to compare the northeast rustbelt and the southern sunbelt. *Protests of desperation* refers to the pattern of activism in Liaoning by veteran state-sector workers, whereas *protests against discrimination* sums up the mode of resistance in Guangdong by young migrant workers employed in private and foreign-owned firms. The two patterns converge in certain dimensions and diverge in others.

Despite many differences in social background and generational and work experiences, I have found that in both regions, worker protests share the characteristics of targeting local officials, cellular activism, fragmentation of interests, and legalistic rhetoric. I argue that these shared dynamics of labor protests can be traced to the overall state strategy and tensions of decentralized legal authoritarianism. Decentralization of economic decision making has turned workers against local governments and apparatuses that now bear the responsibility for enterprise failure and violation of national labor law, social security regulations, and bankruptcy procedures. Moreover, fiscal and economic decentralization, coupled with market competition and an uneven flow of global and domestic investment, has created a kaleido-scope of fine-grained social and economic differentiation across factories in the same locality and across localities. Their interests divided by these local economic forces, workers' targets of action are local power holders because they are the only remaining access points in what is popularly perceived as an agentless and self-regulating market economy.

The common knowledge that the state will not tolerate cross-workplace alliances coupled with the threat of suppression generates self-limiting approaches to protests among workers, who primarily seek to resolve what they see as firm-specific grievances such as layoffs and nonpayment of wages or benefits. Cellular mobilization also thrives in the encompassing environment of Chinese enterprise, where residential quarters and dormi-tories are located within or near the factory or factory complex. These self-contained, all-encompassing communities facilitate communication and the aggregation of interests, especially at moments of mass layoffs or relocation, or when enterprises fail to make good on promised benefits.

Finally, the third common characteristic of protests across the two regions is the ubiquitous invocation of the central government's edicts and legal rights by both groups of workers. It flows from the central government's own emphasis on "rule by law," or a law-based government. Legalism has become simultaneously the hegemonic ideology and the rhetoric of popular resistance. It does not mean that workers already enjoy the rights enshrined in the law books, or that the legal institutions in China effectively secure and protect labor rights. It means only that the law has become a viable terrain of struggle, tantalizing in its promise and empowering in its effect when work-ers occasionally win cases in the unpredictable court system.

Despite these similarities, and despite their shared animosity and oppo-sition to a powerful but corrupt bureaucratic elite, the two groups of work-ers are separated from each other by the persistence of rural-urban dualism in the social structure, the differences in how the local states regulate their employment, and the ways their labor power is socially reproduced beyond wage work. Workers find different leverage under the two labor systems. Rustbelt workers resort to creating public disruption and pressure as a means of political bargaining, whereas migrant workers have no other informal moral economy or institutional power except appealing to labor bureaucracy, the courts, and the rhetoric of legalism. The different ways labor power is socially reproduced for these two groups of workers—workplace-based pensions and housing in the rustbelt and village-based subsistence farming for workers in the sunbelt—lead to different prevailing grievances, with the former group focusing on collective consumption and the latter on wages and working conditions.

Finally, the social origins and collective experiences between the two groups of workers shape the repertoire of their insurgent identities. The older generation of workers who came of age under state socialism and Maoism invoked a rich vocabulary and justice standards drawing on Marxian class analysis and Mao's mass theory. Although the new generation of migrant workers are less conversant in class terms, they share with rustbelt workers the language of rule by law and legal rights to articulate their critique of exploitation. In short, invoking Marxist, Maoist, and liberal political ideology and identities, selecting and combining them in different circumstances, workers demonstrate a lively consciousness of class exploitation, political exclusion, deprivation of legal justice, and outrage against official corruption. The two groups of workers may have arrived at similar sets of insurgent identities through different cultural mediation and historical experiences, but the overlapping albeit not identical repertoire of identities and claims may hold out some possibility for alliance. To date, however, workers' insurgent consciousness exceeds their insurgent capacity. That is, their insurgent identities seem to project a universalistic and inclusive group boundary, yet labor mobilization remains mostly cellular, localized, and fragmented.

By selecting the most excluded and exploited segments of the Chinese working class as the twin foci, this study has left out workers who are more educated and skilled, and are in more formally regulated employment situations. Chinese workers in profitable state-owned enterprises (SOEs), technology-intensive joint ventures, or image-sensitive consumer goods manufacturing are more likely to avoid the most egregious violations of labor rights, such as nonpayment of wages and physical abuse. Employers in these businesses are more compelled to abide by the Labor Law and labor contracts for various reasons. Research has found that big corporations' desire to maintain a stable and semiskilled workforce or cultivate a reputation for good corporate citizenship is conducive to improvement of working conditions. Boy Luthje's study of electronics contract manufacturing in China finds that "these plants differ markedly from low-end assembly workshops

of which many are correctly labeled sweatshops. Wages are usually somewhat higher, and contract manufacturing plants are generally not characterized by the problematic health and safety conditions for which smaller
assembly shops and also many big plants in the region's shoe, garment, and
toy industries have become infamous."[5] The reasons, Luthje suggests, are
twofold. On the one hand, major brand-name information technology manufacturers such as Hewlett-Packard, Dell, Ericsson, and Siemens all have
substantial relations with government authorities as potential customers
for large-scale projects or product development for the Chinese market.
Such relationships "call for a standing of good corporate citizenship which
makes potential troubles regarding working conditions in subcontracting
firms undesirable."[6] On the other hand, contract manufacturing companies
try to cope with the instability of the workforce and to minimize job hop-
ping by offering a range of paternalistic practices such as providing leisure
activities and amusement facilities (such as video-game parlors and cyber-
cafés), and making displays of corporate generosity. Continuity of production requires managerial efforts to minimize potentially conflictual situations, especially when workers do not have any system of interest
representation.

Several studies on the changing industrial relations in SOEs and joint
ventures also indicate an individualization or rationalization of labor conflict
resolution, and a lack of inclination for collective mobilization. Doug
Guthrie, for instance, has found that in Shanghai's medium and large SOEs,
not only did organizations widely adopt organizational features that mimic
Western firms, employees within these firms too were more likely to view
their employment relations through a formal, legal-rational lens.[7] Labor
contracts and the local labor arbitration institutions play a central role in
resolving individual-based contract violations. Collective mobilization is
rarely possible or desirable. Also in Shanghai, Mary Gallagher's study on
urban workers' use of the law in labor disputes discovers that collective
mobilization is rare among those who resort to the legal system for redress
of labor rights violations. These workers are employed in the nonstate sector or in reformed SOEs. The younger ones tend to focus on a more strictly
legalistic interpretation of the dispute, while older workers use a moral discourse and approach the law only after long periods of petitioning.[8] Since
both studies were done in Shanghai, one of the most dynamic growth centers in the Chinese economy, it is possible that general economic prosperity
has engendered more individual-based market solutions among the
aggrieved workers who believe that these solutions are more effective than
collective political or legal ones. How the regional economy, generational

experiences, economic sector, and firm characteristics may affect patterns of labor unrest is an important question with no easy answers, given the hostile terrain of researching labor unrest in China. It is equally difficult to collect systematic aggregate data on the volume of protests, or to obtain in-depth, fine-grained data on the micro-mobilizational dynamics of these events.[9] Based on available materials, it seems that workers in more regulated, technology-intensive sectors in more prosperous regions have more bargaining power and institutional resources to negotiate with their employers, yet are also least likely to pursue collective action because of their relatively privileged position in the labor market.

Besides workers in relatively privileged and regulated employment, many workers find themselves in much less enviable positions. For the millions of workers who still toil in traditional SOEs struggling to stay in business, reform has thrust upon them a new form of dependence. My own research on state industries in Guangzhou in the late 1990s found that middle-aged workers without many educational credentials and lacking market capacity fare worse during the reform period. The elimination of permanent employment and the uneven implementation of pension and welfare reforms have aggravated workers' dependence on these remaining SOE jobs. Their lack of alternative employment opportunities consequently has enhanced managerial authority within the enterprise. Contrary to workers' "organized dependence" on the enterprise and, by extension, the state in the prereform era, I have termed this labor regime in the reform era one of *disorganized despotism*.[10] Owing to workers' continued, albeit transformed, dependence on state factories and the difficulty of finding stable employment in the nonstate sector, SOE workers' discontent, generally about increased shop-floor discipline and relatively low wage levels, did not translate into open defiance, only passive resistance such as goldbricking and hidden sabotage.[11]

Looking ahead, radicalization and pacification of labor struggles are both possible. A looming crisis of landlessness in the countryside, caused by local cadres' coercive requisitioning of rural land, is rapidly removing one of the most significant buffers for subsistence protection among millions of migrant workers. When landless peasants move to the city for jobs, there is no hinterland for retreat to subsistence in times of unemployment or wage arrears. When this avenue of escape back to agricultural subsistence is blocked, labor conflicts are likely to find more explosive expression in cities. For unemployed workers, as we saw in chapter 4, joblessness among middle-aged workers in the state sector may worsen with further globalization and liberalization of the Chinese economy. The adverse effects on workers may be heightened if it develops in tandem with the housing conflicts that have erupted in many cities where local officials' urban redevelopment craze has encroached on homeowners' property rights. At the end of my fieldwork in Liaoning, workers reported their worries about impending relocation and inadequate compensation after the government had announced a plan to redevelop the Tiexi district into a high-technology and commercial district. The rising tide of residents' protests against evacuation and inadequate relocation compensation also indicates that the final form of livelihood security—homeownership—for many retirees and laid-off workers is at risk of being taken away. The convergence of two separate pathways of insurgency cannot be ruled out.

But there is another, opposite scenario of labor politics development. Better enforcement of the Labor Law or property rights may institutionalize and rationalize the resolution of labor conflict. This study has pointed to the potential for the legal system to channel collective mobilization into the relatively routinized, bureaucratic environment of the Labor Bureaus, the arbitration committees, and the courts.[12] The communist regime, for its own legitimacy and survival, may be compelled to crack down on corruption and impose serious judicial and legal reform. We cannot underestimate the determination and effectiveness of the Chinese regime's self-reform to establish a law-based government, after its radical self-transformation from state socialism. Another possible force of change toward a labor rule of law is the pressure generated by workers from below. Workers' expectation of legal justice may grow over time, especially as the social contract can no longer be invoked and if the central government insists on a rule by law to legitimize authoritarianism and restrain subordinate officials. A dialectical view of reality will hold fast to the contradictions of this system of decentralized legal authoritarianism and attend to the ever-emerging effects and possibilities inherent in those contradictions. Legal consciousness may outgrow the illiberal legal system that engendered it, and disparate leaders of cellular mobilization may over time join forces in confronting a common opponent, and in the process overcome the unfavorable conditions that have kept them dispersed in the first place.

POLITICS OF DEINDUSTRIALIZATION: CHINA AND THE GLOBAL RUSTBELT

Decades before Chinese workers in Liaoning's heavy industrial enterprises were let go in massive numbers, their counterparts in the American coal mining industry in Pennsylvania and Appalachia, in the steel industry of

Pittsburgh and Chicago, and later in auto and rubber plants in Midwestern states such as Wisconsin and Ohio, or other low-skill, labor-intensive factories in small-town America had to confront the challenge of deindustrialization and capital relocation. Ethnographies of American working-class communities' sustaining the effects of industrial decline reveal economic, psychological, and moral devastation similar to that experienced in postsocialist China.[13] If the challenges thrust on workers bear striking parallels to one another, however, their responses and leverage in the face of such challenges have sprung from specific local resources and conditions, and are therefore quite varied. The strength of community organizations and the availability of alliances with other community-based social movements or activist groups seem to significantly affect workers' ability to put up a fight, irrespective of immediate results. Civil-society support is conspicuously absent in the Chinese case. Granted that even in the United States, worker struggles usually failed to avert capital's decision to divest, relocate, or shut down factories, there may still be positive long-term effects arising from workers' capacity to ally with other social movement groups in the United States. This has not been the case in China.

Shared Injuries

What Eve Weinbaum wrote about the closing in 1992 of Acme Boot Company in Clarksville, a small Tennessee town, could well be used to describe a typical plant closure in Liaoning. A thriving company that had begun production in 1929, Acme had 1,500 workers with an average age of forty-seven in 1992, who boasted an average company tenure of twenty-five years. Many workers had relatives and friends—even entire families—working in the factory and were shocked to learn that the profitable firm would relocate to Puerto Rico, whose government had offered Acme's financially strapped parent company buildings and generous investment packages. The new plant also stood to benefit from the tax credits allowed by the U.S. tax code applicable to all U.S. territories. Economic and emotional difficulties similar to those experienced by laid-off SOE workers in Liaoning engulfed the Clarksville community. Weinbaum observed, "As in every plant closing, laid-off workers became scared, depressed, and mistrustful. . . . Most workers had believed their jobs to be absolutely secure. They had worked at Acme for their entire adult lives and had no training in anything else." One worker recounted, "When I got laid off, I got depressed, moody. . . . Then you get bitter. It really was very hard. . . . I had a hard time adjusting. I got so depressed that I couldn't even clean my house; I didn't go no place; I didn't even do anything."[14]

244 / Part IV

Similar laments of loss and hopelessness are painfully reminiscent of those in the working-class community following the closure of a Chrysler plant in Kenosha, Wisconsin. Kathryn Dudley gave voice to automobile workers' indignation and rage. Like Chinese workers who emphasized their contribution to constructing socialism and national industry, American workers articulated forceful moral claims for their right to secure employment based on auto workers' contribution to the war effort and national security when the plant was converted to military production during World War II. The sense of betrayal was particularly acute because of what workers saw as the company's capitulation to foreign competition and imports. Dudley, in intriguing parallels with my own findings in China, wrote, "For Kenosha autoworkers, the concept of job security is firmly embedded in a set of cultural assumptions about what American society owes them in return for their productive labor. . . . Industrial communities like Kenosha were among the first to respond to the war call. How . . . can the country now forsake those who have served it so well?"[15]

Like Chinese workers, Kenosha workers pointed to the failure of the rich and powerful to honor the moral commitments that once made America strong. "If the country belongs to the people who have made it strong—all the 'real' Americans—then everyone who works for a living is victimized when jobs are sent out of the country. If the United States government were truly 'of the people, by the people, and for the people,' workers say, it would not allow big corporations to close plants, abandon communities, and dump hardworking people like themselves out onto the streets."[16] No less adamantly than Chinese workers in Liaoning, American workers held the government responsible for breaking an implicit social contract. "Government gains its right to exist as the result of popular consensus and social contract. And its primary duty is to ensure that the average citizen will not be victimized or exploited by ruthless villains, thieves, and lawbreakers. . . . Events in Kenosha signaled to autoworkers that the social contract was unraveling before their very eyes. The United States government, by taking no action to prevent the destruction of American jobs, appears to be abetting the major corporations in their crimes against the people."[17]

When mills closed or went bankrupt, many also lost a major portion of their pensions guaranteed in the union contract. New owners of the old plant may not honor past commitments or have obtained concessions to absolve them of any responsibility for paying benefits. Despite rosy rhetoric from governments and the industrial elite about retraining and new jobs, most rustbelt communities in the wake of deindustrialization see only low-level, nonunion, minimum-wage service jobs without benefits replacing higher-paying unionized jobs in manufacturing. Communities in trauma witness a familiar list of expressions and effects of personal suffering: suicide, divorce, domestic violence, alcoholism, rising mortality rate, disappearing health insurance, depression, and idleness. Women and blacks fare even worse than white male mill workers when industries are in decline.[18] Many a small town in China's northeastern rustbelt has sunk into similar lethargy.

The American Rustbelt

Many workers in mill towns in the rustbelt knew that the decline of their communities was enmeshed in national and international trade policies and competition, currency exchange rates, investment and divestment strategies of big corporations, and domestic party politics and industrial policies. Poverty-stricken blue-collar workers' fight against these forces may seem quixotic, but it happened. Efforts involved have ranged from campaigns for community or worker buyout of mills to the formation of regionwide authorities to promote industrial revival or of national unemployment networks to pressure companies to keep factories open and to lobby national political leaders in Washington, D.C. Community organizations have also opened food pantries and free clinics to provide for unemployed workers' basic needs. Sometimes pressure groups were formed to lobby for state legislation to prevent foreclosures on homes and provide longer coverage periods for unemployment benefits. There were also protests to damage the image of corporations and banks responsible for plant closures. Traditional unions were largely powerless and ineffective, and their concessions on wage and work rules during contract negotiations often undermined rather than promoted worker interests when the plants were eventually shut down. In most of this working-class activism, much of the organizational impetus and capacity has come from grassroots civic groups, church-based groups concerned with social justice, land use, and charity, or regional alliances of these groups. A few examples will illustrate how local groups joined forces with workers and struggled against the formidable tide of plant closures and the enormous difficulties they face in bringing about even small successes.

A prominent example was the Tri-state Conference on Steel (hereafter Tri-state), which grew out of the community struggle in Youngstown, Ohio, against the shutdown of three major steel mills between 1977 and 1979. It was formed in 1981 by labor, church, and community activists in steel communities in Pennsylvania, Ohio, and West Virginia. Their strategies were to educate the public that it was U.S. Steel Corporation's divestment policies, from steel into other lines of business, that caused unemployment, and to develop plans to save steel jobs and reindustrialize the region. Tri-state made several attempts to form a public authority that could exercise the power of "eminent domain" vested in local government to force the sale of private property to a public body out of concern for the common good. In a high-profile effort to save the Dorothy Six ballast furnace at the Duquesne mill in Pittsburgh, scheduled to be demolished as part of U.S. Steel's rationaliza-tion plan, Tri-state mobilized town meetings and managed to fund a feasi-bility study on turning the mill into a worker-owned facility, and members of the local unions volunteered to winterize the furnace. Next, they pres-sured municipal governments to create a Steel Valley Authority (SVA) in order to exercise eminent domain. Local public hearings and popular votes finally brought the SVA into being. Yet SVA failed to find buyers or to secure the $220 million investment needed to keep the mill in operation. Although industrial projects on this scale presented financial hurdles for Tri-state, it was more successful in saving smaller business concerns. From 1989 to 1992, SVA succeeded in building a coalition of residents, church leaders, and local politicians to pressure financial backers into extending loans and grants to turn a failing bakery into a community-worker joint-ownership venture.[19]

Likewise, the Mon Valley Unemployed Committee grew out of disparate civil rights groups and "unemployed committees" in steel unions in the Monongahela River Valley area in Pittsburgh in the early 1980s. They joined together to organize a food bank, a hotline, and demonstrations against mortgage foreclosures and bankruptcy, and demanded extension of the period of eligibility for unemployment benefits. They won a morato-rium on the sheriff's sales of foreclosed homes and raised money to help unemployed workers to make mortgage payments. This regional committee joined with the Philadelphia Unemployed Project to form the National Unemployed Network, drawing similar groups from forty communities in seventeen states in their first national meeting in 1983, and marched on Washington, D.C., in 1985. Yet after several failures to obtain federal mort-gage assistance or to extend the supplementary unemployment compensa-tion program, both the local Mon Valley Unemployment Committee and the National Unemployment Network were gradually demobilized. The reasons were familiar: unemployed workers had little time to spend on political activities and, under pressure to survive, many moved out of the region in search of jobs. Failure to effect political and legislative changes demoralized activists and sapped the sense of injustice and hope that had initially spurred them to action. The committee still ran a hotline dispens-ing information on social services in the early 1990s with funding from the

United Way, Mellon Bank, and various churches and synagogues. It has been converted from a group that effectively helped to "mobilize angry workers who wanted jobs and a decent society into a dispenser of quieting balm on troubled waters."[20]

In 1989, the closing of a General Electric (GE) plant in Morristown, Tennessee, gave birth to a community-based local organization called CATS: Citizens Against Temporary Services. The group identified temporary employment as a systematic trend in the region and pushed for legislation that would regulate contingent work, through lobbying local officials and community campaigns. Ex-GE workers and local activist ministers organized marches and letter-writing campaigns to expose the unfair treatment of contingent and temporary workers hired by big companies through agencies. With help from a coalition of church groups and environmental and community organizations working on economic justice issues, CATS participated in a national network on industrial retention and renewal policies, first filing lawsuits against GE for breach of contract and age discrimination, and then launching a campaign to regulate corporations' use of temporary workers, and against GE's abuse of training funds offered by the local government after old workers were dismissed. Intensive lobbying of the state legislature to prohibit employers from depriving employees of wage and benefits packages based on their categorical status obtained few tangible results. Yet by the mid-1990s, when contingent workers' rights became a national issue, many local groups similar to CATS became part of a national campaign to revise the legal procedures for temporary workers to form unions. Some even participated in the 1999 Seattle demonstrations against the World Trade Organization.[21]

Dale Hathaway asks in his research on the politics of deindustrialization in Pittsburgh, "Can workers have a voice?" His answer is that "workers can have only a very limited voice and that they will have to fight to get that much."[22] Others have reached a similar conclusion that it is a Herculean task for small, disadvantaged communities to mobilize around economic issues. Even though American workers live in a democratic, liberal society, with independent unions, freedom of association and expression, collective leverage on politics as voters, and access to legal due process, they have claimed only very minor victories in the face of plant closures, outsourcing, or downsizing. Most efforts to pass legislation addressing issues of economic justice have been defeated. Corporate and government elites from Pittsburgh to Kenosha to Liaoning, China, have the clout to make major decisions abandoning the traditional base of local economies, shifting from an economy dominated by industry to one structured to serve the needs of corporate headquarters and the high-tech medical, research, and commercial sectors. That goal has been pursued without regard for the effect the transformation would have on ordinary workers. Eve Weinbaum's remark in her intimate account of three Appalachian community struggles can well apply to this book on Chinese workers. "During the 1980s and 1990s ... American prosperity was on the rise and working people—on the surface—were quiescent. But in fact, all across the country, people were struggling with issues of economic justice in their own communities. . . . [I]n many towns across the United States, the battles were often short-lived, and most were unsuccessful. Nobody outside their community paid any attention."[23]

Still, comparing working-class experience in the Chinese and the American rustbelts brings into sharp relief at least one critical difference in the process of labor mobilization and its possible long-term effects. Unemployed workers in both countries lack workplace or labor market bargaining power, and their associational power is drastically if not totally reduced as unions are forced to make incapacitating concessions. Yet an advantage American workers have over their Chinese counterparts is their community associational power. In case after case, from the Youngstown steel mill to those in Chicago and Pittsburgh, from the Firestone rubber and tire plant in Ohio to the Chrysler auto plant in Kenosha and electronics and boot factories in Tennessee, researchers have documented how community resources, residing in the local clergy, church-based social justice organizations, civic or charity groups, environmentalists, and labor activists, have been a critical force in instigating, assisting, and sustaining the mobilization of depressed and outraged workers. The combination of religious or political vision and practical organizing skills keeps alive a sense of hope and possibility. These organizations strengthen bonds among people in the community when work bonds are gone, and help build up the self-confidence that unemployment tears down. The significance of having such labor-community coalitions, even though they have usually failed to avert plant closures or to keep corporations in the locality, is that they are the seeds of sustained political engagement by workers and their communities. Eve Weinbaum, using her case study of ex-GE workers' participation first in a local campaign and then in the anti-WTO protests in Seattle, illustrates the effects of "successful failures"—campaigns that fail to meet their explicit goals at the time, but sow the seeds for later mobilization and pivotal political movements. These successful failures create structures and networks of people who are trained in the process of local struggles to develop the skills, knowledge, and leadership of political action and democratic citizenship. Counter-hegemonic movements most often evolve incrementally from limited and local struggles with small-scale acts and simple demands for reform. But they often also provide rehearsals of opposition that prepare the way for bolder challengers in more propitious moments.[24]

Reading Chinese workers' experiences through the lens of their American counterparts, what stands out is the dire lack of community-based associational power outside of the now defunct socialist work unit. While American unemployed workers confront a probusiness political elite, and their unionism is reduced to irrelevance at times of plant closures, Chinese workers are dealing with the crippling condition of having no viable social movement or civil-society support. Without allies, and under pressure from a repressive state, the seeds sown in these local struggles are deprived of any fertile soil to produce a significant legacy out of their daring activism.

Russia

In the mid-1990s, just when the problem of wage and pension nonpayment began to spread in rustbelt regions in China, some 40 to 60 percent of waged employees in Russia were owed wages between 1994 and 1998.[25] According to the World Bank, one in eight Russian employees were paid in kind, in whole or in part, in 1996. In 1997, overdue wages amounted to about five weeks' wages across the whole economy, and they had approximately doubled each year in real terms since 1992.[26] Nonpayment plagued not just industrial workers and miners, but also "budget-sector" employees such as teachers and the army. Numerous strikes were staged, with some evolving into annual rituals to which the federal and local government responded by scheduling payment proposals in their budgets. National strikes, however, were less predictable or manageable. In March 1997, some 1.8 million people in 1,280 cities participated in a national strike. In February 2003, another all-Russia protest was staged by budgetary workers demanding payment of the wage debt.[27] The root causes of the nonpayment crisis are multiple, involving Russia's economic collapse and the government's lack of funds, the de-monetization of the economy, dependence on the International Monetary Fund, which imposed the priority of tax payments by enterprises over wage payments as a condition of IMF loans, and the pervasive practice by enterprises of using wage debt as a bargaining chip in a game to extract government subsidies. What is of interest to my present study is not how effective or ineffective these protests have been, or what explains workers' participation or nonparticipation.[28] Rather, the existence of even a minimal level of interunion competition between the official trade union federation and the new independent unions has contributed to mobilizing Russian workers, highlighting the predicament of Chinese workers with no alternative to the official union and no leverage from elections to compel politicians to make concessions at least on paper.

BATTLING EXPLOITATION:
CHINA AND THE GLOBAL SUNBELT

In her elegant account of the interactive dynamics of capital relocation and the global labor movement, Beverly Silver maintains that "each time a strong labor movement emerged, capitalists relocated production to sites with cheaper and presumably more docile labor, weakening labor movements in the sites of disinvestments but strengthening labor in the new sites of expansion."[29] Corporate efforts to find a spatial fix for the problem of labor control compel periodic relocation to avoid labor strongholds. Greenfields and sunbelts arise precisely because workers there have less bargaining or associational power than those in brownfields or industrialized areas. China's sunbelt along the southeastern seaboard is just the latest site of capital relocation or "flexible accumulation," preceded by similar experience in Mexico, Korea, and even in treaty-ports in prerevolutionary China. If the appalling and exploitative conditions confronting Chinese workers today are nothing out of the ordinary, workers in other sunbelts have forged other kinds of politics under different circumstances. What has shaped their divergent responses to the global exploitation of labor?

Mexico

Mexico's export-processing factories along its northern border, the *maquiladoras*, have generated a substantial literature on labor conditions typical of many similar export zones in the developing world. Third-world women workers' multifaceted subordination, embedded in global capital, local patriarchy, and managerial sexism, has been incisively and critically exposed. Feminist research has also dispelled the myth of nimble-fingered, docile, passive, and compliant women workers who are uninterested in unions and incapable of resisting corporate and government power.[30] Recently, several multisited ethnographies have most effectively tracked the interconnections of production regimes along global commodity chains, offering powerful comparative insights on the commonalities and differences in labor conditions and politics across manufacturing regions. I shall focus on two of these exemplary studies, Jefferson Cowie's *Capital Moves* (1999), on the electronics industry, and Jane L. Collins's *Threads* (2003), on textile and apparel production. Both follow the paths of transnational corporations as they move from brownfields in the United States to greenfields in Mexico, leaving in their wake both empowering and disempowering effects on working-class communities.

Jefferson Cowie has given a fascinating account of a series of relocations by RCA, a radio and television manufacturer, between the 1920s and the 1990s, from Camden, New Jersey, to Bloomington, Indiana, then to Memphis, Tennessee, and finally to Ciudad Juarez in Mexico. Capital migration, he argues compellingly, has a much longer history than the recent discourse of globalization would seem to suggest. Transnational or offshore relocation may indicate a new level of geographical expansion and flexibility for capital but it also stands as a continuation of earlier patterns and strategies. Moreover, from Camden to Juarez, RCA always looked for women workers to staff "low-skilled" assembly positions, and as they moved out of mature industrial regions, women in these rustbelts bore the brunt of deindustrialization as much as the male unemployed steel or auto workers who stand out in the popular imagination as victims of industrial decline. Also, whether within the United States or across the border in Mexico, the logic of capital mobility remains remarkably the same: it is in search of young, fresh, cheap female labor, usually in locales of oppressive poverty, with weak unionization tradition and little sense of entitlement to jobs or rights. Cowie finds little difference in RCA workers' shop-floor experiences in U.S. and Mexican factories; the tasks, the assembly-line layouts, the gender division of female workers and male supervisors, and the speedup by management and goldbricking by workers—none of these have changed. Yet the external conditions of production present significant obstacles to Mexican workers' developing a degree of worker entitlement similar to that won by their American counterparts decades ago. "An unstable currency, high labor turnover, an authoritarian union structure, and employers that colluded to prevent wage increases all served to check the growing sense of investment in the job, entitlement to the company's consideration, and emboldened class awareness that emerged at the other sites. Only the violence, intimidation, company unionism, and economic devastation of the Great Depression in the Camden case could compare with the obstacles faced by workers on the Mexican frontier."[31]

Cowie's longitudinal study brings to light a very important finding that a single-site and fixed-time-point labor ethnography would fail to capture. In 1995, in the wake of a peso devaluation crisis, two thousand workers participated in a sit-down strike and won a 20 percent wage hike, a return of paid vacation, and the company's commitment to hold fair and open union elections. Looking over a thirty-year period, female workers in *maquiladora* industries have grown in experience, assertiveness, and combativeness.

Progovernment unions' repression of labor disputes only redoubled workers' contentiousness and efforts. Moreover, as the local economy boomed and foreign investment increased in the 1990s, a shortage of experienced workers appeared with more employment opportunities for workers to leave *maquila* factories for other jobs. Finally, shifts in national politics toward a more competitive system also open up political space for unions and citizens groups to compete for worker support. A decorporatization of organized labor has begun with the decline of the progovernment Confederation of Mexican Workers after the historic defeat of the long-ruling PRI (the Institutional Revolutionary Party) in the 2000 election. Although China's rise as a new site of capital relocation would give mobile capital more leverage over Mexican labor, the maturation of workers' mobilization capacity reminds us of a subversive logic or contradiction inherent in capital relocation. That is, as Cowie puts it, "In each location, a glut of potential employees shrank over time into a tightening labor market, once deferential workers organized into a union shop, and years of toil on the shop floor recast docility into a contentious and demanding, if isolated and ambivalent, working class."[32] The lesson is that even under an authoritarian regime, political competition among political parties and unions, coupled with a tightening of the labor market, may enhance the opportunities and resources for plant-based collective action.

Moreover, footloose employers may also spawn community-wide or even transnational activism. Jane Collins's comparative ethnography of two American apparel firms with subcontracting factories in Aguascalientes, central Mexico, finds surprising parallels in the production process and Tayloristic control in both the U.S. and the Mexican firms, with the difference that in factories producing fashion as opposed to casual apparel, workers are subjected to a higher level of stress owing to the simultaneous demands of quality, speed, and efficiency standards monitored by statistical process control. Poverty wage rates, long hours of work, and poor living conditions—all characteristic of third-world export-processing zones—are compounded by subcontracting relations that obfuscate the identity and accessibility of employers in the eyes of the workers. Collins's comparison between these greenfield factories and their American predecessors reveals another distinct disadvantage for Mexican workers. The mobility of capital weakens worker solidarity by preventing the development of webs of social connections and community relations that grow out of companies' long-term embeddedness in a locality, and out of which labor activism grows. Her contrast between the parent company's old factory in Virginia with its new factory in Mexico drives home most clearly the isolation of workers in the latter and the solidarity and moral economic claims harnessed by workers in the former. Ironically, deterritorialized capital also pushes labor and community activists to seek community-based activism. In Mexico's *maquiladora* industries, worker services centers forge worker solidarity across firms and combine workplace and wage demands with concerns for women's reproductive freedom and health services. An increasing number of activist networks have appeared to expand local communities into transnational ones. Prominent examples include the Coalition for Justice in the Maquiladoras (formed by religious, environmental, and women's organizations in the United States, Mexico, and Canada), the Maquila Solidarity Network, and the international anti-sweatshop-movement organizations. Their assistance and support have proved critical to third-world workers' struggle against transnational corporations, as shown in the well-documented cases of labor strife in a Philips–Van Heusen factory in Guatemala and the Walt Disney clothing factory in Haiti.

These two case studies of Mexico powerfully underscore the vulnerability of workers in the global south compared to those in the north, where a more institutionalized social compact and a stronger collective sense of entitlement provide some leverage in labor struggles. In Mexico's export-oriented sector, worker mobilization is enhanced by either elite competition for working-class votes in a more open political system or by transnational and domestic social movement support. Similar dynamics can be found in the South Korean labor movement, certainly one of the most spectacular in Asia. In China, neither of these two facilitating conditions exists.

South Korea

First-person narratives by factory workers during South Korea's early export-oriented industrial takeoff in the 1960s and 1970s graphically reveal the same kind of brutality and wretchedness prevalent on Chinese shop floors in Shenzhen today. Routinely putting in twelve hours per day and forced to work overtime and overnight to fulfill constant rush orders, workers compared their wasted bodies and meaningless lives to those of beasts.

> At night even cattle sleep, but we have to work through the night.
> As everybody knows, we work ten to twelve hours per day, and quite frequently even throughout the whole night. In the morning I barely manage to lift my tired body and carry it to the dusty, noisy, and curse-filled factory. And when I return home at night I am simply too tired even to wash and eat. Repeating this life day after day, I cannot help telling myself, "Oh, I am worse than a machine." I am afraid that I may pass out one day living like this.[33]

In China as in Korea, workers are no strangers to the phenomenon of overwork death, or "alertness pills" given to them by employers to keep them awake during grueling overtime shifts. In both cases, working hard is no guarantee of decent treatment by employers. The labor sociologist Hagen Koo writes,

> In the labor-intensive sectors, the boundaries between the regular shift and overtime was blurred, and the assignment of and payment for over-time often depended on arbitrary decisions by the foremen. . . . In their workplaces, factory workers were constantly subjected to shouts, name calling, reprimands, and vulgar swear words thrown at them by their superiors. . . . By the time they left the factory, their youth had long gone, leaving behind prematurely aged bodies with many nagging diseases acquired from factory work. As workers often lamented, "when all the oil is squeezed out of our bodies, we are thrown out just like trash."[34]

Like the Chinese communist regime, the military regime that presided over South Korea's export-led industrialization was no friend to independent trade unions or workers' rights. In the late 1960s, the government pursued a repressive labor policy, including an antistrike law in foreign-invested firms and increasing restrictions on workers' rights to organize genuinely representative unions and to bargain collectively. The combined pressure of exploitation and suppression led to scores of cases of self-immolation as a key form of working-class resistance during the 1970s. But in the next two decades the Korean unionization struggle flourished and became one of the most militant labor movements in the developing world. Although many factors are relevant in explaining the success of Korean workers in creating their own political institutions, one critical difference between Korean workers in the early days of industrialization and today's young Chinese workers is the presence of grassroots political alliances. Once again, church organizations played critical roles in fostering worker solidarity and consciousness, in this case by sponsoring small-group activities and educational programs for factory women, and by sending clergy to toil alongside workers to become "factory pastors." As Koo points out, the organizational capacity of the church derives from its international networks, internal organizational structure, and ideological legitimacy.[35]

Then in the 1980s, when the military regime turned increasingly repressive toward all kinds of democratic forces, the student movement and oppositional political parties began seeing workers as their potential allies in their battle against the authoritarian state. Students-turned-workers who would later become professional labor activists not only organized large-

scale demonstrations but also changed the demands of the workers' movement from economic issues to organizing new independent unions. The
concentration of factories in a few industrial parks, and the rise of large
heavy industrial enterprises, especially automobile manufacturers, facilitated the transformation from cellular activism into horizontally organized,
interfactory movements in the late 1980s. Amidst political oppression and
economic transformation, Korean intellectuals instigated counter-hegemonic cultural movements, the most influential of which was the *minjung*
movement. This movement contributed tremendously to articulating workers' opposition consciousness. In striking parallel to the new discourse on
ruoshi qunti in China, *minjung* also meant the "people" or the "masses." It
included "all those who were politically oppressed, socially alienated, and
economically excluded from the benefits of economic growth."[36] With a
broad ideological content, and taking various forms—as *minjung* theology,
minjung history, and *minjung* literature—the *minjung* movement asserted
that the real national identity and authentic culture of Korea must be found
in the culture and daily struggles of oppressed commoners. It was therefore
a powerful tool for uniting and mobilizing the diverse social and political
movements. All these factors paved the way for the explosive wave of labor
strikes in 1987, when the military regime surrendered to overwhelming
pressure from the student-led democratization movement to hold democratic elections. Male semiskilled workers in large auto and chemical plants
and white-collar workers then formed the backbone of the unionization
movement that lasted from the late 1980s to the mid-1990s. In the current
period, as the Korean economy moves to a post-Fordist era of flexible accumulation, global competition and strategies have the effect of undermining
the job security of an increasingly disaggregated working class. Democratization has also dissolved the common enemy for the students' and workers'
movements.

Precommunist China's Treaty Ports

If cross-class alliance and social movement support are crucial resources for
nurturing labor's capacity for resistance in late-industrializing authoritarian
regimes, competition among political parties or elite cleavage in authoritarian regimes also stimulate worker activism. To underscore the role of elite
cleavage and competition, a return to the first generation of Chinese industrial workers in the treaty ports of the precommunist era shows interesting
parallels and contrasts between the two periods of "globalization" in China.
This revisit to the Chinese situation should also be an apt last stop in our
brief excursus of international comparison.

Foreign-owned industries first appeared in China in the mid-nineteenth century, following China's defeats in the first and the second Opium Wars and the Sino-Japanese War. Treaty ports along the coast and the major rivers, including Shanghai, Tianjin, Guangzhou (Canton), Ningbo, and Qingdao, were opened to foreign direct investment and trade. British, Japanese, American, Dutch, and French industrialists set up factories along with national Chinese manufacturers and merchants. Artisanal and hand-craft metal workshops and semimechanized family establishments coex-isted with large modern cotton, silk, and flour mills and cigarettes factories. In these cities, women, children, craftsmen, apprentices, outworkers, and casual laborers toiled alongside adult male industrial workers. Many of these workers, like those in today's Chinese cities, were migrants from the countryside who relied on native-place networks and relatives for job intro-ductions. Recruitment was controlled by foremen or forewomen, called the Number Ones, who welded despotic power over the workforce. In Tianjin, a major treaty port in central China, workers faced a workday of ten to twelve hours, spent in perpetual motion.

> The factory is like a sea of machines, belts, wheels, wheels, belts. . . .
> Especially in the weaving and spinning departments, people move in
> a light fog. . . . The people and machines are one body; the machines
> move, and the people follow their motions. While the machines move,
> people don't dare to stop their aching arms and fingers, don't dare to
> stop their exhausted feet.[37]

Again familiar to Chinese workers today, constant danger was involved in working with power-driven machinery for long hours at high speed."In the cotton cleaning department, rapidly rotating blades were the main problem, while in the weaving mill a shuttle could fly off a loom with enough force to kill a nearby worker."[38]

In Shanghai, considered the "Lancashire of China" at the end of World War I, not only were foreign investments most concentrated, but the city was also physically divided into multinational sovereignties. A notorious contract labor system predominated in cotton mills, where contractors, many of whom had ties to the underworld of gangs, bought peasant girls and arranged work for them in different mills. Workers were often sexually abused and mistreated, and their wages deducted by their contractors, whose connection with gangsters allowed them to defeat mill owners' attempt to wrest control over recruitment by establishing a personnel department.[39] Workers were therefore subjected to multiple types of domination and exploitation—foreign imperialist domination, capitalist labor process, and personal dependence on the contractors. Forming sworn brotherhoods and sisterhoods was workers' informal defense against institutional brutality inside the factory gates.

The Chinese working class of this period registered remarkable militancy that played a decisive role in the process of state formation. In her classic study of labor politics of this period, Elizabeth Perry notes that the capacity of Shanghai labor to wreak serious economic damage had lent it strength out of proportion to its actual numbers and its internal fragmentation. The roots of labor's political potency in this period had to do with the competition among multiple political movements and the vibrancy and influence of traditional social organizations, all energized by Chinese nationalism against Japanese and Western imperialism.

The fragmentation of the Chinese working class in Shanghai fostered different modes of politics and multiple insurgent identities. Workers' divisions along skill levels and occupation specializations, often overlapping with divisions according to native-place origins, underlined the formation of different types of organizations amenable to different political movements. So, for instance, the more educated and culturally attuned Jiangnan and Guangdong artisans formed guilds and were susceptible to the appeals of radical students and communist ideology. Unskilled workers from north China, maintaining strong peasant ties and mentality, were uninterested in the political movements of the day but were participants in anti-imperialist demonstrations. The semiskilled machine operatives turned to secret societies, gangsters, and their close ally, the Nationalist Party, for protection and mobility in the city. In other words, the politics of place (native-place origins of workers and their occupation of certain labor market niches) intersected with the politics of production (competition among skilled, semiskilled, and unskilled workers, each with their cultural predispositions and material interests; and gender segregation in the workplace), and the politics of partisanship (competition for worker support between the communists and the nationalists and their respective unions). In the midst of all these domestic conditions that spurred and radicalized labor mobilization, workers also staged general strikes against Japanese, British, and Western imperialism in the 1919 May Fourth Movement, the 1925 May Thirtieth Movement, and against warlordism and inflation in the late 1920s. These strikes convinced communist radicals that their revolution needed the participation of the working class.[40]

In brief, my modest goal in offering these comparisons is to be suggestive of lines of critical inquiry that can overcome a certain blindness to labor's common ground. Aggrieved workers of the world's rustbelts and sunbelts share similar predicaments and the structural weakness of being the subordinate class in a capitalist society. Yet we see also that workers' strategies and capacity to fight against plant closures or exploitation vary greatly, depending on the existence or nonexistence of (1) competition among political elites, parties, or trade unions, (2) skills leverage over integrated production, or (3) community-based associations or social movement allies. We have seen how these factors matter even under repressive, authoritarian regimes. In China, despite the existence of contradictions in the regime's strategies of accumulation and legitimation, there is no competition among political elites requiring them to address working-class grievances or solicit worker support. The bureaucratic-business alliance consolidated in the 1990s contrasts sharply with the fragmentation and localization of labor activism. Grassroots civil-society organizations are growing in number, often financially assisted by international nongovernmental organization (NGO) communities and foundations. Yet the few labor NGOs that exist have proceeded cautiously with a service-oriented, individual-centered, legalistic and educational approach to improve labor's self-protection capacity. Other kinds of activism, by environmentalists, feminists, and students, themselves fledgling communities, have not lent much support to workers' plight.

"AGAINST THE LAW":
THE HIDDEN ALLIANCE OF CHINESE POPULAR UNREST

If the terrain of organized civil society in China is hostile to labor and other subaltern groups, we must not lose sight of a unique site for state-society negotiation and contestation in a globalizing and increasingly capitalistic China—the law. As labor protests mounted throughout the 1990s, villagers also became increasingly agitated and mobilized. Like labor strife, rural popular discontent and resistance had roots in decentralized legal authoritarianism, and peasants also massively appealed to the law as a site for battling venal local officials. In the early 1990s, villagers in interior agricultural provinces reacted to the "three un-rulies" or "peasant burdens" (i.e., illegal taxation, excessive fees, and arbitrary fines) imposed by local cadres. Unlike villagers in coastal provinces with access to overseas investment, good infrastructure, and export markets, agriculture-based provinces in central and western China could not rely on income from township and village enterprises, touted as the engine of takeoff in rural China. Local officials who were made responsible for balancing local budgets under the regime of fiscal decentralization and were not politically accountable to the local population became predatory toward the peasantry. Widespread conflict swept through these agricultural regions, and the State Council issued regulations setting a taxation limit of 5 percent of total annual income and hastened the pace of implementing the Organic Law prescribing village elections for village self-governance.[41] These measures toward legalization, together with the promulgation of the Administrative Litigation Law in 1990, triggered a tidal wave of litigation nationwide. Between 1990 and 2001, the number of cases of administrative litigation exploded, from 13,006 to 100,921 (accepted cases).[42]

Since about 2000, coercive land expropriation has become an additional incendiary issue in many rural areas neighboring big cities. By 2004, an estimated forty million villagers had been dispossessed, left without land, employment, or social security. The new "enclosure movement" that swung into high gear around 2002 has so far requisitioned some 3 percent of total agricultural land area, including much of the most lucrative, under various rubrics of constructing "new development zones," "high-technology parks," or "university towns."[43] Villagers protested against involuntary requisitioning of their contracted land, the meager compensation received, and cadre embezzlement of the land transfer proceeds. Conflicts over the commodification of land-use rights are certain to intensify following the adoption of the 2003 Rural Land Contracting Law. On the one hand, the law legally empowers individual contract-holders as property owners and lays the foundation for a market in rural land-use rights. On the other hand, in response to rural discontent and income disparity, the central government initiated the tax-for-fee reform in 2000 to abolish both the agricultural taxes and the surcharges, keeping only the agricultural product tax. The heightened fiscal pressure on local governments resulting from this reform is likely to lead officials to expand illicit requisitions of farmland.[44]

Rural rebellions frequently begin when some villagers acquire details of the laws and regulations bearing on their interests and rights. When local cadres violate these policies, villagers write complaint letters, visit higher officials, expose local violations of central policy in the media, and mobilize fellow villagers to withhold payment of illegal and arbitrary fees and taxes. Confrontations between these resisters and local cadres have resulted in protracted court battles and in small- and large-scale riots as well as violent crackdowns by local and provincial governments. In recent years, informal groups of rights activists have emerged in a number of localities, and many of these "peasant heroes" who assumed leadership positions are former members of the People's Liberation Army. Shrewdly building networks across villages, even counties, relying on trust, reputation, and verbal communication, they have become more open and organized, with some even succeeding in coordinating cross-village or cross-county actions, inviting crackdowns by armed police forces.[45] Tellingly, as is the case with workers, the law may not be effective in protecting citizens' rights, and rural plaintiffs, much like their urban counterparts, do not necessarily see the law or the courts as a neutral or empowering institution in their fight against official corruption and abuse of power. Still, many continue working through and around the law and its related trappings in the state apparatus.[46]

Besides workers and farmers, the urban middle class has also become legally assertive in defending their property rights increasingly preyed on by the unholy alliance between local officials and financially powerful developers. In Beijing, between 1991 and 2000, some 820,000 people in 260,000 households have been relocated from their homes to make way for urban renewal or city construction. In Shanghai, 2.5 million people in 850,000 households have been relocated. Similarly large-scale demolition and reallocation of urban residents' homes have taken place in major cities across China, including Guangzhou, Nanjing, and Kunming.[47] Owing to the privatization of former welfare housing, as discussed in chapters 2 and 4, and the rapid growth of the real estate market, about 70 percent of urban households owned their homes by the early 2000s.[48] Although land belongs to the state, by law, homeowners have land-use rights for up to seventy years, and demolition and relocation has to be implemented through due process and with reasonable compensation. Local governments see tremendous financial interests in redeveloping built-up areas and transforming them into luxury housing compounds, shopping malls, and commercial high-rises. There have been numerous property disputes, with homeowners contesting the legal grounds for demolition or the amount of financial compensation offered by local governments, which were accused of organizational corruption and profiteering through these land transactions. The 2001 State Council Regulations on Urban Housing Demolition and the 1990 Administrative Litigation Law have been most widely used by aggrieved property owners in their collective lawsuits. Yet their civic activism runs the gamut of petitions, signature campaigns, protests, and sit-in demonstrations. In several high-profile cases, homeowners refused to leave their properties in protests against illegal seizure and inadequate compensation and committed self-immolation and suicide. The Ministry of Construction revealed that conflicts arising from housing demolition resulted in twenty-six deaths and sixteen injuries from January to July 2002 alone.[49]

Perhaps the intensification of property rights struggles by the Chinese middle class is hardly novel or surprising. After all, the bourgeois has been historically the social class that has most ardently championed universal legal rights in its challenge to domination by the landed aristocracy and the crown. In China, we have witnessed the rise of a hidden alliance or an unorganized convergence of the peasantry, the working class, and the propertied middle class toward the terrain of the law. As victims of state-led "accumulation by dispossession" (dispossessed of their land, employment, and property rights), these social classes demand citizens' legal rights and condemn official corruption as illegal. As I was completing this book, I began fieldwork for a new project on the politics of citizenship and the legal rights revolution in urban and rural China. I was struck by the similarity of the demands for legal rights and justice I found among Beijing homeowners and rustbelt workers. Echoing the logic and feelings of rustbelt workers, and mixing moral and legal reasoning, one property owner whose family home was demolished to make way for the 2008 Olympics related his outrage against the district government officials in Beijing.

> Developers, demolition bureau officials, public security, ambulance, police cars, and many demolition workers all surrounded my house. I wrote on the walls of my house in big characters, "The Communist Party and the Eighth Route Army didn't take away a single pin or a penny from ordinary people," "Equality to all before the law," "Ordinary people's homes cannot be violated." . . . In the end, everything was torn down and removed, and they even wanted me to sign a confession letter, forcing me to admit that I obstructed the execution of official duty. My twelve-year-old son and I refused to sign, and they detained us for ten days. . . . I am a Chinese citizen *(gongmin)*, I responded to Chairman Mao's call to construct the Third Front to move to Qinghai, and stayed there for twenty-four years. My two brothers are soldiers serving the Party and protecting our country. Ironically, I cannot even protect our own family home. We are so oppressed. I thought, is this country ruled by the communists? How come the government has become like the nationalists? Are these leaders communist or nationalists?[50]

As in the case of labor activism, the centrality of the law and legalism is salient, and is perhaps a unique Chinese way of popular contention, triggered by the regime's decentralized legal authoritarianism. Even without formal or conscious cross-class alliance against the state, the common and ferocious charge of "against the law" is a powerful and haunting chorus to the Chinese regime.

Methodological Appendix:
Fieldwork in Two Provinces

I have chosen to study two groups of workers in the two provinces that, in rhetorical terms, represent the death of socialism and the birth of capitalism in China. Liaoning is one of the oldest industrial bases in China, with the largest contingent of unemployed workers and retirees in any single province. Guangdong, in contrast, is a booming export powerhouse and the most popular destination for migrant workers. One-third of the country's one hundred million floating population work in Guangdong. Data in this study have come mainly from in-depth interviews with worker representatives and participants in protests, strikes, petitions, and lawsuits. In a few occasions in Liaoning, I was able to observe protests and road blockages on the streets. In Shenzhen, Guangdong, interviews were supplemented by ethnographic observation as access to the Labor Bureau offices, court hearings, labor dispute arbitrations, and mediation between workers and management is more open. This difference in fieldwork access reflects a more open and transparent regulatory regime in the south than in the northeast.

This study evolved quite inadvertently from fieldwork conducted in Guangdong for another project. In 1995, I began a study of the transformation of the labor regime, gender, and class relations in Chinese state industries, after having completed a book on similar issues in the private and foreign-invested sector. That year, 1995, was when the Labor Law was put into effect, implying a fundamental revamping of the socialist employment system and ushering in the labor contract as the legal basis of labor relations for all workers. Over the next couple of years, as I visited factories and conducted interviews with workers, union officials, and managers, it became clear that labor relations within state-owned enterprises were rapidly deteriorating. Very soon, unemployment figures soared to historic heights, leaping from seven million in 1993 to more than twenty million in 1999, with another estimated thirty million "excess workers" who are effectively but not officially unemployed. More alarming to me was the rising number of labor protests in the northeastern and interior provinces, where state factories collapsed in large numbers. It was also around that time, in 1997, that my *guanxi* (social connections) for conducting fieldwork in Guangdong proved increasingly difficult. No matter how hard I tried, I could not get a job in any state factory. And with the help of a friend who was a Liaoning native and who had fed me many stories of worker protests in his home town, Tieling, I shifted my focus from the politics of production to the politics of protests and I moved my field site from Guangdong to Liaoning.

My Tieling friend, whose identity I cannot disclose, first introduced to me to his family members, neighbors, and friends who were involved in bankruptcy disputes, protests, and petitions. Later on, through his network of former classmates and relatives, and some of my own contacts, I managed to interview retirees and laid-off, unemployed, and on-the-job workers in Shenyang. Through other contacts in Beijing, I was able to get in touch with workers involved in the Liaoyang protests in 2002. Altogether, between 1997 and 2003 I conducted more than one hundred fifty interviews in Liaoning. Most workers gave wrenching accounts of their lives and voiced impassioned accusations of mismanagement by enterprise cadres, peppered with nostalgic evocations of their Maoist past. I was intrigued by their historical experience then and now, and by how articulate these workers were in expressing themselves. Finally, beginning in 2002, thanks to a local journalist who had reported extensively on labor issues in Shenzhen, I was able to obtain access to aggrieved migrant workers in Guangdong through his daily work as a reporter. I decided to return to Guangdong, and set out to collect data on migrant workers' strikes, protests, and communities, with the explicit purpose of making a comparison with the situation in the Liaoning. On many occasions, I visited factories and workers' dormitories with my journalist friend and I was introduced as his assistant. Later, my friend quit his job and committed himself full-time to running an independent research and labor advocacy organization, funded by various international foundations and nongovernmental organizations. When workers came to report and seek advice on disputes and lawsuits, I was able to interview and sometimes get involved in and observed the development of these incidents.

The political sensitivity of labor issues has noticeably increased as this research developed, reflecting the intensity of labor challenges staged by workers and the threat perceived by the state. In the northeast, I encountered heightened resistance first from management and local labor bureaus to my request for research interviews. Then toward the latter half of my fieldwork, even workers became understandably reluctant, sometimes also a bit anxious, about being asked to talk with an outsider about their protests and petitions. Each time, it took the reassurance of a mutual acquaintance to break the ice; once the momentum of the conversation was created, they were extraordinarily articulate and honest about their emotions and actions, largely because they felt very righteous in asserting their demands. Many broke down in tears in the course of our conversations, while others could barely contain their indignation and anger. A few were upset by the interviews, which compelled them to mull over strongly suppressed emotions, suffering, and feelings of injustice. The sense of being victimized by injustice was widely shared in the local communities, and workers' desire to have their case heard was very palpable. A few explicitly expressed the hope that the government would listen to academics' opinions and would start doing something for ordinary people.

To avoid official attention to a politically sensitive topic, and to protect my informants, I was not affiliated with any academic institution, nor did I find my subjects through any official or bureaucratic channels. But even as an unaffiliated lone researcher, I could not totally escape the tentacles of what is still basically a police state. One morning in March 2002 in Liaoyang, as I was sitting inside a cab parked in a small alley, waiting to see if workers would come out in protest against the arrest of the four worker representatives leading the spate of citywide protests the week before, six plainclothes police descended and surrounded the cab. They immediately separated me from the cab driver, and we were taken back to the Public Security Bureau for interrogation. It was my first encounter with the police state, and I must admit that I found it a wrenching and fearful experience. They were polite in asking me questions about my identity, my job, my contact, and the reason for my being there. I told them I was a labor researcher and wanted to understand the situation in Liaoyang. After an hour or so of interrogation, they made me sign a "confession" stating all the basic facts about myself, especially the fact that I have been in touch with a Hong Kong–based human rights organization and its officer and have obtained from him the telephone numbers of the worker representatives involved in the protests. In the process of interrogation, it was clear to me that they already knew about the involvement of specific dissident organizations. But I kept asking myself: Did I compromise my informants by providing the police with evidence that they were in alliance with "outside enemies"? Was it ever used as evidence in court?

I do not think anyone can ever answer these questions. All I know is that I have tried my best to protect the identities of all my informants. When the society in which sociologists work does not guarantee freedom of speech and where the state is not constrained by due process of law, who and what procedure can guarantee protection of the human subjects or, for that matter, the researcher herself? The choice is stark but simple: either we remain committed to the scholarly project and try the best we can to overcome political and practical hurdles, or we give up on the possibility of research altogether. My personal choice is self-evident and seems to me unequivocal. The high-handed crackdown by the regime in Liaoyang forced me to wait for a more opportune time to continue my research. One and a half years after the leaders of the Liaoyang protests were sentenced and jailed, my informants were still under police surveillance and my subterranean interviews with them had to be arranged with extreme caution.

What a different world in the southern city of Shenzhen! Labor issues there have become an everyday problem, with workers petitioning routinely in front of the city government or filing lawsuits. Thanks to the high mobility and the rural origin of the workforce, these actions are usually brief episodes without lateral organization or overseas dissident connections. In response, the authorities are less repressive and less concerned about citywide uprisings than those in Liaoyang are.

Notes

CHAPTER 1

1. Interview in Liaoyang, August 5, 2003.

2. Fieldwork in Liaoyang, March 25, 2002. This open letter was dated March 5, 2002, and undersigned by "Bankrupt and Unemployed Workers of Liaoyang Ferro-Alloy Factory."

3. Interview in Liaoyang, March 25, 2002.

4. Murray Scot Tanner, "Protests Now Flourish in China," *International Herald Tribune*, June 2, 2004.

5. Minxin Pei, "Rights and Resistance: The Changing Contexts of the Dissident Movement," in *Chinese Society: Change, Conflict, and Resistance*, ed. Elizabeth J. Perry and Mark Selden, 2d ed. (New York: Routledge, 2003), p. 29.

6. Josephine Ma, "Three Million Took Part in Surging Protests Last Year," *South China Morning Post*, June 8, 2004.

7. Qiao Jian and Jiang Ying, "An Analysis of Labor Demonstrations," in *Analysis and Forecast on China's Social Development (2005)*, ed. Ru Xin, Lu Xueyi, and Li Peilin (Beijing: Social Science Academic Press, 2005), p. 300 [in Chinese].

8. Howard French, "Land of 74,000 Protests (But Little Is Ever Fixed)," *New York Times*, August 24, 2005; Joseph Kahn, "Pace and Scope of Protests in China Accelerated in '05," *New York Times*, January 20, 2005.

9. Research Department, All China Federation of Trade Unions, *Chinese Trade Union Statistics Yearbook, 2001* (Beijing: China Statistics Press, 2002), pp. 67, 90 [in Chinese].

10. John Giles, Albert Park, and Cai Fang, "How Has Economic Restructuring Affected China's Urban Workers?" *China Quarterly* 185 (March 2006): 61–95.

11. There are various estimates of the size of the unemployed population. Li Qiang, a leading sociologist on unemployment surveys, put the figure at 27.258 million in 2002. See Li Qiang, "Urban Unemployment in China and Its Countermeasures" (manuscript, Tsinghua University, Beijing). The Labor Science Institute of the Ministry of Labor and Social Security gives an accumulated

total of 25 million laid-off workers and 12.83 million unemployed between 1998 and 2001. See Labor Science Research Institute, Ministry of Labor and Social Security of China, *Blue Book of Chinese Employment, 2002* (Beijing: China Labor and Social Security Publishing House, 2003), p. 25 [in Chinese].

12. Lu Xueyi, "Balancing Rural-Urban Relations for the Sake of Rural Residents," in *Analysis and Forecast on China's Social Development, 2005*, ed. Ru Xin, Lu Xueyi, and Li Peilin (Beijing: Social Sciences Academic Press, 2004), p. 184 [in Chinese].

13. Shenzhen City Labor Bureau, *Shenzhen Labor Statistics Yearbook, 1998–1999* (Beijing: China Labor and Social Security Publishing House, 2000), p. 103 [in Chinese]; Shenzhen City Labor Bureau, *Shenzhen Labor Statistics Yearbook, 2000–2001* (Beijing: China Labor and Social Security Publishing House, 2002), pp. 109, 115 [in Chinese].

14. Shenzhen City Labor Bureau, *Constructing Harmonious Labor Relations* (Beijing: China Labor and Social Security Publishing House, 2000), p. 170 [in Chinese].

15. Shenzhen Labor Relations Department, Shenzhen City Labor Bureau, "A Survey Report on Shenzhen Labor Dispute Arbitration Handling," in *A Collection of Shenzhen Labor Studies Scientific Papers, 1997–1998*, vol. 1, ed. Shenzhen City Labor Bureau and Shenzhen Labor Studies Association (Beijing: China Labor and Social Security Publishing House, 1999), pp. 259–65 [in Chinese].

16. Murray Scot Tanner, *Chinese Government Reponses to Rising Social Unrest*, testimony presented to the U.S.-China Economic and Security Review Commission on April 14, 2005, Rand Corporation Testimony Series (Santa Monica: Rand Corporation, 2005).

17. Guangdong Provincial Statistics Bureau, *Guangdong Statistical Yearbook, 2002* (Beijing: China Statistics Press, 2003) [in Chinese].

18. Anthony Kuhn, "A High Price to Pay for a Job," *Far Eastern Economic Review* (Hong Kong) 167, no. 3 (January 22, 2004): 30.

19. Fieldwork in Shenzhen, April 16, 2002.

20. This case was reported in Philip P. Pan, "Chinese Workers' Rights Stop at the Courtroom Door," *Washington Post*, June 28, 2002.

21. Beverly J. Silver, *Forces of Labor: Workers' Movements and Globalization since 1870* (Cambridge: Cambridge University Press, 2003), p. 20.

22. Michael Burawoy, "Where Next for Labor?" *Critical Solidarity* 3, no. 3 (December 2003): 2–4.

23. Reinhard Bendix, "The Citizenship of the Lower Classes," in *Force, Fate, and Freedom: On Historical Sociology* (Berkeley and Los Angeles: University of California Press, 1984), chap. 5.

24. Margaret R. Somers, "Deconstructing and Reconstructing Class Formation Theory: Narrativity, Relational Analysis, and Social Theory," in *Reworking Class*, ed. John R. Hall (Ithaca, N.Y.: Cornell University Press, 1997), pp. 73–106.

25. Rick Fantasia, *Cultures of Solidarity* (Berkeley and Los Angeles: University of California Press, 1988).

26. Somers, "Deconstructing and Reconstructing Class Formation Theory."

27. Roger V. Gould, *Insurgent Identities: Class, Community, and Protest in Paris from 1848 to the Commune* (Chicago: University of Chicago Press, 1995).

28. Sun Liping, "Social Transition: Developing a New Sociological Agenda," *Sociological Research* 1 (2005): 1–24 [in Chinese].

29. The literature is massive but see, in particular, Craig Calhoun, *The Question of Class Struggle: Social Foundations of Popular Radicalism during the Industrial Revolution* (Chicago: University of Chicago Press, 1982); William P. Sewell, *Work and Revolution in France: The Language of Labor from the Old Regime to 1848* (New York: Cambridge University Press, 1980); Michael P. Hanagan, *The Logic of Solidarity* (Urbana: University of Illinois Press, 1980); Joan W. Scott, *The Glassworkers of Carmaux: French Craftsmen and Political Activism in a Nineteenth-Century City* (Cambridge, Mass.: Harvard University Press, 1974); and Ira Katznelson and Aristide Zolberg, eds., *Working-Class Formation: Nineteenth-Century Patterns in Western Europe and the United States* (Princeton, N.J.: Princeton University Press, 1986).

30. Michael Burawoy, *The Politics of Production* (London: Verso, 1985).

31. See, for instance, Linda Cook, *The Soviet Social Contract and Why It Failed: Welfare Policy and Workers' Politics from Brezhnev to Yeltsin* (Cambridge, Mass.: Harvard University Press, 1993).

32. Andrew G. Walder, *Communist Neo-traditionalism: Work and Authority in Chinese Industry* (Berkeley and Los Angeles: University of California Press, 1986).

33. Susan L. Shirk, *The Political Logic of Economic Reform in China* (Berkeley and Los Angeles: University of California Press, 1993), p. 149.

34. David Zweig, *Internationalizing China* (Ithaca, N.Y.: Cornell University Press, 2002).

35. Jean Oi, *Rural China Takes Off* (Berkeley and Los Angeles: University of California Press, 1998).

36. Dali L. Yang, *Beyond Beijing: Liberalization and the Regions in China* (London: Routledge, 1997).

37. Gabriella Montinola, Yingyi Qian, and Barry R. Weingast, "Federalism, Chinese Style: The Political Basis for Economic Success," *World Politics* 48, no. 1 (1995): 50–81; Yuanzheng Cao, Yingyi Qian, and Barry R. Weingast, "From Federalism, Chinese Style, to Privatization, Chinese Style," *Economics of Transition* 7, no. 1 (1999): 103–31.

38. Minxin Pei, *China's Trapped Transition: The Limits of Developmental Autocracy* (Cambridge, Mass.: Harvard University Press, 2006). See also Xiaobo Lü, "Booty Socialism, Bureau-preneurs, and the State in Transition: Organizational Corruption in China," *Comparative Politics* 32, no. 3 (2000): 273–94.

39. Dingxin Zhao, *The Power of Tiananmen: State and Society Relations and the 1989 Beijing Student Movement* (Chicago: University of Chicago Press, 2001).

40. Kevin J. O'Brien and Lianjiang Li, *Rightful Resistance in Rural China* (Cambridge: Cambridge University Press, 2006), p. 2.

41. Zheng Yongnian, "From Rule by Law to Rule of Law?" *China Perspectives* 25 (September–October 1999): 31–43.

42. Quoted in Stanley Lubman, *Bird in a Cage: Legal Reform in China* (Stanford, Calif.: Stanford University Press, 1999), p. 127.

43. Silver, *Forces of Labor.*

44. Hong Dayong, "The Development of Chinese Urban Poverty Alleviation Work since Economic Reform," *Sociological Research* 1 (2003): 78 [in Chinese].

45. *Ming Pao* (Hong Kong), July 24, 1998 [in Chinese].

46. William P. Alford, "A Second Great Wall? China's Post–Cultural Revolution Project of Legal Construction," *Cultural Dynamics* 11, no. 2 (1999): 198–99.

47. Ethan Michelson, "Unhooking from the State: Chinese Lawyers in Transition" (Ph.D. diss., Department of Sociology, University of Chicago, 2003), p. 264.

48. Fieldwork in Shenzhen, April 15, 2003.

49. Vivienne Shue, "Legitimacy Crisis in China?" in *State and Society in 21st-Century China: Crisis, Contention, and Legitimation,* ed. Peter Hays Gries and Stanley Rosen (New York: Routledge/Curzon, 2004), p. 29. Marc Blecher has written about depressed workers in Tianjin who subscribe to market hegemony and accept the inequality and predicaments they face as inevitable. See Marc Blecher, "Hegemony and Workers' Politics in China," *China Quarterly* 170 (2002): 283–303.

50. Wang Feng, "Housing Improvement and Distribution in Urban China: Initial Evidence from China's 2000 Census," *China Review* 3, no. 2 (Fall 2003): 134.

51. Michael Burawoy, "The Functions and Reproduction of Migrant Labor: Comparative Materials from Southern Africa and the United States," *American Journal of Sociology* 81, no. 5 (1976): 1050–87.

52. Silver, *Forces of Labor.*

53. Jennifer Chun, "Public Dramas and the Politics of Justice: Comparison of Janitors' Union Struggles in South Korea and the United States," *Work and Occupations* 32, no. 4 (November 2005): 486–503.

54. Ira Katznelson, "Working-Class Formation: Constructing Cases and Comparisons," in *Working Class Formation,* ed. Ira Katznelson and Aristide Zolberg (Princeton, N.J.: Princeton University Press, 1986), pp. 3–41.

55. Somers, "Deconstructing and Reconstructing Class Formation Theory," p. 93.

56. Dipesh Chakrabarty, *Rethinking Working-Class History: Bengal, 1890–1940* (Princeton, N.J.: Princeton University Press, 1989), p. 218.

57. Göran Therborn, *The Ideology of Power and the Power of Ideology* (London: Verso, 1980), pp. 17, 21.

58. James R. Townsend, *Political Participation in Communist China* (Berkeley and Los Angeles: University of California Press, 1967).

59. Elizabeth J. Perry, *Challenging the Mandate of Heaven: Social Protest and State Power in China* (Armonk, N.Y.: M. E. Sharpe, 2002), introduction.

60. See, for instance, Charles Tilly, *Stories, Identities, and Political Change* (Lanham, Md.: Rowman and Littlefield, 2002).

61. David Harvey, *Spaces of Hope* (Berkeley and Los Angeles: University of California Press, 2000), p. 102.

62. Ranajit Guha, *Elementary Aspects of Peasant Insurgency in Colonial India* (Durham, N.C.: Duke University Press, 1999), p. 11.

63. Harvey, *Spaces of Hope*, p. 120.

64. Quoted in Fantasia, *Cultures of Solidarity*, p. 17.

CHAPTER 2

1. Moishe Postone, *Time, Labor, and Social Domination* (Cambridge: Cambridge University Press, 1993); Jeffery M. Paige, "Abstract Subjects: 'Class,' 'Race,' 'Gender,' and Modernity" (manuscript, University of Michigan, 2000); Dipesh Chakrabarty, *Provincializing Europe: Postcolonial Thought and Historical Difference* (Princeton, N.J.: Princeton University Press, 2000).

2. Karl Polanyi, *The Great Transformation: The Political and Economic Origins of Our Time* (Boston: Beacon Press, 1957).

3. Andrew G. Walder, *Communist Neo-traditionalism: Work and Authority in Chinese Industry* (Berkeley and Los Angeles: University of California Press, 1986).

4. Ibid.

5. John Logan, Fuqin Bian, and Yanjie Bian. "Tradition and Change in the Urban Chinese Family: The Case of Living Arrangements," *Social Forces* 76, no. 3 (1998): 851–82; Ping Ping, "Gender Strategy in the Management of State Enterprises and Women Workers' Dependency on Enterprises," *Sociological Research* 1 (1998): pp. 55–62 [in Chinese].

6. Elizabeth J. Perry, "Shanghai's Strike Wave of 1957," *China Quarterly* 137 (1994): 1–27.

7. Elizabeth J. Perry, "Labor's Love Lost: Worker Militancy in Communist China," *International Labor and Working-Class History* 50 (1996): 64–76; Elizabeth J. Perry and Li Xun, *Proletarian Power: Shanghai in the Cultural Revolution* (Boulder, Colo.: Westview Press, 1997); Andrew G. Walder, "The Chinese Cultural Revolution in the Factories: Party-State Structures and Patterns of Conflict," in *Putting Class in Its Place: Worker Identities in East Asia*, ed. Elizabeth J. Perry, China Research Monograph 48 (Berkeley: University of California, Berkeley, Institute of East Asian Studies, 1996), pp. 167–98.

8. Sebastian Heilmann, "The Social Context of Mobilization in China: Factions, Work Units, and Activists during the 1976 April Fifth Movement," *China Information* 8 (1993): 1–19.

9. Charles Hoffmann, *The Chinese Worker* (Albany: State University of New York Press, 1974).

10. Liang Zai and Zjongdong Ma, "China's Floating Population: New Evidence from the 2000 Census," *Population and Development Review* 30, no. 3 (2004): 467–88.

11. Liu Kaiming, *Migrant Labor in South China* (Beijing: Xinhua Publishing House, 2003) [in Chinese].

12. Cai Fang, ed., *Chinese Population and Labor Issues Report, 2002: Rural*

and Urban Employment Problems and Strategies (Beijing: Social Science Literature Press, 2002), p. 60 [in Chinese].

13. Linda Cook, *The Soviet Social Contract and Why It Failed: Welfare Policy and Workers' Politics from Brezhnev to Yeltsin* (Cambridge, Mass.: Harvard University Press, 1993); Wenfeng Tang and William L. Parish, *Chinese Urban Life under Reform: The Changing Social Contract* (Cambridge: Cambridge University Press, 2000).

14. Gordon White, "The Politics of Economic Reform in Chinese Industry: The Introduction of the Labor Contract System," *China Quarterly* 111 (1987): 365–89.

15. Thomas P. Bernstein, *Up to the Mountains and down to the Villages: The Transfer of Youth from Urban to Rural China* (New Haven, Conn.: Yale University Press, 1977).

16. White, "Politics of Economic Reform in Chinese Industry."

17. Susan L. Shirk, "Recent Chinese Labor Policies and the Transformation of Industrial Organization in China," *China Quarterly* 88 (1981): 575–93.

18. Mary E. Gallagher, *Contagious Capitalism: Globalization and the Politics of Chinese Labor* (Princeton, N.J.: Princeton University Press, 2005).

19. Luigi Tomba, *Paradoxes of Labor Reform: Chinese Labor Theory and Practice from Socialism to Market* (London: Routledge/Curzon, 2002).

20. Edward X. Gu, "Labor Market Reforms: Central Government Policy," *Chinese Law and Government* 34, no. 1 (2001): 5–15.

21. Dai Jianzhong and Zhu Min, "A Survey Report on Labor Relations in Private Enterprises and Women Workers' Problems" (manuscript, Beijing Academy of Social Science, 1999) [in Chinese].

22. Virginia E. Ho, *Labor Dispute Resolution in China: Implications for Labor Rights and Legal Reform,* China Research Monograph 59 (Berkeley: University of California, Berkeley, Institute of East Asian Studies, 2003).

23. Mary E. Gallagher, "'Use the Law as Your Weapon!': Institutional Change and Legal Mobilization in China," in *Engaging the Law in China: State, Society, and Possibilities for Justice,* ed. Neil J. Diamant, Stanley B. Lubman, and Kevin J. O'Brien (Stanford, Calif.: Stanford University Press, 2005), pp. 54–83; Ching Kwan Lee, "Pathways of Labor Insurgency," in *Chinese Society: Change, Conflict, and Resistance,* ed. Elizabeth J. Perry and Mark Selden, 2d ed. (London: Routledge, 2003), pp. 41–61.

24. Gallagher, "'Use the Law as Your Weapon!'"; Lee, "Pathways of Labor Insurgency."

25. For details of these regulations, see Hillary K. Josephs, *Labor Law in China: Choice and Responsibility* (Seattle: Butterworth Legal Publishers, 1990); and Ho, *Labor Dispute Resolution in China.* For procedural details of mediation, arbitration, and litigation, see Virginia E. Ho, "Labor Law in China's Reform Era: The Evolving Legal Framework for Labor Rights," in *The Labor of Reform,* ed. Mary E. Gallagher, Ching Kwan Lee, and Albert Park (manuscript, University of Michigan, 2005). The Labor Safety and Health Law was implemented in May 2003; the Labor Contract Law, the Collective Contract Law, and the Law on

Settlement of Labor Disputes are in the drafting and planning process. See Mary E. Gallagher and Jiang Junlu, eds., *Chinese Labor Legislation*, special issue of *Chinese Law and Government* (forthcoming).

26. Elizabeth J. Perry, "From Native Place to Workplace: Labor Origins and Outcomes of China's *Danwei* System," in *Danwei: The Changing Chinese Workplace in Historical and Comparative Perspective*, ed. Xiaobo Lü and Elizabeth J. Perry (Armonk, N.Y.: M. E. Sharpe, 1997), pp. 42–59; World Bank: *Old Age Security: Pension Reform in China* (Washington, D.C.: World Bank, 1997), pp. 15–16. For a somewhat different interpretation of the origin of welfare and pensions, see Mark W. Frazier, *The Making of the Chinese Industrial Workplace: State, Revolution, and Labor Management* (Cambridge: Cambridge University Press, 2002).

27. World Bank, *Old Age Security*, p. 5.

28. Edward X. Gu, "Dismantling the Chinese Mini-welfare State? Marketization and the Politics of Institutional Transformation, 1979–1999," *Communist and Post-Communist Studies* 34 (2001): 91–111.

29. Zheng Chenggong, *Evolution and Assessment of China's Social Security System* (Beijing: Renmin University Press, 2002), pp. 87–88 [in Chinese].

30. Greg O'Leary, "The Making of the Chinese Working Class," in *Adjusting to Capitalism: Chinese Workers and the State*, ed. Greg O'Leary (Armonk, N.Y.: M. E. Sharpe, 1998), p. 57.

31. Feng Genxin, *The Twenty-first-Century Chinese Urban Social Security System* (Zhengzhou: Henan People's Press, 2001), p. 80 [in Chinese]; World Bank, *Old Age Security*, p. 24.

32. Clara Li, "Thousand of Migrants Cash in Pension Plan," *South China Morning Post*, July 10, 2002. Li reports that many migrants, having no intention of retiring in Shenzhen, withdraw funds on leaving their employer or returning home. The Shenzhen Employee Social Insurance Policy stipulates that temporary residents can qualify for pensions if they contribute to pension funds for at least fifteen years.

33. National Bureau of Statistics of China, *China Labor and Social Security Yearbook, 2002* (Beijing: China Statistics Press, 2003), p. 256, [in Chinese].

34. Feng, *Twenty-first-Century Chinese Urban Social Security System*, p. 80 [in Chinese]; World Bank, *Old Age Security*, p. 34.

35. *Southern Metropolis News*, January 16, 2002 [in Chinese].

36. Liu Kaiming, "Listening to Workers' Complaints" (report, Institute of Contemporary Observation, Shenzhen, 2004), p. 44 [in Chinese].

37. Research Department, All China Federation of Trade Unions, *Chinese Trade Union Statistics Yearbook, 2000* (Beijing: China Statistics Press, 2001), p. 90 [in Chinese].

38. John Giles, Albert Park, and Cai Fang, "How Has Economic Restructuring Affected China's Urban Workers?" *China Quarterly* 185 (March 2006): 61–95.

39. Ibid.

40. National Bureau of Statistics of China, *China Labor and Social Security Yearbook, 2002*, p. 256 [in Chinese].

41. Ding Yuanzhu, Hu Angang, and Wang Shaoguang, "Behind China's Wealth Gap," *South China Morning Post*, October 31, 2002; Hu Angang, *State of the Country Report* (Beijing: Tsinghua University Press, 2002) [in Chinese]. The China Social Stability Research Unit surveys in 2000 and 2001 (cited in Hu, *State of the Country Report*) revealed that ordinary citizens consider corruption, unemployment, and peasant burdens (i.e., illegal taxation, excessive fees, and arbitrary fines) to be three major causes of social instability. A 1999 survey of fifty-six mayors in China reported that unemployment was perceived as the most significant threat to social stability.

42. Lin Justin Yifu, Fang Cai, and Zhou Li, *State-Owned Enterprise Reform in China* (Hong Kong: Chinese University Press, 2001).

43. *Xiagang* literally means "stepping down from the post."

44. Mo Rong, "Employment Conditions Are Still Difficult," in *The Blue Book of Chinese Society, 2002*, ed. Ru Xin, Lu Xueyi, and Li Peilin (Beijing: Social Science Documentation Publishing House, 2002), pp. 165–74 [in Chinese].

45. Cheng Lianxing, *A Study of Anti-unemployment Policies in China (1958–2000)* (Beijing: Social Science Documentation Publishing House, 2002) [in Chinese].

46. Dorothy Solinger, "Why We Cannot Count the 'Unemployed,'" *China Quarterly* 167 (2001): 671–88. Solinger argues that the term *laid-off* applies only to workers at state-owned enterprises, but most surveys of laid-off workers include workers shed from urban collectives as well.

47. Li Qiang, *A Comparative Study of Unemployment and Layoffs* (Beijing: Tsinghua University Press, 2001), p. 3 [in Chinese]; Tang Jun, "Joining WTO and Employment Policies and Strategies," in *WTO: Labor Rights and Protection*, ed. China College of Labor Movement, Institute of Labor Relations (Beijing: Workers' Press, 2001), pp. 181–99 [in Chinese]; Giles, Park, and Cai, "How Has Economic Restructuring Affected China's Urban Workers?" Giles, Park, and Cai find that the unemployment rate was 12.9 percent in 2001, up from 7.2 percent in 1996.

48. Labor Science Institute, Ministry of Labor and Social Security of China, *The Blue Book of Chinese Employment, 2002* (Beijing: Social Science Documentation Publishing House, 2003), p. 94 [in Chinese].

49. Dorothy J. Solinger, "Labour Market Reform and the Plight of the Laid-off Proletariat," *China Quarterly* 170 (June 2002): 304–26.

50. Giles, Park, and Cai, "How Has Economic Restructuring Affected China's Urban Workers?"

51. Hong Dayong, "The Development of Chinese Urban Poverty Alleviation Work since Economic Reform," *Sociological Research* 1 (2003): 77 [in Chinese].

52. Labor Science Institute, Ministry of Labor and Social Security of China, *The Blue Book of Chinese Employment, 2002*, pp. 84–92 [in Chinese].

53. Tang Jun, "Selections from Report on Poverty and Anti-poverty in Urban China," *Chinese Sociology and Anthropology* 36, nos. 2–3 (2003–4): 28.

54. Feng, *Twenty-first-Century Chinese Urban Social Security System*, pp. 269–70 [in Chinese].

55. *China Labor* 8 (2002): 9.

56. Hong, "Development of Chinese Urban Poverty Alleviation Work since Economic Reform," p. 78.

57. Zheng, *Evolution and Assessment of China's Social Security System*, p. 123 [in Chinese].

58. Feng, *Twenty-first-Century Chinese Urban Social Security System*, p. 154 [in Chinese].

59. Gu, "Dismantling the Chinese Mini-welfare State?"

60. Ibid.

61. Giles, Park, and Cai, "How Has Economic Restructuring Affected China's Urban Workers?"

62. Fulong Wu, "Changes in the Structure of Public Housing Provision in Urban China," *Urban Studies* 33, no. 9 (1996): 1601–27.

63. Ibid.

64. Yaping Wang and Alan Murie, "The Process of Commercialization of Urban Housing in China," *Urban Studies* 33, no. 6 (1996): 971–89.

65. Yaping Wang and Alan Murie, "Social and Spatial Implications of Housing Reform in China," *International Journal of Urban and Regional Research* 24, no. 2 (2000): 397–417.

66. Yaping Wang, "Housing Reform and Its Impacts on the Urban Poor in China," *Housing Studies* 15, no. 6 (2000): 845–64; Wang and Murie, "Social and Spatial Implications of Housing Reform in China."

67. Gu, "Dismantling the Chinese Mini-welfare State?"; Wu, "Changes in the Structure of Public Housing Provision in Urban China."

68. Ping, "Gender Strategy in the Management of State Enterprises and Women Workers' Dependency on Enterprises"; Logan, Bian, and Bian, "Tradition and Change in the Urban Chinese Family."

69. Wu Weiping, "Migrant Housing in Urban China," *Urban Affairs Review* 38, no. 1 (2002): 90–119 [in Chinese].

70. Chris Smith, "Living at Work: Management Control and the Chinese Dormitory Labor System in China," *Asia Pacific Journal of Management* 20, no. 3 (2002): 333–58.

71. For a brief account of the emergence of independent unions since 1989, see Lee, "Pathways of Labor Insurgency"; for information on individuals arrested and sentenced for organizing independent unions, see Amnesty International, "People's Republic of China: Labor Unrest and the Suppression of the Rights to Freedom of Association and Expression" (ASA 17/015/2002, Amnesty International, April 30, 2002, posted online at http://web.amnesty.org/library/index/engasa170152002), pp. 9–10.

72. Wook Baek Seung, "The Changing Trade Unions in China," *Journal of Contemporary Asia* 30, no.1 (2000): 46–66.

73. Gallagher and Jiang, *Chinese Labor Legislation*.

74. National Bureau of Statistics of China, *China Labor and Social Security*

Yearbook, 2000 (Beijing: China Statistics Press, 2001) [in Chinese]. After an organization campaign in 1999, the unionization rate among private and foreign-invested enterprises has reportedly jumped from 7 to 40 percent. See Philip P. Pan, "When Workers Organize, China's Party-Run Unions Resist," *Washington Post*, October 15, 2002. But the official *Beijing Review* reports that a 2004 nationwide survey conducted by the National People's Congress found less than 10 percent of foreign-funded enterprises have established trade unions. See "Coming to Terms with Unions," *Beijing Review*, December 9, 2004, pp. 32–33.

75. Erik Eckholm, "Petitioners Urge China to Enforce Legal Rights," *New York Times*, June 2, 2003.

76. Feng Chen, "Between the State and Labor: The Conflict of Chinese Trade Unions' Dual Institutional Identity," *China Quarterly* 176 (2003): 1006–28.

77. Seung, "Changing Trade Unions in China," p. 60.

78. Ching Kwan Lee, "From Organized Dependence to Disorganized Despotism: Changing Labor Regimes in Chinese Factories," *China Quarterly* 157 (1999): 44–71; in his Zhejiang survey, Wook Baek Seung shows that 41.5 percent of union cadres were recruited from the ranks of management, 35.8 percent from the ranks of full-time Party cadres, and only 11.3 percent from the ranks of workers; 77.8 percent of union cadres held Party membership. See Seung, "Changing Trade Unions in China."

79. Anita Chan, "Labor Relations in Foreign-Funded Ventures: Chinese Trade Unions and the Prospects for Collective Bargaining," in *Adjusting to Capitalism: Chinese Workers and the State*, ed. Greg O'Leary (Armonk, N.Y.: M. E. Sharpe, 1998), pp. 122–49; China Labor Watch, *Reebok's Human Rights Standard and Chinese Workers' Working Conditions* (New York: China Labor Watch, 2002); Mary E. Gallagher, "An Unequal Battle," *China Rights Forum*, Summer 1997, p. 15.

80. Qi Li and Bill Taylor, "ACFTU Membership Organizing Strategies" (manuscript, All China Federation of Trade Unions, 2002); Seung, "Changing Trade Unions in China."

81. Jeanne L. Wilson, "'The Polish Lesson': China and Poland, 1980–1990," *Studies in Comparative Communism* 23, nos. 3–4 (1990): 259–79.

82. Chang Kai, "On Enacting Legislation Regarding Unfair Labor Practices," *Social Science in China* 5 (September 2000): 71–82 [in Chinese]; Qiao Jian, "Employees Confronting Reform," in *The Blue Book of Chinese Society, 2002*, ed. Ru Xin, Lu Xueyi, and Li Peilin (Beijing: Social Science Documentation Publishing House, 2002), pp. 243–51 [in Chinese].

83. Research Department, All China Federation of Trade Unions, *Survey of the Status of Chinese Staff and Workers in 1997* (Beijing: Xiyuan Press, 1997), p. 218 [in Chinese].

84. Seung, "Changing Trade Unions in China," p. 62.

85. Stephen Crowley and David Ost, eds., *Workers after Workers' States: Labor and Politics in Postcommunist Eastern Europe* (Lanham, Md.: Rowman and Littlefield, 2001).

86. Katherine Verdery, *The Vanishing Hectare: Property and Value in Post-socialist Transylvania* (Ithaca, N.Y.: Cornell University Press, 2003), pp. 74–75.

87. Lisa Rofel, *Other Modernities: Gendered Yearnings in China after Socialism* (Berkeley and Los Angeles: University of California Press, 1999), p. 122.

88. Gordon White, "Restructuring the Working Class: Labor Reform in Post-Mao China," in *Marxism and the Chinese Experience*, ed. Arif Dirlik and Maurice Meisner (Armonk, N.Y.: M. E. Sharpe, 1989), pp. 159–60.

89. White, "Politics of Economic Reform in Chinese Industry."

90. Shirk, "Recent Chinese Labor Policies and the Transformation of Industrial Organization in China."

91. White, "Restructuring the Working Class," pp. 159–60.

92. Kalpana Misra, *From Post-Maoism to Post-Marxism: The Erosion of Official Ideology in Deng's China* (New York: Routledge, 1998), chap. 4.

93. Randall Peerenboom, *China's Long March toward Rule of Law* (Cambridge: Cambridge University Press, 2002), chap. 3.

94. *China Labor Daily*, March 4, 1997, and November 14, 1996 [in Chinese].

95. Wang Zheng, "Gender, Employment, and Women's Resistance," in *Chinese Society: Change, Conflict, and Resistance*, ed. Elizabeth J. Perry and Mark Selden, 2d ed. (London: Routledge, 2003), pp. 158–82.

CHAPTER 3

1. Margot Schueller, "Liaoning: Struggling with the Burdens of the Past," in *China's Provinces in Reform: Class, Community, and Political Culture*, ed. David S. G. Goodman (London: Routledge, 1997), pp. 93–126.

2. The rate of 30 to 40 percent was cited by Antoine Kernen and Jean-Louis Rocca in "The Reform of State-Owned Enterprises and Its Social Consequences in Shenyang and Liaoning," *China Perspectives* 27 (January–February 2000): 35–51. In internal documents available to labor scholars in China, I have seen a provincial average of 30 percent. In Liaoyang, locals put the unemployment rate at 60 percent.

3. Waves of unemployment plagued the country in 1953, 1961, 1970, and 1978 for different economic and political reasons. For instance, during the Cultural Revolution period, an estimated 17 million youths were unemployed, and the Party responded with rustification, or the "send down" movement. See Li Peilin, "Unemployment Management in Old Industrial Bases," in *China's Economic Opening and Changes in Social Structure*, ed. Hu Yaosu and Lu Xueyi (Beijing: Social Sciences Academic Press, 1998), pp. 83–105 [in Chinese].

4. Cheng Lianxing, *A Study of Anti-unemployment Policies in China (1958–2000)* (Beijing: Social Science Documentation Publishing House, 2002), p. 62 [in Chinese].

5. Li Qiang, *A Comparative Study of Unemployment and Layoffs* (Beijing: Tsinghua University Press, 2001), p. 3 [in Chinese]; Tang Jun, "Joining WTO and Employment Policies and Strategies," in *WTO: Labor Rights and Protection*, ed. China College of Labor Movement, Institute of Labor Relations (Bei-

jing: Worker's Publishing House,), pp. 181–99 [in Chinese]. Dorothy Solinger has argued convincingly that there is no way to count accurately and comprehensively the actual number of the "unemployed," given the elasticity of the definition used by the Chinese government and the complex and layered categorization of unemployed workers. See Dorothy Solinger, "Why We Cannot Count the 'Unemployed,'" *China Quarterly* 167 (2001): 671–88.

6. A popular estimate is that there would be a 25 percent loss of employment opportunities in the initial three to five years after entry into the WTO. Most job losses would occur in the automobile, chemical, machinery, and telecommunications industries. See, for instance, Mo Rong, "Employment Conditions Are Still Difficult," and Li Peilin, "Possible Changes in Chinese Society after Joining the WTO," both in *The Blue Book of Chinese Society, 2002*, ed. Ru Xin, Lu Xueyi, and Li Peilin (Beijing: Social Science Documentation Publishing House, 2002), pp. 165–74, 57–65 [in Chinese].

7. Vivien Pik-Kwan Chan, "Deprived Groups May Be Greatest Threat to Society," *South China Morning Post*, February 6, 2002.

8. Liaoning Academy of Social Sciences, "A Study on Liaoning's Strategy and Implementation of the Reemployment Project" (manuscript, Liaoning Academy of Social Sciences, December 1999) [in Chinese].

9. See Solinger, "Why We Cannot Count the 'Unemployed.'"

10. By 1996, the failure to shift from military to civilian production led to a loss of 2.4 billion yuan, and 50 percent of military enterprises were unable to pay wages to their workers. See Wang Ao, *Strategic Transfer of Labor in Liaoning's Development Process*, special consultation report (Shenyang: Liaoning Academy of Social Sciences, 2000) [in Chinese].

11. Liaoning Urban Employment Research Team, "Conditions and Strategies of Liaoning's Urban Population and Employment," *Management World* 5 (1998): 69–76 [in Chinese].

12. Research Department, All China Federation of Trade Unions, *Chinese Trade Union Statistics Yearbook, 2001* (Beijing: China Statistics Press, 2002) [in Chinese].

13. State Letters and Visits Bureau, *People's Letters and Visits (Remin Xinfang)* 7 (2001): 13–16 [in Chinese]. This is the official journal of the State Letters and Visits Bureau.

14. Liaoning Province Politics and Law Committee, "The Prevention and Management of Mass Incidents amidst Reform of State-Owned Enterprises," in *A Collection of Essays on Maintaining Social Stability*, ed. Central Committee Politics and Law Committee Research Department (Beijing: Legal Press, 2001), pp. 109–19 [in Chinese].

15. Ibid., p. 121.

16. Ibid., p. 130.

17. Research Department of All-China Federation of Trade Unions, *China Trade Unions Statistics Yearbook, 2001* (Beijing: China Statistics Press, 2002), p. 67.

18. John Giles, Albert Park, and Cai Fang, "How Has Economic Restructur-

ing Affected China's Urban Workers?" *China Quarterly* 185 (March 2006): 61–95. In postcommunist Russia as well as some Eastern European countries, wage nonpayment has reached epidemic proportions and is a major cause of labor protests. See Debra Javeline, *Protest and the Politics of Blame: The Russian Response to Unpaid Wages* (Ann Arbor: University of Michigan Press, 2003); Padma Desai and Todd Idson, *Work without Wages: Russia's Nonpayment Crisis* (Cambridge, Mass.: MIT Press, 2000); and Simon Clarke, "Trade Unions and the Non-payment of Wages in Russia," *International Journal of Manpower* 19, nos. 1–2 (1998): 68–83. The Chinese situation may be less serious in terms of sectors and proportion of workers affected, but given the context of heightened wealth inequality and the lack of democratic processes, the Chinese nonpayment crisis could have more significant political effects. Interestingly, Chinese economists have witnessed the emergence of a "nonpayment economy" in China. "Commercial buyers make purchases, and then refuse to pay. Borrowers take out loans, and then default. Banks accept deposits, and then squander them in ill-advised lending. In each case the victim is left without recourse. . . . What results is neither utter lawlessness nor an absence of growth. Instead, there exists a subtle pattern of unclear rules, low levels of trust, and frequent efforts to skirt the boundaries of legal strictures" (Edward Steinfeld, "Chinese Enterprise Development and the Challenge of Global Integration," in *East Asian Networked Production*, ed. Shahid Yusuf [New York: World Bank, forthcoming]).

19. Mark Frazier, "China's Pension Reform and Its Discontents," *China Journal* 51 (2004): 97–114.

20. Yang Yiyong and Xin Xiaobai, "A Report on Layoffs and Reemployment," in *Analysis and Forecast of the Social Situation in China, 1999*, ed. Ru Xin et al. (Beijing: Social Sciences Academic Press, 1999), pp. 248–49 [in Chinese].

21. Zheng Chenggong, *Evolution and Assessment of China's Social Security System* (Beijing: Renmin University Press, 2002), p. 96 [in Chinese].

22. Interview in Shenyang, July 4, 2003.

23. This jingle appeared on a banner in a protest by five hundred retired workers at Anshan's Third Metallurgical Construction Company on April 16, 1998. *Financial Times*, Asia Intelligence Wire, May 1, 1998.

24. On Liaoyang, see Agence France-Presse photo accompanying article by Jasper Becker, "Workers in a State of Disunion," *South China Morning Post*, March 23, 2002. For a vivid report on a protest in Harbin, Heilongjiang, see Jasper Becker, "The Dark Side of the Dream," *South China Morning Post*, October 12, 1997.

25. Interview in Shenyang, December 25, 2002.

26. Interview in Shenyang, July 4, 2003.

27. Ibid.

28. Ibid.

29. Interview in Shenyang, December 24, 2002.

30. See Elisabeth Rosenthal, "Workers' Plight Brings New Militancy in China," *New York Times*, March 10, 2003.

31. Zheng, *Evolution and Assessment of China's Social Security System*, p. 96.

32. Interview in Shenyang, December 26, 2003.

33. Ibid.

34. State Letters and Visits Bureau, *People's Letters and Visits* 1 (2001): 20–22 [in Chinese].

35. For Changchun, see www.epochtimes.com/gb/2/11/5/n242299.htm; for Daqing, see www.china-labour.org.hk/iso/article.adp?article_id=4364; for Liaoyang, see www.china-labour.org.hk/iso/article.adp?article_id=3562 ; and for Tianjin, see www.china-labour.org.hk/iso/article.adp?article_id=4887

36. Interview in Shenyang December 25, 2003.

37. Interview in Shenyang, July 6, 2003.

38. Interview in Shenyang, July 4, 2003.

39. Solinger offers a detailed and illuminating discussion of the Chinese terminology of unemployment in "Why We Cannot Count the 'Unemployed.' "

40. Eva Hung and Stephen Chiu, "The Lost Generation: Life Course Dynamics and *Xiagang* in China," *Modern China* 29, no. 2 (2003): 204–36.

41. Interview in Shenyang, January 7, 2000. For similar comments by Guangzhou state workers, see Ching Kwan Lee, "The Labor Politics of Market Socialism," *Modern China* 24, no. 1 (1998): 3–33; and Hung and Chiu, "Lost Generation."

42. Interview in Tieling, January 7, 2000.

43. Interview in Tieling, January 31, 2002.

44. Interview in Tieling, May 1999.

45. A copy of the petition letter obtained from a worker representative in June 1999.

46. Interview in Tieling, May 1999.

47. Ibid.

48. Interviews in Tieling, July 5, 1999, and January 31, 2002.

49. This strategy of factory occupation is quite widespread. See Feng Chen, "Industrial Restructuring and Workers' Resistance in China," *Modern China* 29, no. 2 (2003): 237–62.

50. Interview in Tieling, June 30, 1999.

51. Ibid. Contrary to what the worker said, the single-time payment was not an official policy in 1999. If anything, it was explicitly denounced in the official media.

52. James Kynge, "Riots in Chinese Mining Town," *Financial Times*, April 3, 2000.

53. Foreign Broadcast Information Service, CHI-97-198, July 17, 1997.

54. See, for instance, Craig Smith, "Blasts Kill 18 in Textile City South of Beijing," *New York Times*, March 17, 2001; Elizabeth Rosenthal, "Factory Closings in China Arouse Workers' Fury," *New York Times*, August 31, 2000; and "Factory Managers Killed in Pay Rows," *South China Morning Post*, February 25, 2002.

55. Interviews with worker representatives of the Liaoyang protests were

clandestine, because the interviewees reported police surveillance of their daily activities. In referencing these interviews, I have changed the dates and locations of the interviews and have avoided specific references to workers' personal characteristics. A detailed account of the Liaoyang incident can be found in "The Liaoyang Protest Movement of 2002–3, and the Arrest, Trial, and Sentencing of the 'Liaoyang Two,'" *China Labor Bulletin*, Hong Kong (July 2003).

56. Group interview with five workers in Liaoyang, August 5, 2003.

57. "Angry Workers Besiege City Hall," *South China Morning Post*, May 17, 2000; "PRC Police, Steel Workers Clash over Unpaid Wages," Foreign Broadcast Information Service, CHI-2000-0516. Also, An Open Letter to Provincial Governor Bo Xilai, March 5, 2002.

58. Group interview with five workers in Liaoyang, August 5, 2003.

59. In a letter to the Liaoyang People's Government dated June 25, 2002, signed by more than one hundred Liaotie workers, workers explained in detail the reasons for their economic demands, including why they did not accept the government's proposal to transfer severance compensation to workers' social security accounts. They wanted both severance pay and social security, and wanted them kept separate.

60. Group interview with five workers in Liaoyang, August 5, 2003.

61. Ibid.

62. Ibid.

63. John Pomfret, "With Carrots and Sticks, China Quiets Protestors," *Washington Post*, March 22, 2002.

64. Personal communication from Philip P. Pan, a *Washington Post* reporter.

65. Group interview with five workers in Liaoyang, August 5, 2003.

66. Ibid.

67. Ibid.

68. Ibid.

69. Philip P. Pan offers a nuanced and moving investigative report on the fate of the worker leaders in "Three Chinese Workers: Jail, Betrayal, and Fear," *Washington Post*, December 28, 2002. See also Philip P. Pan, "China Tries Labor Leaders amid Protest," *Washington Post*, January 16, 2003.

70. Erik Eckholm, "Two Promoters of Worker Protests in China Get Prison Sentences," *New York Times*, May 10, 2003.

71. *Party Discipline Monthly* (*Dang Feng Yue Bao*) 5 (2003): 18–22 [in Chinese].

72. In Yao's defense statement, his lawyer denied charges that Yao was a member of the China Democracy Party (CDP) and stated that when Yao went to CDP meetings, he opposed its platform of overthrowing the Communist Party's one-party regime. Defense statement prepared by Mo Shaoping, Beijing, June 21, 2003.

73. Personal communication from Li Erjin, who studied a military enterprise in Shenyang where high officials explicitly mentioned this new policy prompted by unrest in Liaoyang and other places in Liaoning. See Li Erjin, "The Making

of the Xiagang Worker List" (M.Phil. thesis, Department of Sociology, Tsinghua University, Beijing, 2003) [in Chinese].

74. Jiang Xueqin, "Fighting to Organize," *Far Eastern Economic Review* 164, no. 35 (September 6, 2001): 72–75; Matthew Forney and Neil Gough, "Working Man Blues," *Time Asia*, April 1, 2002; Stephen Philion, "The Discourse of Workers' Democracy in China as a Terrain of Ideological Struggle" (Ph.D. diss., Department of Sociology, University of Hawaii, 2004).

75. See also Yongshun Cai, "The Resistance of Chinese Laid-Off Workers in the Reform Period," *China Quarterly* 170 (2002): 327–44.

76. Philip P. Pan, "China's Seething Workers: Oil Industry Layoffs Spark Widespread Demonstrations," *Washington Post*, April 24, 2002.

77. The Beijing leadership has been so alert to the rise of social violence perpetrated by workers and peasants that a high-level interdepartmental steering group was said to have been set up in 2003 by the Hu-Wen leadership to handle quasi-terrorist social violence such as poisoning, assassination, bombing, hijacking, and arson. Willy Wo-Lap Lam, "Beijing Faces Winter of Discontent" (CNN, September 30, 2003, posted online at www.cnn.com/2003/WORLD/asiapcf/east/09/29/willy.column/index.html).

78. Derek Sayer, *Capitalism and Modernity* (London: Routledge, 1991), p. 2.

79. Rogers Brubaker and Frederick Cooper, "Beyond 'Identity,'" *Theory and Society* 29, no. 1 (2000): 17.

80. Interview in Tieling, June 1999, textile mill.

81. Group interview with five workers in Liaoyang, August 5, 2003.

82. Elizabeth J. Perry, *Challenging the Mandate of Heaven: Social Protest and State Power in China* (Armonk, N.Y.: M. E. Sharpe, 2002), p. xxiv.

83. A letter addressed "To the Comrades of the Central Disciplinary Committee," dated June 15, 2002, and signed by "All Former Liaotie Workers."

84. Interview in Shenyang, June 1999.

85. State Letters and Visits Bureau, *People's Letters and Visits* 9 (2001): 42–44; James R. Townsend, *Political Participation in Communist China* (Berkeley and Los Angeles: University of California Press, 1967), p. 177.

86. Interview in Tieling, January 31, 2002.

87. Chen, "Industrial Restructuring and Workers' Resistance in China"; Elizabeth J. Perry, "Crime, Corruption, and Contention," in *The Paradox of China's Post-Mao Reform*, ed. Merle Goldman and Roderick MacFarquhar (Cambridge, Mass.: Harvard University Press, 1999), pp. 308–32; Hurst and O'Brien, "China's Contentious Pensioners."

88. Göran Therborn, *The Ideology of Power and the Power of Ideology* (London: Verso, 1980).

CHAPTER 4

1. Raymond Williams, *Marxism and Literature* (Oxford: Oxford University Press, 1977), p. 132.

2. David Harvey, *Spaces of Hope* (Berkeley and Los Angeles: University of California Press, 2000).

3. Deborah S. Davis, "From Welfare Benefits to Capitalized Asset: The Re-commodification of Residential Space in Urban China," in *Housing and Social Change: East-West Perspectives*, ed. Ray Forrest and James Lee (New York: Routledge, 2003), pp. 183–96.

4. Wang Feng, "Housing Improvement and Distribution in Urban China: Initial Evidence from China's 2000 Census," *China Review* 3, no. 2 (2003): 121–43.

5. Sian Victoria Liu, "Social Positions: Neighborhood Transitions after *Danwei*," in *Working in China: Ethnographies of Labor and Workplace Transformation*, ed. Ching Kwan Lee (London: Routledge, 2006), pp. 38–55.

6. Davis, "From Welfare Benefits to Capitalized Asset."

7. Yaping Wang and Alan Murie, "The Process of Commercialisation of Urban Housing in China," *Urban Studies* 33, no. 6 (1996): 971–89.

8. Interview in Shenyang, August 15, 1999.

9. Interview in Shenyang, July 4, 2003.

10. Interview in Shenyang, July 6, 2003.

11. Interview in Shenyang, July 5, 2003.

12. Martin King Whyte, "Postscript: Filial Support and Family Change," in *China's Revolutions and Intergenerational Relations*, ed. Martin King Whyte (Ann Arbor: University of Michigan Press, 2003), pp. 303–11.

13. Interview in Liaoning, August 5, 2003.

14. John Giles, Albert Park, and Cai Fang, "How Has Economic Restructuring Affected China's Urban Workers?" *China Quarterly* 185 (March 2006): 61–95.

15. Interview in Shenyang, August 15, 1999.

16. Yongshun Cai, "Civil Resistance and Rule of Law in China: The Case of Homeowners' Rights Defense," in *Grassroots Political Reform in Contemporary China*, ed. Merle Goldman and Elizabeth J. Perry (Cambridge, Mass.: Harvard University Press, forthcoming).

17. Steven Harrell remarks that the Chinese socialist revolution has transformed the meaning of work. Only wage jobs in state units were considered real work, or *gongzuo*. Reform has upset the boundary between paid and unpaid work, work inside and outside the home, and so on. He maintains that in the reform era, there is more disagreement on what constitutes real work. See Steven Harrell, "The Changing Meanings of Work in China," in *Re-drawing Boundaries: Work, Households, and Gender in China*, ed. Barbara Entwisle and Gail E. Henderson (Berkeley and Los Angeles: University of California Press, 2000), pp. 67–76.

18. Giles, Park, and Cai, "How Has Economic Restructuring Affected China's Urban Workers?"

19. Labor Science Institute, Ministry of Labor and Social Security, *The Blue Book of Chinese Employment, 2002* (Beijing: China Labor and Social Security Press, 2003), p. 147 [in Chinese].

20. Ibid., p. 153.

21. Interview in Shenyang, July 6, 2003.

22. Interview in Shenyang, March 31, 2002.

23. Interview in Shenyang, January 6, 2000.

24. The demographer Wang Feng has found that 34.2 percent of male urban retirees and more than 20 percent of female urban retirees were working in the mid-1990s in Baoding, a city in Hubei province. He argued that these rates were typical of other Chinese cities in the 1990s. Wang Feng, "Privilege or Punishment? Retirement and Reemployment among the Chinese Urban Elderly," in *China's Revolutions and Intergenerational Relations,* ed. Martin King Whyte (Ann Arbor: University of Michigan Press, 2003), pp. 61–84.

25. Interview in Shenyang, July 4, 2003.

26. Interview in Shenyang, July 4, 2003.

27. Interview in Tieling, July 8, 1999.

28. Interview in Shenyang, July 5, 2003.

29. See chapter 2 for details.

30. *China Labor* 8 (2002): 9.

31. Giles, Park, and Cai, "How Has Economic Restructuring Affected China's Urban Workers?"

32. Tang, "Selections from Report on Poverty and Anti-poverty in Urban China," p. 28.

33. Interview in Shenyang, May 20, 1999.

34. Azizur Rahman Khan and Carl Riskin, *Inequality and Poverty in China in the Age of Globalization* (Oxford: Oxford University Press, 2001).

35. Jeff Goodwin, James M. Jasper, and Francesca Polletta, "Why Emotions Matter," in *Passionate Politics: Emotions and Social Movements,* ed. Jeff Goodwin, James M. Jasper, and Francesca Polletta (Chicago: University of Chicago Press, 1992), pp. 1–24.

36. Interview in Shenyang, January 7, 2000.

37. Interview in Tieling, July 7, 1999.

38. Interview in Shenyang, May 18, 1999.

39. Interview in Shenyang, May 20, 1999.

40. Interview in Tieling, February 2, 2002.

41. Interview in Shenyang, May 18, 1999.

42. Interview in Shenyang, January 6, 2000.

43. Interview in Shenyang, January 7, 2000, with a forty-nine-year-old woman textile-mill worker.

44. Interview in Shenyang, January 7, 2000, with a forty-eight-year-old woman textile-mill worker.

45. Interview in Shenyang, January 7, 2000, with a forty-five-year-old woman textile-mill worker.

46. Interview in Shenyang, July 4, 2003.

47. Interview in Shenyang, January 8, 2000.

48. Interview in Shenyang, July 5, 2003.

49. Interview in Tieling, February 1, 2002.

50. Interview with Liaoyang protest participants, August 5, 2003.

51. Interview in Shenyang, July 6, 2003.

52. Interview in Shenyang, May 18, 1999.

53. Ching Kwan Lee, "The 'Revenge of History': Collective Memories and Labor Protests in Northeastern China," *Ethnography* 1, no. 2 (2000): 217–37.

54. This ambivalence is found not just among workers, but also among villagers, women, and ethnic minorities. See Ching Kwan Lee and Guobin Yang, eds., *Re-envisioning the Chinese Revolution: The Politics and Poetics of Collective Memories in Contemporary China* (Washington, D.C.: Woodrow Wilson Center Press and Stanford University Press, 2007).

55. Marc Blecher, "Hegemony and Workers' Politics in China," *China Quarterly* 170 (2002): 283–303.

56. William Hurst and Kevin J. O'Brien, "China's Contentious Pensioners," *China Quarterly* 170 (2002): 345–60.

CHAPTER 5

1. Fieldwork in Shenzhen, May 7, 2002, and interview on May 10, 2002.

2. Fieldwork in Shenzhen, May 7, 2002.

3. Interviews in Shenzhen, March 23 and May 29, 2002.

4. Katherine Verdery, "A Transition from Socialism to Feudalism? Thoughts on the Postsocialist State," in *What Was Socialism, and What Comes Next?* (Princeton, N.J.: Princeton University Press, 1996), p. 221.

5. William P. Alford, "A Second Great Wall? China's Post–Cultural Revolution Project of Legal Construction," *Cultural Dynamics* 11, no. 2 (1999): 193–213.

6. Pierre Bourdieu, "The Force of Law: Toward a Sociology of the Juridical Field," *Hastings Law Journal* 38 (1987): 805–53.

7. What counts as "radical" in the Chinese context may look tame to an outside observer or in another sociopolitical system. By *radical*, I do not mean revolution or violence. I adopt workers' local understanding of what constitutes "radical" action, which in China includes public disobedience that disrupts social order, holding rallies and demonstrations without official approval, and forming loose or formal organizations among workers across factories. I thank Al Feuerwerker for insisting that I clarify my usage of the term.

8. Joe Studwell, article in *China Economic Quarterly* 1, no. 1 (2001): 23.

9. Shenzhen Statistics and Information Bureau, *Shenzhen Statistical Handbook* (Shenzhen: Shenzhen Statistics and Information Bureau, 2001), p. 76 [in Chinese]. In 2000, 37 percent of all industrial migrant labor in China worked in Guangdong. See Public Safety Administration Bureau, ed., *A Compilation of National Temporary Population Statistical Data.* (Beijing: Masses Publishing House, 2000), p. 2 [in Chinese].

10. Institute of Contemporary Observation, "Legal Protection and Assistance Network for Labor in Guangdong: A Research Report" (manuscript, Institute of Contemporary Observation, January 2002), p. 2 [in Chinese].

11. Ching Kwan Lee, *Gender and the South China Miracle: Two Worlds of Factory Women* (Berkeley and Los Angeles: University of California Press, 1998).

12. For a critique of my book and my response regarding issues of class, gender, and worker rebellion, see the symposium in *Journal of Labor Studies* 27, no. 2 (2002).

13. Clara Li, "Abuse of Workers Revealed," *South China Morning Post*, January 17, 2002.

14. *Southern Metropolitan News*, April 7, 2002, p. 3 [in Chinese]; *South China Morning Post*, April 8, 2002, p. 7. For a similar incident, see *Shenzhen Legal Daily*, December 2, 2001, p. 1 [in Chinese]. For a summary report on several cases of deaths in Shenzhen caused by overwork, see *China Youth Daily*, October 22, 2001. Also see Philip P. Pan, "Worked Till They Drop: Few Protections for China's New Laborers," *Washington Post*, May 13, 2002; and *Guangzhou Daily*, June 13, 2001 [in Chinese], on a female worker's miscarriage after months of overtime work.

15. Shenzhen City Labor Bureau, *Constructing Harmonious Labor Relations* (Beijing: China Labor and Social Security Publishing House, 2000), p. 169 [in Chinese].

16. Shenzhen City Labor Bureau, *Establishing Marketized Employment Institutions* (Beijing: China Labor and Social Security Publishing House, 2000) [in Chinese].

17. *Shenzhen Legal Daily*, December 18, 2000, cited in Liu Kaiming, *Migrant Labor in South China* (Beijing: Xinhua Publishing House, 2003), p. 210 [in Chinese].

18. Shenzhen City Labor Bureau, *Shenzhen Labor Statistics Yearbook, 1998–1999* (Beijing: China Labor and Social Security Publishing House, 2000), p. 103 [in Chinese]; Shenzhen City Labor Bureau, *Shenzhen Labor Statistics Yearbook, 2000–2001* (Beijing: China Labor and Social Security Publishing House, 2002), pp. 109, 115 [in Chinese].

19. Clara Li, "Shenzhen Gets a Bad Name with Workers It Does Not Want," *South China Morning Post*, January 15, 2002.

20. *Shenzhen Special Zone Daily*, May 1, 2002 [in Chinese].

21. Shenzhen Labor Relations Department, Shenzhen City Labor Bureau, "A Survey Report on Shenzhen Labor Dispute Arbitration Handling," in *A Collection of Shenzhen Labor Studies Scientific Papers, 1997–1998*, vol. 1, ed. Shenzhen City Labor Bureau and Shenzhen Labor Studies Association (Beijing: China Labor and Social Security Publishing House, 1999), pp. 259–65 [in Chinese].

22. Philip P. Pan, "Getting Paid in China: Matter of Life and Death," *Washington Post*, February 13, 2003.

23. Dai Jianzhong and Zhu Min, "A Survey Report on Labor Relations in Private Enterprises and Women Workers' Problems" (manuscript, Beijing Academy of Social Science, 1999) [in Chinese].

24. Fieldwork in Shenzhen, May 9, 2002.

25. Interview in Shenzhen, May 12, 2002.

26. Chen He, "Boss Forces Workers to Kneel," *Entrepreneurs* 1 (1997): 9–10 [in Chinese].

27. Che Xiaowei and Wang Pan, "Eighty Women Workers Were Strip Searched," *China Employment* 9 (2002): 35–36 [in Chinese].

28. *Southern Metropolitan News,* August 3, 2001 [in Chinese]. Posted online at http://news.sina.com.cn/c/2001–08–03/319656.html.

29. Tan Yibo, "Shenzhen Electronics Factory Illegally Detains Workers: One Death, Six Injured," *China Labor Daily,* June 20, 1998, p. 2 [in Chinese].

30. Reuters, June 28, 2002.

31. *Guangzhou Youth Daily,* February 3, 1999, reports that in 1997, there were more than 10,800 cases of workplace injuries in two industrial districts alone in Shenzhen.

32. "More Than One Hundred Cases of Industrial Injuries to Be Tried," *Southern Weekend,* November 26, 1999, p. 1 [in Chinese].

33. Amnesty International, "People's Republic of China: Labor Unrest and the Suppression of the Rights to Freedom of Association and Expression" (ASA 17/015/2002, Amnesty International, April 30, 2002, posted online at http://web.amnesty.org/library/index/engasa170152002); Joseph Khan, "China's Workers Risk Limbs in Export Drive," *New York Times,* April 7, 2003.

34. Joseph Khan, "Workplace Deaths Rise in China Despite New Safety Legislation," *New York Times,* October 24, 2003.

35. Interview in Shenzhen, September 17, 1999.

36. Interview in Shenzhen, March 2001.

37. Interview in Shenzhen, March 2001.

38. Interview in Shenzhen, April 13, 2002.

39. Anita Chan, *China's Workers under Assault* (Armonk, N.Y.: E. M. Sharpe, 2001), pp. 14–15.

40. Interview in Shenzhen, April 16, 2002.

41. Interview in Shajing, April 7, 2002.

42. Interview in Shenzhen, April 16, 2002.

43. Interview in Longgang, Shenzhen, March 2001.

44. Interview in Shenzhen, May 2, 2002.

45. Shi Meixia, "Causes and Policies Regarding Spontaneous Incidents in Labor Relations," in *Report of Chinese Labor Science Studies, 1997–1999,* ed. Labor Science Institute, Labor and Social Security Bureau (Beijing: China Labor and Social Security Publishing House, 2000), pp. 166–216.

46. Interview in Shenzhen, May 17, 2002.

47. Interview in Shenzhen, March 23, 2002.

48. Stanley Lubman, *Bird in a Cage: Legal Reform in China* (Stanford, Calif.: Stanford University Press, 1999).

49. For a discussion of the basic procedures of labor dispute resolution, see Virginia E. Ho, *Labor Dispute Resolution in China: Implications for Labor Rights and Legal Reform,* China Research Monograph 59 (Berkeley: University of California, Berkeley, Institute of East Asian Studies, 2003).

50. As of 2000, enterprise mediation committees handled less than 25 percent of the total number of reported disputes handled by arbitration committees.

See ibid., p. 60. The general absence of these two grassroots-level units in non-state workplaces means that migrant workers in Shenzhen approach the Labor Bureau directly. The two clerks at the arbitration application department mediated 465 cases in 1999 alone. See Shenzhen City Labor Bureau, *Constructing Harmonious Labor Relations*, p. 175.

51. Interview in Shenzhen, May 10, 2002.

52. I ran into this mass petition on May 9, 2002, and conducted the interview with this worker representative on May 10, 2002.

53. Research Department, All China Federation of Trade Unions, *Chinese Trade Union Statistics Yearbook, 1998* (Beijing: China Statistics Press, 1999), table 2–36 [in Chinese].

54. Interview in Shenzhen, May 12, 2002.

55. Interview in Nanshan district, Shenzhen, April 22, 2002.

56. Interview with five worker representatives, Nanshan district, Shenzhen, March 23, 2002.

57. Observation of the negotiation on May 1, 2002, Shenzhen.

58. Ho, *Labor Dispute Resolution in China*, pp. 69–70.

59. Interviews in Shenzhen, April 12 and May 15, 2002.

60. Interviews in Shenzhen, May 10 and 17, 2002.

61. Shenzhen City Labor Bureau, *Constructing Harmonious Labor Relations*, chap. 5.

62. Interview in Shenzhen, April 22, 2002.

63. In Baoan district, where there is a migrant labor population of about 2.5 million, the legal aid center was first established in 1997, giving advice and legal representation to several hundred migrant workers. For instance, in 2000, 266 migrant workers received assistance, out of a total of 422 clients. In 2001, 156 migrant workers out of a total of 399 clients received assistance. Many of these involved industrial injury compensation and wages. The local hotline "148" and legal aid reception room received more than two thousand counseling inquiries each of these years. These figures were obtained in an interview with a director of the Baoan Legal Aid Center on March 4, 2002.

64. Cited in Ho, *Labor Dispute Resolution in China*, p. 169.

65. Shenzhen seemed to differ from the national pattern: it was reported that less than 10 percent of arbitrated cases reached the court of first instance in Shenzhen. Ibid., p. 79.

66. Interview in Shenzhen, March 23, 2002.

67. Interview in Shenzhen, May 12, 2002.

68. During the National People's Congress in 2002, local-level court officials in Guangdong complained about a lack of financial and professional support. In the city of Gaozhou in Guangdong, for instance, only eight of the ninety-three judges and legal assistants had been trained in legal studies at the university level, "while others are officers transferred from other public bodies or from the military, as the government is downsizing the armed forces," revealed one official. The Supreme Court president Xiao Yang announced a five-year retraining program and admitted that many judges were unfamiliar

with the concepts of nonprejudicial treatment and transparent legal procedures. Local protectionism was also highlighted as a common problem. See Vivien Pik-Kwan Chan, "Get Qualified or Go, Judges Told," *South China Morning Post*, March 13, 2002.

69. Intervie in Shenzhen, December 25, 2000.

70. For a general overview of the legal profession, see William P. Alford, "Tasseled Loafers for Barefoot Lawyers: Transformation and Tension in the World of Chinese Legal Workers," in *China's Legal Reforms*, ed. Stanley Lubman (Oxford: Oxford University Press, 1996), pp. 22–38.

71. Ethan Michelson, "Chinese Lawyers at Work: The Practice of Law as an Obstacle to Justice," in *Working in China: Ethnographies of Labor and Workplace Transformation*, ed. Ching Kwan Lee (London: Routledge, 2006), pp. 169–87.

72. *Shenzhen Legal Daily*, October 25, 2001 [in Chinese]. In Longgang district, for instance, in November and December 2001, the government claimed to have charged twenty unregistered lawyers with practicing illegally. Another twenty-four bogus lawyers were charged in Shenzhen itself during a campaign at the end of 2001. Some of them purportedly worked through labor service stations set up by the local government representative from Hubei and were accused by the Shenzhen government of accepting fees for their supposedly free services and for encouraging workers to stage a sit-in and strike. See *Shenzhen Legal Daily*, December 11, 2001, and January 4, 2002 [in Chinese].

73. Interview in Shenzhen, April 20, 2002.

74. This case was reported in Pan, "Chinese Workers' Rights Stop at Courtroom Door."

75. Interview with three worker representatives in Shenzhen, May 23, 2002.

76. Interview in Shenzhen, May 14, 2003.

77. Chris Smith, "Living at Work: Management Control and the Chinese Dormitory Labor System in China," *Asia Pacific Journal of Management* 20, no. 3 (2002): 333–58.

78. Raymond W. K. Lau, "China: Labor Reform and the Challenge Facing the Working Class," *Capital and Class* 61 (1997): 45–81; Trini Leung, "Labor Fights for Its Rights," *China Perspectives* 19 (1998): 6–21.

79. Li Minqi, "Response to Lau's 'China: Labor Reform and the Challenge Facing the Working Class,'" *Capital and Class* 65 (1998): 22.

80. Ibid.

81. In September 2006, I cohosted a weeklong labor NGO workshop with the sociologist Shen Yuan at Tsinghua University. Fourteen organizations from Guangdong, Sichuan, Shangdong, and Beijing participated. NGO activists estimated that there are about fifty labor NGOs active in China. For a brief discussion of several more established NGOs in the Pearl River Delta, see Ching Kwan Lee, "Is Labor a Political Force in China?" in *Grassroots Political Reform in Contemporary China*, ed. Merle Goldman and Elizabeth J. Perry (Cambridge, Mass.: Harvard University Press, forthcoming).

82. "Reforming Fee Regulation on Migrants," *China Employment* 4 (2002): 4–10 [in Chinese].

83. Erik Eckholm, "Petitioners Urge China to Enforce Legal Rights," *New York Times,* June 2, 2003.

84. Roger V. Gould, *Insurgent Identities: Class, Community, and Protest in Paris from 1848 to the Commune* (Chicago: University of Chicago Press, 1995).

85. Interview in Shenzhen, May 9, 2006.

86. See Lee, *Gender and the South China Miracle;* and Lei Guang, "Guerrilla Workfare: Migrant Decorators, State Power, and the Moral Economy of Work in China," in *Working in China: Ethnographies of Labor and Workplace Transformation,* ed. Ching Kwan Lee (New York: Routledge, 2006), pp. 56–76.

87. Interview in Shenzhen, Guangdong, December 25, 2000.

88. Interview in Shenzhen, Guangdong, December 26, 2000.

89. Interview in Shenzhen, May 17, 2002.

90. Interview in Shajin, Shenzhen, March 3, 2002.

91. Li Zhang shows that even migrant garment traders who can compensate for their low social status (arising from their rural *hukou*) by conspicuous consumption are subject to expulsion during unpredictable government campaigns. See Li Zhang, "Urban Experiences and Social Belonging," in *Popular China: Unofficial Culture in a Globalizing Society,* ed. Perry Link, Richard P. Madsen, and Paul G. Pickowicz (Lanham, Md.: Rowman and Littlefield, 2002), pp. 275–99.

92. Interview in Shenzhen, May 9, 2002.

93. Ibid.

94. The first appearance of the term in the *People's Daily* was on January 21, 1995, in an article announcing the need to use a national compensation law to protect the rights of vulnerable groups such as the handicapped, women, and children. Later, around 1999, academics and policy makers concerned with social welfare, charity, and volunteer work gradually expanded the reference of the term to include social groups disadvantaged by the reform process rather than by personal and physical predicaments. Since then, the term tends to include both socially and physically impaired groups, especially unemployed and migrant workers in the cities. Li Erjin, " 'Ruoshi Qunti' in the *People's Daily,* 1995–2002" (research note, Department of Sociology, Tsinghua University, Beijing, August 2002) [in Chinese].

95. Thireau and Huan, "The Moral Universe of Aggrieved Chinese Workers."

CHAPTER 6

1. Michael Burawoy, "The Functions and Reproduction of Migrant Labor: Comparative Materials from Southern Africa and the United States," *American Journal of Sociology* 81, no. 5 (1976): 1050–87.

2. Interview in Shenzhen, May 17, 2002.

3. Samuel P. S. Ho and George C. S. Lin, "Emerging Land Markets in Rural and Urban China: Policies and Practices," *China Quarterly* 175 (2003): 681–707. There is ambiguity in the law as to which organization represents farmers' collectives, leading to an increasing volume of land disputes relating to requisition

and land boundary assessment. The term *village collective* can variously mean the administrative village (the former commune), the small group (previously the production team), or the township government. See Peter Ho, "Who Owns China's Land? Policies, Property Rights, and Deliberate Institutional Ambiguity," *China Quarterly* 166 (2001): 394–421; and Yongshun Cai, "Collective Ownership or Cadres' Ownership? The Non-agricultural Use of Farmland in China," *China Quarterly* 175 (2003): 662–80.

4. Ho and Lin, "Emerging Land Markets in Rural and Urban China," p. 689 n. 20. Two types of adjustments have been reported: big and small. When big adjustments are made, all farmland is taken back and then reallocated so households get different plots of land. With small adjustments, households with added or lost members receive land from or return land to the village.

5. Rachel Murphy, *How Migrant Labor Is Changing Rural China* (Cambridge: Cambridge University Press, 2002), p. 74. (1 mu = 0.1647 acres.)

6. Interview in Shenzhen, May 8, 2003.

7. Interview in Shenzhen, May 20, 2003.

8. Interview in Shenzhen, May 9, 2003.

9. Interview in Shenzhen, May 17, 2003.

10. These figures are reported in Liu Kaiming, "Social Structure of Rights Deprivation: A Report on a Collective Labor Dispute Investigation" (report, Institute of Contemporary Observation, 2004) [in Chinese].

11. Bai Nangsheng and Song Hungyuan, *Return to the Village or Enter the City?* (Beijing: China Finance and Economics Publishing House, 2002), p. 23 [in Chinese].

12. Yang Junxiong, "Peasant Employment Is the Primary Question after Subsistence Is Achieved," in *Hot Topics in Chinese Peasant Studies in 2001*, ed. Xian Zhude (Beijing: China Statistics Press, 2001), p. 29 [in Chinese].

13. Rural Economy Research Center, Ministry of Agriculture, ed., *Chinese Rural Studies Report (2002)* (Beijing: China Finance and Economics Publishing House, 2002), p. 88 [in Chinese].

14. Thomas P. Bernstein and Xiaobo Lü, *Taxation without Representation in Contemporary Rural China* (New York: Cambridge University Press, 2003), pp. 48–49.

15. James Kynge, "Chinese Workers Transform Fortunes of Home Towns," *Financial Times*, November 9, 2003.

16. Bai Nansheng and He Yupeng, "Return to the Village or Going Out?" *Sociological Research (Shehuixu Yanjiu)* 3 (2002): 64–78 [in Chinese].

17. Interview in Renshou County, Sichuan, July 16, 2003.

18. Interview in Renshou County, Sichuan, July 17, 2003.

19. Interview in Shenzhen, May 8, 2003.

20. Interview in Shenzhen, May 16, 2003.

21. Interview in Sichuan, July 23, 2003.

22. Interview in Shenzhen, May 16, 2003.

23. Interview in Shenzhen, May 17, 2003.

24. Interview in Renshou County, Sichuan, July 16, 2003.

25. Murphy, *How Migrant Labor Is Changing Rural China,* chap. 4.

26. Sally Sargeson, "Subduing 'the Rural House-Building Craze': Attitudes towards Housing Construction and Land Use Controls in Four Zhejiang Villages," *China Quarterly* 169 (2002): 945.

27. Interview in Shenzhen, May 6, 2003.

28. Interview in Sichuan, July 17, 2003.

29. Interview in Shenzhen, May 17, 2003.

30. Mark Selden, *The Political Economy of Chinese Development* (Armonk, N.Y.: M. E. Sharpe, 1993).

31. Kate Zhou, *How Farmers Changed China* (Boulder, Colo.: Westview Press, 2000).

32. Myron L. Cohen, "Cultural and Political Inventions in Modern China: The Case of the Chinese 'Peasant,'" *Daedalus* 122, no. 2 (1993): 151–70.

33. Lu Xueyi, "Balancing Rural-Urban Relations for the Sake of Rural Residents," in *Analysis and Forecast on China's Social Development, 2005,* ed. Ru Xin, Lu Xueyi, and Li Peilin (Beijing: Social Sciences Academic Press, 2004), pp. 175–86 [in Chinese].

34. Interview in Renshou, Sichuan, July 18, 2003.

35. Interview in Shenzhen, May 9, 2003.

36. Interview in Shenzhen, May 16, 2003.

37. Interview in Renshou, Sichuan, July 17, 2003.

38. Interview in Renshou, Sichuan, July 16, 2003.

39. Interview in Shenzhen, April 13, 2002.

40. For a detailed account of the Renshou incident, see Bernstein and Lü, *Taxation without Representation in Contemporary Rural China,* pp. 130–37. My brief description of the causes of peasant discontents is based on two interviews with the peasant leader Xiang Wenqing in Sichuan and Shenzhen in July and August 2003. He was released in June 2002, after nine years in prison for his role in the Renshou incident. Some of the details he offered differ from the description in Bernstein and Lü's book.

41. Bernstein and Lü, *Taxation without Representation in Contemporary Rural China,* pp. 199–205.

42. Interview in Renshou, Sichuan, July 18, 2003.

43. Kevin J. O'Brien, "Rightful Resistance," *World Politics* 49, no. 1 (1996): 31–55; Kevin J. O'Brien, "Villagers, Elections, and Citizenship in Contemporary China," *Modern China* 27, no. 4 (2001): 407–35; Kevin J. O'Brien and Lianjiang Li, "The Politics of Lodging Complaints in Rural China," *China Quarterly* 143 (1995): 756–83.

44. Interview in Shenzhen, May 9, 2003.

45. Interview in Shenzhen, May 16, 2003.

46. Interview in Shenzhen, April 13, 2002.

47. Interview in Shenzhen, March 17, 2002.

48. Interview in Shenzhen, April 7, 2002.

49. Interview in Shenzhen, May 20, 2003.

50. Interview in Shenzhen, May 8, 2003.

51. Ibid.

52. Interview in Shenzhen, April 13, 2002.

53. Interview in Shenzhen, April 13, 2002.

54. Interview in Shenzhen, May 9, 2003.

55. The image of the countryside as a wasteland of stagnation is common among migrant workers. See Yan Hairong, "Spectralization of the Rural: Reinterpreting the Labor Mobility of Rural Young Women in Post-Mao China," *American Ethnologist* 30, no. 4 (2003): 1–19.

56. Interview in Shenzhen, May 16, 2003.

57. Interview in Shenzhen, May 15, 2003.

58. Interview in Shenzhen, May 9, 2003.

59. Interview in Shenzhen, April 13, 2002.

60. Interview in Shenzhen, May 16, 2003.

61. Interview in Shenzhen, May 9, 2003.

62. Interviews in Shenzhen, May 8, 2003, and May 21, 2002.

63. Murphy, *How Migrant Labor Is Changing Rural China*, chap. 6.

64. Interview in Shenzhen, May 8, 2003.

65. Bai and He, "Return to the Village or Going Out?" p. 70.

66. Murphy, *How Migrant Labor Is Changing Rural China*, p. 128. Yet she emphasizes the "added moisture" content of these official statistics and the difficulty in obtaining reliable data on businesses whose existence is always ephemeral and in flux.

67. See Gillian Hart, *Disabling Globalization* (Berkeley and Los Angeles: University of California Press, 2002), chap. 6; David Harvey, "Accumulation by Dispossession," in *The New Imperialism* (New York: Oxford University Press, 2005), pp. 127–82; and Massimo De Angelis, "Marx's Theory of Primitive Accumulation: A Suggested Reinterpretation" (manuscript, University of East London, March 1999, posted online at http://homepages.uel.ac.uk/M.DeAngelis/PRIMACCA.htm).

CHAPTER 7

1. Friedrich Engels, *The Condition of the Working Class in England*, trans. and ed. W. O. Henderson and W. H. Chaloner (New York: Macmillan, 1958), pp. 184–86.

2. Interview in Shenzhen, December 25, 2000.

3. David Bensman and Roberta Lynch, *Rusted Dreams: Hard Times in a Steel Community* (New York: McGraw-Hill, 1987), p. 6.

4. Interview in Tieling, January 31, 2002.

5. Boy Luthje, "Global Production, Industrial Development, and New Labor Regimes in China: The Case of Electronics Contract Manufacturing" (paper presented at the conference "The Labor of Reform: Employment, Workers' Rights, and Labor Law in China," University of Michigan, Ann Arbor, March 21–22, 2003).

6. Ibid.

294 / Notes to Pages 240–243

7. Doug Guthrie, *Dragon in a Three-Piece Suit: The Emergence of Capitalism in China* (Princeton, N.J.: Princeton University Press, 1999).

8. Mary E. Gallagher, "Following in the Steps of Qiu Ju? Law and Morality at the Chinese Workplace" (presentation at Stanford University, February 24, 2005).

9. The significance of the regional economy is suggested, but not sufficiently substantiated with data, in William Hurst, "Understanding Contentious Collective Action by Chinese Laid-Off Workers: The Importance of Regional Political Economy," *Studies in Comparative International Development Studies* 39, no. 2 (2004): 94–120.

10. Ching Kwan Lee, "From Organized Dependence to Disorganized Despotism: Changing Labor Regimes in Chinese Factories," *China Quarterly* 157 (1999): 44–71.

11. Ching Kwan Lee, "The Labor Politics of Market Socialism: Collective Inaction and Class Experiences among State Workers in Guangzhou," *Modern China* 24, no. 1 (1998): 3–33.

12. Anita Chan has pointed to another source of change: domestic and international pressures on the official unions to adopt a more responsive role toward workers' grievances. I disagree with her assessment about the significance and potential of official unions and share the views of Mary Gallagher. For these different assessments of the official unions, see Anita Chan, "Recent Trends in Chinese Labor Issues: Signs of Change," *China Perspectives* 57 (2005): 23–31; and Mary E. Gallagher, " 'Time Is Money, Efficiency Is Life': The Transformation of Labor Relations in China," *Studies in Comparative International Development* 39, no. 2 (2004): 11–44.

13. On coal mining, see Thomas Dublin, *When the Mines Closed: Stories of Struggles in Hard Times* (Ithaca, N.Y.: Cornell University Press, 1998); and John Gaventa, *Power and Powerlessness: Quiescence and Rebellion in an Appalachian Valley* (Urbana: University of Illinois Press, 1980). On the steel industry, see Dale A. Hathaway, *Can Workers Have a Voice? The Politics of Deindustrialization in Pittsburgh* (University Park: Pennsylvania State University Press, 1993); and Bensman and Lynch, *Rusted Dreams*. On automobile and rubber plants, see Kathryn Marie Dudley, *The End of the Line: Lost Jobs, New Lives in Postindustrial America* (Chicago: University of Chicago Press, 1994); and Gregory Pappas, *The Magic City: Unemployment in a Working-Class Community* (Ithaca, N.Y.: Cornell University Press, 1989). On the electronics, apparel, and textile industries, see Jefferson Cowie, *Capital Moves: RCA's Seventy-Year Quest for Cheap Labor* (New York: New Press, 2001); Eve S. Weinbaum, *To Move a Mountain: Fighting the Global Economy in Appalachia* (New York: New Press, 2004); and Jane L. Collins, *Threads: Gender, Labor, and Power in the Global Apparel Industry* (Chicago: University of Chicago Press, 2003).

14. Weinbaum, *To Move a Mountain*, p. 133.

15. Dudley, *End of the Line*, p. 137.

16. Ibid., p. 141.

17. Ibid., p. 148.

18. Dudley, *End of the Line*, chap. 4; Pappas, *Magic City*.

19. Hathaway, *Can Workers Have a Voice?*, chap. 3; John Portz, *The Politics of Plant Closings* (Lawrence: University Press of Kansas, 1990), chap. 5.

20. Hathaway, *Can Workers Have a Voice?*, p. 149.

21. Weinbaum, *To Move a Mountain*, chap. 5.

22. Hathaway, *Can Workers Have a Voice?*, p. 201.

23. Weinbaum, *To Move a Mountain*, p. 4.

24. Ibid., pp. 267–70.

25. Padma Desai and Todd Idson, *Work without Wages: Russia's Nonpayment Crisis* (Cambridge, Mass.: MIT Press, 2000), p. 50; John S. Earle and Klara Z. Sabirianova, "How Late to Pay? Understanding Wage Arrears in Russia," *Journal of Labor Economics* 20, no. 3 (2000): 661–707.

26. Simon Clarke, "Trade Unions and the Non-payment of Wages in Russia," *International Journal of Manpower* 19, nos. 1–2 (1998): 69.

27. Foreign Broadcast Information Service, SOV-2003-0226.

28. To answer these questions, see, for instance, Debra Javeline, *Protest and the Politics of Blame: The Russian Response to Unpaid Wages* (Ann Arbor: University of Michigan Press, 2003).

29. Beverly J. Silver, *Forces of Labor: Workers' Movements and Globalization since 1870* (Cambridge: Cambridge University Press, 2003), p. 41.

30. Leslie Salzinger, *Genders in Production: Making Workers in Mexico's Global Factories* (Berkeley and Los Angeles: University of California Press, 2003); Suan Tiano, *Patriarchy on the Line: Labor, Gender, and Ideology in the Mexican Maquila Industry* (Philadelphia: Temple University Press, 1994); Leslie Sklair, *Assembling for Development: The Maquila Industry in Mexico and the United States* (San Diego: University of California, San Diego, Center for US-Mexican Studies, 1993); Maria-Patricia Fernandez-Kelly, *For We Are Sold, I and My People: Women and Industry in Mexico's Frontier* (Albany: State University of New York Press, 1983); Diane Elson and Ruth Pearson, "Nimble Fingers Make Cheap Workers: An Analysis of Women's Employment in Third World Export Manufacturing," *Feminist Studies* 8 (1981): 87–107; Louise Lamphere, *From Working Daughters to Working Mothers* (Ithaca, N.Y.: Cornell University Press, 1987); Lourdes Beneria and Martha Roldan, *The Crossroads of Class and Gender* (Chicago: University of Chicago Press, 1987).

31. Cowie, *Capital Moves*, p. 154.

32. Ibid., p. 4.

33. Hagen Koo, *Korean Workers: The Culture and Politics of Class Formation* (Ithaca, N.Y.: Cornell University Press), p. 54.

34. Ibid., pp. 53, 56.

35. Ibid., chap. 4.

36. Ibid., p. 143.

37. Gail Hershatter, *The Workers of Tianjin, 1900–1949* (Stanford, Calif.: Stanford University Press, 1986), pp. 151–52.

38. Ibid., p. 155.

39. Emily Honig, *Sisters and Strangers: Women in the Shanghai Cotton*

Mills, 1919–1949 (Stanford, Calif.: Stanford University Press, 1986), pp. 139, 144.

40. Elizabeth J. Perry, *Shanghai on Strike: The Politics of Chinese Labor* (Stanford, Calif.: Stanford University Press, 1993).

41. Thomas P. Bernstein and Xiaobo Lü, *Taxation without Representation in Contemporary Rural China* (New York: Cambridge University Press, 2003).

42. Kevin J. O'Brien and Lianjiang Li, "Suing the Local State: Administrative Litigation in Rural China," in *Engaging the Law in China: State, Society and Possibilities for Justice*, ed. Neil J. Diamant, Stanley B. Lubman, and Kevin O'Brien (Berkeley and Los Angeles: University of California Press, 2005), p. 32.

43. Lu Xueyi, "Balancing Rural-Urban Relations for the Sake of Rural Residents," in *Analysis and Forecast on China's Social Development, 2005*, ed. Ru Xin, Lu Xueyi, and Li Peilin (Beijing: Social Sciences Academic Press, 2004), pp. 175–86 [in Chinese]

44. Sally Sargeson, "Full Circle? Rural Land Reforms in Globalizing China," *Critical Asian Studies* 36, no. 4 (2004): 637–56. Also, Peter Ho, "Introduction," in *Developmental Dilemmas: Land Reform and Institutional Change in China*, ed. Peter Ho (London: Routledge, 2005), p. 16.

45. Yu Jianrong, "An Explanation of Farmers' Defense of Rights," *Sociological Research* 2 (2004): 49–55 [in Chinese]; Yu Jianrong, "Peasants' Organized Resistance and Political Risk: A Case Study of One Hunan County," *Strategy and Management* 3 (2003): 1–16 [in Chinese]; Yu Jianrong, "Organized Peasant Resistance in Contemporary China" (lecture delivered at Fairbank Center, Harvard University, December 4, 2003).

46. O'Brien and Li, "Suing the Local State."

47. Yongshun Cai, "Civil Resistance and Rule of Law in China: The Case of Homeowners' Rights Defense," in *Grassroots Political Reform in Contemporary China*, ed. Merle Goldman and Elizabeth J. Perry (Cambridge, Mass.: Harvard University Press, forthcoming); Li Zhang, "Forced from Home: Property Rights, Civic Activism, and the Politics of Relocation in China," *Urban Anthropology* 33, nos. 2–4 (2004): 247–81.

48. Cai, "Civil Resistance and Rule of Law in China."

49. Ibid.

50. Interview in Beijing, April 22, 2005.

Bibliography

Alford, William P. "A Second Great Wall? China's Post–Cultural Revolution Project of Legal Construction." *Cultural Dynamics* 11, no. 2 (1999): 193–213.
———. "Tasseled Loafers for Barefoot Lawyers: Transformation and Tension in the World of Chinese Legal Workers." In *China's Legal Reforms*, ed. Stanley Lubman, pp. 22–38. Oxford: Oxford University Press, 1996.
Amnesty International. "People's Republic of China: Labour Unrest and the Suppression of the Rights to Freedom of Association and Expression." ASA 17/015/2002, Amnesty International, April 30, 2002. Posted online at http://web.amnesty.org/library/index/engasa170152002.
"Angry Workers Besiege City Hall." *South China Morning Post*, May 17, 2000.
Bai Nansheng and He Yupeng. "Return to the Village or Going Out?" *Sociological Research* 3 (2002): 64–78 [in Chinese].
Bai Nansheng and Song Hungyuan. *Return to the Village or Enter the City?* Beijing: China Finance and Economics Publishing House, 2002 [in Chinese].
Becker, Jasper. "The Dark Side of the Dream." *South China Morning Post*, October 12, 1997.
———. "Workers in a State of Disunion." *South China Morning Post*, March 23, 2002.
Bendix, Reinhard. "The Citizenship of the Lower Classes." In *Force, Fate, and Freedom: On Historical Sociology*, chap. 5. Berkeley and Los Angeles: University of California Press, 1984.
Beneria, Lourdes, and Martha Roldan. *The Crossroads of Class and Gender*. Chicago: University of Chicago Press, 1987.
Bensman, David, and Roberta Lynch. *Rusted Dreams: Hard Times in a Steel Community*. New York: McGraw-Hill, 1987.
Bernstein, Thomas P. *Up to the Mountains and down to the Villages: The Transfer of Youth from Urban to Rural China*. New Haven, Conn.: Yale University Press, 1977.
Bernstein, Thomas P., and Xiaobo Lü. *Taxation without Representation in Contemporary Rural China*. New York: Cambridge University Press, 2003.

Blecher, Marc. "Hegemony and Workers' Politics in China." *China Quarterly* 170 (2002): 283–303.

Bourdieu, Pierre. "The Force of Law: Toward a Sociology of the Juridical Field." *Hastings Law Journal* 38 (1987): 805–53.

Brubaker, Rogers, and Frederick Cooper. "Beyond 'Identity.'" *Theory and Society* 29, no. 1 (2000): 1–47.

Burawoy, Michael. "The Functions and Reproduction of Migrant Labor: Comparative Materials from Southern Africa and the United States." *American Journal of Sociology* 81, no. 5 (1976): 1050–87.

———. *The Politics of Production.* London: Verso, 1985.

———. "Where Next for Labor?" *Critical Solidarity* 3, no. 3 (December 2003): 2–4.

Cai Fang, ed. *Chinese Population and Labor Issues Report, 2002: Rural and Urban Employment Problems and Strategies.* Beijing: Social Science Literature Press, 2002 [in Chinese].

Cai, Yongshun. "Civil Resistance and Rule of Law in China: The Case of Home Owners' Rights Defense." In *Grassroots Political Reform in Contemporary China,* ed. Merle Goldman and Elizabeth J. Perry. Cambridge, Mass.: Harvard University Press, forthcoming.

———. "Collective Ownership or Cadres' Ownership? The Non-agricultural Use of Farmland in China." *China Quarterly* 175 (2003): 662–80.

———. "The Resistance of Chinese Laid-Off Workers in the Reform Period." *China Quarterly* 170 (2002): 327–44.

Calhoun, Craig. *The Question of Class Struggle: Social Foundations of Popular Radicalism during the Industrial Revolution.* Chicago: University of Chicago Press, 1982.

Cao Siyuan. "Bankruptcy Law in China." *Harvard China Review* 1, no. 1 (1998).

Cao, Yuanzheng, Yingyi Qian, and Barry R. Weingast. "From Federalism, Chinese Style, to Privatization, Chinese Style." *Economics of Transition* 7, no. 1 (1999): 103–31.

Chakrabarty, Dipesh. *Provincializing Europe: Postcolonial Thought and Historical Difference.* Princeton, N.J.: Princeton University Press, 2000.

———. *Rethinking Working-Class History: Bengal, 1890–1940.* Princeton, N.J.: Princeton University Press, 1989.

Chan, Anita. *China's Workers under Assault.* Armonk, N.Y.: E. M. Sharpe, 2001.

———. "Labor Relations in Foreign-Funded Ventures: Chinese Trade Unions and the Prospects for Collective Bargaining." In *Adjusting to Capitalism: Chinese Workers and the State,* ed. Greg O'Leary, pp. 122–49. Armonk, N.Y.: M. E. Sharpe, 1998.

———. "Recent Trends in Chinese Labor Issues: Signs of Change." *China Perspectives* 57 (2005): 23–31.

Chan, Vivien Pik-Kwan. "Deprived Groups May Be Greatest Threat to Society." *South China Morning Post,* February 6, 2002.

————. "Get Qualified or Go, Judges Told." *South China Morning Post*, March 13, 2002.

Chang Kai. "On Enacting Legislation Regarding Unfair Labor Practices." *Social Science in China* 5 (September 2000): 71–82 [in Chinese].

Che Xiaowei and Wang Pan. "Eighty Women Workers Were Strip Searched." *China Employment* 9 (2002): 35–36 [in Chinese].

Chen, Feng. "Between the State and Labor: The Conflict of Chinese Trade Unions' Dual Institutional Identity." *China Quarterly* 176 (2003): 1006–28.

————. "Industrial Restructuring and Workers' Resistance in China." *Modern China* 29, no. 2 (2003): 237–62.

Chen He. "Boss Forces Workers to Kneel." *Entrepreneurs* 1 (1997): 9–10 [in Chinese].

Cheng, Lianxing. *A Study of Anti-unemployment Policies in China (1958–2000).* Beijing: Social Science Documentation Publishing House, 2002 [in Chinese].

China Labor Watch. *Reebok's Human Rights Standard and Chinese Workers' Working Conditions.* New York: China Labor Watch, 2002.

Chun, Jennifer. "Public Dramas and the Politics of Justice: Comparison of Janitors' Union Struggles in South Korea and the United States." *Work and Occupations* 32, no. 4 (November 2005): 486–503.

Clarke, Simon. "Trade Unions and the Non-payment of Wages in Russia." *International Journal of Manpower* 19, nos. 1–2 (1998): 68–83.

Cohen, Myron L. "Cultural and Political Inventions in Modern China: The Case of the Chinese 'Peasant.'" *Daedalus* 122, no. 2 (1993): 151–70.

Collins, Jane L. *Threads: Gender, Labor, and Power in the Global Apparel Industry.* Chicago: University of Chicago Press, 2003.

"Coming to Terms with Unions." *Beijing Review,* December 9, 2004, pp. 32–33.

Cook, Linda. *The Soviet Social Contract and Why It Failed: Welfare Policy and Workers' Politics from Brezhnev to Yeltsin.* Cambridge, Mass.: Harvard University Press, 1993.

Cowie, Jefferson. *Capital Moves: RCA's Seventy-Year Quest for Cheap Labor.* New York: New Press, 2001.

Crowley, Stephen, and David Ost, eds. *Workers after Workers' States: Labor and Politics in Postcommunist Eastern Europe.* Lanham, Md.: Rowman and Littlefield, 2001.

Dai Jianzhong and Zhu Min. "A Survey Report on Labor Relations in Private Enterprises and Women Workers' Problems." Manuscript, Beijing Academy of Social Science, 1999 [in Chinese].

Davis, Deborah S. "From Welfare Benefits to Capitalized Asset: The Re-commodification of Residential Space in Urban China." In *Housing and Social Change: East-West Perspectives,* ed. Ray Forrest and James Lee, pp. 183–96. New York: Routledge, 2003.

De Angelis, Massimo. "Marx's Theory of Primitive Accumulation: A Suggested Reinterpretation." Manuscript, University of East London, March 1999.

Posted online at http://homepages.uel.ac.uk/M.DeAngelis/PRIMACCA .htm.

Desai, Padma, and Todd Idson. *Work without Wages: Russia's Nonpayment Crisis.* Cambridge, Mass.: MIT Press, 2000.

Ding Yuanzhu, Hu Angang, and Wang Shaoguang. "Behind China's Wealth Gap." *South China Morning Post,* October 31, 2002.

Dublin, Thomas. *When the Mines Closed: Stories of Struggles in Hard Times.* Ithaca, N.Y.: Cornell University Press, 1998.

Dudley, Kathryn Marie. *The End of the Line: Lost Jobs, New Lives in Postindustrial America.* Chicago: University of Chicago Press, 1994.

Earle, John S., and Klara Z. Sabirianova. "How Late to Pay? Understanding Wage Arrears in Russia." *Journal of Labor Economics* 20, no. 3 (2000): 661– 707.

Eckholm, Erik. "Petitioners Urge China to Enforce Legal Rights." *New York Times,* June 2, 2003.

———. "Two Promoters of Worker Protests in China Get Prison Sentences." *New York Times,* May 10, 2003.

Editorial Board, Law Yearbook of China. *Law Yearbook of China, 2004.* Beijing: Press of Law Yearbook of China, 2005.

Elson, Diane, and Ruth Pearson. "Nimble Fingers Make Cheap Workers: An Analysis of Women's Employment in Third World Export Manufacturing." *Feminist Studies* 8 (1981): 87–107.

Engels, Friedrich. *The Condition of the Working Class in England,* trans. and ed. W. O. Henderson and W. H. Chaloner. New York: Macmillan, 1958.

"Factory Managers Killed in Pay Rows." *South China Morning Post,* February 25, 2002.

Fantasia, Rick. *Cultures of Solidarity.* Berkeley and Los Angeles: University of California Press, 1988.

Feng Genxin. *The Twenty-first-Century Chinese Urban Social Security System.* Zhengzhou: Henan People's Press, 2001 [in Chinese].

Fernandez-Kelly, Maria-Patricia. *For We Are Sold, I and My People: Women and Industry in Mexico's Frontier.* Albany: State University of New York Press, 1983.

Forney, Matthew, and Neil Gough. "Working Man Blues." *Time Asia,* April 1, 2002.

Frazier, Mark W. "China's Pension Reform and Its Discontents." *China Journal* 51 (2004): 97–114.

———. *The Making of the Chinese Industrial Workplace: State, Revolution, and Labor Management.* Cambridge: Cambridge University Press, 2002.

French, Howard. "Land of 74,000 Protests (But Little Is Ever Fixed)." *New York Times,* August 24, 2005.

Gallagher, Mary E. *Contagious Capitalism: Globalization and the Politics of Chinese Labor.* Princeton, N.J.: Princeton University Press, 2005.

———. "Following in the Steps of Qiu Ju? Law and Morality at the Chinese Workplace." Presentation at Stanford University, February 24, 2005.

————. " 'Time Is Money, Efficiency Is Life': The Transformation of Labor Relations in China." *Studies in Comparative International Development* 39, no. 2 (2004): 11–44.

————. "An Unequal Battle." *China Rights Forum,* Summer 1997, p. 15.

————. " 'Use the Law as Your Weapon!': Institutional Change and Legal Mobilization in China." In *Engaging the Law in China: State, Society, and Possibilities for Justice,* ed. Neil J. Diamant, Stanley B. Lubman, and Kevin J. O'Brien, pp. 54–83. Stanford, Calif.: Stanford University Press, 2005.

Gallagher, Mary E., and Jiang Junlu, eds. *Chinese Labor Legislation.* Special issue of *Chinese Law and Government* (forthcoming).

Gaventa, John. *Power and Powerlessness: Quiescence and Rebellion in an Appalachian Valley.* Urbana: University of Illinois Press, 1980.

Giles, John, Albert Park, and Cai Fang. "How Has Economic Restructuring Affected China's Urban Workers?" *China Quarterly* 185 (March 2006): 61–95.

Goodwin, Jeff, James M. Jasper, and Francesca Polletta. "Why Emotions Matter." In *Passionate Politics: Emotions and Social Movements,* ed. Jeff Goodwin, James M. Jasper, and Francesca Polletta, pp. 1–24. Chicago: University of Chicago Press, 1992.

Gould, Roger V. *Insurgent Identities: Class, Community, and Protest in Paris from 1848 to the Commune.* Chicago: University of Chicago Press, 1995.

Gu, Edward X. "Dismantling the Chinese Mini-welfare State? Marketization and the Politics of Institutional Transformation, 1979–1999." *Communist and Post-Communist Studies* 34 (2001): 91–111.

————. "Labor Market Reforms: Central Government Policy." *Chinese Law and Government* 34, no. 1 (2001): 5–15.

Guang, Lei. "Guerrilla Workfare: Migrant Decorators, State Power, and the Moral Economy of Work in China." In *Working in China: Ethnographies of Labor and Workplace Transformation,* ed. Ching Kwan Lee, pp. 56–76. London: Routledge, 2006.

Guangdong Provincial Statistics Bureau. *Guangdong Statistical Yearbook, 2002.* Beijing: China Statistics Press, 2003 [in Chinese].

Guha, Ranajit. *Elementary Aspects of Peasant Insurgency in Colonial India.* Durham, N.C.: Duke University Press, 1999.

Guthrie, Doug. *Dragon in a Three-Piece Suit: The Emergence of Capitalism in China.* Princeton, N.J.: Princeton University Press, 1999.

Hanagan, Michael P. *The Logic of Solidarity.* Urbana: University of Illinois Press, 1980.

Harrell, Steven. "The Changing Meanings of Work in China." In *Re-drawing Boundaries: Work, Households, and Gender in China,* ed. Barbara Entwisle and Gail E. Henderson, pp. 67–76. Berkeley and Los Angeles: University of California Press, 2000.

Hart, Gillian. *Disabling Globalization.* Berkeley and Los Angeles: University of California Press, 2002.

Harvey, David. "Accumulation by Dispossession." In *The New Imperialism*, pp. 127–82. New York: Oxford University Press, 2005.

———. *Spaces of Hope*. Berkeley and Los Angeles: University of California Press, 2000.

Hathaway, Dale A. *Can Workers Have a Voice? The Politics of Deindustrialization in Pittsburgh*. University Park: Pennsylvania State University Press, 1993.

Heilmann, Sebastian. "The Social Context of Mobilization in China: Factions, Work Units, and Activists during the 1976 April Fifth Movement." *China Information* 8 (1993): 1–19.

Hershatter, Gail. *The Workers of Tianjin, 1900–1949*. Stanford, Calif.: Stanford University Press, 1986.

Ho, Peter. "Introduction." In *Developmental Dilemmas: Land Reform and Institutional Change in China*, ed. Peter Ho. London: Routledge, 2005.

———. "Who Owns China's Land? Policies, Property Rights, and Deliberate Institutional Ambiguity." *China Quarterly* 166 (2001): 394–421.

Ho, Samuel P. S., and George C. S. Lin. "Emerging Land Markets in Rural and Urban China: Policies and Practices." *China Quarterly* 175 (2003): 681–707.

Ho, Virginia E. *Labor Dispute Resolution in China: Implications for Labor Rights and Legal Reform*. China Research Monograph 59. Berkeley: University of California, Berkeley, Institute of East Asian Studies, 2003.

———. "Labor Law in China's Reform Era: The Evolving Legal Framework for Labor Rights." In *The Labor of Reform*, ed. Mary E. Gallagher, Ching Kwan Lee, and Albert Park. Manuscript, University of Michigan, 2005.

Hoffmann, Charles. *The Chinese Worker*. Albany: State University of New York Press, 1974.

Hong Dayong. "The Development of Chinese Urban Poverty Alleviation Work since Economic Reform." *Sociological Research* 1 (2003): 78 [in Chinese].

Honig, Emily. *Sisters and Strangers: Women in the Shanghai Cotton Mills, 1919–1949*. Stanford, Calif.: Stanford University Press, 1986.

Hu Angang. "Chinese Microeconomic Index, 1997–2002: An Analysis of the Previous Administration's Performance and Recommendations for the New Administration." *Hebei Journal* 4 (2003) [in Chinese].

———. "The Current State of China's Economic and Social Development: Analysis and Recommendations." *Reform* 5 (2002) [in Chinese].

———. *State of the Country Report*. Beijing: Tsinghua University Press, 2002 [in Chinese].

Hung, Eva, and Stephen Chiu. "The Lost Generation: Life Course Dynamics and Xiagang in China." *Modern China* 29, no. 2 (2003): 204–36.

Hurst, William. "Understanding Contentious Collective Action by Chinese Laid-Off Workers: The Importance of Regional Political Economy." *Studies in Comparative International Development Studies* 39, no. 2 (2004): 94–120.

Hurst, William, and Kevin J. O'Brien. "China's Contentious Pensioners." *China Quarterly* 170 (2002): 345–60.

Institute of Contemporary Observation. "Legal Protection and Assistance Network for Labor in Guangdong: A Research Report." Manuscript, Institute of Contemporary Observation, January 2002 [in Chinese].

Javeline, Debra. *Protest and the Politics of Blame: The Russian Response to Unpaid Wages.* Ann Arbor: University of Michigan Press, 2003.

Jiang, Xueqin. "Fighting to Organize." *Far Eastern Economic Review* 164, no. 35 (September 6, 2001): 72–75.

Josephs, Hillary K. *Labor Law in China: Choice and Responsibility.* Seattle: Butterworth Legal Publishers, 1990.

Katznelson, Ira. "Working-Class Formation: Constructing Cases and Comparisons." In *Working Class Formation: Nineteenth-Century Patterns in Western Europe and the United States,* ed. Ira Katznelson and Aristide Zolberg, pp. 3–41. Princeton, N.J.: Princeton University Press, 1986.

Katznelson, Ira, and Aristide Zolberg, eds. *Working-Class Formation: Nineteenth-Century Patterns in Western Europe and the United States.* Princeton, N.J.: Princeton University Press, 1986.

Kernen, Antoine, and Jean-Louis Rocca. "The Reform of State-Owned Enterprises and Its Social Consequences in Shenyang and Liaoning." *China Perspectives* 27 (January–February 2000): 35–51.

Khan, Azizur Rahman, and Carl Riskin. *Inequality and Poverty in China in the Age of Globalization.* Oxford: Oxford University Press, 2001.

Khan, Joseph. "China's Workers Risk Limbs in Export Drive." *New York Times,* April 7, 2003.

———. "Pace and Scope of Protests in China Accelerated in '05." *New York Times,* January 20, 2005.

———. "Workplace Deaths Rise in China Despite New Safety Legislation." *New York Times,* October 24, 2003.

Koo, Hagen. *Korean Workers: The Culture and Politics of Class Formation.* Ithaca, N.Y.: Cornell University Press.

Kuhn, Anthony. "A High Price to Pay for a Job." *Far Eastern Economic Review* (Hong Kong) 167, no. 3 (January 22, 2004): 30.

Kynge, James. "Chinese Workers Transform Fortunes of Home Towns." *Financial Times,* November 9, 2003.

———. "Riots in Chinese Mining Town." *Financial Times,* April 3, 2000.

Labor Science Institute, Ministry of Labor and Social Security of China. *The Blue Book of Chinese Employment, 2002.* Beijing: China Labor and Social Security Press, 2003 [in Chinese].

Lam, Willy Wo-Lap. "Beijing Faces Winter of Discontent." CNN, September 30, 2003. Posted online at www.cnn.com/2003/WORLD/asiapcf/east/09/29/willy.column/index.html.

Lamphere, Louise. *From Working Daughters to Working Mothers.* Ithaca, N.Y.: Cornell University Press, 1987.

Lau, Raymond W. K. "China: Labor Reform and the Challenge Facing the Working Class." *Capital and Class* 61 (1997): 45–81.

Lee, Ching Kwan. "From Organized Dependence to Disorganized Despotism:

Changing Labor Regimes in Chinese Factories." *China Quarterly* 157 (1999): 44–71.

———. *Gender and the South China Miracle: Two Worlds of Factory Women.* Berkeley and Los Angeles: University of California Press, 1998.

———. "Is Labor a Political Force in China?" In *Grassroots Political Reform in Contemporary China,* ed. Merle Goldman and Elizabeth J. Perry. Cambridge, Mass.: Harvard University Press, forthcoming.

———. "The Labor Politics of Market Socialism: Collective Inaction and Class Experiences among State Workers in Guangzhou." *Modern China* 24, no. 1 (1998): 3–33.

———. "Pathways of Labor Insurgency." In *Chinese Society: Change, Conflict, and Resistance,* ed. Elizabeth J. Perry and Mark Selden, pp. 41–61. 2d ed. London: Routledge, 2003.

———. "The 'Revenge of History': Collective Memories and Labor Protests in Northeastern China." *Ethnography* 1, no. 2 (2000): 217–37.

Lee, Ching Kwan, and Guobin Yang, eds. *Re-envisioning the Chinese Revolution: The Politics and Poetics of Collective Memories in Contemporary China.* Washington, D.C.: Woodrow Wilson Center Press and Stanford University Press, 2007.

Leung, Trini. "Labor Fights for Its Rights." *China Perspectives* 19 (1998): 6–21.

Li, Clara. "Abuse of Workers Revealed." *South China Morning Post,* January 17, 2002.

———. "Shenzhen Gets a Bad Name with Workers It Does Not Want." *South China Morning Post,* January 15, 2002.

———. "Thousand of Migrants Cash in Pension Plan." *South China Morning Post,* July 10, 2002.

Li Erjun. "The Making of the Xiagang Worker List." M.Phil. thesis, Department of Sociology, Tsinghua University, Beijing, 2003 [in Chinese].

———. "'Ruoshi Qunti' in the *People's Daily,* 1995–2002." Research note, Department of Sociology, Tsinghua University, Beijing, August 2002 [in Chinese].

Li, Minqi. "Response to Lau's 'China: Labor Reform and the Challenge Facing the Working Class.'" *Capital and Class* 65 (1998): 21–34.

Li Peilin. "Possible Changes in Chinese Society after Joining the WTO." In *The Blue Book of Chinese Society, 2002,* ed. Ru Xin, Lu Xueyi, and Li Peilin, pp. 57–65. Beijing: Social Science Documentation Publishing House, 2002 [in Chinese].

———. "Unemployment Management in Old Industrial Bases." In *China's Economic Opening and Changes in Social Structure,* ed. Hu Yaosu and Lu Xueyi, pp. 83–105. Beijing: Social Sciences Academic Press, 1998 [in Chinese].

Li, Qi, and Bill Taylor. "ACFTU Membership Organizing Strategies." Manuscript, All China Federation of Trade Unions, 2002.

Li Qiang. *A Comparative Study of Unemployment and Layoffs.* Beijing: Tsinghua University Press, 2001 [in Chinese].

———. "Urban Unemployment in China and Its Countermeasures." Manuscript, Tsinghua University, Beijing.

Liang Zai and Zjongdong Ma. "China's Floating Population: New Evidence from the 2000 Census." *Population and Development Review* 30, no. 3 (2004): 467–88.

Liaoning Academy of Social Sciences. "A Study on Liaoning's Strategy and Implementation of the Reemployment Project." Manuscript, Liaoning Academy of Social Sciences, December 1999 [in Chinese].

Liaoning Province Politics and Law Committee. "The Prevention and Management of Mass Incidents amidst Reform of State-Owned Enterprises." In *A Collection of Essays on Maintaining Social Stability,* ed. Central Committee Politics and Law Committee Research Department. Beijing: Legal Press, 2001 [in Chinese].

Liaoning Statistics Bureau. *Liaoning Statistics Yearbook, 1999.* Beijing: China Statistics Bureau, 2000 [in Chinese].

———. *Liaoning Statistics Yearbook, 2000.* Beijing: China Statistics Bureau, 2001 [in Chinese].

———. *Liaoning Statistics Yearbook, 2001.* Beijing: China Statistics Bureau, 2002 [in Chinese].

———. *Liaoning Statistics Yearbook, 2002.* Beijing: China Statistics Bureau, 2003 [in Chinese].

———. *Liaoning Statistics Yearbook, 2003.* Beijing: China Statistics Bureau, 2004 [in Chinese].

———. *Liaoning Statistics Yearbook, 2004.* Beijing: China Statistics Bureau, 2005 [in Chinese].

Liaoning Urban Employment Research Team. "Conditions and Strategies of Liaoning's Urban Population and Employment." *Management World* 5 (1998): 69–76 [in Chinese].

"The Liaoyang Protest Movement of 2002–3, and the Arrest, Trial, and Sentencing of the 'Liaoyang Two.'" *China Labor Bulletin,* Hong Kong (July 2003).

Lin Justin Yifu, Fang Cai, and Zhou Li. *State-Owned Enterprise Reform in China.* Hong Kong: Chinese University Press, 2001.

Liu Kaiming. "Listening to Workers' Complaints." Report, Institute of Contemporary Observation, Shenzhen, 2004 [in Chinese].

———. *Migrant Labor in South China.* Beijing: Xinhua Publishing House, 2003 [in Chinese].

———. "Social Structure of Rights Deprivation: A Report on a Collective Labor Dispute Investigation." Report, Institute of Contemporary Observation, Shenzhen 2004 [in Chinese].

Liu, Sian Victoria. "Social Positions: Neighborhood Transitions after *Danwei.*" In *Working in China: Ethnographies of Labor and Workplace Transformation,* ed. Ching Kwan Lee, pp. 38–55. London: Routledge, 2006.

Logan, John, Fuqin Bian, and Yanjie Bian. "Tradition and Change in the Urban

Chinese Family: The Case of Living Arrangements." *Social Forces* 76, no. 3 (1998): 851–82.

Lü, Xiaobo. "Booty Socialism, Bureau-preneurs, and the State in Transition: Organizational Corruption in China." *Comparative Politics* 32, no. 3 (2000): 273–94.

Lu, Xueyi. "Balancing Rural-Urban Relations for the Sake of Rural Residents." In *Analysis and Forecast on China's Social Development, 2005*, ed. Ru Xin, Lu Xueyi, and Li Peilin, pp. 175–86. Beijing: Social Sciences Academic Press, 2004 [in Chinese].

Lubman, Stanley. *Bird in a Cage: Legal Reform in China*. Stanford, Calif.: Stanford University Press, 1999.

Luthje, Boy. "Global Production, Industrial Development, and New Labor Regimes in China: The Case of Electronics Contract Manufacturing." Paper presented at the conference "The Labor of Reform: Employment, Workers' Rights, and Labor Law in China," University of Michigan, Ann Arbor, March 21–22, 2003.

Ma, Josephine. "Three Million Took Part in Surging Protests Last Year." *South China Morning Post*, June 8, 2004.

Michelson, Ethan. "Chinese Lawyers at Work: The Practice of Law as an Obstacle to Justice." In *Working in China: Ethnographies of Labor and Workplace Transformation*, ed. Ching Kwan Lee, pp. 169–87. London: Routledge, 2006.

———. "Unhooking from the State: Chinese Lawyers in Transition." Ph.D. diss., Department of Sociology, University of Chicago, 2003.

Misra, Kalpana. *From Post-Maoism to Post-Marxism: The Erosion of Official Ideology in Deng's China*. New York: Routledge, 1998.

Mo Rong. "Chinese Urban Unemployment Rate Already at 7 Percent—Appropriate Measures Must Be Taken." *Research Forum* 20 (2001) [in Chinese].

———. "Employment Conditions Are Still Difficult." In *The Blue Book of Chinese Society, 2002*, ed. Ru Xin, Lu Xueyi, and Li Peilin, pp. 165–74. Beijing: Social Science Documentation Publishing House, 2002 [in Chinese].

Montinola, Gabriella, Yingyi Qian, and Barry R. Weingast. "Federalism, Chinese Style: The Political Basis for Economic Success." *World Politics* 48, no. 1 (1995): 50–81.

"More Than One Hundred Cases of Industrial Injuries to Be Tried." *Southern Weekend*, November 26, 1999, p. 1 [in Chinese].

Murphy, Rachel. *How Migrant Labor Is Changing Rural China*. Cambridge: Cambridge University Press, 2002.

National Bureau of Statistics of China. *China Industrial Economic Statistical Yearbook, 2004*. Beijing: China Statistics Press, 2005 [in Chinese].

———. *China Labor and Social Security Yearbook, 1995*. Beijing: China Statistics Press, 1996 [in Chinese].

———. *China Labor and Social Security Yearbook, 1996*. Beijing: China Statistics Press, 1997 [in Chinese].

———. *China Labor and Social Security Yearbook, 1997*. Beijing: China Statistics Press, 1998 [in Chinese].

————. *China Labor and Social Security Yearbook, 1998.* Beijing: China Statistics Press, 1999 [in Chinese].

————. *China Labor and Social Security Yearbook, 1999.* Beijing: China Statistics Press, 2000 [in Chinese].

————. *China Labor and Social Security Yearbook, 2000.* Beijing: China Statistics Press, 2001 [in Chinese].

————. *China Labor and Social Security Yearbook, 2001.* Beijing: China Statistics Press, 2002 [in Chinese].

————. *China Labor and Social Security Yearbook, 2002.* Beijing: China Statistics Press, 2003 [in Chinese].

————. *China Statistical Yearbook, 1997.* New York: Praeger, 1998.

————. *China Statistical Yearbook, 1998.* New York: Praeger, 1999.

————. *China Statistical Yearbook, 1999.* New York: Praeger, 2000.

————. *China Statistical Yearbook, 2001.* New York: Praeger, 2002.

————. *China Statistical Yearbook, 2002.* New York: Praeger, 2003.

————. *China Statistical Yearbook, 2003.* New York: Praeger, 2004.

————. *China Statistical Yearbook, 2004.* New York: Praeger, 2005.

O'Brien, Kevin J. "Rightful Resistance." *World Politics* 49, no. 1 (1996): 31–55.

————. "Villagers, Elections, and Citizenship in Contemporary China." *Modern China* 27, no. 4 (2001): 407–35.

O'Brien, Kevin J., and Lianjiang Li. "The Politics of Lodging Complaints in Rural China." *China Quarterly* 143 (1995): 756–83.

————. *Rightful Resistance in Rural China.* Cambridge: Cambridge University Press, 2006.

————. "Suing the Local State: Administrative Litigation in Rural China." In *Engaging the Law in China: State, Society and Possibilities for Justice,* ed. Neil J. Diamant, Stanley B. Lubman, and Kevin O'Brien, pp. 31–53. Berkeley and Los Angeles: University of California Press, 2005.

Oi, Jean. *Rural China Takes Off.* Berkeley and Los Angeles: University of California Press, 1998.

O'Leary, Greg. "The Making of the Chinese Working Class." In *Adjusting to Capitalism: Chinese Workers and the State,* ed. Greg O'Leary, pp. 48–74. Armonk, N.Y.: M. E. Sharpe, 1998.

Paige, Jeffery M. "Abstract Subjects: 'Class,' 'Race,' 'Gender,' and Modernity." Manuscript, University of Michigan, 2000.

————. "Conjuncture, Comparison, and Conditional Theory in Macrosocial Inquiry." *American Journal of Sociology* 105, no. 3 (1999): 781–800.

Pan, Philip P. "China Tries Labor Leaders amid Protest." *Washington Post,* January 16, 2003.

————. "China's Seething Workers: Oil Industry Layoffs Spark Widespread Demonstrations." *Washington Post,* April 24, 2002.

————. "Chinese Workers' Rights Stop at Courtroom Door." *Washington Post,* June 28, 2002.

————. "Getting Paid in China: Matter of Life and Death." *Washington Post,* February 13, 2003.

———. "Three Chinese Workers: Jail, Betrayal, and Fear." *Washington Post,* December 28, 2002.

———. "When Workers Organize, China's Party-Run Unions Resist." *Washington Post,* October 15, 2002.

———. "Worked Till They Drop: Few Protections for China's New Laborers." *Washington Post,* May 13, 2002.

Pappas, Gregory. *The Magic City: Unemployment in a Working-Class Community.* Ithaca, N.Y.: Cornell University Press, 1989.

Peerenboom, Randall. *China's Long March toward Rule of Law.* Cambridge: Cambridge University Press, 2002.

Pei, Minxin. *China's Trapped Transition: The Limits of Developmental Autocracy.* Cambridge, Mass.: Harvard University Press, 2006.

———. "Rights and Resistance: The Changing Contexts of the Dissident Movement." In *Chinese Society: Change, Conflict, and Resistance,* ed. Elizabeth J. Perry and Mark Selden, pp. 20–40. 2d ed. London: Routledge, 2003.

Perry, Elizabeth J. *Challenging the Mandate of Heaven: Social Protest and State Power in China.* Armonk, N.Y.: M. E. Sharpe, 2002.

———. "Crime, Corruption, and Contention." In *The Paradox of China's Post-Mao Reform,* ed. Merle Goldman and Roderick MacFarquhar, pp. 308–32. Cambridge, Mass.: Harvard University Press, 1999.

———. "From Native Place to Workplace: Labor Origins and Outcomes of China's *Danwei* System." In *Danwei: The Changing Chinese Workplace in Historical and Comparative Perspective,* ed. Xiaobo Lü and Elizabeth J. Perry, pp. 42–59. Armonk, N.Y.: M. E. Sharpe, 1997.

———. "Labor's Love Lost: Worker Militancy in Communist China." *International Labor and Working-Class History* 50 (1996): 64–76.

———. *Shanghai on Strike: The Politics of Chinese Labor.* Stanford, Calif.: Stanford University Press, 1993.

———. "Shanghai's Strike Wave of 1957." *China Quarterly* 137 (1994): 1–27.

Perry, Elizabeth J., and Li Xun. *Proletarian Power: Shanghai in the Cultural Revolution.* Boulder, Colo.: Westview Press, 1997.

Philion, Stephen. "The Discourse of Workers' Democracy in China as a Terrain of Ideological Struggle." Ph.D. diss., Department of Sociology, University of Hawaii, 2004.

Ping Ping. "Gender Strategy in the Management of State Enterprises and Women Workers' Dependency on Enterprises." *Sociological Research* 1 (1998): 55–62 [in Chinese].

Piven, Frances Fox, and Richard A. Cloward. *Poor People's Movements.* New York: Viking, 1979.

Polanyi, Karl. *The Great Transformation: The Political and Economic Origins of Our Time.* Boston: Beacon Press, 1957.

Pomfret, John. "With Carrots and Sticks, China Quiets Protestors." *Washington Post,* March 22, 2002.

Portz, John. *The Politics of Plant Closings.* Lawrence: University Press of Kansas, 1990.

Postone, Moishe. *Time, Labor, and Social Domination.* Cambridge: Cambridge University Press, 1993.

"PRC Police, Steel Workers Clash over Unpaid Wages." Foreign Broadcast Information Service, CHI-2000-0516.

Public Safety Administration Bureau, ed. *A Compilation of National Temporary Population Statistical Data.* Beijing: Masses Publishing House, 2000 [in Chinese].

Qiao Jian. "Employees Confronting Reform." In *The Blue Book of Chinese Society, 2002,* ed. Ru Xin, Lu Xueyi, and Li Peilin, pp. 243–51. Beijing: Social Science Documentation Publishing House, 2002 [in Chinese].

Qiao Jian and Jiang Ying. "An Analysis of Labor Demonstrations." In *Analysis and Forecast on China's Social Development (2005),* ed. Ru Xin, Lu Xueyi, and Li Peilin. Beijing: Social Science Academic Press, 2005 [in Chinese].

"Reforming Fee Regulation on Migrants." *China Employment* 4 (2002): 4–10 [in Chinese].

Research Department, All China Federation of Trade Unions. *Chinese Trade Union Statistics Yearbook, 1998.* Beijing: China Statistics Press, 1999 [in Chinese].

———. *Chinese Trade Union Statistics Yearbook, 2000.* Beijing: China Statistics Press, 2001 [in Chinese].

———. *Chinese Trade Union Statistics Yearbook, 2001.* Beijing: China Statistics Press, 2002 [in Chinese].

———. *Survey of the Status of Chinese Staff and Workers in 1997.* Beijing: Xiyuan Press, 1997 [in Chinese].

Rofel, Lisa. *Other Modernities: Gendered Yearnings in China after Socialism.* Berkeley and Los Angeles: University of California Press, 1999.

Rosenthal, Elisabeth. "Factory Closings in China Arouse Workers' Fury." *New York Times,* August 31, 2000.

———. "Workers' Plight Brings New Militancy in China." *New York Times,* March 10, 2003.

Ru Xin, Lu Xueyi, and Li Peilin, eds. *The Blue Book of Chinese Society, 2002.* Beijing: Social Science Documentation Publishing House, 2002 [in Chinese].

Rural Economy Research Center, Ministry of Agriculture, ed. *Chinese Rural Studies Report, 2002.* Beijing: China Finance and Economics Publishing House, 2002 [in Chinese].

Ryoshin Minami and Xue Jinjun. "Estimation of Population and Labor Force in China: 1949–1999." *Chinese Journal of Population Science* 3 (2002) [in Chinese].

Salzinger, Leslie. *Genders in Production: Making Workers in Mexico's Global Factories.* Berkeley and Los Angeles: University of California Press, 2003.

Sargeson, Sally. "Full Circle? Rural Land Reforms in Globalizing China." *Critical Asian Studies* 36, no. 4 (2004): 637–56.

———. "Subduing 'the Rural House-Building Craze': Attitudes towards Housing Construction and Land Use Controls in Four Zhejiang Villages." *China Quarterly* 169 (2002): 927–55.

Sayer, Derek. *Capitalism and Modernity.* London: Routledge, 1991.

Schueller, Margot. "Liaoning: Struggling with the Burdens of the Past." In *China's Provinces in Reform: Class, Community, and Political Culture,* ed. David S. G. Goodman, pp. 93–126. London: Routledge, 1997.

Scott, Joan W. *The Glassworkers of Carmaux: French Craftsmen and Political Activism in a Nineteenth-Century City.* Cambridge, Mass.: Harvard University Press, 1974.

Selden, Mark. *The Political Economy of Chinese Development.* Armonk, N.Y.: M. E. Sharpe, 1993.

Seung, Wook Baek. "The Changing Trade Unions in China." *Journal of Contemporary Asia* 30, no. 1 (2000): 46–66.

Sewell, William P. *Work and Revolution in France: The Language of Labor from the Old Regime to 1848.* New York: Cambridge University Press, 1980.

Shenzhen City Labor Bureau. *Constructing Harmonious Labor Relations.* Beijing: China Labor and Social Security Publishing House, 2000 [in Chinese].

———. *Establishing Marketized Employment Institutions.* Beijing: China Labor and Social Security Publishing House, 2000 [in Chinese].

———. *Shenzhen Labor Statistics Yearbook, 1998–1999.* Beijing: China Labor and Social Security Publishing House, 2000 [in Chinese].

———. *Shenzhen Labor Statistics Yearbook, 2000–2001.* Beijing: China Labor and Social Security Publishing House, 2002 [in Chinese].

Shenzhen Labor Relations Department, Shenzhen City Labor Bureau. "A Survey Report on Shenzhen Labor Dispute Arbitration Handling." In *A Collection of Shenzhen Labor Studies Scientific Papers, 1997–1998,* vol. 1, ed. Shenzhen City Labor Bureau and Shenzhen Labor Studies Association, pp. 259–65. Beijing: China Labor and Social Security Publishing House, 1999 [in Chinese].

Shenzhen Statistics and Information Bureau. *Shenzhen Statistical Handbook.* Shenzhen: Shenzhen Statistics and Information Bureau, 2001 [in Chinese].

Shi Meixia. "Causes and Policies Regarding Spontaneous Incidents in Labor Relations." In *Report of Chinese Labor Science Studies, 1997–1999,* ed. Labor Science Institute, Labor and Social Security Bureau, pp. 166–216. Beijing: China Labor and Social Security Publishing House, 2000 [in Chinese].

Shirk, Susan L. *The Political Logic of Economic Reform in China.* Berkeley and Los Angeles: University of California Press, 1993.

———. "Recent Chinese Labor Policies and the Transformation of Industrial Organization in China." *China Quarterly* 88 (1981): 575–93.

Shue, Vivienne. "Legitimacy Crisis in China?" In *State and Society in 21st-Century China: Crisis, Contention, and Legitimation,* ed. Peter Hays Gries and Stanley Rosen, pp. 24–49. New York: Routledge/Curzon, 2004.

Silver, Beverly J. *Forces of Labor: Workers' Movements and Globalization since 1870.* Cambridge: Cambridge University Press, 2003.

Sklair, Leslie. *Assembling for Development: The Maquila Industry in Mexico and the United States.* San Diego: University of California, San Diego, Center for US-Mexican Studies, 1993.

Smith, Chris. "Living at Work: Management Control and the Chinese Dormitory Labor System in China." *Asia Pacific Journal of Management* 20, no. 3 (2002): 333–58.

Smith, Craig. "Blasts Kill 18 in Textile City South of Beijing." *New York Times*, March 17, 2001.

Solinger, Dorothy. "Labour Market Reform and the Plight of the Laid-off Proletariat." *China Quarterly* 170 (June 2002): 304–26.

———. "Why We Cannot Count the 'Unemployed.'" *China Quarterly* 167 (2001): 671–88.

Somers, Margaret R. "Deconstructing and Reconstructing Class Formation Theory: Narrativity, Relational Analysis, and Social Theory." In *Reworking Class*, ed. John R. Hall, pp. 73–106. Ithaca, N.Y.: Cornell University Press, 1997.

State Letters and Visits Bureau. *People's Letters and Visits (Remin Xinfang)* 1 (2001) [in Chinese].

———. *People's Letters and Visits (Remin Xinfang)* 7 (2001) [in Chinese].

———. *People's Letters and Visits (Remin Xinfang)* 9 (2001) [in Chinese].

Steinfeld, Edward. "Chinese Enterprise Development and the Challenge of Global Integration." In *East Asian Networked Production*, ed. Shahid Yusuf. New York: World Bank, forthcoming.

Sun Liping. "Social Transition: Developing a New Sociological Agenda." *Sociological Research* 1 (2005): 1–24 [in Chinese].

Tan Yibo. "Shenzhen Electronics Factory Illegally Detains Workers: One Death, Six Injured." *China Labor Daily*, June 20, 1998 [in Chinese].

Tang Jun. "Joining WTO and Employment Policies and Strategies." In *WTO: Labor Rights and Protection*, ed. China College of Labor Movement, Institute of Labor Relations, pp. 181–99. Beijing: Workers' Press, 2001.

———. "Selections from Report on Poverty and Anti-poverty in Urban China." *Chinese Sociology and Anthropology* 36, nos. 2–3 (2003–4).

Tang, Wenfang, and William L. Parish. *Chinese Urban Life under Reform: The Changing Social Contract*. Cambridge: Cambridge University Press, 2000.

Tanner, Murray Scot. *Chinese Government Reponses to Rising Social Unrest*. Testimony presented to the U.S.-China Economic and Security Review Commission on April 14, 2005. Rand Corporation Testimony Series. Santa Monica: Rand Corporation, 2005.

———. "Protests Now Flourish in China." *International Herald Tribune*, June 2, 2004.

Tarrow, Sidney. *Power in Movement*. New York: Cambridge University Press, 1994.

Therborn, Göran. *The Ideology of Power and the Power of Ideology*. London: Verso, 1980.

Thireau, Isabelle, and Huan Linshan. "The Moral Universe of Aggrieved Chinese Workers: Workers' Appeals to Arbitration Committees and Letters and Visits Offices." *China Journal* 50 (2003): 83–103.

Thompson, E. P. *The Making of the English Working Class.* New York: Vintage, 1963.

Tiano, Suan. *Patriarchy on the Line: Labor, Gender, and Ideology in the Mexican Maquila Industry.* Philadelphia: Temple University Press, 1994.

Tilly, Charles. *Stories, Identities, and Political Change.* Lanham, Md.: Rowman and Littlefield, 2002.

Tomba, Luigi. *Paradoxes of Labor Reform: Chinese Labor Theory and Practice from Socialism to Market.* London: Routledge/Curzon, 2002.

Townsend, James R. *Political Participation in Communist China.* Berkeley and Los Angeles: University of California Press, 1967.

Verdery, Katherine. "A Transition from Socialism to Feudalism? Thoughts on the Postcolonial State." In *What Was Socialism, and What Comes Next?* Princeton, N.J.: Princeton University Press, 1996.

———. *The Vanishing Hectare: Property and Value in Postsocialist Transylvania.* Ithaca, N.Y.: Cornell University Press, 2003.

Walder, Andrew G. "The Chinese Cultural Revolution in the Factories: Party-State Structures and Patterns of Conflict." In *Putting Class in Its Place: Worker Identities in East Asia,* ed. Elizabeth J. Perry, pp. 167–98. China Research Monograph 48. Berkeley: University of California, Berkeley, Institute of East Asian Studies, 1996.

———. *Communist Neo-traditionalism: Work and Authority in Chinese Industry.* Berkeley and Los Angeles: University of California Press, 1986.

Wang Ao. *Strategic Transfer of Labor in Liaoning's Development Process.* Special Consultation Report. Shenyang: Liaoning Academy of Social Sciences, 2000 [in Chinese].

Wang Feng. "Housing Improvement and Distribution in Urban China: Initial Evidence from China's 2000 Census." *China Review* 3, no. 2 (2003): 121–43.

———. "Privilege or Punishment? Retirement and Reemployment among the Chinese Urban Elderly." In *China's Revolutions and Intergenerational Relations,* ed. Martin King Whyte, pp. 61–84. Ann Arbor: University of Michigan Press, 2003.

Wang, Yaping. "Housing Reform and Its Impacts on the Urban Poor in China." *Housing Studies* 15, no. 6 (2000): 845–64.

Wang, Yaping, and Alan Murie. "The Process of Commercialization of Urban Housing in China." *Urban Studies* 33, no. 6 (1996): 971–89.

———. "Social and Spatial Implications of Housing Reform in China." *International Journal of Urban and Regional Research* 24, no. 2 (2000): 397–417.

Wang Zheng. "Gender, Employment, and Women's Resistance." In *Chinese Society: Change, Conflict, and Resistance,* ed. Elizabeth J. Perry and Mark Selden, pp. 158–82. 2d ed. London: Routledge, 2003.

Weinbaum, Eve S. *To Move a Mountain: Fighting the Global Economy in Appalachia.* New York: New Press, 2004.

White, Gordon. "The Politics of Economic Reform in Chinese Industry: The Introduction of the Labor Contract System." *China Quarterly* 111 (1987): 365–89.

———. "Restructuring the Working Class: Labor Reform in Post-Mao China." In *Marxism and the Chinese Experience,* ed. Arif Dirlik and Maurice Meisner. Armonk, N.Y.: M. E. Sharpe, 1989.

Whyte, Martin King. "Postscript: Filial Support and Family Change." In *China's Revolutions and Intergenerational Relations,* ed. Martin King Whyte, pp. 303–11. Ann Arbor: University of Michigan Press, 2003.

Williams, Raymond. *Marxism and Literature.* Oxford: Oxford University Press, 1977.

Wilson, Jeanne L. "'The Polish Lesson': China and Poland, 1980–1990." *Studies in Comparative Communism* 23, nos. 3–4 (1990): 259–79.

Won, Jaeyoun. "Withering Away of the Iron Rice Bowl? The Reemployment Project of Post-Socialist China." *Studies in Comparative International Development* 39, no. 2 (2004): 71–93.

World Bank. *Old Age Security: Pension Reform in China.* Washington, D.C.: World Bank, 1997.

Wu, Fulong. "Changes in the Structure of Public Housing Provision in Urban China." *Urban Studies* 33, no. 9 (1996): 1601–27.

Wu Weiping. "Migrant Housing in Urban China." *Urban Affairs Review* 38, no. 1 (2002): 90–119 [in Chinese].

Yan Hairong. "Spectralization of the Rural: Reinterpreting the Labor Mobility of Rural Young Women in Post-Mao China." *American Ethnologist* 30, no. 4 (2003): 1–19.

Yang, Dali L. *Beyond Beijing: Liberalization and the Regions in China.* London: Routledge, 1997.

Yang, Junxiong. "Peasant Employment Is the Primary Question after Subsistence Is Achieved." In *Hot Topics in Chinese Peasant Studies in 2001,* ed. Xian Zhude. Beijing: China Statistics Press, 2001 [in Chinese].

Yang Yiyong. *Unemployment Shockwave: A Report on the Future of Employment in China.* Beijing: Jinri Publishing House, 1997 [in Chinese].

Yang Yiyong and Xin Xiaobai. "A Report on Layoffs and Reemployment." In *Analysis and Forecast of the Social Situation in China, 1999,* ed. Ru Xin et al. Beijing: Social Sciences Academic Press, 1999 [in Chinese].

Yu Jianrong. "An Explanation of Farmers' Defense of Rights." *Sociological Research* 2 (2004): 49–55 [in Chinese].

———. "Organized Peasant Resistance in Contemporary China." Lecture delivered at Fairbank Center, Harvard University, December 4, 2003.

———. "Peasants' Organized Resistance and Political Risk: A Case Study of One Hunan County." *Strategy and Management* 3 (2003): 1–16 [in Chinese].

Zhang, Li. "Forced from Home: Property Rights, Civic Activism, and the Politics of Relocation in China." *Urban Anthropology* 33, nos. 2–4 (2004): 247–81.

———. "Urban Experiences and Social Belonging." In *Popular China: Unofficial Culture in a Globalizing Society,* ed. Perry Link, Richard P. Madsen, and Paul G. Pickowicz, pp. 275–99. Lanham, Md.: Rowman and Littlefield, 2002.

Zhao, Dingxin. *The Power of Tiananmen: State and Society Relations and the 1989 Beijing Student Movement.* Chicago: University of Chicago Press, 2001.

Zheng Chenggong. *Evolution and Assessment of China's Social Security System*. Beijing: Renmin University Press, 2002 [in Chinese].

Zheng Yongnian. "From Rule by Law to Rule of Law?" *China Perspectives* 25 (September–October 1999): 31–43.

Zhou, Kate. *How Farmers Changed China*. Boulder, Colo.: Westview Press, 2000.

Zhou, Xueguang. "Unorganized Interests and Collective Action in China." *American Sociological Review* 58 (1993): 54–73.

Zweig, David. *Internationalizing China*. Ithaca, N.Y.: Cornell University Press, 2002.

Index

Text: 10/13 Aldus
Display: Aldus
Compositor: BookMatters, Berkeley
Indexer: Jeanne C. Moody